THE BEAUTY OF
ENGLAND

THE BEAUTY OF
ENGLAND

English Castles by
Richard Humble

Great English Houses by
Russell Chamberlin

English Rivers & Canals
by Paul Atterbury

**SPRING
BOOKS**

First published in Great Britain by
George Weidenfeld & Nicolson Limited
under the titles

English Castles (published in 1984)
Copyright © Richard Humble 1984

Great English Houses (published in 1983)
Copyright © Russell Chamberlin 1983

English Rivers & Canals (published in 1984)
Copyright © Paul Atterbury 1984

This edition first published in 1988 by Spring Books
An imprint of Octopus Publishing PLC
Michelin House, 81 Fulham Road
London SW3 6RB

ISBN 0 600 55842 8

Printed by Mandarin Offset in Hong Kong

CONTENTS

GREAT ENGLISH HOUSES

THE MIDDLE AGES

THE FIFTEENTH CENTURY

THE SIXTEENTH CENTURY

Norham

Bamburgh
Dunstanburgh
Alnwick
Warkworth

Newcastle

Carlisle

Durham

Brougham
Barnard Castle
Brough
Richmond
Bolton
Scarborough
Helmsley
Pickering
Skipton
York

THE NORTH COUNTRY

Conisbrough

Peveril
Lincoln

Beeston
Newark
Tattershall

THE MIDLANDS

Castle
Rising
Caister
Norwich

Acton
Burnell
Ashby-de-la-Zouch
Bridgnorth
EAST ANGLIA
Stokesay
Dudley
Ludlow
Orford
Warwick
Framlingham

Castle
Hedingham
Goodrich
Colchester
Berkhamsted

Berkeley
Hadleigh

Windsor
London
Donnington
Upnor
Farleigh
Rochester
Hungerford
THE
SOUTH COUNTRY
THE
Nunney
Farnham
SOUTH-EAST
Walmer
Deal
THE
Old Sarum
Bodiam
Saltwood
Dover
SOUTH-WEST
Portchester
Arundel
Okehampton
Sherborne
Lewes
Tintagel
Christchurch
Hurst
Pevensey
Launceston
Berry
Corfe
Carisbrooke
Pomeroy
Restormel
Totnes
Yarmouth
Pendennis
Dartmouth
St Mawes

ENGLISH CASTLES

Richard Humble

Warkworth Castle,
Northumberland.

'THE BONES OF THE KINGDOM'

Author's note

All castles in this section are 'real' castles – that is, 'large fortified buildings or sets of buildings, strongholds' – and not, as the *Concise Oxford Dictionary* continues, 'mansions that were once such'. This excludes all great houses with 'castle' names like Castle Howard in Yorkshire, splendid neo-Victorian confections like Castle Drogo in Devon, or comparatively modern renovations like Hever Castle in Kent. (Readers interested in castles as stately residences rather than as fighting strongholds are recommended to the second section in this book, 'Great English Houses'.)

Nor have I included much older fortifications from the Bronze and early Iron Ages, all of them undoubted strongholds, which also happen to be called castles. (The best-known of these and undoubtedly the most majestic is the gigantic triple ring of Maiden Castle in Dorset.) These great Celtic ring fortifications are nevertheless well worth visiting in their own right.

Instruments of royal power

The first true castles in England were sited and built during and immediately after the Norman Conquest of 1066–72 – to hasten the defeat of the English population and keep it firmly under the control of the King and his trusted lieutenants, the new ruling caste. Royal control, direct or delegated, was the primary role of the castle in England; and this role never changed over the next six hundred years, even after the arrival of gunpowder and cannon. From the second half of the eleventh century to the first half of the seventeenth, castles remained both symbols and instruments of royal power in England, enabling that power to be exercised by force whenever necessary. This was why the victorious Parliamentarians, after beating King Charles I in the English Civil War of 1642–8, reduced to ruins (or 'slighted') all the major castles which had been held for the King during the fighting. The 'ruins that Cromwell knocked about a bit' were not created in blind revenge or unthinking vandalism, but as a deliberate attempt to destroy the provincial underpinning of royalist power in England.

Reduced to ruins after its long Civil War siege, Corfe Castle still dominates the natural gap through the Purbeck Hills in south-east Dorset.

A linear castle developed from a central motte-and-bailey : Arundel in Sussex, showing how the western curtain wall abuts with the keep on its motte.

Windsor, a close cousin to Arundel, but with the Round Tower on its motte completely enclosed by the curtain wall. St George's Chapel is on the left.

The republican victory of 1649 was short-lived: ten years of military dictatorship were more than enough to see the English welcoming Charles II home from exile in the summer of 1660. Nevertheless, the Civil War had accomplished a decisive and final shift of power from Crown to Parliament. After the Restoration, with Parliament holding the national purse strings, the castles of England could never return to their former status as the front-line bastions of royal power throughout the land. Nor were aristocratic families, returning to or taking over estates once governed from great castles, motivated to repair the ruins and restore every castle to its former glory. The taste was now for elegant and spacious mansions with the accent on grace and comfort rather than defence.

Stone and brick castles, however, were built to last, and it would have taken much longer than a couple of centuries of redundancy and neglect to wipe them off the English landscape. (Remember that Hadrian's Wall, the coast-to-coast northern frontier of the Roman Empire, survived nearly 1,500 years of being used as a convenient stone quarry, before archaeologists and preservationists began seriously trying to save what was left.) By the late eighteenth century castles were back in fashion – not so much for their historical interest, but as picturesque ornaments of the English landscape.

A new role: landscape ornaments

The eighteenth-century landscape gardeners, looking at the natural features of the land with a new eye, used castle ruins to enhance the beautiful gardens and estates being laid out as settings for the great houses of England's ruling class. This was a less

ironical or ignominious fate than it seems. Every castle in the land had been deliberately sited to command the surrounding landscape, even though this had been done with military rather than aesthetic purposes in mind. The landscape gardeners of the eighteenth century were the first to exploit the fact that there is no such thing as a castle with a bad view – which makes castles so rewarding for visitors today.

Indeed, in the later eighteenth and nineteenth centuries the demand for castle ruins far outran supply of the genuine article, making this period the golden age for the construction of fake ruins, or follies. Theirs is a fascinating story in itself, but sadly follies, like mansions and Celtic hill-forts, fall outside the scope of this book.

This new appreciation of castles as 'landscape improvers' was assisted by prodigious changes in the landscape itself, wrought in the same period by England's Agricultural Revolution. By the end of the eighteenth century thousands of square miles of new farming land had been brought under cultivation, stripped of the forests which had carpeted England practically from sea to sea as little as two hundred years before. Further acreage had been won by the taming of waste land and the draining of marshes. This tidying-up of the English countryside, which by the 1870s resulted in England being the most efficient farming nation in the world, helped invest the castles of England with a natural prominence in the landscape which had never before been so marked.

The Victorian achievement

All this went hand in glove with the nineteenth-century 'Gothic Revival' of interest in the Middle Ages, with best-selling novels like Sir Walter Scott's *Ivanhoe* boosting popular interest in castles and their past. It helped make the nineteenth and early twentieth centuries the last great period of castle-building in England. Business fortunes made in commerce and industry were translated into mock medieval castles, often complete with drawbridge or portcullis. In these replica castles, Victorian tastes were furnished in Gothic flamboyance, with results ranging from the beautiful to the cheerfully appalling. In general it is fair to say that Victorian neo-medieval architects achieved far less dire results with castles than they did with ancient churches or university buildings. (At Oxford the new-look Balliol College, apparently modelled on the imposing railway terminus buildings appearing in the cities, attracted the deathless comment '*C'est magnifique, mais ce n'est pas la gare.*') Two outstanding examples of nineteenth-century renovation work on famous medieval castles are included in these pages: **Arundel** (p. 44) and **Windsor** (p. 50).

To this enthusiastic fostering of interest in England's medieval buildings, the Victorians added a transport revolution spanning the length and breadth of the land. Travel by rail, with over 20,000 miles of railway completed by 1890, was made possible by the most comprehensive public transport network ever seen in England (or ever likely to be). The expansion of the railways left no spot in Britain more than an hour's journey from a railway station. Cheap and easy excursion travel by rail created a domestic tourist industry which expanded out of all measure after the advent of the motor car and family touring by road. And castles have always ranked among the most popular assets of England's tourist industry.

Visiting castles

One very good reason why castles are such marvellous places to visit is because, as mentioned above, there is no such thing as a castle with a bad view; building a castle without an all-round panorama of the surrounding countryside would have been as pointless as building an underground lighthouse. Then there is the variety. No two English castles are the same – not even 'series castles' built in the same period and to the same basic specifications, like Henry VIII's south coastal chain from Deal to Pendennis. In each case, the demands of the site and the availability of materials produced a building with its own unique combination of features. Castles *had* to be different one from the other, to make them as hard as possible to capture: one of the most important functions of the castle was to present attackers with a unique set of problems to which there was no stock solution.

Castles were blatant statements of the owners' worldly wealth and power. They were places where laws were enforced and punishment dealt out, often in hideous measure; where men trained for war and, not infrequently, fought, and were killed or horribly wounded. They were also places of squalor and disease, especially when resisting long sieges. But this is only part of the story: castles were also places where people of both high and low social status

From the later fourteenth century; 'keyhole' gunports were built into town walls and new castles such as Bodiam in order to deter attackers.

The imposing Newel Staircase at Tattershall in Lincolnshire. Broad glazed windows show the fifteenth-century accent on domestic comfort.

played sports, feasted, made music, and lived life to the full.

An enduring test of great architecture is that neither human destructiveness nor the passing of the centuries manage to dispel the original purpose of the builders. Ruined abbeys like Glastonbury, Tintern or Fountains remain cloaked in reverence, but with castles – even brutally blitzed specimens like **Corfe** (p. 62) – it is the worldliness which has survived. Where churches exist to funnel one's imagination towards God and the next life, castles let the imagination run riot about the mundane details of living in former ages. All this can make castles a lot more fun to visit.

Far more often than not, a castle visit involves a good deal of clambering about, in or on mysterious and exciting ruins, and children particularly love spiral staircases up towers pierced with firing-slits. Tell them to watch out for spiral stairs which turn to the right. These were specially designed to favour defenders beating a fighting retreat to the upper levels. The right-hand turn obliged attackers to fight their way up with their sword arms uncomfortably close to the central spine of the staircase, while the defenders were left with plenty of room for downward cutting and thrusting. Once up, and making the round of the battlements or enjoying the view from the top of a tower keep, visitors are automatically cast in the role of sentries on watch; but this was also where the castle's upper crust would come to enjoy a breath of fresh air and a gentle stroll, well above the bustle and smells at ground level.

If the castle has a Great Hall with walls still standing, look for the rows of sockets which held the

One of the earliest castle amenities : outfalls for garderobes *(latrines), built into the castle's outer wall above the ditch or moat.*

cross-beams of upper floors and galleries. Before you leave the hall, notice the distance from the kitchens and wonder if cooked food ever arrived still hot on the tables in the hall.

As for that classic castle feature, the dungeon, bear in mind that not every underground chamber was necessarily a prison or torture-chamber. During a siege the safest place for women, children and wounded was underground. And large underground store-rooms were often built to take inflammable items, such as firewood, which could not be left lying around in the open where enemy fire-missiles could set them ablaze. On the ground and upper levels, if you find what looks like a one-man cell built into the wall with no exit but a downward drain, it was probably a simple *garderobe* ('protect-your-clothes') or latrine, sluiced out with the occasional bucket of water when it became too ripe.

This section is intended to whet the appetite for castle-visiting in England by providing nationwide coverage of the range of castle types open to the public. The best individual castle histories and architectural descriptions are to be found in the excellent booklets on sale at castles in the care of the Department of the Environment, the National Trust or private ownership. But when visiting castles for the first time, a certain amount of general knowledge about castles and their time is most useful. The following information will help visitors to recognize basic castle types and layouts.

MOTTE-AND-BAILEY

The first castles (c. 1066–1189)
Norman kings: William I (1066–87), William II (1087–1100), Henry I (1100–35), Stephen (1135–54); Henry II, first Angevin king (1154–89)

Founded, according to tradition, in 911, the Duchy of Normandy was the first European society since the Roman Empire to perfect the regular use of fortifications in war. The Normans used their *castella*, from which the word 'castle' derives, to guarantee the security of base areas and to dominate newly-won territory. By about 1050, the Normans had developed an 'instant' castle which could be built at great speed using local peasant labour and timber. This consisted of a mound of earth thrown up from a circular ditch, with the top ringed by a wooden stockade and a two- or three-storey wooden tower (*donjon*) in the middle. This mound, usually about 50 feet (15 m) high, was called the *motte*, and it was encircled at ground level by another ditch and stockade enclosing an outer defensive area known as a *bailey*. Where the size of the castle and the lie of the land permitted, additional security would be provided by adding a second or outer bailey. All surrounding trees and undergrowth outside the outer bailey stockade would then be swept away to leave an unimpeded all-round view from the castle, making surprise attacks impossible.

These castles were carefully sited to command key roads, river crossings and strategic high ground. The better chosen the castle site, the more dangerous it was for an enemy force to ignore the castle and bypass it, for this was an invitation to the castle garrison to sally out and attack the enemy's communications. The castle's prime role was to deny the enemy freedom of movement: to force him to sit down for a siege instead of moving on to achieve his true objective.

How long a motte-and-bailey castle could hold out depended on two factors: the size of the garrison and of its stock of provisions, and how much the attackers knew about reducing castles. The latter proved the decisive factor in Norman-occupied England, where castles on the Norman model were a frightening novelty. Vivid scenes in the earlier sections of the Bayeux Tapestry show professionals at work: Duke William's knights attacking Dol and Dinan Castles in Brittany. Even allowing for artist's licence, it is clear that the trick was to start by overrunning the bailey, forcing the garrison to retreat up the wooden ramp leading from the bailey to the motte. (Attacking the motte first would enable the garrison to counter-attack from the bailey.) Once the garrison was safely holed up inside the motte defences, its attention was fixed by feint attacks up the ramp while flanking parties crept forward to fire the motte's stockade, leaving the garrison with no option but surrender.

Fire was always the greatest enemy of these 'first-generation' wooden castles, but the beauty of the

A classic example of the Norman motte-and-bailey: Pleshey Castle in Essex, which never made the twelfth-century transition to stone defences.

system was that the motte-and-bailey foundation site, once created, could not be so easily destroyed. It was an easy job to recommission a burned-out castle by building new wooden defences. William I's first motte-and-bailey castle at York, built in 1068, was burned out in the Northern Rising of September 1069 but rebuilt before the end of the year; and **Clifford's Tower** (p. 126) still squats on the original Norman motte thrown up 915 years ago. The confusion of the defeated English is reflected by

How to attack a motte-and-bailey, from the Bayeux Tapestry: Duke William's men are shown firing the keep palisade of Dinan Castle in Brittany.

the familiar words 'dungeon' and 'moat', with their accepted meanings of underground chamber and water-filled ditch – both of which are about as far from the original *donjon* and *motte* as it is possible to get.

The earliest picture of a motte-and-bailey castle being built in England is in the Bayeux Tapestry: the construction of the castle at Hastings, built to protect Duke William's base camp after his army landed at Pevensey on 28 September 1066. The tapestry shows a working party of peasants with

The earliest contemporary picture of Norman stone defences on a motte: Duke William's castle at Bayeux, with William shown arriving at centre.

mattocks and shovels, closely supervised by armed Normans. The labourers are shovelling stones and soil to build up the motte which, unlike other, older castles shown in the tapestry, is layered. This is presumably a deliberate reference to the alternating layers of gravel and rammed earth of the motte's core. Wherever possible, Norman engineers would site a castle where a natural hillock or knoll offered a solid foundation for the motte, because it took decades for the mounded earth to settle. Medieval records from all over England are packed with references to castle damage caused by soil subsidence, usually with the motte as main culprit.

The motte-and-bailey castle remained the basic 'instant' castle type long after the Norman Conquest, well into the latter years of the twelfth

The Bayeux Tapestry depicts the building of the first Norman motte-and-bailey on English soil: Hastings, built to protect the Norman beach-head.

century. As well as serving as a strategic weapon during campaigns of conquest and retribution, the castle was the focal point of royal power as delegated to the king's vassals on their estates, or manors. When effective royal rule broke down, as during the 'Anarchy' in the mid-twelfth century under King Stephen, the result would be an epidemic of castle-building, as petty lords kicked over the traces and strengthened their local power-bases in the shires. One of the first tasks confronting the tough young Henry II when he succeeded Stephen in 1154 was to bring his vassals to heel, destroying these unauthorized or 'adulterine' castles by the score. This is one reason why there are hundreds of motte-and-bailey sites across mainland Britain, and also in Ireland, the invasion of which was launched under Henry II in 1170. Most of these sites are now overgrown and recognizable only by the grassy hump of the motte – the stamp of the Norman conqueror and his heirs.

England's most sophisticated shell keep : Clifford's Tower at York. Its graceful outline is created by four interlocking circular towers.

The transition to stone: shell keeps
Clifford's Tower at York (p. 126), **Arundel** (p. 44), **Windsor** (p. 50), and **Pickering** (p. 125) are perfect examples of how an original motte-and-bailey site formed the core of later and much more elaborate stone-built castles. In all cases this expansion began with the fireproofing of first gener-

ation motte-and-bailey castles, with stone *curtain walls* replacing the original bailey stockades and a circular *shell keep* instead of the wooden donjon tower on top of the motte.

But it is at smaller castles, of less strategic importance or where the lie of the land forbade such expansion, that the original motte-and-bailey format can best be appreciated. **Totnes** (p. 71), **Launceston** (p. 80) and **Restormel** (p. 73) all lie tucked away in the South-West, far from the military frontiers with Wales and Scotland where castle expansion and strengthening was most naturally favoured. All three are shell keeps, or motte-and-bailey castles rebuilt in stone in the twelfth and early thirteenth centuries: fossil specimens, as it were, of England's first castles.

The first stone castles:
tower keeps
(c. 1080–1189)

Although the ubiquitous motte-and-bailey was the basic 'front-line' castle of the Norman Conquest and its aftermath, the Normans never relied on it exclusively. While it was easy to build and repair, the motte-and-bailey was also much too vulnerable to fire (both accidental and deliberate), and too small for much more than the most immediate needs of local defence. By the end of William I's reign, therefore, the most important of the king's stone strongholds were being constructed on an entirely different plan. These were the massive, multi-storey *tower keeps*, screened from direct assault by baileys and later enclosed by more elaborate stone defence-works. The classic eleventh-century tower keeps are the Conqueror's **White Tower** at London (p. 28) and the keep at **Colchester** (p. 84), followed by the twelfth-century tower keeps at **Rochester** (p. 36) and **Dover** (p. 34).

The Norman tower keep is the ultimate statement of the Conquest: brute force come to stay. This, one feels, is what the *Anglo-Saxon Chronicle* had in mind with its bitter verse epitaph of William I, which begins 'He had castles built, and poor men stark oppressed'. These tower keeps are sheer, two-to three-storey blocks of masonry, impossible to contemplate at close quarters without a catch of the breath; even the very best photographs rarely capture their brooding menace. The walls are 90–100 feet high (27.5–30.5 m) and enormously thick – 15 feet (4.6 m) in the White Tower, 21 feet (6.4 m) at Dover. For additional strength their lower levels were packed with earth, with an outside staircase flush with the wall leading to a single entrance on the first storey. This would be closed for defence with a massive wooden door, most probably two-ply, with the grain of the two layers running at right-angles to each other to create an axe-proof slab. The quickest way through this would be a fire started with brushwood bundles and buckets of pitch – which the defenders would naturally attempt to put out with water dumped from the battlement and upper storeys.

The net result was a murderous bottleneck which attackers had to attempt to pierce under a hail of missiles from the battlement, the upper storeys, and the flat-sided turrets jutting out from the corners of the keep. Any attacking force which did manage to burn down the door and force its way into the first storey immediately came up against a mighty cross-wall dividing the keep's interior in two, leaving all the work of breaking and entering to be done again; and again on the upper storeys, assuming that the decimated attackers had not already been wiped out or forced to retreat by a counter-attack.

Brutally effective against frontal attack, the tower keep achieved economy in defence by forcing attackers to expose themselves to concentrated fire-power at a single point. But the tower keep had four great weaknesses: its corners, which were always vulnerable to the tactic of mining. Drive a long tunnel under one of the keep's corners, pack the end with wood and set it ablaze, and the resulting cave-in would bring the rubble-packed masonry above down with a run, creating a gaping breach.

This happened at Rochester in the winter of 1215, when King John besieged a rebel garrison in the castle. After a two-month siege the keep was still holding out long after the bailey defences had been overrun, and John ordered his miners into action. The King's famous choice of fuel for the completed mine consisted of 40 bacon pigs 'of the sort least good for eating'. The blazing bacon fat did the trick and Rochester's south-east corner turret collapsed in ruin – but even then the defenders did not give up. Alerted to what was coming, probably by the usual mine-detecting method (bowls of water whose surface would tremble from the shock-waves of the miners' picks), the garrison had pulled back beyond the internal cross-wall of the keep, and fought on. But the defenders were now cut off from their last food stocks, and only a few days were needed for the work of the slowest, surest siege weapon of all – hunger – to compel their surrender.

The Rochester siege of 1215 is a perfect demonstration of the strengths and weaknesses of the tower keep. When Rochester's ruined corner tower was rebuilt, it was in the much stronger rounded cross-section which became the hallmark of castle-building in the thirteenth and fourteenth centuries.

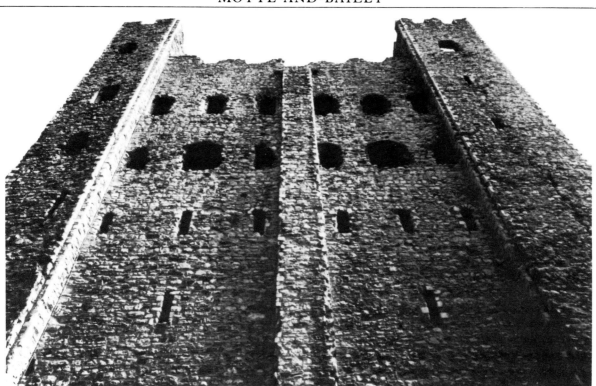

The soaring mass of the immense tower keep at Rochester in Kent, built in the early twelfth century as a bishop's palace as well as a stronghold.

'Hermit-crab' castles (c. 1070–1154)

In addition to motte-and-bailey castles and tower keeps, the Normans were never slow to plant castles on sites where there were existing defence-works, dating back to Roman times and before. These may be thought of as 'hermit-crab' castles, where the genius of Norman castle-building took over the abandoned shells of ancient strongholds and gave them a new lease of life. Three fine examples of these 'hermit-crab' castles are **Old Sarum** (p. 57), **Pevensey** (p. 40) and **Portchester** (p. 54).

Old Sarum was where William I disbanded his army in 1070, after his terrible punitive campaign against the Northern rebels which left Yorkshire a blackened desert. In the centre of the circular Celtic earthwork and ditch a second ring was dug and a motte raised in the middle: a circular 'bullseye' motte-and-bailey, converted to a stone castle in the reign of Henry I. The Celtic outer ring was renovated to shelter a cathedral town (the site of the cathedral can also be inspected when visiting this fine castle). But this arrangement did not prove successful; the churchmen objected to living under the constant military jurisdiction of the castle, and a

new cathedral was founded on the site of modern Salisbury, 1½ miles (2·4 km) south of Old Sarum castle, in 1220.

Pevensey and Portchester, however, were girdled with the mighty stone ramparts characteristic of the coastal fortresses built by the Romans to defend the 'Saxon Shore' against Saxon raids in the fourth century AD. These fortresses consisted of huge curtain walls studded with rounded projecting bastions. At both sites, the Normans built a tower keep at one corner of the Roman walls, cutting off part of the enclosed space to form an inner bailey. Similar work was begun at a third 'Saxon Shore' fortress in Suffolk: Burgh Castle, 2 miles (3·2 km) west of modern Yarmouth on the Waveney river. At Burgh a motte and bailey were sited at the southeast corner of the Roman perimeter, but here the transition to stone was never achieved. When a castle was eventually completed in the area it was at **Caister**, 4 miles (6·5 km) north of Burgh, in the early fifteenth century. Visitors to Caister (p. 95) should try to find time for a quick look at Burgh, a good example of a Norman castle 'graft' which did not take.

THE GREAT YEARS OF CASTLE BUILDING

Linear and concentric castles (c. 1189–1377)
Angevin kings: Richard I (1189–99), John (1199–1216); Plantagenet kings: Henry III (1216–72),
Edward I (1272–1307), Edward II (1307–27) and Edward III (1327–77)

The period from the mid-twelfth to the mid-thirteenth centuries was a 'melting-pot' century in English castle development, prompted by a flood of new ideas on castle defences from the Continent and, thanks to the Crusades, from the Middle East. They added up to the removal of obvious weak spots in the defence system by strengthening the main gate and the outer curtain wall. The latter was also extended, so that the keep was now surrounded by outer defences instead of merely being the strongest point of the perimeter.

After the tower keeps of the first century of castle-building came the tower gatehouse, developed as the strongest sector of the curtain wall – and invariably, if the castle did not have an earlier keep, the strongest part of the whole castle. 'Murder holes', in the ceiling of the gatehouse porch through which all the castle's traffic passed, enabled rocks, red-hot irons and showers of red-hot sand to be rained down on any attackers foolhardy enough to try to break through. Curtain walls were extended and rebuilt with projecting towers from which attackers, no matter from which direction they tried to approach, would be caught in a crossfire from the walls. And, wherever feasible, water-filled moats were added as the most effective answer to mining.

Step by step, all these improvements led steadily towards the great concentric and linear castles of the late thirteenth century, in which outer and inner defences formed an integrated whole and the original function of a central keep became redundant. A remarkably early specimen of these 'keepless' castles is **Framlingham** in Suffolk (p. 88), built between 1178 and 1213. Here all the eggs were put in one basket: a gigantic curtain wall studded with thirteen rectangular flanking towers, and no keep.

Yet Framlingham was the exception which proved the rule; in general the tower keep, either free-standing or spliced into an angle of the curtain wall, remained a favourite standby of English castle-building until the early fifteenth century. Few other basic elements of castle architecture underwent so many drastic changes, all aimed at improving strength and habitability. **Orford** tower keep (p. 87), is another startling East Anglian novelty dating from the second half of the twelfth century. There is little to indicate that Orford was built in the same period, and to the orders of the same king (Henry II) as the massive rectangular keep at Dover. Orford was actually completed in 1173, over ten years *before* Dover; yet the two are as different as chalk from cheese. The Orford keep is polygonal

Framlingham in Suffolk, perhaps the most impressive early attempt at a 'keepless' castle, with thirteen rectangular towers studding the curtain wall.

Strengthening the tower keep: Conisbrough, South Yorkshire, with six flanking towers rising from a battered or inward-sloping base.

outside, cylindrical inside, and braced by three rectangular flanking towers: a handsome blend of elegance and strength. Nor is Orford an isolated one-off design, like Framlingham. There is a similar tower keep at **Conisbrough** in Yorkshire (p. 118), cylindrical with *six* rectangular flanking towers, and smaller polygonal keeps are to be found at Chilham in Kent, Odiham in Hampshire and Tickhill in Yorkshire.

The next logical step after polygonal and cylindrical tower keeps braced with external flanking towers was the fully cylindrical keep. This offered the best all-round streamlining against battering with rocks by siege artillery, and presented the strongest cross-section to mining operations. Yet the *round keep*, as distinct from the shell keep, is the greatest rarity of all in English castles (there are seven in Wales: Bronllys and Tretower in Breconshire, Dynevor in Carmarthenshire, Dolbadarn in Caernarvonshire, Pembroke, and Caldicot and Skenfrith in Monmouthshire). The best surviving example is at **Launceston** in Cornwall (p. 80), where a round keep was built inside the shell keep. England has nothing like the huge cylindrical tower keep of Richard I's Château Gaillard, built in 1197–8 to keep the French out of Normandy, which resembles nothing so much as a Saturn I rocket in stone. The reason for this is that by the middle thirteenth century, when the cylindrical keep might have been expected to be the latest trend, English castle design was already drifting faster and faster towards the symmetrical, concentric and linear types which either enclosed existing keeps, or rendered the building of new ones unnecessary.

The finest examples of concentric castle-building in Britain fall outside the scope of this book. They are the graceful giants built to the orders of Edward I (1272–1307) to keep the conquered Welsh under the English thumb – Caernarvon, Conway, Beaumaris and Harlech. But the preparatory work for these magnificent achievements in stone – all of which were designed and built 'in one' – had been done in England. The English prototype for the great Edwardian concentric castles, in which the baileys (or *wards*) enclose each other, was achieved with the expansion of the Tower of London in the reign of Henry III (1216–72). Henry's son, Edward I, completed the job by adding the Tower's outer curtain wall and flanking towers. Another superb conversion dating from Edward I's reign is **Goodrich** in Hereford and Worcester (p. 100), where the

The twelfth-century tower keep of Goodrich (Hereford and Worcester), enclosed by later curtain defences to create a powerful concentric castle complex.

curtain wall and towers enclose a late twelfth-century square keep.

But the idea of adding full circuits of curtain walls and towers was also applied to castles sited for the domination of high ground or ridges, where big contour changes made concentric designs impossible. The result here was the linear castle, best typified by **Windsor** (p. 50) and **Arundel** (p. 44), where the wards are enclosed in a chain instead of one inside the other. Linear defences were also adopted at **Warkworth** (p. 146), dominated by an imposing cruciform stone tower built on the original motte in the fourteenth century.

It was in these years that the fortified outwork known as the *barbican* was introduced. At its best, the barbican, which always blocked the approach to the main gatehouse, was a 'mini-castle' pushed forward from the outer castle defences. Sometimes this was extended to provide not double but triple security from surprise attack. At London the barbican (the now-vanished Lion Tower) covered the twin outer defences of the Middle Tower, which in turn covered the main landward entrance through Edward I's outer curtain: the Byward Tower. At **Pickering** (p. 125) the entire southern or Outer Ward served as a barbican, screening the main castle defences. Other barbican defences of differing types, all best contrived to suit the needs of the site and of the existing defences of the time, can be seen at **Donnington** (p. 48), **Dunstanburgh** (p. 144), **Helmsley** (p. 128), **Richmond** (p. 120) and **Scarborough** (p. 122).

FROM CASTLES TO FORTIFIED HOUSES

(c. 1350–1485)
Plantagenet kings: Edward III (1327–77), Richard II (1377–99);
Lancastrian kings: Henry IV (1399–1413), Henry V (1413–22),
Henry VI (1422–61); Yorkist kings: Edward IV (1461–83), Richard III (1483–5)

All these far-reaching improvements to castle defences may be said to have reached their peak by the middle of the fourteenth century, and they carried English medieval castle-building to its zenith of effectiveness. The last of the great Plantagenet castle-builders was Edward III, who showed all his grandfather's flair and more. Sadly, Edward III's superb castle at Queenborough on the Isle of Sheppey no longer exists; but its foundations have been excavated, proving it to have been beyond doubt the most powerful and sophisticated concentric castle ever built on English soil.

Built in 1361, Queenborough was circular: a ring of curtain wall unadorned with towers, save at the main gatehouse on the western side, which was flanked by twin towers. Queenborough's circular core was guarded by six towers, with the only way in through a second gatehouse halfway round the circle from the first. Cross-walls divided the inner defences into nine separate compartments, each intended to support its neighbours. The innermost circle was left clear, enabling garrison troops to shift easily to the most endangered sector. That vital amenity of any castle, the well, was plumb in the middle. Parallel walls inside the first gatehouse and outside the second, connecting the outer and inner curtains, left attackers with no freedom of movement at all. At Queenborough, therefore, the concentric castle reached its ultimate form: a perfect killing-bottle for intruders.

By the late fourteenth century, the defences of castles like Queenborough had become so strong that sieges aimed at rapid capture – commonplace throughout the late eleventh, twelfth and early thirteenth centuries – had become largely a waste of effort. But this did not mean that castle development came to an abrupt halt. Mere defensibility against attack had long ceased to be the castle's only reason for existence. They were no longer merely local fortresses for the king and his barons, 'the bones of the kingdom', as the chronicler William of Newburgh had called them back in the eleventh century. Improved habitability had always gone hand in

The dream castle – Bodiam in East Sussex, built under royal licence in the later fourteenth century. The wide moat kept enemy cannon at maximum range.

hand with improved defensibility; as residences of the country's royalty and aristocracy, castles were focal points of society. In other words, English medieval castles were bound to reflect any important changes in English medieval society, and between the accession of Edward III in 1327 and the defeat and death of Richard III in 1485, English society underwent more change than at any time since the Norman Conquest.

The Conqueror's system had been based on land tenure by the provision of military service on demand, with a peasantry fettered by bondage at the bottom of the feudal pyramid. But as the king's government moved away from purely military concerns and took on the functions of a civil government it needed annual injections of tax money drawn from all over the country. In less than a generation after the Conquest, cash rents had begun to replace military service, and by the second half of the fourteenth century this process had broken through to the bottom layer of the pyramid. The

Fireplaces and large windows for domestic comfort, built into the strong fifteenth-century tower of Ashby-de-la-Zouch in Leicestershire.

direct cause was a series of plague epidemics (not limited to the appalling 'Black Death' visitation in 1348–9) which reduced the population by nearly 30 per cent, causing an instant, nationwide labour shortage. For the first time ever, peasant labourers were in a position to push a series of runaway wage demands. But as wages soared, so did taxation (to pay for the wars in France), with the inevitable backlash of resentment against grasping landlords and Crown officials.

There is no space here to describe the resultant Peasants' Revolt of 1381, when the labourers of Kent and Essex marched on London to demand justice against their oppressors from the young King Richard II. Suffice it to say that the great royal castles of **Colchester**, **Rochester** and the **Tower of London** itself proved utterly useless as bastions against the Revolt. Garrisons which would probably have held out bravely against foreign invaders surrendered without a fight rather than be lynched by their own countrymen, and it will never be known for certain how much subversion and fifth-column work was involved. And the lesson was not forgotten. Though the Peasants' Revolt was the closest England came to the mass peasant risings (*Jacqueries*) suffered by France, the fear of repeated outbreaks inevitably left its mark on the ensuing century of castle-building in England.

The trauma of the Revolt confirmed a long-standing tendency of lords to fortify their manor houses against the possibility of local disturbances, making the late fourteenth and fifteenth centuries the heyday of the *domus defensabilis* or 'defensible home'. Because the need for security never eclipsed the need for more domestic comfort and grandeur, perhaps a better translation would be 'fortified stately home'. As with larger castles, these fortified manor houses consist of two basic types: those whose development spanned hundreds of years, and those (usually of the fifteenth or early sixteenth century) which were built in one go. Two fine examples of the former are **Ashby-de-la-Zouch** (p. 105) and **Stokesay** (p. 110). Perhaps the most impressive example of a fifteenth-century fortified manor, prompting the instinctive reaction 'Now that's what I *call* a castle!', is the massive brick tower of **Tattershall** (p. 103).

Castles and the coming of cannon

One of the greatest myths about castles is that the advent of gunpowder and cannon rendered them obsolete virtually overnight. This was true enough in the case of walled towns, but in general castles remained remarkably cannon-proof until, in the sixteenth and seventeenth centuries, the art of casting reliable heavy cannon was perfected. (Even with the high-velocity artillery of the Second World War, it was found that medieval fortifications needed a surprising amount of battering before they cracked.) When cannon arrived in the fourteenth century, castles adapted to this new military development, as they had always done. With its curtain wall and round corner towers, **Bodiam** in Sussex (p. 42) looks like a miniature concentric castle of the late thirteenth century. In fact it is a fortified manor house, built by licence of Richard II in 1385 – complete with 'keyhole' firing ports for cannon.

The first real test of cannon against castles came in the Wars of the Roses, fought intermittently between the factions of York and Lancaster between 1455 and 1485. About the only generalization which can be made about this confused conflict is that when castles fell to besiegers equipped with cannon – as did **Bamburgh** (p. 140) and the **Tower of London** (p. 28), to take just two examples – it was rarely due solely to the destructiveness of the artillery. The old factors of siege warfare still applied: the readiness of the defences, the extent of provision stockpiles, the likelihood of relief – not to

Majesty in brick : the splendid tower of Tattershall in Lincolnshire – like Bodiam in Sussex, restored by the munificence and dedication of Lord Curzon.

mention the chance of the garrison commander trying to save his neck by a timely surrender and quick change of sides – all added up to the state of the garrison's morale. The campaigns of the Wars of the Roses were nearly all settled by decisive field actions, such as St Albans, Northampton or Towton. At no stage was the result of such a battle reversed or even cancelled by an ensuing siege, with or without cannon.

This was particularly true of Henry Tudor's all-or-nothing march to victory on Bosworth Field in 1485 – a campaign in which castles and sieges played no part. It could be said that Bosworth, the last battle of the Wars of the Roses, symbolized the conflict as a whole. It was ultimately decided by which leading families, all with castles as their home bases, supported which claimant to the throne. The Wars of the Roses did *not* prove the obsolescence of castles in general – only of castles which were not, or could not be, equipped to reply to cannon with cannon.

THE TUDOR CASTLES

Platforms for geometric fire-power
Henry VIII (1509–47), Edward VI (1547–53),
Mary (1553–8), Elizabeth I (1558–1603)

The sixteenth century saw the last phase of royal castle-building in England, and in many ways it was the most extraordinary of them all. It certainly entitles Henry VIII to be ranked with his most famous castle-building forebears: Edward I, Henry II and William I. Henry's castles formed the most comprehensive system of coastal defence created since the Roman 'Saxon Shore' forts some 1,200 years earlier. Like his flagship, the recently re-covered *Mary Rose* with its mixed armament of longbows and heavy guns, the castles of Henry VIII were a perfect synthesis of medieval and modern principles, tailored to the age of the cannon.

With the exception of the square block and straight-sided bastion of Yarmouth on the Isle of Wight, Henry VIII's castles were of circular or 'clover-leaf' (overlapping circles) design. Both of the two soundest late medieval principles were incorporated: a single gateway commanded by 'murder-holes' and a concentric layout, with outer and inner defences separated by a ditch or passage, itself commanded from both sides by walls loop-holed for archery or musketry. The castle walls were squat and solid, presenting no easy target to enemy gunners, while covering every line of fire.

These castles were built to defend all vital anchorages of the King's other new creation: the Fleet, of which *Mary Rose* is the unique memorial. **Deal** (p. 32) and **Walmer** (p. 37) were sited to cover the anchorage of the Downs between the mainland and the Goodwin Sands. The main envisaged enemy was France, in alliance with the Holy Roman Empire. Henry's fears of a French attack were proved to be well founded by the French landing on the Isle of Wight in 1545 – the occasion of the tragic loss of *Mary Rose* – after which **Yarmouth** (p. 60) was built. In the South-West, the entrance to Falmouth Bay was covered from either side by **Pendennis** (p. 74) and **St Mawes** (p. 76).

These are the finest surviving examples of Henry VIII's castles, but they were by no means the only ones he built. There were five others at the Thames narrows of Tilbury and Gravesend, none of which have survived. And, like all great castle-builders, Henry VIII improved on the old as well as creating the new. He added three bastions to the outer defences at Dover, one of which (Moates Bulwark) still jabs like a defiant spear-head towards the line of attack from inland. And at London he added two massive semicircular bastions (Legge's Mount and the Brass Mount) to the northern angles of the Tower's outer curtain wall.

Under Elizabeth I (1558–1603), with the threat of Spanish instead of French invasion, there was widespread extending of castle fire-power by the addition of outer earthworks and bastions for the mounting of guns. One new Elizabethan castle, however, was **Upnor** (p. 38), built on the Medway to protect the Fleet base at Chatham.

The Civil War and after: an enduring legacy
The last fighting chapter in the story of England's castles was written in the English Civil War (1642–9), which saw more castles besieged in seven years than during the entire thirty years of the Wars of the Roses. These sieges are the best witness to the versatility of the castle over the centuries; it is remarkable how many Civil War sieges were conducted not against castles of the latest (Tudor) type, but against castles with pedigrees going right back to Norman motte-and-bailey days, like **Arundel**. The record was held by **Corfe**, stoutly defended for King Charles by the indomitable Lady Bankes from August 1644 to February 1646. Even then Corfe was not taken by direct attack, but by a fifth column of Parliamentarian troops admitted during fake negotiations. Corfe had been a famous Saxon royal residence a hundred years before the Norman Conquest – one of the very oldest 'bones of the kingdom'.

The active life of the castles certainly did not end with the Civil War. Henry VIII's castles were overhauled during the Napoleonic Wars, both for coastal defence and for the accommodation of French prisoners. The last bastion defence was hastily added to the Tower of London to keep out Chartist rioters in the early years of Queen

Tudor gun platform: Henry VIII's 'cloverleaf' castle at Deal in Kent, built low in a deep moat to command the Fleet anchorage of the Downs.

Victoria's reign; it was somewhat pointedly demolished by a German bomb in October 1940, and not replaced. This was the year before Hitler's Deputy, Rudolf Hess, was imprisoned in the Tower. In May 1940 the 'Miracle of Dunkirk' was improvised from Admiral Ramsay's HQ in **Dover Castle**, while inside the ancient Roman defences of **Pevensey**, machine-gun nests were cunningly constructed against the expected German invasion. Until the liberation of France four years later, Dover remained within range of German heavy guns – still the 'front door of England', as it had been 720 years before, when defended by Hubert de Burgh against French invaders and quisling barons.

THE SOUTH-EAST

THE TOWER OF LONDON

Department of the Environment
BR Fenchurch Street Station/4 mins walk;
BR Liverpool Street Station/78 bus; BR London Bridge
Station/47 bus to Tower Bridge Road/6 mins walk *or* 42 *or* 78 bus;
Green Line Coach to Minories Coach Station;
LT Underground, Circle or District Line, to Tower Hill Station

A casual visit to the Tower (say two hours or less) is really a waste of time and money; a day is hardly enough to do justice to its many attractions, any one of which – the Crown Jewels, the Armouries, St John's Chapel, the Royal Fusiliers Museum, the Changing of the Guard – would be well worth a visit on its own. Here we are concerned only with the Tower as a *castle*, and a unique specimen it is: the biggest, most complete concentric castle in all England, with William the Conqueror's White Tower at its core.

Visitors normally approach the Tower on foot, walking south from Tower Hill, with a good view of the green sweep of the dry Moat bed on the left, Edward I's outer curtain wall with Henry III's curtain wall beyond (both thirteenth-century), and

The Tower of London from the south, looking across the Thames from Tower Bridge, with Traitor's Gate and Bloody Tower to the left.

the pinnacles of the eleventh-century White Tower rising in the centre. One glance is enough to grasp the function of the concentric castle: successive belts of defence, getting tougher all the way in. As with nearly every English castle, the first mental exercise is to imagine the daunting effect of those cliffs of stone without the trees, none of which would have been permitted to grow in medieval times.

When passing through the Ticket Office, try to imagine the drawbridge which led into the Tower's now-vanished barbican: the semicircular Lion Tower, where the Royal Menagerie was housed from Henry III's time to 1834 (making the Tower England's oldest zoo). You then have to imagine a second drawbridge connecting the Lion Tower with the Middle Tower, the only surviving defences of the barbican. From the Middle Tower a causeway bridge leads over the Moat to the Byward Tower, the main entrance through Edward I's outer curtain wall into the Outer Ward. This entrance was closed by a portcullis, which can still be seen above. Beyond the Byward Tower is the Bell Tower, the south-western corner of Henry III's inner curtain wall.

The modern-day Tower Wharf, with its splendid park of antique artillery, makes it hard to realize that the Tower's second main entrance was by water, direct from the Thames. This was via the watergate: the famous 'Traitor's Gate' under St Thomas's Tower. Contrary to popular belief, Traitor's Gate is not of Tudor vintage (though most of the famous names who passed through it were). Like the rest of the outer curtain defences, St Thomas's Tower was built in the thirteenth century by Edward I.

The steps leading up from Traitor's Gate are directly in front of the main gatehouse tower piercing Henry III's curtain wall. This is the Bloody Tower (complete with portcullis), dominated to the right by the circular Wakefield Tower. The Bloody Tower's original name was the Garden Tower because it led to the Constable's garden in the Inner Ward; the 'Bloody' derives from the supposed murder there of the 'Princes in the Tower' (the young sons of Edward IV) on Richard III's orders in 1483. For good measure, the 8th Earl of Northumberland committed suicide in the Bloody Tower in 1585 – a grim blend of Tudor mythology and reality.

Through the Bloody Tower, the splendid mass of the White Tower dominates the Inner Ward in looming isolation – but it did not do so originally. A

The essence of Norman architecture: solid columns and rounded arches in St John's Chapel, White Tower.

look at the map is needed to understand the original layout. Extending eastward from the White Tower, a small bailey was anchored at its south-east corner on a bastion of the ancient city wall of Roman London. This has now disappeared. When Henry III enclosed the White Tower in his curtain wall, he also connected keep and curtain by running a wall north from the Wakefield Tower (parallel with the Roman city wall) and joined it to the White Tower with a twin-tower gatehouse (Coldharbour Tower). As the original entrance to the White Tower was on the south side and not, as today, on the north, it was therefore completely enclosed by an *Inmost Ward*. It only needed Edward I's outer curtain and barbican to complete an approach to the White Tower of appalling complexity (Lion Tower/Middle Tower/Byward Tower/Bloody Tower/Coldharbour Gate/White Tower): Plantagenet castle-building at its most ingenious.

Not even the beautifully displayed armour, weapons and other exhibits on view in the White Tower are more impressive than the enormous

The most famous Norman keep in England: London's White Tower, rising grimly beyond the river-front defences.

thickness of the keep's masonry. Look for the hallmark of the Norman tower keep: the massive cross-wall dividing the building in two. And on no account forget to visit the Chapel of St John in the White Tower, one glance at which will tell you more about the Normans and their architecture than a thousand books.

The Tower's attractions are well signposted and there is no need to describe them all here. Photography and sketching are permitted, 'provided no obstruction or nuisance is caused', but no photography is allowed in the Jewel House, a prohibition which can come as a bitter surprise to the unprepared. Appropriately enough, the best place from which to see the Changing of the Guard is the site of the Block, just north of Tower Green. Yeoman warders conduct regular guided tours, and the Tower also has good restaurant, snack bar and toilet facilities.

One final word of advice, particularly to visitors with young children. Close encounters with the famous Tower ravens are best avoided: an ingratiating croak has been known to be the prelude to a swift chop with a beak that can really hurt.

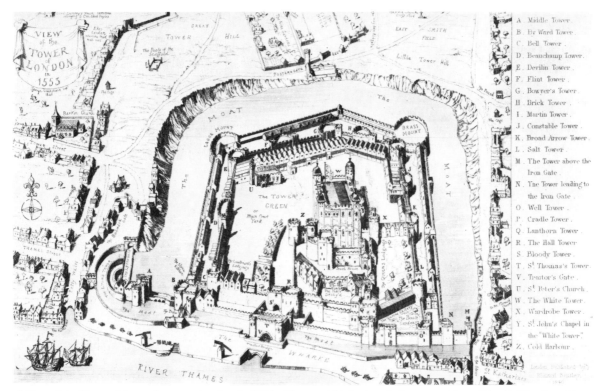

A plan of the Tower defences in 1553, showing the White Tower still joined to the inner curtain wall by Coldharbour Tower (Z) and the Wardrobe Tower (X).

SALTWOOD, KENT

Privately owned
1 mile (1·6 km) NE of Hythe;
A20/M20 from Maidstone/Ashford
or Dover/Folkestone

Saltwood is a privately-owned castle, so do not go along without checking opening times (normally Sundays and Bank Holidays from late May to September). Castle and grounds represent a joint triumph of Victorian castle preservation and subsequent private ownership; the grounds are very beautiful.

This castle is an Angevin reconstruction (1160) on an eleventh-century foundation and, like so many castles, is associated with one notorious event above all others. Though Saltwood technically belonged to the archbishopric of Canterbury, it became a front-line position in Henry II's fatal quarrel with Archbishop Thomas à Becket. Despite repeated requests from Becket, the King took no steps to prevent one of his more aggressive barons,

Rannulf de Broc, from establishing himself at Saltwood with a private army. They used Saltwood to store crops looted from the archbishopric's estates; but this crude persuasion failed to cow the defiant Archbishop. As the well-known power base of de Broc and his thugs, Saltwood was the rendezvous for the four knights who slipped away from Court, crossing the Channel to murder Becket and win the King's favour. It was from Saltwood that the conspirators rode to Canterbury on the day of Thomas à Becket's notorious martyrdom, 29 December 1170.

Subsequently confirmed as the property of Canterbury, Saltwood reverted to royal ownership 370 years later, when it was presented to Henry VIII by Archbishop Cranmer. By then the castle's value as a fortification had long since disappeared, though it had received several additions since the twelfth century. Of these the most important was the splendid fourteenth-century gatehouse – the residential part of the castle today. Saltwood is therefore a perfect example of how improved residential comfort often went hand-in-hand with improved defensibility.

Saltwood Castle in Kent as it looked before its reconstruction as a private residence, showing the imposing fourteenth-century gatehouse.

DEAL, KENT

Department of the Environment
By A258, 7 miles (11·3 km) NNE from Dover
or A257/A258 from Canterbury via Sandwich

Of the surviving 'stone battleships' built by Henry VIII, Deal is particularly impressive for two reasons: the shoreline it was built to command has remained stable over the centuries, and the castle itself was never converted to a residence to the extent of its neighbour Walmer. You therefore see this geometric masterpiece virtually as completed in 1540, under the spur of the French invasion scare of 1539. Deal was built at great speed (about 18 months) with masonry cannibalized from the dissolved Carmelite Priory, under the direction of Stefan von Haschenperg (Henry's 'Deviser of Buildings' from 1537 to 1543). Henry himself took an active part in designing his new fortifications, particularly their tapered gunports – 'splays as the king's grace hath devised'.

Deal was designed for all-round fire-power, with overlapping circuits of six semicircular bastions each commanding a 60-degree arc of fire. The castle was built to present as little and as low a target as possible, like a modern battle tank in a 'hull-down' position. It would have been impossible for enemy gunners to get a fair shot at the outermost walls, sunk below ground level in a deep dry moat, without coming under converging fire from the upper storeys. The moat floor is commanded by an unbroken ring of 53 gunports, again with overlapping arcs of fire; and a smaller ring of gunports commands the narrow ward or ditch separating the outer defences from the keep. Deal's defences are loopholed with over 145 ports for cannon and handguns. Few castles anywhere, of any period, have had so much fire-power built into them.

But notice how all the best medieval features are still present at Deal: fully concentric defences, with no entrance at moat-floor level apart from a postern to allow sorties; a single entrance at ground-floor level, with a main door impossible to attack without passing under five 'murder-holes'; and outer defences virtually impossible for attackers to convert, at any point, into a strongpoint for an assault on the inner defences. The only way to reach the keep

The approach to Deal, covered by embrasures and circular gunports in the outer gatehouse wall.

The floor of the moat was covered by interlocking lines of fire from the gunports.

Murder holes in the brick vault of the gatehouse.

entrance is by traversing one-third of an enclosed ward, every inch of which could be swept by fire, as could every inch of the wall of the keep. Underground store-rooms and the all-important well lie under the keep. And all designed for a garrison fewer than 50 strong.

Deal was garrisoned during the Armada crisis of 1588, and held for the King in the English Civil War. It surrendered, after two sieges, when all hope of relief had gone (August 1648), but was far too important to destroy, and remained an operational fortress for the rest of the seventeenth century. An interesting parallel with the Tower of London is that eighteenth-century attempts to extend Deal's living quarters were destroyed by German bombs in the Second World War, and omitted in subsequent restoration work.

DOVER, KENT

Department of the Environment

Dover marks the start of the transition from the Norman tower keeps of the eleventh and early twelfth centuries to the concentric castles of the thirteenth. Like the Tower of London, Dover is a 'growth' castle: a keep-and-curtain design with later improvements spanning four centuries, the last being added by Henry VIII.

There are no superlatives adequate for Dover: it has to be seen to be believed. When completed at the end of the twelfth century by Henry II's great architect Maurice the Engineer, Dover was one of the strongest castles in Christendom, and it still looks it. The might of the central defences is seen to excellent advantage because the keep and inner

Dover Castle complex, with Henry II's keep and inner curtain at the centre and the main entrance (Constable's Gate) at lower right.

curtain are not obscured by trees, as at the Tower of London. The castle is dominated by the enormous keep at its heart: basically a cube (98 ft by 98 ft/ 29·9 m by 29·9 m) set on a battered (inward-sloping) plinth, with square towers at each corner. The keep is ringed by Henry II's curtain wall, with ten rectangular flanking towers and two twin-tower gatehouses. Each of these gatehouses was originally

The main strongpoint of Dover's outer defences: the defiant sweep of Constable's Tower, enclosing the main gate of the same name.

The massive, cube-shaped block of Dover Castle keep, solidly based on a battered (inward-sloping) plinth.

protected by a barbican, of which only the northern one has survived.

An outer curtain, extended to the cliff edge, was added under King John in the thirteenth century. These new defences, with their D-shaped flanking towers, served Dover well during its most famous siege, by the French, in 1216–17, when the whole of south-east England from Lincoln to the Channel (including London and the Tower) passed temporarily under French control after the death of John. In this crisis, Hubert de Burgh's resolute defence of Dover, imperilling the French cross-Channel supply route and inspiring a growing resistance movement in the south, was vital in

persuading the French to cut their losses and quit England.

Unlike the Tower of London, whose outer curtain defences were completed under Edward I, Dover's defences reached their widest extent in the thirteenth century under Edward's father, Henry III. He abandoned John's northern gateway (which had been mined during the great siege) and built the splendid Constable's Gate on the west side – still the main entrance to Dover Castle today. The final modifications to Dover's outer defences – Henry VIII's bastions and the scarping of the east side for battery-fire defence – were made in the sixteenth and seventeenth centuries.

The Parliamentarians took Dover with comparative ease in the Civil War, but would have been most unlikely to have destroyed it even if it had resisted a bitter siege. Dover's magnificent state of preservation, as the cream of twelfth- and early thirteenth-century castle-building, was guaranteed down the centuries by the supreme importance of its site on the White Cliffs – 'the front door of England'.

ROCHESTER, KENT

Department of the Environment
A2 from London, Dartford; M2 from Dover,
Canterbury; A29/M2 from Maidstone

Ruined, floorless and roofless though it is today, Rochester is still a superb castle to visit. It is one of the most impressive Norman and Angevin tower keeps in all England, ranking with Dover and the White Tower at London. Rochester comes between these two in date: it was built in the latter years of Henry I, the Conqueror's youngest son, by William de Corbeil, Archbishop of Canterbury, who received the King's licence to build a 'fortification or tower' at Rochester in 1127.

Taller than either the White Tower or Dover, with a ground-to-parapet height of 113 feet (34·5 m) (the four flanking towers are 12 feet (3·7 m) higher), Archbishop William's tower keep was intended to transform the earlier castle at Rochester. Built between 1087 and 1089, this was the work of Bishop Gundulf, the Conqueror's Clerk of Works, whose greatest masterpiece was the White Tower. Like the White Tower, Gundulf's castle at Rochester used the old Roman city walls as foundations for the bailey defences, and these in turn were retained to screen Archbishop William's huge new tower keep.

Archbishop William's keep was no mere stronghold. It was intended to function as an archbishop's palace, with apartments and amenities for his retinue and guests. No other great castle of the period contains so many built-in facilities for a large civilian establishment (such as garderobes for sanitation, of which Rochester has an abnormally large number). On the second floor, the level of the Great Hall (notice the row of sockets for the massive floor-beams), the keep's defensive cross-wall was pierced with an arcade – making it useless for defence at this level, but adding greatly to the living space. You can still see the well-head running up the centre pier of this arcade, providing each floor of the castle with its own water supply. Thus Rochester is startling proof of how early the castle's basic role as stronghold was combined with its other role as lordly residence.

The castle chapel was not enclosed within the main walls, but instead was situated in the upper storey of a forebuilding extending from the north wall. The approach to the main door of the keep, below the chapel, was through an outer entrance

The tower keep of Rochester, showing the round flanking tower built to replace the one destroyed by mining in the 1215 siege.

tower at the side. This makes the forebuilding of Rochester keep a clumsy forerunner of the barbicans and tower gatehouses of later castles.

Yet Rochester's real problem was that too much trust was put in the strength of the keep without enough attention being given to the outer defences. Unlike, say, the Tower of London, Rochester was never taken in hand by a royal castle-builder tough enough to encroach ruthlessly on the surrounding township in order to give the keep an effective belt of concentric curtain walls. The rebuilding of Gundulf's curtain wall undertaken by Henry III, Edward III and Richard II was cosmetic rather than corrective. By 1400 Rochester was too obsolete to justify the expense of keeping it in repair, and was already far gone in decay. Though its mighty stone shell has survived five centuries, a glorious monument to Norman castle-building, the castle's rebuilt corner tower always bore witness to the vulnerability of tower keeps when inadequately screened.

WALMER, KENT

Department of the Environment
(For directions, see Deal, p. 30)

Walmer Castle is easy to find: 1 mile (1·6 km) south of Deal, to whose castle Walmer was the nearest link in Henry VIII's defence chain along the South Coast. The two make an interesting contrast because Walmer, unlike Deal, was extensively rebuilt in the eighteenth century to become the official residence of the Lord Warden of the Cinque Ports. The current incumbent is H M Queen Elizabeth the Queen Mother. The most famous of past Lord Wardens to live at Walmer was the Duke of Wellington, and the wealth of Wellington memorabilia at Walmer makes it an ideal visit for all fans of the Iron Duke who are also interested in castles.

Walmer is open daily, except for the brief periods when the Lord Warden happens to be in residence; and none of the reconstruction work which created its state rooms has erased or marred the basic layout of Henry VIII's castle, built at the same time as Deal (1539–40). Walmer has a much simpler layout than Deal, being a four-fold, instead of a six-fold, cloverleaf, with three tiers of guns to Deal's five. Walmer's round keep (also with well and storerooms at its core) is a simple masonry drum, without projecting bastions. But there is the same lowering of the castle's bottom tier below ground level, with gunports commanding the floor of a deep moat; and the same well-defended main gatehouse and death-trap courtyard between main wall and keep, designed to be swept by defensive fire.

The Wellington memorabilia (including the original Wellington boots) are on the first floor. In fine weather, visitors to Walmer can walk out of the Dining Room onto the gun platforms to enjoy the view from the northern and eastern bastions.

Modern gardens and Tudor gunports in the moat of Walmer Castle, today the residence of the Lord Warden of the Cinque Ports.

UPNOR, KENT

Department of the Environment
A228 from Chatham/Rochester via Frindsbury;
2 miles (3·2 km) from Rochester, signposted

Rochester and Upnor Castles lie so close together that both can be visited easily in a morning, and this is a most appropriate association. Rochester was one of the first stone castles built in England, and Upnor one of the last, some 450 years later, in the reign of Elizabeth I. Both had unhappy histories as defensive strongpoints, because each was the result of misapplied principles. Rochester was weak because it relied too much on the inherent strength of the tower keep, and lacked well-spaced outer defences. Upnor, on the other hand, owed its weakness to too much confidence in too little fire-power – the belief that the guns of a single small fort could render the tidal Medway impassable to a seaborne enemy. And both castles failed dismally, more than once, when put to the test.

Upnor's position still *looks* formidable enough, commanding the dog-leg in the Medway leading from the lower estuary to Chatham. The castle was really a blockhouse, built between 1559 and 1567 to secure the new Fleet base at Chatham, but it saw no action in Elizabeth's reign. In the Civil War it was held for Parliament from 1642 to 1648, when it was taken by men of Chatham dockyard in the King's name. This was less of a Royalist rising than a disgruntled riot, and it was a humiliating event for a strongpoint of such importance; the Royalist 'garrison' lost heart as soon as proper troops turned up and demanded their surrender.

As with Rochester's need for proper concentric defences after the great siege of 1216, Upnor's need after the Civil War was for the addition of flanking batteries to raise its fire-power. But what Upnor got was near-total neglect, paid for in abundance when the Dutch Fleet swept up the Medway (June 1667) to attack the English fleet there. Pepys' *Diary* tells how 'the good old castle built by Queen Elizabeth' did its feeble best, though the Dutch warships 'made no more of Upner's shooting than of a fly'; and that 'Upner played hard with their guns at first, but slowly afterward, either from the men being beat off [by Dutch landing parties] or their powder spent.' In true British style, the Medway stable-door was properly bolted *after* the fiasco of 1667, with the addition of downstream batteries making Upnor redundant.

Upnor Castle survived, with extensive modification, as a residence, but though it lacks the bristling menace of earlier Deal it is a most attractive Tudor castle, out of the ordinary and well worth a visit.

Built under Elizabeth I to protect the Fleet anchorage in the Medway, Upnor Castle proved to have too little fire-power to beat off the Dutch in 1667.

LEWES, EAST SUSSEX

Sussex Archaeological Society
A27 from Brighton; A259/A27 from Hastings
via Bexhill and Eastbourne;
A26 from Tunbridge Wells;
A275 from East Grinstead

Lewes is another first-generation Norman castle. It was the seat of one of William I's most trusted lieutenants, William de Warenne, who was granted extensive estates in Sussex after the Conquest. William de Warenne's castle was built to command the valley of the Sussex Ouse – as its contemporary, Roger de Montgomery's castle at Arundel, was built to command the valley of the Arun. How well Warenne succeeded may be judged from the superb views over the town and surrounding countryside which the visitor enjoys from Lewes Castle.

William de Warenne seems to have attempted a most ambitious novelty at Lewes: a castle centred on two mottes instead of the usual one. A more orthodox design was obviously chosen when the time came to convert the defences to stone, with a shell keep erected on only one of the mottes. Curtain defences were added in the thirteenth century, and an enormous barbican – the best-preserved part of the castle ruins today – in the early fourteenth.

The story of Lewes as an active castle ended unusually early, with the extinction of the Warenne line in 1347 and the depopulation of Sussex in the Black Death of 1348. In the years of recovery, Lewes Castle was eclipsed from the west by Arundel and from the east (after 1385) by Bodiam, remaining abandoned and increasingly ruinous, and used inevitably as a quarry by the townsmen. There was no halt to the process of dilapidation until the nineteenth century, when the Sussex Archaeological Society intervened to preserve what was left of this finely-sited castle.

Lewes Castle: a shell keep completed on only one of the original two mottes.

PEVENSEY, EAST SUSSEX

Department of the Environment
A259 from Eastbourne and from Hastings via Bexhill

Pevensey is a fine specimen of a 'hermit-crab' castle, with the walls of a Roman coastal fortress used as outer bailey defences for a Norman castle. Pevensey's Romano-British name was *Anderida*, and according to the *Anglo-Saxon Chronicle* it was stormed with great slaughter by the invading South Saxons in AD 491. That is the last recorded instance of Pevensey falling to a direct attack, for over the intervening 1,500-odd years, though often besieged and occasionally surrendered, Pevensey has never been taken by direct assault. This makes it a decided rarity among English castles.

After the Conquest, William I granted Pevensey to his half-brother, Robert de Mortain, who set about the conversion of the Roman defences into a castle. He began by building a simple tower keep in the south-eastern curve of the oval described by the Roman walls, enclosing this keep with a ditch and palisade to form an inner bailey. By 1088 Pevensey Castle was already strong enough to hold out against William II in the revolt against the new King by Count Robert's brother, Odo of Bayeux, until starved into surrender. King Stephen, besieging Pevensey in 1147, also failed to storm the castle because of the strength of its 'most ancient walls'. With the accession of Henry II in 1154, Pevensey became a Crown castle and the great years of

Pevensey's moat, and the north and east towers screening the inner bailey.

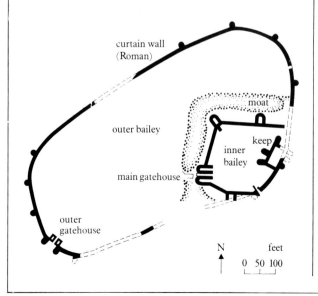

building began: a late twelfth-century keep with massive rounded projecting towers was added, and subsequently enclosed by a thirteenth-century curtain wall. This was studded with three D-shaped flanking towers and a twin-tower gatehouse.

Pevensey's two most famous sieges in its final form were against the supporters of Simon de Montfort in 1264 (holding out for Henry III) and against Richard II in 1399 (holding out for Henry, Duke of Lancaster, afterwards Henry IV). But despite its undoubted strength, records show that Pevensey was an expensive castle to maintain; this, combined with the receding of the sea coast which lessened the castle's strategic importance, led to a

Pevensey Castle keep from the east, standing outside the circuit of the curtain wall of the Roman 'Saxon Shore' fortress.

story of sustained neglect from the end of the fourteenth century. By 1500 Pevensey Castle had been abandoned, and though surveyed in 1573 was dismissed as not worth the immense cost of repair. An emplacement for two guns was built behind the fallen wall of the outer bailey for the Armada invasion crisis of 1588, but there was no role for Pevensey in the English Civil War.

Pevensey's keep suffered worst from continual quarrying over the centuries, but the immense strength of the masonry has preserved most of the ancient Roman walls and the inner bailey curtain and towers. The castle's last private owner, the Duke of Devonshire, presented it to the nation in 1925, and preservation work began at last. In the Second World War, however, camouflaged machine-gun positions were sited among the ruins and a blockhouse (now removed) was built in the main entrance. Most of these twentieth-century defences were left deliberately, as witness to Pevensey's unique longevity as a stronghold.

The basement of Pevensey's north tower, in the inner bailey, with a separate stairway leading up the tower's interior.

BODIAM, EAST SUSSEX

National Trust
E of A229, 3 miles (4·8 km) S of Hawkhurst;
A21 from Tunbridge Wells, A229 from Maidstone,
A229 from Hastings, A267/A265 from Hailsham via Heathfield

Inside the south-east drum tower at Bodiam. The square holes supported the floor beams of the upper storey.

Bodiam has a unique place among English castles, and one look will tell you why. This is everyone's dream of a medieval castle – compact, symmetrical, with towers and battlements of a stone which looks particularly beautiful in late afternoon or evening sunshine, apparently floating at the centre of a wide encircling moat. Without the distractions of a bustling modern town on its doorstep, Bodiam seems timeless. If ever a castle makes readers of Malory think of Sir Lancelot's beloved castle, Joyeuse Garde, it is Bodiam.

Despite all appearances, Bodiam is more of a fortified manor than a castle. Its builder, Sir Edward Dalyngrigge, was licensed in October 1385 to 'fortify and crenellate his manor house ... and to construct and make thereof a castle in defence of the

adjacent countryside and for resistance against our enemies'. Like Henry VIII's coastal castles, Bodiam was built to block a French invasion which never came. The castle is a rarity; a strongpoint of national defence 'contracted out' by the Crown (or, in more depressing modern terms, defence on the cheap). Bodiam's new role also indicates the speed with which the ancient Cinque Port of Rye was, by the late fourteenth century, losing all value as a naval base for coastal defence. The new Bodiam Castle was intended to block any French advance inland from Rye up the Rother Valley.

Though never put to the test against French invaders, Bodiam's defences were shrewdly contrived. The wide moat kept the walls outside the effective range of the primitive cannon of the day;

The spacious and elegant screen passage flanking the lord's hall at Bodiam, viewed from the north.

Bodiam's wide moat would have prevented enemy siege gunners from bombarding the walls at point-blank range.

Bodiam was designed to be cannon-proof as well as mine-proof. The original causeway across the moat led first to a barbican (the remains of which can still be seen) then made a right-turn towards the castle gate. This last stretch of causeway was swept by the castle's own guns, firing through 'keyhole' ports built into the twin towers of the gatehouse. Yet Bodiam was always more of a residence than a fortress; the green courtyard of today was once packed with the lord's apartments, servants' quarters, store-rooms and kitchens, with most advanced chimney ducts built into the outer walls, and a generous allocation of windows.

Though hastily surrendered to the Parliamentarians in the Civil War, Bodiam was viciously slighted by the victors and remained a ruin for the next two and a half centuries. From 1917, Bodiam's fighting shell was painstakingly re-created at great expense under the direction of Lord Curzon, who presented this model of castle restoration to the nation in 1925.

The gatehouse of Bodiam Castle, flanked by 'keyhole' gunports for defensive fire, and with a restored portcullis above the gate.

43

ARUNDEL, WEST SUSSEX

Privately owned
A3100/A283/A284 from Guildford via Petworth and Pulborough;
A24/A29/A284 from Dorking via Pulborough; A27 from
Portsmouth via Chichester, from Brighton via Worthing

Arundel falls into the same category as the Tower of London and Windsor: a castle replete with attractions, for which too brief a visit is really a waste of time and money. It has been the residence of the Dukes of Norfolk for 500 years; when the 300-year-old Fitzalan dynasty became extinct in 1580, the castle and title passed to the Howard family.

The similarity between the layouts (and indeed the modern fabrics) of Arundel and Windsor is very striking. Both are extensive Victorian reconstructions of medieval linear castles, which were in turn extensions of first-generation motte-and-bailey castles with shell keeps. The restoration of Arundel was completed in 1903, and although the internal result is a particularly impressive masterpiece of the

The bridge across the ditch to the Bevis Tower at Arundel, showing how the curtain wall is angled sharply inwards to connect with the keep.

nineteenth-century Gothic Revival, the work started with the preservation of the twelfth-century shell keep on its motte and the thirteenth-century curtain wall and barbican.

Arundel, with a chalk spur commanding the valley of the river Arun, had been a natural site for a Norman motte-and-bailey. Its conversion to a stone castle began almost at once, and the most impressive survival from Arundel's first stone defences is the squat tower gatehouse, known as Earl Roger's Tower (named after Earl Roger de Montgomery, who died in 1094). The twin barbican towers screening Earl Roger's Tower were added, with the

The machicolated south tower at Arundel, part of the extensive rebuilding carried out under the Dukes of Norfolk in the nineteenth century.

Arundel Castle on its commanding ridge, viewed from the south-west across the river Arun.

outer curtain wall, by Richard, first of the Fitzalan Earls of Arundel (1289–1302). But this did not create a truly concentric castle, with the keep fully enclosed by the curtain wall. Arundel's western curtain wall is angled sharply inward to join the keep, leaving the latter as part of the outer defences – a notable weakness.

Arundel withstood two famous sieges in the twelfth century: one by Henry I attacking the rebel Earl Robert in 1102 (Arundel fell in three months), and one by King Stephen attacking his rival, Henry I's daughter Matilda (Arundel held out and Matilda escaped). But the castle's third and worst siege was in the Civil War. After its capture by the Royalists in December 1643 the Parliamentarians promptly besieged Arundel, before its new garrison had put itself in a proper state of defence. An unusually heavy series of artillery bombardments caused extensive damage to the western defences (you can still see the marks of Roundhead shot on the Barbican towers) and the Royalists surrendered on 5 January 1644. Arundel was then further wrecked by deliberate slighting and became steadily more ruinous until restoration work started with the 11th Duke in 1789. The painstaking work of restoring Arundel's medieval defences to their original appearance was the enduring achievement of Henry, 15th Duke of Norfolk, between 1890 and 1903. *(See also p. 272)*

Another fine result of the nineteenth-century rebuilding of Arundel: the Dining Room.

45

FARNHAM, SURREY

Department of the Environment
A31, 9 miles (14·5 km) w of Guildford;
M3 to Junction 4, then 7 miles (11·3 km) south
via Frimley, Farnborough, Aldershot, A3011

Farnham was one of the more important manors of the medieval bishopric of Winchester. The first Farnham Castle in stone was one of five built without Crown licence by Henry of Blois (Bishop of Winchester 1129–71) during the civil wars of his brother King Stephen. This square stone keep on a conical motte was destroyed by Henry II in 1155. There is no documentary evidence for the rebuilding of Farnham Castle as a shell keep ringed by a curtain wall, but this seems to have been accomplished, this time very much under royal licence, between about 1180 and 1200.

This is the oldest part of Farnham Castle as it stands today, and it is extraordinary on two counts. Firstly, most of the old masonry is quarried local chalk – the least suitable of all materials, one might think, from which to build a castle. This chalk is

Though clad in a seventeenth-century facade with nineteenth-century additions above, the core of Farnham Castle gatehouse is of medieval origin.

either rubble bound with mortar (as in the foundations of the original keep) or blocks faced in later years with sandstone or brick, which explains the 'patchy' look of Farnham's masonry. And the second surprise is the shell keep itself – enclosing the whole motte instead of merely crowning it, with the gap between shell wall and motte later filled in. By about 1300 the gap had vanished, filled to the level of the top of the motte, creating a massive drum-like structure. The keep's central well-shaft (which can still be inspected) was sunk through the heart of the now-buried motte. The outer face of the keep is studded with six shallow, rectangular flanking towers reminiscent of Framlingham, with the south-eastern tower doubling as the keep's gatehouse.

The wedge-shaped area of the original bailey was preserved in the outer walled courtyard, around which were packed the living apartments, hall, kitchen and chapel appropriate to a bishop's household. Entry to this complex is via the splendid brick tower built by Bishop Waynflete in 1470–5,

The entrance to the keep at Farnham Castle is a murderous bottleneck equipped for portcullis defences and overhead fire through a murder hole.

46

The keep of Farnham Castle, an original motte enclosed in a shell wall, with the interior subsequently filled in.

probably inspired by the contemporary brick masterpiece of Tattershall.

Farnham surrendered to the invading French in the war of 1216–17, but was recaptured ten months later (March 1217). In the Civil War, Farnham was taken and briefly held by the Royalists (November 1642), then recaptured and held by the Parliamentarians until January 1645, when Royalist raiders surprised the garrison and took possession for a day before retreating. Being held by Parliament for most of the war did not, however, save Farnham's keep from being slighted (deliberately wrecked) in 1648 'so as not to be defensible or tenable by an enemy if surprised'. (The resultant gap can be seen on the east side.) Farnham returned to the bishopric of Winchester with the Restoration of 1660. It remained the residence of the bishops of Winchester until 1927, and of the bishops of Guildford until 1955 – a continuous occupation which happily saved this fine castle from further decay.

OTHER CASTLES TO VISIT

Allington, Kent
Finely restored late thirteenth-century reconstruction on earlier site; today owned by Carmelite Order.

Chilham, Kent
Polygonal twelfth-century keep; gardens only open to public.

Eynsford, Kent
Impressive twelfth-century curtain wall; only $\frac{1}{2}$ mile (800 metres) N of Lullingstone Roman Villa.

Hever, Kent
Finely restored fourteenth-century fortified manor, of Henry VIII/Anne Boleyn fame.

Sissinghurst, Kent
Tudor fortified manor, more mansion than fortifications. Beautiful gardens.

Guildford, Surrey
Shell of Norman keep.

Bramber, West Sussex
Much-slighted twelfth-century castle of former great prominence on south coast – a noted 'leaning tower' castle.

Hastings, East Sussex
Cliff-top shell of stone replacement for William I's first castle on English soil.

THE SOUTH COUNTRY

DONNINGTON, BERKSHIRE

Department of the Environment
1½ miles (2·4 km) NW of Newbury;
B4494 from Newbury, A34 from M3, Junction 13

Donnington is a castle of the same vintage as Bodiam: a fortified manor of the late fourteenth century, brought into being by licence of Richard II in 1386. It was the scene of one of the longest and most dramatic sieges of the Civil War, during which the main part of the castle was battered to destruction. Only the twin-tower gatehouse has survived, but it dominates the landscape for miles.

Donnington was a manor in Saxon times, as attested by Domesday Book. In 1386 it was held by Richard de Abberbury, a knight in the service of Edward the 'Black Prince' who had been chosen as one of the young Richard II's guardians, subsequently serving at the royal Court as chamberlain to Queen Anne. This service earned him Richard's licence to 'build anew and fortify with stone and lime, and crenellate a certain Castle on his own land at Donyngton'. The result was an oblong curtain wall enclosing the manor buildings and courtyard, with round flanking towers at the corners and a square flanking tower halfway along each of the long sides. These outer defences were completed after the magnificent, three-storey tower gatehouse, of which two cylindrical towers have survived virtually intact. The remnants of outer barbican walls can be seen outside the gatehouse entrance.

Unscathed by the Wars of the Roses, in 1568 Donnington earned a visit from Queen Elizabeth I, for which the old drawbridge before the barbican was replaced by a fixed bridge. In 1586 Camden's *Britannia* described Donnington as 'a small but very neat castle, seated on the banks of a woody hill, having a fair prospect and windows in all sides very lightsome'. But this attractive picture was shattered for good by the Civil War. In September 1643 King Charles sent Colonel John Boys to garrison Donnington (abandoned by its Parliamentarian owner) with 200 foot, 25 horse and guns. Boys's first task was to employ local labour to surround Donnington with earthworks and artillery bastions in the latest style. In this he succeeded so well that Donnington resisted five successive Parliamentarian sieges and bombardments between July 1644 and March 1646. The castle was twice relieved by the King's army and Boys, knighted by a grateful monarch, launched repeated sorties against the Parliamentarians.

By the spring of 1646, however, Donnington's garrison was in poor shape. The whole of the curtain wall and its towers had been battered to rubble, leaving only the gatehouse standing. There was no hope of further relief; but Boys did not surrender until he had passed an envoy through the Parliamentarian lines to obtain the King's written permission to do so. Only then did Boys make his surrender, receiving the full honours of war, on 1 April 1646. Donnington's garrison marched out 'bagge and baggage, muskets charged and primed, mache in Coke, bullet in mouthe, drumes beatinge and Collurers ffleyinge. Every man taken wth hime as much amunishion as hee could Carrye. As honourable Conditions as Could be given.'

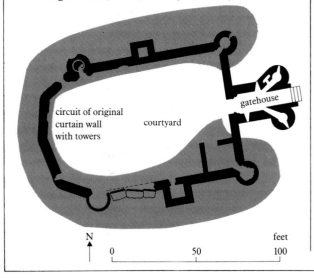

circuit of original
curtain wall
with towers

courtyard

gatehouse

N

feet
0   50   100

The twin towers of Donnington's gatehouse – all that was left from the Civil War siege which battered the rest of the castle to ruins.

WINDSOR, BERKSHIRE

M4 from London, Reading to Junction 6; A308 from Staines;
A332 from Camberley; A355 from Beaconsfield via Slough

Windsor has two overriding claims to fame: it is the biggest inhabited castle in the world, and the only royal castle to have been used continually as such for the past 500 years. England's only other royal castle of similar size and antiquity, the Tower of London, is the finest concentric castle in England; Windsor is England's finest linear castle, with the baileys or wards enclosed in a row instead of one inside the other.

Windsor started life in the aftermath of the Norman Conquest as one of the cordon of castles sited by William I to cover the approaches to London and the south-east, his original power base in England. The site on the ridge above the major waterway of the Thames was an important one, and the lie of the land permitted two baileys, one higher than the other. This layout is preserved today in Windsor's Upper and Lower Wards, with the keep on its motte – the Round Tower – enclosed by the Middle Ward.

Though Windsor's intimate connection with the royal family has made it probably the best-known and most popular English castle today, it would have been a very different story eight centuries ago. Easily the most hated element of Norman supremacy was the strict preservation of all forests as royal hunting estates, with savage punishment meted out to any who dared hunt the king's game or fell the trees which sheltered it. Hunting remained the true 'sport of kings' throughout the Middle Ages (even the saintly Edward the Confessor was a fanatical huntsman) and Windsor became a favourite hunting lodge of the Norman kings.

Henry II began both the improved fortification of Windsor (shell keep and curtain wall) and its conversion into a royal residence. By 1193 Windsor, seized by the rebel Prince John during his brother Richard's imprisonment in Germany, was strong enough to sit out a siege by forces loyal to Richard. Windsor was King John's headquarters during the tense negotiations leading to the signing of Magna Carta at nearby Runnymede in June 1215, and was again successfully defended in a three-months' siege during the civil war which followed. These were Windsor's only two sieges, and the damage inflicted by them was speedily repaired by the strengthening of the defences and expansion of the royal apartments under Henry III in the thirteenth century.

By 1300 Windsor had reached a stage of development that would be familiar to modern visitors, and the castle was a favourite royal residence. But its great days as a national institution began in the fourteenth century with the reign of Edward III, the first of the only two English monarchs born at Windsor (the other being Henry VI). Edward III fostered what might be called the national cult of St George, embodied in his foundation of the knightly Order of the Garter which has had its seat at Windsor ever since. The Order's glorious Chapel of

*The glorious fan vaulting and
heraldic banners of
St George's Chapel.*

The superb skyline panorama of Windsor Castle, dominated by the Round Tower, with St George's Chapel to the left.

St George, one of the most beautiful buildings in England, was begun by the Yorkist King Edward IV in the late fifteenth century and completed by Henry VIII in 1528. Henry VIII also ordered the building of the imposing main entrance familiar to visitors today.

Windsor was lucky in the Civil War: it could easily have gone the way of Donnington, destroyed in repeated sieges, but instead was held for Parliament throughout the war and never attacked. Charles I was confined there in December 1648 before being transferred to London for his trial and execution in the following month. So far from consigning Windsor to oblivion, the regicides unwittingly helped enhance Windsor's royal aura by burying the 'Martyr King' there. The restored Charles II held summer court at Windsor, where the royal apartments were again rebuilt and redecorated; later Windsor was the favourite residence of George III (1760–1820), who was buried there, setting a precedent followed by every English monarch since.

Windsor's magnificent appearance today is due primarily to the much-maligned George IV (1820–30). Determined to rebuild the castle as a sumptuous and imposing modern palace, he gave the architect Jeffry Wyatville that most difficult of tasks, to transform without destroying, and took a close personal interest in the work. Wyatville's triumphant success ranks as one of the greatest achievements of English nineteenth-century architecture. He rightly concentrated on the Round Tower as the heart of the castle, and managed to double its height without making the result grotesque. You have to look very hard to see the join between Henry II's shell keep and Wyatville's addition, the latter with its circuit of machicolation (projecting arches) unobtrusively suggestive of a royal crown. Another master-stroke was the choice of facing stone for the outer walls, which looks natural and timeless, rather than sham.

Like the Tower of London, Windsor merits more than a short visit. The State Apartments in the Upper Ward are not always open to the public, and it is worth checking in advance because they should not be missed. Military buffs must not overlook the Queen's Guard and Waterloo Chambers; Queen Mary's Dolls' House always delights young children; and it should be unthinkable to visit Windsor without at least entering St George's Chapel.

The Long or Queen's View at Windsor, looking from

the Great Park towards the State Apartments.

PORTCHESTER, HAMPSHIRE

Department of the Environment
6 miles (9·6 km) from Portsmouth,
off A27 to Fareham/Southampton

Portchester is the most complete 'hermit-crab' castle of the late eleventh and early twelfth century. It lies on the north shore of Portsmouth Harbour, whose waters still protect the east wall at high tide. The castle's outer bailey walls are those of the best-preserved of all the late Roman 'Saxon Shore' fortresses built along the east and south coasts in the third and fourth centuries AD. The medieval castle dates from Henry I's reign (1100–35) and seems to have been built under his supervision. The north-eastern corner of the Roman walls was replaced with an exceptionally fine twelfth-century tower keep, enclosed by a rectangular inner bailey. The inner bailey walls were protected by a right-angled moat crossed by a drawbridge.

In its heyday, Portchester's capacious Roman walls accommodated a small town. Eventually the town grew too big for the confining walls and began to migrate to the more spacious site of present-day Portsmouth; but for 300-odd years Portchester remained one of the most important royal castles of the Norman and Angevin kings. Its unique position, with 'one foot on shore and one on sea', made it ideal for mustering and embarking armies destined for service in Normandy. Edward III shipped his army from Portchester for the Crécy campaign of 1346, and Henry V did the same for the Agincourt campaign of 1415. In many ways, Portchester was a miniature duplicate of the Tower of London; the keep was used as both state treasury and state

Portchester Castle, with a twelfth-century keep and inner bailey built into an angle of the Roman 'Saxon Shore' fortress.

The enduring masonry and drum-shaped flanking towers of the outer, late Roman walls at Portchester.

prison, and Richard II built a palace within the inner bailey.

Yet Portchester's role as an effective royal castle was cut short with surprising speed; as early as 1441 it was written off as 'ruinous and feeble'. There were two real reasons for Portchester's redundancy: its continuing eclipse by nearby Portsmouth, and the more fundamental problem that there was no way of up-dating the defences to bring it into line with more modern developments in fortification. It remained virtually a ghost castle until Charles I sold it off to private ownership in 1632. Held for Parliament throughout the Civil War, Portchester suffered the ignominy of being used as a barracks. But the castle was still leased back by the Crown for use as a prisoner-of-war camp in the Dutch Wars of the later seventeenth century, the Seven Years War in the eighteenth century, and the Revolutionary and Napoleonic Wars.

A fascinating castle to visit, if only because of the great antiquity of its defences, Portchester shows Norman ingenuity in castle-building at its best. It is a unique specimen of a twelfth-century castle which, with results fatal to itself, failed to evolve.

The unusually complete tower of Portchester's twelfth-century keep.

HURST, HAMPSHIRE

Department of the Environment
A337/B3058 to Milford on Sea from
Southampton via Lyndhurst;
approach to castle by ferry from Keyhaven,
or on foot from Milford on Sea, 2½ miles (4 km)

Hurst Castle is one of Henry VIII's 'intermediary' coastal castles, built between the French invasion scare of 1539–40 and the French descent on the Isle of Wight in 1545. Of all Henry VIII's castles it is the one with the most spectacular site, if less directly accessible by car than most of the others. American visitors will probably think of Fort Sumter at Charleston. Although Hurst does not stand on a natural island, like Sumter, it has an equally commanding position: out at the end of a 2½-mile (4-km) shingle spit extending into the western entrance to the Solent from Milford on Sea, at the Solent's narrowest point.

With Calshot, 12 miles (19·3 km) north-east at the entrance to Southampton Water, Hurst Castle represents the first stage of Henry VIII's plan to render Southampton and Portsmouth secure from assault by sea. It is unlikely that the King ever believed that this could be done merely with forts like Hurst, sited only on the mainland. But it needed the stimulus of the French invasion of 1545 – in which Hurst played no part – for the building of additional defences on the Isle of Wight. Hurst's later counterpart across the Solent on the Isle of Wight, creating an unpleasant crossfire against any enemy fleet attempting to penetrate the Solent from the west, was Yarmouth. The complementary role intended for Hurst and Yarmouth may be compared with that of Pendennis and St Mawes in Cornwall.

Hurst was held for Parliament in the Civil War and at the end of 1648 served briefly as a prison for Charles I during his transfer from Carisbrooke to Windsor, London and execution. Always a fighting castle pure and simple, Hurst lacked any apartments fit for royal visitors and Charles was deeply depressed by his dank and gloomy surroundings. Pondering on the chances of assassination during his stay at Hurst, Charles bitterly called the castle 'a place fit for such a purpose'.

Subsequent modifications to the castle are the result of Hurst's enduring service as a coastal strongpoint over four centuries. Its excellent site caused it to be manned again in both world wars.

Henry VIII's castle at Hurst, thrust out into the narrows of the western Solent at the end of a narrow spit of shingle.

OLD SARUM, WILTSHIRE

Department of the Environment
A345, 2 miles (3·2 km) N of Salisbury

Old Sarum is like Portchester: a 'hermit-crab' Norman castle planted amid fortifications of an earlier age, which lost its strategic value when the town it was intended to dominate migrated to a new site. It is a useful reminder that medieval castles never existed in isolation, but were woven tightly into the social fabric of the age. Any dramatic changes at local level inevitably resulted in change to the local castle – in the case of Old Sarum, a terminal one.

Old Sarum is first and foremost a Celtic fortification, but it does not seem to have been a Roman township. Sarum's old ramparts were certainly defended again in AD 552, when the West Saxons defeated a Romano-British force there – a reminder of how long it took Roman Britain to give way to the invading Anglo-Saxons. As a Saxon township or *burh*, fortified to survive in the long wars against the Danes, *Serebrig* was important enough for kings to hold court there, and to be assigned a mint. But Old Sarum Castle followed the Norman Conquest.

Military genius that he was, William I never overlooked a geographically useful site, and his attention seems to have been drawn there before 1070, when he disbanded his army at Old Sarum after crushing the Northern Rebellion. In 1075 he chose it as the new seat for the old bishopric of Sherborne, which stretched from Windsor to Lyme Regis. The new cathedral was begun at Old Sarum and completed in 1092 – promptly to be destroyed in a storm. In the reign of Henry I, Bishop Roger of Sherborne, one of the great administrators of the Norman era, planned a permanent replacement not only for the cathedral but also for the motte-and-bailey castle which had occupied the centre of Old Sarum since the 1060s.

Like the bull's-eye of a target, Bishop Roger's new castle dominated the circular enclosure within the old Celtic ringwork, with a deep circular dry ditch surrounding a broad motte crowned with a circular curtain wall. Unlike Pevensey or Portchester there was no keep at Old Sarum, but the stout outer wall of the Bishop's Palace, taking up the north-western quadrant of the inner bailey, was clearly intended to serve the same purpose as the walls of the Pevensey and Portchester keeps. What made Old Sarum startlingly different from other castles of the same date was the fact that the Bishop's Palace was completed *first*, with the curtain wall being completed later in the twelfth century. There are very strong parallels between Old Sarum and Bishop Roger's other castle, Sherborne, also built between 1107 and 1139.

Old Sarum was neither a fortified cathedral town, nor a fighting castle equipped with apartments and suited to a leading civilian role, but a wholly experimental mix of the two – and the experiment did not work. At Old Sarum, Church interests prevailed over the military. The cathedral clergy bitterly objected to living almost like prisoners, under the jurisdiction of the castle. In 1219 not only royal but papal approval was given for the building of a new cathedral – the birth certificate of modern Salisbury. The rapid development of the new cathedral town left Old Sarum Castle high and dry, stripped of the dual role which Bishop Roger had built into it a hundred years before. By the mid-thirteenth century, with its existence now futile and its maintenance costs soaring, Old Sarum was already withering on the vine – just as Portchester was to do, for almost precisely the same reasons, 200 years later.

When visiting Old Sarum, it is fascinating to speculate as to what would have happened to the castle's development without its fatal connection with the cathedral. For here, inside the ancient Celtic ringwork, may be seen the first, fumbling attempt at a concentric castle layout – a failed experiment a century ahead of its time.

Like the bull's-eye of a target: Old Sarum keep, protected by ditch and low motte, surrounded by the ancient Celtic ringwork enclosing the cathedral site.

CARISBROOKE, ISLE OF WIGHT

Department of the Environment
1 mile (1·6 km) sw of Newport;
buses from Newport to Yarmouth and Freshwater;
local bus service to castle in summer months

*The imposing gatehouse of Carisbrooke Castle,
thrusting outward from the western
curtain wall.*

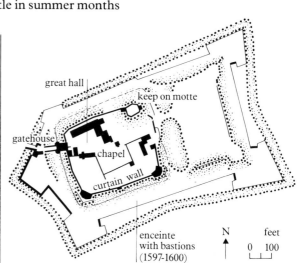

Doubtless Carisbrooke Castle will always be associated with the ten-month captivity of Charles I in 1647–8, after the final defeat of his cause in the English Civil War. But it is also a perfect model of the evolution of English castle history, from its beginnings in the eleventh century to the seventeenth.

As the Isle of Wight's most important castle, Carisbrooke has the unusual distinction of having been kept in excellent repair for nine centuries without a break. The castle began as a standard Norman motte-and-bailey, constructed by William FitzOsbern in the 1060s. Between 1107 and 1136 this was converted to a stone shell keep and curtain wall, in the form of an oblong with rounded corners spliced to the motte and keep at the north-western corner. These defences were unusually strong because of the height of the steep banks sloping away outside the curtain wall; there was no need for a ditch or moat. A chapel, great hall and other service accommodation were added in the thirteenth century, when the north-east curtain wall was strengthened, and a barbican was added to the gatehouse through the western wall. This was converted to a typically fourteenth-century twin-tower gatehouse in 1335–6.

Carisbrooke's defences were overhauled so as to fit the castle for the 'cannon era' in the last 13 years of the sixteenth century, the work beginning at the time of the Armada crisis (1587–8). The south-east and south-west towers of the curtain wall received pointed outer bastions, and a completely new set of enclosing ramparts was built round the entire castle, with 'arrow-head' artillery bastions at the corners. These final embellishments completed Carisbrooke Castle as it appears today.

Carisbrooke's medieval history was uneventful; it only stood one siege, by King Stephen's forces in 1136, in which it sustained little damage because its water supply failed, forcing the rebel Baldwin de Redvers to surrender. In the fourteenth century the Hundred Years War gave rise to a succession of

The Governor's House at Carisbrooke (now the Isle of Wight Museum) with the castle keep on its motte in the left background.

Looking down from Carisbrooke's keep and motte to where the eastern curtain wall resumes its circuit.

attacks by French raiders, all of which were beaten off. At the outset of the Civil War the Royalist Governor, the Earl of Portland, was neatly removed by order of Parliament before he could garrison Carisbrooke for Charles I, and the Parliamentarians retained the castle throughout the war.

The irony of Charles I's famous imprisonment at Carisbrooke is that he went there voluntarily, after escaping from Hampton Court in November 1647. The Governor was the nephew of one of the King's chaplains and Charles believed him to be a Royalist sympathizer at heart. But any sympathy the Governor might have had was dispelled when he discovered that Charles was secretly negotiating to renew the Civil War with the aid of an invading Scottish army. From then on (December 1647– September 1648) Charles remained a prisoner at Carisbrooke, making a hopeless bungle of an enterprising plan to free him (which failed when Charles discovered, too late, that the bars on his bedchamber window were too narrow for him to squeeze through!).

One of the most famous sights of Carisbrooke is the donkey-powered windlass drawing water from the well in the courtyard. This was added during the castle's final expansion in the reign of Elizabeth I.

YARMOUTH, ISLE OF WIGHT

Department of the Environment
A3054 from Newport; B3401 from Carisbrooke

Yarmouth was one of Henry VIII's last castles, built to supplement the Isle of Wight's defences after the French invasion of 1545. It was sited so that with Hurst, on the other side of the Solent, it could subject any enemy attempt to penetrate the western Solent to a punishing crossfire.

Yarmouth presents a total contrast to the rounded 'cloverleafs' of Deal and Walmer. It marks the mid-sixteenth century transition from rounded bastions to the straight-sided fortifications of the late sixteenth and seventeenth centuries, which reached their peak of development with the French military engineer Vauban in the reign of Louis XIV. The new vogue for straight-sided fortifications exploited the fact that cannons fire in straight lines, and that a correctly angled fortress layout relying on straight lines required fewer guns to defend it than one with rounded bastions. This, of course, was a refinement of a principle which had dominated castle design from its medieval beginnings: the fact that a symmetrical castle layout required a smaller garrison than an unbalanced one. Yarmouth's original garrison was a master gunner, a porter, and 17 soldiers.

The layout of Yarmouth is simplicity itself: a canted square, with the north-western corner pointing out to sea and the south-eastern, inland corner protected by an 'arrow-head' bastion. Two triangular gun platforms were added to the seaward corner in about 1632 to increase crossfire against attacks from the sea.

Like Carisbrooke, Yarmouth had a Royalist commander at the outbreak of the Civil War but surrendered on demand, and remained in Parliamentarian hands throughout the conflict. The castle remained a coastal battery throughout the late seventeenth and eighteenth centuries, and the Napoleonic Wars. It was finally disarmed in 1885, used as a Coast Guard signalling station until 1901, and commandeered for service use in both world wars, extending its active life to 400 years.

The courtyard of Henry VIII's castle at Yarmouth, looking west to the stairway leading up to the main gun platform.

CHRISTCHURCH, DORSET

Department of the Environment
A35 from Bournemouth, Southampton;
A337 from Lymington;
A338/B3347 from Salisbury via Ringwood

Christchurch was originally a first-generation motte-and-bailey, sited, like Arundel and Lewes, to command the lower reaches of a river – in this case the Avon – on the Channel coast. Although it is extensively ruined and there is comparatively little to see, Christchurch is still worth a brief visit when passing through the Bournemouth region. For this is a rare example of a square stone keep – not a shell keep – built on an earlier artificial motte, and the twelfth-century walls have survived. The other important surviving unit is the Castle Hall, or Constable's House, which was built in the castle bailey (now the gardens of the King's Arms Hotel) at the same time as the keep, instead of being a later addition. Though roofless, the enormously thick walls of the Constable's House show that it was built as a 'mini-keep': part of the defences of the castle, not merely living quarters. The hall itself, with original windows and round chimney, is on the first floor. Here, then, is an unusually early example of improved defensibility and domestic comfort advancing together.

*A window in the shell of
the Constable's House, in the bailey of
Christchurch Castle.*

There is a strong parallel between Christchurch and Old Sarum, and it is to be found in the town's famous Norman priory close by the castle. This is another example (as at Old Sarum and, above all, at Durham) of an important piece of Church property taking precedence over the local castle, and effectively preventing it from evolving further than its twelfth-century stage of development.

*Christchurch Castle keep from the south-east – a most unusual example of a stone keep built on an earlier,
artificial motte.*

CORFE, DORSET

Privately owned
A351 from Wareham

Corfe is the Old English word for 'gap' or 'pass', in this case describing the natural gap in the range of hills traversing the peninsula known as the Isle of Purbeck, south of Wareham. The castle stands on a natural hillock commanding the gap, and was the site of a royal residence long before the Norman Conquest. At Corfe, on 18 March 978, the young King Edward 'The Martyr' was murdered – allegedly at the instigation of his stepmother Elfrida, in order to put his half-brother Ethelred 'The Unready' on the throne. The *Anglo-Saxon Chronicle* lamented that 'no worse deed than this for the English people was committed since first they came to Britain'. At Corfe the murder is still commemorated by the massive, twin-towered gateway known as the Martyr's Gate, built on the reputed scene of the crime.

The Martyr's Gate was probably the outer entrance to the keep built at Corfe by William I; but the castle evolved rapidly on this natural site, with a lower ward being added outside the upper. What you see today are the ruins of the castle's near-total rebuilding in the late fourteenth and early fifteenth century, the Martyr's Gate now being the gatehouse between the Lower and Upper Wards. The result was an immensely strong linear castle, which shares with Pevensey the rare distinction of never having been taken by assault.

In the twelfth century, long before it had reached its full strength, Corfe had joined the list of castles unsuccessfully besieged by King Stephen in the wars of the Anarchy. Corfe later added to its notoriety by becoming the favourite castle of King John. Here, John is said to have starved to death 22 French nobles who had backed the claim to the throne of John's nephew Arthur. It was also at Corfe

Corfe seen from the east, showing the long wall enclosing the castle's lower ward.

The shattered but still magnificent King's Tower at Corfe, victim of particularly thorough Parliamentarian slighting after the Civil War.

that John strung up a local prophet, Peter the Hermit, who had been so unwise as to forecast the King's downfall; before his execution the unfortunate Peter was dragged to Wareham and back on a hurdle.

Remaining in permanent occupation, Corfe survived the Wars of the Roses and in 1572 was granted to Sir Christopher Hatton, one of Queen Elizabeth's favourite young men. Hatton not only repaired the defences to meet the Armada crisis but considerably expanded Corfe's amenities as a Tudor mansion. But the castle's finest hour was its magnificent defence by Lady Bankes in the Civil War, from August 1644 to February 1646. When the siege began, Corfe was the only remaining Royalist stronghold between London and Exeter; but the castle remained a thorn in the side of the Parliamentarian cause for another 18 months. When Corfe fell – to treachery, after a fifth column had been slipped inside the walls during negotiations – Parliament wasted no time in exacting an efficient revenge, voting for the castle's demolition within the week (5 March 1646).

The resulting work, carried out more ruthlessly than with any other Parliamentarian slighting, destroyed the keep (King's Tower) to such an extent that its original layout can only be guessed at. Yet even when the wreckers had done their worst, Corfe could not be deprived of the rugged splendour which still awaits the visitor today.

The solid-looking gatehouse of Sherborne Old Castle.

SHERBORNE, DORSET

Department of the Environment
A30 from Shaftesbury, Yeovil; A352 from Dorchester;
A357/A3030 from Blandford Forum

Sherborne has two castles, but only one is a medieval site. The new castle dates from the sixteenth century and was built by Sir Walter Raleigh when he found it impossible to convert the old castle to a mansion. (There is a story that Raleigh was enjoying a quiet smoke in the garden of the new castle when a servant, terrified by the novelty of tobacco, hurled water over his master in the belief that he was on fire.)

Sherborne Old Castle was built by Bishop Roger in 1107–39, and the keep defences are very similar to those of its contemporary, Old Sarum: more of an enclosed courtyard, a prototype inner ward, than the usual square or rectilinear keeps of the period. It is easy to see why the twelfth-century chronicler William of Malmesbury, praising Bishop Roger's genius as an architect, wrote that his buildings seemed to be carved from a single stone.

Though Old Sarum Castle suffered the most from the transfer of the bishopric from Sherborne in 1075, the evolution of the latter castle was also cramped by the flourishing Abbey which remained on the site of the former cathedral. In the Civil War Sherborne suffered a similar fate to Donnington, undergoing two destructive sieges and taking a heavy battering from the Parliamentarian artillery. It finally surrendered on 15 August 1645, and was at least spared further extensive slighting.

OTHER CASTLES TO VISIT

Southsea (Portsmouth), Hampshire
Coast-defence castle of Henry VIII, from which he watched *Mary Rose* go down in 1545.

Old Wardour, Wiltshire
Late fourteenth-century fortified manor, twice besieged in Civil War; fine gardens.

Portland, Dorset
Coast-defence castle of Henry VIII.

The courtyard of Sherborne Old Castle, showing the extensive remains of the early twelfth-century stronghold.

THE SOUTH-WEST

NUNNEY, SOMERSET

Department of the Environment
A361, 3 miles (4·8 km) sw of Frome

Nunney is one of the most impressive fortified manors in the whole of England. Like Bodiam, built slightly later, the castle today is reduced to its curtain-wall shell. This features four enormous round towers at the corners, each crowned with a ring of machicolations (projecting arches through which missiles could be dropped on attackers at the foot of the wall). But Nunney has few of the graceful, balanced proportions of Bodiam; in plan it seems to have been squeezed together like a concertina to fit on a small, raft-like island skirted by a moat only 30 feet (9·1 m) wide. Reduced to its essentials, Nunney consists of two pairs of flanking towers connected by walls 40 feet (12·2 m) long. It has a look suggestive of many French châteaux of the fourteenth century, and was in fact built in 1373 by Sir John de la Mare with the proceeds of loot from the French wars.

A comparison of Nunney with Bodiam shows how rapidly warfare was changing in the late fourteenth century, for Nunney is clearly a 'pre-

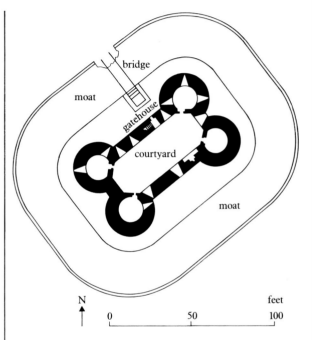

cannon' castle. Bodiam, built only 15 years later, not only has a wide lake-moat to force enemy gunners to shoot at extreme range, but it is also equipped with gun-ports through which to shoot back. Lacking both these amenities, Nunney was left in poor stead when defended by the Royalists during the English Civil War. With no defence in depth as at Donnington or Corfe, Nunney surrendered after a mere two-day bombardment. The Nunney garrison could certainly have held out much longer by retreating up the towers, which would have endured a good deal of battering; but there was no heart in the defence. The last Royalist field army had been broken at Naseby three months before, there was no possibility of relief, and the commander offered an easy surrender if he could be retained in command afterwards. The offer was rejected, but happily the early surrender spared Nunney from slighting on anything like the scale of Corfe.

The military threat of Nunney's tower machicolations is belied by the large windows in the connecting curtain walls.

The modest moat offered little real security to the walls of Nunney.

FARLEIGH HUNGERFORD, SOMERSET

Department of the Environment
A366, 3 miles (4·8 km) w of Trowbridge

Farleigh Hungerford is a straightforward fortified manor house of the late fourteenth century, square in outline with two wards. The principal surviving buildings are the tower and the extremely interesting chapel, with its weapons, armour, effigy tombs and fifteenth-century wall paintings. The castle was built between 1370 and 1380 by Sir Thomas Hungerford, steward to John of Gaunt, Duke of Lancaster, and second Speaker of the House of Commons.

The most scandalous story attached to Farleigh Hungerford relates to the tower, in which an early Tudor Hungerford kept his third wife locked up for four years on suspicion of infidelity. He tried to kill her by poison and starvation, neither of which succeeded, and was himself executed by Henry VIII for treason *and* unnatural vice, in that order.

The Hungerfords, a family noted for political acumen, managed to keep their property out of the crossfire during both the Wars of the Roses and the English Civil War. But the castle fell into ruin together with the family, and in 1689 was gambled

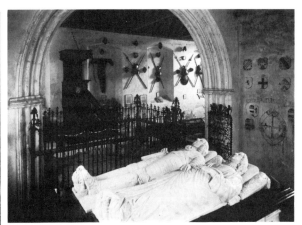

The family chapel at Farleigh Hungerford, with its weapon displays, tomb effigies and wall paintings, is not to be missed.

away with no fewer than 27 other manors by Edward Hungerford, who died in poverty. Subsequently it was neglected until its preservation in the nineteenth century, when picturesque ruins became part of fashionable taste.

The fourteenth-century fortified manor of Farleigh Hungerford, looking across the courtyard towards the gatehouse and chapel.

BERRY POMEROY, DEVON

Privately owned
1½ miles (2·4 km) s of A381, Newton Abbot/Totnes,
or 1 mile (1·6 km) N of A385, Totnes/Paignton

The ruins of Berry Pomeroy Castle, cloaked in woodland on the edge of a ravine, should not be visited on a bright sunny day. They are seen to best advantage in dark and ominous weather. For Berry Pomeroy is one of the most mysterious castles in the country: no one knows for sure how it came to its end, and the ruins are haunted.

Berry Pomeroy takes its name from the de la Pomerai family which held it until 1548, when the castle was sold to Edward Seymour, Lord Protector in the minority of Edward VI. Under Elizabeth I and the early Stuarts, the Seymours spent prodigious sums in converting Berry Pomeroy's apartments into what was, by all contemporary accounts, one of the most splendid and luxuriously furnished private mansions in the country. The castle escaped damage or destruction in the western campaigns of the Civil War, and seems to have reached a zenith of splen-dour in the reign of James II (1685–8). In November 1688 William of Orange, after landing at Brixham with his army, stayed at Berry Pomeroy at the start of his march to London and the Crown. But at some unspecified date over the next 12 years Berry Pomeroy was completely destroyed in a disastrous fire. There was fearful talk of the castle having been set ablaze by lightning, which in that witchcraft-haunted century carried immense overtones of divine or diabolical wrath. Commenting on the mystery in his *Worthies of Devon* (1701) the vicar John Prince wrote merely that 'all this Glory lieth in the Dust, buried in its own Ruines'.

Four of Berry Pomeroy's ghosts deserve special mention. There is Henry de Pomerai, one of the castle's founding fathers, who committed the most unknightly deed of killing a herald and later stabbed himself to death. Margaret de Pomeroy was locked up and starved to death by a jealous sister for falling in love with the same man. Another woman was killed with her lover by an outraged brother when caught at a secret tryst. But most to be feared is another lady ghost who walks in the woods. She killed her illegitimate baby, and appalling luck befalls all who see her.

The gatehouse of ghost-ridden Berry Pomeroy Castle, mysteriously destroyed by fire in the seventeenth century.

DARTMOUTH, DEVON

Department of the Environment
A380/A381/B3207 from Exeter via Newton Abbot
and Totnes; A3022 from Torbay with ferry

Few English south coast ports have a longer naval tradition than Dartmouth, where fleets mustered for the Crusades of the twelfth century, the French wars of the fourteenth, and the D-Day armada in 1944. There are two castles at Dartmouth, one of which is a ruined coastal blockhouse built in 1481. The more interesting of the two, however, is about 100 years older. It was built in Richard II's reign (1377–99) to defend the Dart estuary against raids from the sea. Strictly speaking, this older Dartmouth Castle is not a true castle, in that it was never a royal or lordly residence, or designed for a permanent garrison; but it is included here as one of the best examples of how medieval fortifications were, from the late fourteenth century, adapted to the advent of cannon.

Like Tintagel in Cornwall (p. 77) Dartmouth Castle shows that medieval castle-builders did not invariably look for the likeliest high ground, then build on top of it. This is a strongpoint tailored to the face of the cliff, with landward security provided by the cliff itself. The fortifications consist of a 'V' of battlements 110 feet (33·5 m) across at the base, pointing out towards the estuary, with a squat tower at the squared-off point. The tower was built to mount guns firing through large rectangular openings, rather than the 'keyhole' ports which were modifications of the traditional arrow-slit.

At Dartmouth, therefore, we find England's oldest coastal battery, in startling contrast to the traditional appearance of the contemporary Bodiam. Despite their manifest differences Dartmouth and Bodiam are both examples of Richard II's flair for securing 'defence on the cheap', Bodiam being built as a licensed fortified manor, and Dartmouth by the town corporation.

Though it must be repeated that Dartmouth was not a true castle, it had all the hallmarks of the most effective English castles – above all adaptability for a long service life. Its value in coastal defence saved it from peacetime neglect, or deliberate slighting in the Civil War; the curtain wall was pierced with eight embrasures for additional fire-power in the eighteenth century, and it served in both world wars.

Dartmouth Castle, tailored into the cliff face on the west bank (left in the picture) of the river Dart to command the seaborne approach to the port.

TOTNES, DEVON

Department of the Environment
A38/B3210 from Plymouth;
A380/A381 from Exeter via Newton Abbot;
A381 from Salcombe, Kingsbridge

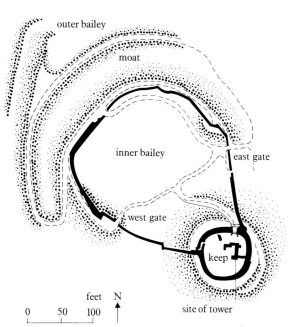

Totnes town stands at the head of the navigable reaches of the river Dart, at the junction of three valleys, and was therefore a natural site for a castle after the Norman Conquest. The first lord of Totnes, Judhael, was a Breton high in the favour of William I, by whom he was granted over a hundred manors in Devon. To command the town, Judhael built up a natural knoll into a castle motte, rendering it waterproof by sheathing it with clay and adding a pear-shaped bailey below. In its surviving form, Totnes Castle preserves the complete outline of Judhael's defence perimeter, right down to the stone foundation of the original wooden donjon on top of the motte. The ditch which formerly ringed the foot of the motte is now filled in and incorporated into the small gardens of the houses which cluster round the entire south side of the motte. As usual, visitors must imagine the castle uncluttered by the tall old trees obscuring the view over the bailey on the north side and the town houses built right up to the foot of the motte on the south.

Though never attacked or besieged, and devoid of military value long before the Civil War, Totnes Castle was an unusually active pawn in West Country medieval power politics. It passed through no fewer than eight changes of ruling family between the late eleventh century and the early sixteenth. The castle's conversion to a stone shell keep and walled bailey began under Reginald de Braose in 1219, but the work was poorly executed and soon became ruinous. The much more solid stonework visible today is the result of a complete rebuilding by William de la Zouch, on the orders of Edward II in the last year of his reign (1326–7). This reconstruction effectively preserved Totnes as one of England's most perfect shell keeps with a complete set of crenellations, the larger ones pierced for archery. From the keep's intact walkway visitors enjoy superb all-round views over Totnes town and the south Devon countryside.

A classic fossil specimen of the Norman motte-and-bailey : the shell keep at Totnes, with merlons pierced for defensive fire.

OKEHAMPTON, DEVON

Department of the Environment
A30, between Launceston and Exeter

Okehampton Castle stands on a knoll about half a mile west of the town, on the lower slopes of northern Dartmoor, and its extensively ruined state is the result of over three centuries of use as a local quarry. Though long overgrown, its fine site is now kept clear and rendered well worth a visit when travelling to or from Cornwall along the Exeter–Launceston road.

The castle began as a twelfth-century motte-and-bailey, converted to stone in the thirteenth century. Lying as it did far from the sea or the turbulent frontier zones of the Welsh and Northern marches, Okehampton was always more of a residence than a fighting stronghold. It was the original seat of the powerful Courtenay family and its ruins reveal a high proportion of residential buildings. The castle's further development was cut short when the Courtenays moved their family seat to Powderham Castle at Kenton in the 1390s.

Already badly run down, Okehampton Castle was finally abandoned after the execution of Henry Courtenay, Marquis of Exeter, by Henry VIII on a trumped-up treason charge in December 1538. The dominant element of the ruins today is, as usual, the keep. The configuration of the site suggests that if the Courtenays had stayed at Okehampton this castle could well have developed on the lines of Corfe, with upper and lower wards extending down the hill, though it would never have achieved the same massive strength.

The splintered ruins of the keep of Okehampton Castle, family seat of the powerful Courtenays until their move to Powderham in the late fourteenth century.

RESTORMEL, CORNWALL

Department of the Environment
1½ miles (2·4 km) N of Lostwithiel, A390 from
St Austell and Liskeard; B3269 from Bodmin

Though none of its outer defences have survived, Restormel is nevertheless one of the most beautifully proportioned shell keeps in England. The first castle was built by Baldwin FitzTurstin in about 1100 to command the crossing over the river Fowey; the conversion to stone defences began under Robert de Cardinan at the end of the twelfth century, with extensive inner development about 50 years later under Richard of Cornwall, contemporary with the rebuilding of Launceston.

The main strength of Restormel was clearly not the height of the motte, but the enormous width (50 feet/15·2 m) and depth of the ditch. The keep itself is one of the biggest of its type in the land, being some 50 feet wider in diameter (outer wall to outer wall) than those at Totnes and Launceston. This yielded space for generous accommodation within the keep: the walls of these inner chambers are still standing, giving Restormel the distinctive plan view of a spoked wheel. The chambers are ranged round the circular inner courtyard on two levels, the ground level being reserved for guardroom and storage. The entire upper storey was reserved for the lord of the castle and his family, with the chambers of the lord and lady on the north-west sector being faced by the hall on the south-east. The square tower jutting out to the north-east was the castle chapel. The sockets for the floor-beams of the upper storey can still be seen, as can others on the outer wall, below the parapet. These were to support *hoards* – temporary wooden galleries rigged in time of siege, from which attackers could be bombarded at the foot of the wall.

Other curiosities at Restormel include the deep underground chambers in the outer courtyard, the lord's private stair from the chamber south of the chapel to the walkway, and, in the hall beyond, the vertical speaking-tube built into the wall, leading up to the walkway. The kitchen beside the hall served food via a hatch in the wall and had a generous built-in fireplace – a remarkably advanced facility for a castle of this period.

Restormel had been abandoned long before the Civil War but, unlike most West Country medieval castles, briefly held a Parliamentarian garrison. This was speedily ejected by the Royalist army of Sir Richard Grenville in 1644, but the castle saw no further action. The skill with which the castle site, long overgrown, was cleared, has preserved one of the most interesting of all English castles of the thirteenth century.

*The elegant shell keep of Restormel: looking towards the castle entrance
on its low, broad motte.*

PENDENNIS, CORNWALL

Department of the Environment
Falmouth – A39 from Truro,
A393 from Redruth, A394 from Helston

Pendennis Castle is another of Henry VIII's gun platforms, begun in 1539 and magnificently sited on Pendennis Point, the peninsula extending southeast of Falmouth town. Together with St Mawes across the water to the east, Pendennis was built to defend Falmouth and the fine anchorage of Carrick Roads.

It is a concentric circular castle, without the 'cloverleafs' which distinguish Deal and Walmer. The lie of the land, with a steep drop to the sea which the castle's guns were intended to sweep, ruled out 'sinking' the castle in a deep moat, but the upper gun embrasures were rounded to deflect shot. The keep was given splayed ports for 13 guns firing on two floors; and at ground level the curtain wall was pierced with 14 embrasures. An outer blockhouse, known as 'Little Dennis', was built at the very tip of the promontory.

Pendennis was transformed in the last five years of Elizabeth's reign, after a damaging Spanish raid

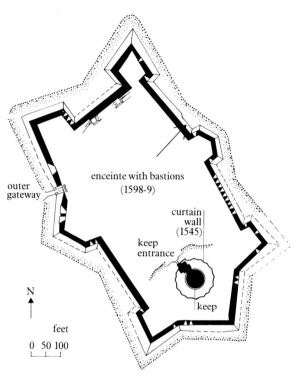

The Tudor Royal Arms, fulsomely displayed at Pendennis over the gateway to the keep.

on Penzance had given timely warning that Pendennis would hardly be able to repel a similar attack in force. Henry VIII's castle was girdled with an *enceinte*, or connecting rampart-with-bastions for extra artillery, with a steep-sided ditch all round; Little Dennis was similarly strengthened. In this new guise, as the most modern and best-armed castle held by the Royalists, Pendennis earned the undying fame of being the last English castle to surrender in the Civil War of 1642–6.

Untouched by the earlier campaigns in the staunchly Royalist West, Pendennis played host to Queen Henrietta Maria and Charles, Prince of Wales, before receiving the full weight of the Parliamentarian onslaught under General Fairfax in March 1646. The ensuing five-month siege reiterated the lesson that any beleaguered castle or strongpoint is only as strong as the will of its garrison commander. Colonel John Arundell, Governor at Pendennis, was 70 years old and had seen

Henry VIII's keep at Pendennis. The approach bridge and original castle entrance are on the landward side, to the left.

Queen Elizabeth review her troops at Tilbury in Armada year (1588). Undeterred by the precipitate surrender of neighbouring St Mawes on 12 March 1646, Arundell told Fairfax that 'I will here bury myself before I deliver up this castle to such as fight against His Majesty'. After Arundell rejected a second surrender demand on 17 April, Fairfax ordered the close blockade of Pendennis by land and sea. Hunger, not enemy force, beat Pendennis in the end, though Arundell held on until the last hope of receiving relief and supplies had gone. He finally surrendered on 17 August 1646, his emaciated garrison marching out with the full honours of war.

Pendennis was much too important a coastal stronghold to be slighted after the Civil War. It remained in service, housing VIP state prisoners and enemy prisoners-of-war, and was manned in both world wars.

The southernmost extremity of the Pendennis defensive perimeter: the blockhouse of Little Dennis, perched above the water at the headland's tip.

ST MAWES, CORNWALL

Department of the Environment
A390/B3287/A3078 from St Austell;
A39/B3289 from Redruth

This is the smaller partner of Pendennis, built by Henry VIII in 1540 to create a crossfire against enemy ships trying to break into Carrick Roads. The castles face one another, and each can plainly be seen through the gunports of the other.

In March 1646 St Mawes surrendered to the Roundheads without firing a shot, leaving the Pendennis garrison to win glory in a famous siege; but this comparison is not really fair. St Mawes was always the poor relation of Pendennis. St Mawes was a much smaller castle, and when the time came to strengthen the defences of Pendennis in the 1590s, the cost of keeping 400 workmen employed on the new outworks for 18 months could not be duplicated across the water at St Mawes. As a result St Mawes remained more of a blockhouse than a castle fit for all-round defence, and was wholly unequipped to fight off an attack from the landward side, especially by the veteran army of Fairfax.

A gunner's eye view of St Mawes through a Pendennis gunport, showing how the two castles were intended to keep Carrick Roads closed to enemy shipping.

St Mawes Castle is not only smaller than its partner Pendennis, but was never given the outer defences necessary to endure a full-dress siege.

Scandalous though it will always remain to fanatical Royalists, the prompt surrender of St Mawes preserved what is probably the most attractive of Henry VIII's smaller castles. It is a mirror-image of the round keep of Pendennis, complete with rounded-edge embrasures to deflect shot. St Mawes remained in service as a coastal blockhouse for the next 300 years, and was manned again for service in the two world wars.

TINTAGEL, CORNWALL

Department of the Environment
A395/A39/B3266/B3263 from Launceston via Camelford
and Trewarmett; A39/B3263 from Bude via Boscastle;
A389/B3266/B3263 from Bodmin via Camelford and Trewarmett

As the locals would cheerfully agree, Tintagel is the centre of the 'King Arthur industry' and has been for the past 800 years, ever since Geoffrey of Monmouth wrote his *History of the Kings of Britain* (1136). This splendid romance tells how Arthur was conceived at Tintagel by the lovely Duchess Ygerna of Cornwall, after the arts of Merlin the enchanter had smuggled King Uther Pendragon through the castle's impregnable defences, disguised as the Duke. In the late fifteenth century Sir Thomas Malory, hauling all the Arthurian and Holy Grail legends together in his immortal book *Le Morte d'Arthur*, described the saviour of Britain as having been born at Tintagel as well as conceived there. More recently, the splendidly convincing 'Merlin' trilogy of Mary Stewart has brilliantly refurbished the Tintagel connection with Arthur. The legend lives on, as does the debate as to whether or not a 'real' King Arthur ever existed.

The hard facts are few, but well enough established. A perfectly credible sequence of Anglo-Saxon victories over the demoralized British, all in Kent, Sussex and Hampshire, is recorded in the *Anglo-Saxon Chronicle* from AD 445 to 530, when the West Saxons took the Isle of Wight. Then there is a most interesting 20-year gap before the next Saxon victories in the south and west. This gap coincides with the early Celtic stories of Arthur's great victory (at 'Mount Badon', wherever that may be) which stopped the Saxons in their tracks and won the British peace for a generation. If the British war leader who cut through the Anglo-Saxon record of conquest *was* called Arthur, there is no reason at all why he should not have been born at Tintagel (or, for that matter, buried at Glastonbury, where the monks supposedly discovered his tomb in the Abbey precincts in about 1190). But it is absolutely certain that the surviving castle ruins at Tintagel date from the twelfth and thirteenth centuries and can have no direct connection with a British war leader of the early sixth.

Tintagel Castle was built in about 1145 by Reginald, Earl of Cornwall, bastard son of Henry I. It is England's earliest linear castle built in stone,

The modern bridge over the vanished causeway, providing access to the curtain wall and inner ward of Tintagel Castle.

Though the legends endure, the surviving ruins of Tintagel's thirteenth-century defences have no possible connection with any real King Arthur.

The gateway and curtain wall securing Tintagel's inner ward. Holes in the wall once supported fighting platforms for the garrison.

with lower, upper and inner wards in a row; but its exploitation of the spectacular local landscape makes it like no other castle in the kingdom. This landscape consists of a steep headland, connected by a knife-blade of rock to a small island. The castle is divided between the mainland and the island, with the restricted landward approach and sheer cliffs all round making it impossible either to mine or to take by storm.

Like the shell keeps of Launceston and Restormel, Tintagel passed to Earl Richard of Cornwall in the early thirteenth century and he extensively rebuilt the castle; today's ruins date mainly from this reconstruction. The access paths used by modern visitors were built after 1852, when Tintagel was opened to a public fired with Arthurian fantasies by Tennyson's blank-verse *Morte d'Arthur*. The original narrow causeway connecting the upper ward with the inner ward on the island no longer exists, but the modern pathway still gives a vivid

The keep at Launceston, showing how the shell wall round the later round tower provided the defenders with three levels on which to fight.

until 1840, when they were transferred to Bodmin. The noisome town jail in the bailey was then thankfully removed and the present gardens laid out. Quakers will not need reminding that their founding father, George Fox, was jailed at Launceston in 1656 for distributing 'seditious' tracts (also for refusing to take off his hat when hauled before the court).

OTHER CASTLES TO VISIT

Dunster, Somerset
Fortified manor, extensively rebuilt from sixteenth to nineteenth centuries; owned by Luttrell family since 1375.

Taunton, Somerset
Extensively rebuilt stronghold of the town's defence by Parliament in the Civil War. Houses excellent County Museum.

Compton, Devon
Fourteenth-century fortified manor, extensively rebuilt in nineteenth century; owned by Gilbert family since 1329.

Lydford, Devon
Castle begun in 1195 to dominate spectacular Lydford Gorge; mainly thirteenth-century remains.

St Michael's Mount, Cornwall
Spectacular island (at high tide) castle, originally a Benedictine priory; besieged in both Wars of the Roses and English Civil War. (*See also p. 180*)

EAST ANGLIA

CASTLE HEDINGHAM, ESSEX

Privately owned
1 mile (1·6 km) N of Sible Hedingham;
A604 from Colchester via Halstead;
B1058 from Sudbury; A1017/A131 from Braintree

Castle Hedingham is a privately owned castle, open to the public on Bank Holidays and three afternoons a week from May to September. It is a magnificent twelfth-century tower keep of three storeys, standing almost 100 feet (30·5 m) high and dominated by two corner turrets, built in about 1140 to command the crossing over the river Colne, 17 miles (27·3 km) upstream from Colchester. The bridge over the ditch, across which the castle is reached, is a much later addition of about 1500.

Castle Hedingham dominated one of the many estates held in East Anglia by the earls of Oxford, the de Vere family, which had a turbulent medieval history. Richard de Vere fought for Simon de Montfort at the Battle of Lewes (14 May 1265), in the civil war against Henry III. In the Wars of the

The massive twelfth-century arch spanning the Great Hall at Castle Hedingham. The restored flooring gives a vivid idea of life in these looming strongholds.

The fine tower keep of Castle Hedingham, dominated by its two corner turrets. The first storey main gate is approached by a stairway on the left.

Roses the family fought for Lancaster, with a notable lack of success. In February 1462 John de Vere, the twelfth earl, and his eldest son were sentenced for treason by the Yorkist Earl of Worcester, Constable of England, and executed. Eight years later, in the Lancastrian backlash which temporarily restored Henry VI, John, the thirteenth earl, had the satisfaction of passing the death sentence on Worcester in turn. But this was the same de Vere who helped lose the Battle of Barnet for Lancaster in April 1471, by losing his bearings in a fog and attacking the troops of his own side!

While at Castle Hedingham, do not miss the Church of St Nicholas – another masterpiece of Norman architecture of the twelfth century, built about 50 years after the castle.

COLCHESTER, ESSEX

Borough of Colchester
A12 from London via Chelmsford and Ipswich;
A134 from Sudbury; A604 from Harwich

Colchester prides itself on being 'Britain's oldest recorded town', and with good reason: it has seen a remarkable continuity of occupation since the Bronze Age. The Romans called it *Camulodunum* and built an enormous temple here to the Emperor Claudius, whose legions had launched the Roman invasion of Britain in AD 43. Alfred the Great's son Edward, advancing north-east from the Thames to drive the Danes out of East Anglia in the early tenth century, built a rampart round Colchester as a fortified town or *burh*. It was to be expected that the Normans would not overlook Colchester's value as the southern anchor of East Anglia. At Colchester they built the only stone tower keep other than London's White Tower to date from the reign of the Conqueror. And not the least of Colchester's claims to historical fame is that it boasts the most enormous castle keep not only in England, but in Europe.

Colchester was built by Eudo, *dapifer* or steward both to William I and to his two sons, William II and Henry I. As with the White Tower at London, Eudo's castle was sited in the old Roman city. In a way Colchester ranks as a 'hermit-crab' castle because, while not making use of standing Roman walls for its outer defences, the Norman castle nevertheless occupies a Roman site: the massive plinth foundation of the long-destroyed Temple of Claudius, which can still be seen beneath the castle vaults.

Colchester's Great Keep measures a staggering 171 feet by 146 feet (52·1 m by 44·5 m), yielding a ground area 63 per cent bigger than that of the later keep at Dover; and although only two of the castle's original four storeys have survived, it is still an impressive fortress. The castle was involved in a few dramatic actions in the Middle Ages, being surrendered during the French occupation of the south-east in 1216–17 and again during the Peasant's Revolt of 1381. Its finest hour came in 1648, during the renewed fighting of the Second Civil War. Stubbornly defended by the Royalists, Colchester beat off the attacks of Fairfax and the veterans of the New Model Army from 13 June to 28 August, when Sir Charles Lucas was forced to capitulate. The Parliamentarian general, incensed

Colchester Castle, the biggest twelfth-century great keep in Europe, built on the site of the Roman temple of Claudius.

The doorway at Colchester.

by what he regarded as a wanton shedding of blood, showed none of the chivalry he had displayed at Pendennis in 1646: the surrender terms were harsh and Lucas and another Royalist commander were shot. But not even Roundhead vengeance could level Colchester's great keep. Today it houses the fascinating collection of the Colchester and Essex Museum.

HADLEIGH, ESSEX

Department of the Environment
A13 from Basildon and Southend-on-Sea;
castle is 1 mile (1·6 km) w of BR Leigh-on-Sea

Hadleigh Castle lies in a small enclave of open country, hemmed in by the urban sprawl of Canvey Island and South Benfleet to the south and west, and Leigh and Southend to the north and east. Though extensively ruined, the castle still preserves the main layout of an early thirteenth-century manorial castle – the transition period from keep-and-curtain to fully concentric designs. It was begun in 1231 on one of the south Essex estates of the great Angevin crown official Hubert de Burgh, Dover's defender against the French in the war of 1216–17, and justiciar of England during the early reign of Henry III. Though he never lost the popular aura of a national hero, Hubert was still a greedy and ambitious man, who at the peak of his power held estates in 15 counties. But he fell from royal favour in 1232, his estates were confiscated, and Hadleigh Castle was finally completed later in Henry III's reign.

Despite its apparently useful site overlooking the northern shore of the Thames estuary, Hadleigh never flourished as a castle worthy of sustained expense in maintenance. It is notable for having served as a temporary home for Anne of Cleves after she was divorced by Henry VIII. Nearly 200 years later, having been reduced to thoroughly picturesque ruins by ground subsidence, the castle became a favourite subject for the landscape painter John Constable. One of Constable's most powerful studies of Hadleigh Castle is in the Tate Gallery in London.

The castle as landscape ornament in the Romantic period : one of John Constable's studies of Hadleigh Castle's ruins commanding the Essex flatlands.

ORFORD, SUFFOLK

Department of the Environment
A12/B1084 from Ipswich via Woodbridge;
A12/B1078 from Saxmundham via Wickham Market

Lying only 12 miles (19.3 km) from Framlingham, Orford Castle (completed about 30 years earlier) is another Suffolk masterpiece of a twelfth-century castle – but in near-total contrast. These two are a perfect demonstration of how completely different neighbouring English castles of the same period could be. This difference is epitomized by the only parts of the two castles to have survived. At Framlingham the curtain wall and flanking towers have outlived the domestic buildings inside. At Orford the original outer curtain and towers have vanished, leaving only the splendid tower keep, the combined defensive and residential core of the castle. Again, Framlingham was a baronial castle, the fortification of which was actively restrained by Henry II. The King wanted no nearby rival to his splendid new creation, the royal castle at Orford.

Orford is unique because it is the earliest English castle for which detailed documentary evidence of the construction has survived. This evidence is preserved in the Pipe Rolls, the cash-flow records of the royal exchequer. They show that between 1165 and 1173, when it was completed, Henry II spent more money on Orford than on any other castle. Henry built Orford fast, with no expense spared, because on his accession there had been no royal castles in East Anglia, and he wanted to keep the powerful Hugh Bigod in check. Orford Castle immediately proved its worth by holding out in 1173–4 during the rebellion of Henry's eldest son, Henry 'The Young King'. Bigod not only backed the Young King but brought over an army of mercenaries from Flanders – who kept well away from Orford, however. Though briefly surrendered to Prince Louis of France in the war of 1216–17, Orford remained a royal castle until 1336, when Edward III granted it in perpetuity to Robert de Ufford, Earl of Suffolk. As with Framlingham, East Anglia's adherence to the Parliamentarian cause saved Orford from battle damage in the Civil War.

Orford Castle represents attempts to strengthen keeps by rounding off the corners which, without the alternative development of concentric castles, would have resulted in many more cylindrical

A masterpiece from the reign of Henry II: Orford's polygonal keep, the core of one of the strongest royal castles in East Anglia.

keeps. But though Orford's keep stands in splendid isolation today, it is important to remember that the bailey curtain wall and towers that screened it originally completed a defensive complex scarcely less formidable than Henry II's later achievement at Dover. These bailey defences were still more or less intact in 1600, but decayed steadily over the next 200 years. (The last section of the bailey wall collapsed 'with a tremendous crash' on the night of 1 July 1841.)

The weirdest story connected with Orford is that of the 'Orford Merman', dredged up in the nets of local fishermen in the 1170s and hauled to the castle for examination. He is described in a contemporary chronicle as 'naked and like a man in all his members', covered with hair and with a long shaggy beard. 'Whether he would or could not, he would not talk, although oft-times hung up by his feet and harshly tortured.' Given this brutal taste of life ashore, it is hardly surprising that 'later on, being negligently guarded, he secretly fled to the sea and was never afterwards seen.'

FRAMLINGHAM, SUFFOLK

Department of the Environment
A12/B116 from Ipswich via Wickham Market;
A45/A1120/B119 from Bury St Edmunds via Stowmarket

With its intact cliff of curtain wall and fine views over beautiful Suffolk countryside from its ramparts and towers, most people would probably rank Framlingham as the most impressive castle in East Anglia. Certainly it is one of the most interesting of England's twelfth-century castles, being the earliest recognizable attempt at a 'keepless' castle – the forerunner of the concentric castles of the following century.

As a Norman manor, Framlingham was first granted by Henry I to Roger Bigod in 1100–1. Roger broke with convention by not strengthening the manor with a motte-and-bailey castle. He contented himself instead with a wooden hall surrounded by a palisade and ditch, enclosed by a 'wrap-around' bailey on three sides and an artificial lake on the fourth. Henry II, wanting no rivals to his castle at Orford, ordered Roger's son Hugh Bigod, first Earl

The western walkway at Framlingham, with the ornate twisted decorative chimneys – all that remains of the splendid sixteenth-century Great Hall.

of Norfolk, to dismantle Framlingham's palisades in 1175; but the second earl, Roger Bigod II, wasted no time in rebuilding Framlingham in stone when Henry II died in 1189. The curtain wall and towers date from this reconstruction.

The Bigods held Framlingham until 1306, when it was taken under Crown control. It was later granted to the Mowbrays, first dukes of Norfolk (1375–1476), and passed to the related Howards; but the third Howard duke, falling foul of Henry VIII, lost Framlingham in forfeiture to the Crown.

Framlingham's main gate, surmounted by the Howard coat of arms. The 3rd Howard duke rebuilt the gateway between 1525 and 1550.

The bridge over the moat, leading to the main gate in Framlingham's southern wall. The walkway can be seen through the gap in the battlements to the right.

Henry's son Edward VI gave the castle to his half-sister, Mary, and it was at Framlingham that Mary mustered her supporters before moving on London to oust Lady Jane Grey in 1553. Queen Mary restored Framlingham to the Howards, but by the end of the sixteenth century, after the fourth duke had been executed for treason by Elizabeth (1572), the castle was back in Crown hands. James I again restored Framlingham to the Howards (1613), who sold it to Sir Robert Hitcham in 1635; and Hitcham bequeathed the castle to Pembroke College, Cambridge (1636), on condition that a poor-house be built on the site of the old Great Hall. East Anglia's adherence to the Parliamentarian cause saved Framlingham from Civil War damage; and finally, in 1913, Pembroke College entrusted Framlingham to the nation. It all added up to a highly colourful if non-violent history, preserving a fine set of castle defences virtually intact.

Framlingham's glory is its irregular oval curtain wall and 13 rectangular flanking towers, connected by a walkway open to visitors. Fine 'twisted' chimneys of ornate brick serve as a reminder of the Tudor mansion which the castle became under the Howards. Looking down on the Inner Court from the walkway it is easy to see Framlingham as a fore-runner not only of the concentric castles of the thirteenth century, but also of the fortified manors of the fourteenth and fifteenth.

Looking west from Framlingham's walkway towards the lake, with the interior of the ruined Prison Tower in the foreground.

The cliff-like curtain wall and towers of Framlingham,

seen to particularly fine advantage from the west, across the lake.

CASTLE RISING, NORFOLK

Department of the Environment
3 miles (4·8 km) NE King's Lynn; A1078/A149 from King's Lynn;
A149 from Hunstanton; A148 from Fakenham; A47/A149 from Norwich

Castle Rising is a hulking brute of a castle: one of the largest rectangular keeps in the country, with its mass only accentuated by its low height of under 60 feet (18·3 m). It was built by William d'Albini in the mid-twelfth century, later passing to the redoubtable Warennes.

Despite its intimidating strength, the outside walls of this 'great keep' are quite richly decorated with arcading which can have served no military purpose. The first-floor main entrance is protected by a forebuilding reminiscent of the one at Rochester – an anticipation of the later barbican.

The staircase leading to Castle Rising's main gate: how an attacker would have seen it from inside the 'killing bottle' of the forebuilding.

The squat mass of Castle Rising's twelfth-century great keep is graced with decorative stonework, and the main gate screened by a forebuilding.

The generous ground area permitted the incorporation of the castle's domestic amenities – great hall and kitchens, a gallery and a chapel – on only two floors. This was a simple way of achieving a more solid mass and making mining less effective. The castle's outworks were completed on an equally massive scale and can still be traced.

Castle Rising will always be associated with Queen Isabelle of France, Edward III's mother. Having deposed her husband Edward II, and having raised no recorded objection to his appalling murder at Berkeley, Isabelle had governed the country in the name of her son, in collusion with her lover Mortimer (January 1327–October 1329). This state of affairs ended abruptly when Mortimer was toppled by a *coup d'état* headed by the young King, with Mortimer seized in the Queen's chamber and hauled off to London for summary trial and execution. Edward III then gave his mother Castle Rising as her sole remaining estate. Apart from the occasional journey with her son's approval, Isabelle remained at Castle Rising, frequently visited by Edward, until her death there 28 years later in 1358.

A closer look at the extensive stone decorations on the exterior of Castle Rising keep.

NORWICH, NORFOLK

Borough of Norwich

Norwich Castle is another huge, early twelfth-century 'great keep', a massive rectangle of masonry 96 feet by 76 feet (29·3 m by 23·2 m), which replaced the original post-Conquest stockade of 1067 in 1125. The Norwich keep was originally screened by outworks, but whereas those of the White Tower in London continued to expand into the neighbouring city, those at Norwich were devoured by the increasing prosperity of the medieval town. Like Castle Rising, Norwich keep's outer walls are decorated with patterns of blank arcading – carefully restored by the Norwich city fathers in 1833–9.

And yet, as with the great keeps of Rochester, London and Colchester, the strength of Norwich Castle proved of little use during the Peasants'

*Looking across Norwich City towards
the commanding silhouette
of the castle.*

Revolt of 1381. Assembling on Mousehold Heath outside Norwich, the rebels led by Geoffrey Litster demanded and got the surrender of both city and castle (17 June 1381). Hailed as 'King of the Commons', Litster feasted in state in the castle while his followers looted the city. But their timing was wrong: the Revolt had already collapsed in the south-east. When the fighting Bishop of Norwich, Henry Despenser, marched on Norwich a week later, Litster and his adherents fled from the city. (They were overtaken at North Walsham, where Litster was solemnly absolved of his sins and hanged without further ado.)

Much the same happened 168 years later during

Blank arcading on the exterior of Norwich Castle, a reminder of the fine work in castle preservation achieved by the city fathers in the nineteenth century.

'Kett's Revolt' (1549) when Robert Kett, a respected local landowner, assumed the leadership of Norfolk peasantry reduced to beggary by the greedy enclosure of common land. Though Norwich city and castle again capitulated to the insurgents, Kett kept his followers in good order, in camp on Mousehold Heath. But it did him little good when they were smashed by German mercenaries hired by the Earl of Warwick. Exempted from pardon, Kett was hanged from the battlements of Norwich Castle – a great-hearted man still remembered in Norfolk with almost a folk-hero's dues.

Norwich Castle is yet another example of the excellent work done by the Victorians in castle preservation. In 1894, having been used for centuries as the city prison, the castle became the city museum instead. Here in the old keep is one of the finest city museums in England, with excellent displays of local archaeological finds, natural history and works of art.

CAISTER, NORFOLK

Privately owned
1 mile (1·6 km) w of Caister-on-Sea;
A1064 from Great Yarmouth;
A47/A1064 from Norwich via Acle

Caister is a fifteenth-century fortified manor in brick, and one of the finest specimens of its kind. Privately owned, it is open to the public from May to September, and a motor museum is one of its many attractions.

The castle belongs to the period when private castle-building under royal licence was rapidly falling off. There had been 52 such licences in the reign of Richard II (1377–99), and 11 in the reigns of

Caister is a classic fifteenth-century defensible home, with large windows for maximum light as well as circular gunports commanding the moat.

Henry IV and Henry V (1399–1422). Under Henry VI (1422–60) there were only five, of which Caister was one. It was built by one of the most famous Lancastrian soldiers, Sir John Fastolf (nothing to do with Shakespeare's Falstaff, with whom any resemblance is not only accidental but unlikely in the extreme), and financed by the immense ransom extorted for the Duc d'Alencon, captured by Fastolf in one of the battles of the Hundred Years War at Verneuil in 1424. Moated and rectangular in plan, Caister was completed with separate summer and winter halls. Its surviving tower originally had no less than five storeys of rooms.

Caister will be familiar to all who have read the 'Paston Letters', that unique record of a remarkable family's life and times in fifteenth-century England. Fastolf may or may not have been related to John Paston, whom he called 'cousin', but he certainly became deeply indebted to Paston's sharpness in business and the law, and bequeathed Caister to Paston in 1457. The Duke of Norfolk coveted the castle for himself and indignantly disputed the will. In 1470 he resorted to direct action, besieging Caister with 3,000 men against 30 when he was supposed to be pacifying the country for the temporarily restored Henry VI. Not surprisingly, the Pastons were evicted, but thanks to their legal acumen and persistence recovered Caister afterwards.

OTHER CASTLES TO VISIT

Pleshey, Essex
Classic Norman motte-and-bailey site which never made the transition to stone defences.

Baconsthorpe, Norfolk
Late fifteenth-century fortified manor, considerably marred by quarrying in the seventeenth century.

THE MIDLANDS

BERKHAMSTED, HERTFORDSHIRE

Department of the Environment
MI from London to Junction 5, then A41 via Watford,
Hemel Hempstead; A355/A416 from Beaconsfield via Chesham;
MIO/A41 from St Albans via Hemel Hempstead

Unlike the Romans, who raised a mighty monument to their conquest of Britain (at Richborough in Kent, where its foundations can still be seen), the Normans created no specific memorial to the Conquest of 1066; but if one exists it is to be found at Berkhamsted Castle. For Berkhamsted is where the war of the Conquest ended – where the *Witan*, the lords of Anglo-Saxon England, came out from London to make formal submission to Duke William after his march through southern England from the field of Hastings. The new manor of Berkhamsted was presented by William I to his half-brother Robert of Mortain, who built one of the most ambitious 'first-generation' motte-and-bailey castles to have survived in recognizable form to the present day.

Berkhamsted is a castle where the decay of the later stonework, so far from erasing the entire complex, has left an impressive amount of the original works showing. The castle is a larger than usual motte-and-bailey, with a twelfth-century replacement shell keep on the motte and about half of the bailey curtain wall remaining. But the most remarkable aspect of Berkhamsted's surviving defences is the outer girdle of earthworks and the unique double moat – not only one of the oldest, but easily the most original system of water defences of any English castle.

However, combat experience in Berkhamsted's most dramatic siege proved that the castle's double moat lay too close to the bailey. In the civil war of 1216 a besieging army, well armed with siege catapults, battered down the bailey defences and rendered the castle indefensible in a mere 14 days.

*Berkhamsted's unique
double moat.*

WARWICK, WARWICKSHIRE

Privately owned

Warwick Castle falls into the same category as Bodiam and Tattershall: everyone's ideal of what a medieval castle *should* look like. It has survived unslighted by vandals, unmarred by battle damage, and superbly preserved: a monument to the great Beauchamp earls of Warwick, who raised the castle to its peak of glory in the fourteenth and fifteenth centuries.

As a thriving Old English royal *burh* of the tenth and early eleventh centuries, Warwick was pre-destined to receive a Norman castle during the Conquest. The first motte-and-bailey was sited there in 1067, safeguarding William I's march to York to cow the northern English earls into sub-mission. The outlines of the original motte and bailey can still be seen. The castle went through the standard transition to stone defences in the twelfth and thirteenth centuries, but its present-day appearance dates from the late fourteenth century, when it was almost completely rebuilt by the Beauchamp earls as both an improved stronghold and a luxury residence.

The residential apartments are in the south range – the Great Hall with its fine collection of armour, the state dining room, and the library. The great towers stand on the north side of the rebuilt bailey, with its gatehouse and barbican flanked by Caesar's Tower and Guy's Tower. These have the pro-nounced machicolations already mentioned in con-nection with Nunney, built in the same period. The strength of the castle's fighting north front is sustained by the water defence of the river Avon in front of the residential south side.

Warwick is no mere shell of a once-proud castle: it is a magnificently preserved fortified home, full of interest, to which a brief visit cannot do justice.

Warwick Castle from Castle Bridge : a superb monument to the Beauchamp earls of Warwick, who completely rebuilt it in the late fourteenth century.

BERKELEY, GLOUCESTERSHIRE

Privately owned
From Bristol, M5 to Junction 14, then A38/B4509;
from Gloucester, M5 to Junction 13, then A38/B4066;
from Cirencester, A419 via Stroud to Frampton Severn, then A38/B4066

If Windsor is remarkable as the oldest royal residential castle in England, Berkeley is its counterpart: the oldest residential castle in England to have been held by the same family for the past 800 years. (Berkeley's family tradition is actually a century older than that of Windsor, which really only dates from the rebuilding by Henry III, whereas Berkeley passed to Robert FitzHarding in the reign of Henry II.) Berkeley will probably go on being remembered, however, for the terrible screams heard outside the castle when Edward II was foully murdered there in September 1327. And this is a pity, for here is one of England's most beautiful castles, both in itself and in its countryside setting.

Berkeley is a thirteenth- and fourteenth-century residential rebuilding of an eleventh-century motte-and-bailey founded by William FitzOsbern (died 1071), the steward of Normandy, who was created Earl of Hereford by William I and entrusted with the security of the southern Welsh border zone. The castle's conversion to shell keep and stone curtain wall began under Robert FitzHarding, forebear of

*Enormous barrels in
the vaulted beer
cellar.*

the Berkeley family of today, who received the castle from Henry II in 1154. Like Farnham in Surrey Berkeley's shell keep is a rarity. It was built round the foot of the motte instead of the top, but whereas Farnham's shell keep was filled in to create a solid drum, that of Berkeley was subsequently excavated,

*Berkeley Castle, a stronghold and residence with an unbroken history of family residence
dating back 800 years.*

One of Berkeley's magnificent drawing rooms, known as the Long Drawing Room to distinguish it from the Small Drawing Room.

Berkeley's main gate, surmounted by the family arms, placed in a tower facing the inner courtyard.

with the motte entirely removed to create a circular courtyard.

Berkeley's keep contains the famous room where Edward II was imprisoned and eventually murdered after his deposition in 1327 – a crime which, as the castle guide-book carefully explains, was none of the Berkeley family's doing. It looks rather nice today, with interesting furniture and plenty of light admitted through snug-looking windows, but its present-day look is that created by the rebuilding of Berkeley in 1340–50. By all accounts Edward was penned in a cell made noisome by the cesspit below, into which rotting carcasses were thrown in hopes that the fumes would kill him off. The agents of Mortimer and Queen Isabelle were disappointed, however, for Edward was physically very tough and survived. In the end, the story goes, he was over-powered in the night, pinned down and had his bowels burned out with a red-hot poker 'putte thro the secret place posterialle'.

None of this notoriety, however, can detract from the beauty and grandeur of Berkeley: one of England's best-preserved castles, a living achievement by a remarkable family to whom we owe a great debt of gratitude. *(See also p. 163)*

GOODRICH, HEREFORD & WORCESTER

Department of the Environment
M5/M50 to Ross-on-Wye;
A40 from Ross-on-Wye, Monmouth

A stronghold of the Welsh frontier, Goodrich Castle still crowns the skyline, blocking the crossing of the River Wye.

A frontier fortress from its origin, reaching its peak strength in the Welsh wars of Edward I, Goodrich is an excellent model of castle evolution, from the tower keep of the eleventh and twelfth centuries to the concentric castle defences of the thirteenth. What makes this castle really impressive, however, is its dramatic site: crowning the heights above the river Wye, the old frontier between Norman England and the fiercely independent principality of Wales.

Goodrich Castle gets its name from 'Godric's Castle', the Godric in question being Godric Mappestone, who built the first Norman stronghold there at the close of the eleventh century. This can still be seen at the core of Goodrich's defences: a small, square tower keep of three storeys. In the

reign of King John, Goodrich passed to one of the greatest warriors of the age, loyal servant to Henry II, Richard I, John and the young Henry III: William the Marshal, the 'Good Knight', and arguably the inspiration for the Sir Lancelot in medieval romance. The Marshal gave Goodrich an ambitious curtain wall outside the west and north sides, extended by a dry ditch to the east and south.

From about 1280, however, during the decisive conquest of Wales by Edward I, the King's uncle William de Valence rebuilt Goodrich again as a square, concentric castle on an entirely new plan. The original tower keep was now enclosed on the south side of a central courtyard. Thrusting out from the corners of the outer curtain were four cylindrical flanking towers, each flaring out at the foot into a solid battered square base. Each of these towers was designed as a fortress in itself. It would have been useless for an attacker to storm or breach the curtain wall (assuming such a feat were possible); every tower would have to be taken in turn. The result was one of the strongest English castles of the age.

Three and a half centuries were to pass before

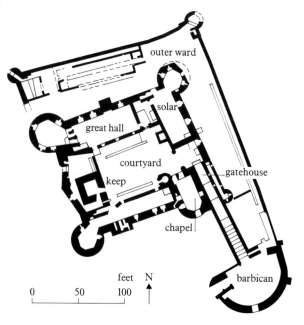

feet   N

0   50   100

The private apartments: the floor level of the upper-storey solar can be traced on the wall to the right; to the left is the well-head.

Goodrich's mighty walls met the fire-power of modern artillery, which the castle was unable to mount itself. Twice besieged in the Civil War, the castle held out valiantly for King Charles in 1646, commanded by Sir Henry Lingen, until the south walls were breached by a Parliamentarian siege gun by the name of 'Roaring Meg'. (She is still to be seen beside Hereford Cathedral, on Castle Green.) Even after 'Roaring Meg's' depredations, Lingen's garrison fought on until the Parliamentarians captured the well-head and cut off the defenders' water supply. But even Parliamentarian battle damage and post-war slighting and quarrying could not detract from what Wordsworth, a regular visitor to the Wye valley, was to call 'the noblest ruin in Herefordshire'.

DUDLEY, WEST MIDLANDS

Borough of Dudley
9 miles (14·5 km) w of Birmingham

With the best will in the world, it is hard to imagine Dudley Castle as it was in its fourteenth-century heyday, for modern Dudley is the 'Capital of the Black Country', hemmed in on all sides by industrial sprawl. This is where coal started to be used for smelting iron in the seventeenth century, with hideous results for the landscape. It has been said of Dudley that no fewer than seven counties could be seen from the castle's Norman keep – air pollution permitting. The Clean Air Acts, however, have wrought miracles over the past 20 years, and Dudley is still an excellent place for a family visit because it has a zoo: an appropriate attraction for a castle, as it is consistent with medieval tradition (even the Tower of London once had its zoo, in the now-vanished Lion Tower).

The first Dudley Castle was a post-Conquest motte-and-bailey, but this was destroyed on Henry II's orders in 1174 when its overlord, Roger de Mowbray, unwisely backed the rebellion of Henry 'The Young King' and the invading Scots. The new castle was that decided rarity, a tower keep on a motte, proving the natural firmness of the site. By 1324 Dudley had developed into a sufficiently important castle to be coveted by Edward II's popularly hated favourite, Hugh Despenser. He got his hands on Dudley by the simple expedient of keeping the rightful owner, John de Sutton, in prison until the castle was handed over.

Dudley stands on an imposing limestone bluff, and the 200-foot (61-m) slopes below the castle are served by a chair-lift. The Norman keep is screened by extensive fourteenth-century outer defences, with a courtyard surrounded by a massive curtain wall. Two drum towers and a fine barbican survived a Civil War siege in 1644 and the Parliamentarian slighting that followed in 1646; and further damage was caused by a bad fire in 1750. This was the only important castle of its type in the old county of Worcestershire.

Dudley Castle
from the air.

TATTERSHALL, LINCOLNSHIRE

National Trust
12 miles (19·3 km) NE of Sleaford, A153

To describe the magnificent castle at Tattershall, which at first sight looks like a giant tower keep, as a mere 'fortified manor' seems almost ludicrously inadequate; but this is in fact the most accurate definition. This soaring masterpiece in brick was

The beautiful brick-vaulted gallery at Tattershall, with heraldic bosses bearing the arms of (from front to back) Tateshale, Deincourt, and Cromwell.

The great brick tower of Tattershall, built by the 3rd Lord Cromwell in 1434–45, seen from the south-east.

built in 1434–45 by Ralph, 3rd Baron Cromwell, who was Treasurer of England under Henry VI from 1433 to 1443. Later it passed to the Earls of Lincoln from 1573 to 1693, after which it lay unoccupied until American speculators began shipping it piecemeal to the United States in 1910. Lord Curzon, saviour of Bodiam, thereupon intervened, bought Tattershall himself and restored it, with its outer defences, to its former glory. The castle was bequeathed to the National Trust in 1925.

Lord Curzon's extensive excavations during the restoration of Tattershall revealed the foundations of the original stone castle, built in 1231 by Ralph de Tateshale, after whom the manor was named. But the restoration work also revealed the outer defences which Cromwell had added: an inner ward ringed by a bank and moat, and an outer ward ringed by a second bank, a second moat and yet a third bank. The great tower itself has four storeys (plus an enormous basement area), the fourth storey consisting of a covered gallery below roof level with a parapet walk above. The 'great chamber' on the second storey, above the first-storey 'great hall', doubled as sitting-room and bedroom for the lord of the castle; the entire third storey seems to have been set aside for the women of the household.

At Tattershall, therefore, we find the wheel turned full circle from the dark and comfortless tower keeps of the eleventh and twelfth centuries: all the virtues of strength, increased by concentric outer defences, are combined here with the luxury of any orthodox great house of the period.

LINCOLN, LINCOLNSHIRE

Borough of Lincoln

Cobb Hall, the two-storey dungeon tower in the north-eastern angle of Lincoln's curtain wall, where executions were carried out until 1859.

Before the frontier of Roman Britain was pushed north to the line of Hadrian's Wall, Lincoln had been the base of the 9th Legion: a walled legionary fortress. Some nine centuries later the walls of Roman Lincoln were still recognizable (if not fully defensible) at the time of the Norman Conquest.

Wishing in 1068 to site a particularly strong castle at Lincoln, William I ordered the building of a 'hermit-crab' motte-and-bailey, using the south-west corner of the old Roman walls. The motte and keep were not enclosed by the bailey, but instead were incorporated a third of the way along the southern bailey wall. The area of the bailey (still known as the Bail) was extensive: Domesday Book recorded that no fewer than 166 houses were swept away during the building of the castle. The conversion to stone in the twelfth century produced a shell keep – the Lucy Tower – on the motte, incorporated in a now-formidable walled perimeter. The castle originally had two gateways, one in the west and the other in the east. The western gateway was subsequently blocked, but can still be seen, delineated by a massive Norman arch; the eastern gateway was retained as the main castle entrance, transformed by a massive twin-tower gatehouse in the fourteenth century. This followed on from the thirteenth-century addition of a two-storey flanking tower, Cobb Hall, at the castle's north-eastern corner. Though loopholed for defence it was used as a jail – the iron rings for securing prisoners to the walls are still there – and as an execution chamber as late as 1859.

Lincoln Castle's finest hour was in the civil war of 1216–17, when it represented the high-water mark of the French Prince Louis' ambitions in England. The castle was resolutely defended for the boy king Henry III by a gallant old lady: Nicolaa de la Haye, the widowed holder of Lincoln's hereditary constableship. She held on at Lincoln until a relieving army, commanded by the aged veteran, William the Marshal, arrived on the scene. While the Marshal's forces drove the surprised French into the confines of the city, Nicolaa's garrison sortied to catch the invaders between hammer and anvil – a victory so easy that the triumphant English remembered it as the 'Fair of Lincoln' (20 May 1217).

The English Civil War, however, yielded no such glory. On 6 May 1644, Lincoln Castle was stormed by Parliamentarian forces using the most basic of tactics: escalade, a rush to the walls with storming-ladders. As soon as the Parliamentarians gained the wall the Royalists turned and ran, and the castle fell. For this Charles II had only himself to blame. Eager for any method of raising revenue without calling Parliament, he had sold off the land traversed by the defensive ditch outside the wall, on which houses had subsequently been built. This made it all the easier for his enemies to gain the foot of the wall and capture what had formerly been one of the strongest city castles in the land.

ASHBY-DE-LA-ZOUCH, LEICESTERSHIRE

Department of the Environment
A50 from Leicester via Coalville and Burton-upon-Trent;
A512 from Loughborough; A453 from Nottingham

Ashby-de-la-Zouch is most famous as the scene of the great tournament in Sir Walter Scott's *Ivanhoe*, at which the champions of the scheming Prince John are put to shame by the loyal Ivanhoe and Locksley the archer. Scott, however, seems to have picked on Ashby more for its swashbuckling name than for any real historical connection with the early 1190s, when it was still an unremarkable Norman manor. In the twelfth century the manor was held by the Zouch family, who named it after their home in Brittany. It was probably little more than a walled manor in the mid-fifteenth century, when the huge kitchen was added.

Ashby only attained real prominence after 1461, when Edward IV granted it to the Hastings family. It was Lord Hastings who added the splendid tower, which still survives, along with parts of the walls and solar, which has a fine fireplace and ornate mullioned windows. Under the command of Henry Hastings, Lord Loughborough, Ashby received the defeated King Charles after Naseby (June 1645), and later held out for the King in a siege lasting over a year. This achievement, however, literally brought about Ashby's ruin: an extensive slighting which this fortified manor, with the exception of the tower, could not withstand.

The remains of the tower residence at Ashby-de-la-Zouch. Stronger than Tattershall tower, it was built by Lord Hastings in the reign of Edward IV.

NEWARK, NOTTINGHAMSHIRE

Borough of Newark
A1 from Grantham, Worksop;
A46 from Lincoln, Leicester

Newark Castle is one of the most savagely slighted victims of the English Civil War, in which it served as the main Royalist stronghold in the north-east Midlands from December 1643 to May 1646. Assigned to the bishopric of Lincoln in the post-Conquest settlement, the original motte-and-bailey castle of Newark was rebuilt as a stone tower by Bishop Alexander in 1125. After 1139, when the castle passed to the Crown, the huge and elaborate north gatehouse was added, followed by the south-west corner turret and the extensive crypt, with eight bays.

Like Corfe, Newark was a favourite castle of King John, who withdrew there to die in October 1216. In the civil war which ensued, Newark was garrisoned and held for the boy king Henry III by John's mercenaries; in the following year, it served as the advanced base for William the Marshal's brilliant relief of Lincoln Castle.

In the fourteenth and fifteenth centuries the castle was modified as a residence, the great hall being lit by three large windows in the west wall, and two towers added to the corners of the same wall.

In the Civil War, after Newark had been captured by Royalist cavalry in December 1643, it was a thorn in the side of the Parliamentarian cause for two and a half years, constantly inhibiting Parliamentarian strategy with the threat of a Royalist advance into the Parliamentarian heartland of East Anglia. It was half-heartedly besieged in March 1644, the year of the Parliamentary victory at Marston Moor, but the garrison was speedily relieved by Prince Rupert. The final siege was begun in November 1645, when the Parliamentarians were aided by a Scots Presbyterian expeditionary force. The garrison commander, Lord Bellasis, surrendered on the King's orders in May 1646. He and his men were granted the honours of war, but the ensuing slighting left only the west side of the castle standing – a viciously mutilated yet still imposing ruin.

Newark Castle, where King John withdrew to die in 1216. Having been held for Charles I in the Civil War, it was mercilessly slighted by the Parliamentarians.

PEVERIL, DERBYSHIRE

Department of the Environment
A625, Sheffield/Castleton; A6/A625, Manchester/
Stockport/New Mills/Whaley Bridge/Castleton

Midway between the modern conurbations of Manchester to the west and Sheffield to the east, Peveril is another castle well-known to fans of Sir Walter Scott, with a starring role in *Peveril of the Peak*. It was always a castle of limited national importance by virtue of its small size and isolation, but it was nevertheless an essential possession for any lord wanting to control the central Peak District and its lead mines.

Peveril is worth the long climb to reach its eyrie-like triangular site, protected on two sides by sheer crags (the south-east side has no wall) and to the northern front – the longer side of the triangle – by steep slopes dropping away to the road. Apart from the amazing views it offers, Peveril is interesting because it is one of the handful of eleventh-century stone castles built, from its beginnings, with a curtain wall. The western and northern walls also have small projecting turrets to permit a measure of lateral fire along the foot of the wall.

Peveril's curtain wall was built by William Peveril in 1090; but its small square keep is a later addition (1176). This was too small to accommodate a garrison in anything like comfort, and traces of a modest hall have been found close to the keep.

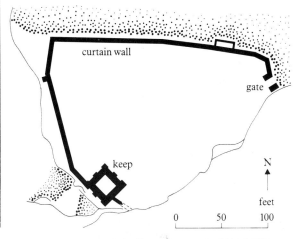

Peveril Castle, one of the very few eleventh-century castles with a stone curtain wall.

BEESTON, CHESHIRE

Department of the Environment
A51/A49 from Chester and Crewe

Beeston Castle stands on an immense crag 500 feet (152 m) high – one of the most daunting natural castle sites anywhere in England. It was always a stronghold pure and simple, and could never have evolved into a residential and administrative centre like Ludlow. One of the most impressive sections of the defences is the frowning pair of semicircular towers flanking the gateway. Among its most pressing problems, however, was that of the water supply, as indicated by the prodigious depth (370 feet/113 m) of the well shaft.

Beeston was built by Ranulf de Blundeville, Earl of Chester, who died in 1232. It was later occupied by Simon de Montfort, and served as a refuge for those of his followers who managed to escape the defeat of de Montfort's army at Evesham in 1265. Later, according to popular belief, Richard II, hastening back from Ireland in 1399 to meet the invasion of his usurping cousin Henry of Bolingbroke (afterwards Henry IV), buried his treasure at Beeston before falling into his enemies' hands. The castle's ruinous condition is due to Parliamentarian slighting after the Civil War – no doubt carried out all the more viciously because Beeston had been the scene of a humiliating Parliamentarian defeat, when a 'forlorn hope' storming party of eight Royalists managed to scale the north wall and bluff the 80-strong garrison into surrender. Beeston then remained in Royalist hands for two years before being blockaded into surrender.

The massive twin towers of Beeston's gatehouse. The castle was the scene of a daring Royalist assault in the English Civil War.

ACTON BURNELL, SHROPSHIRE

Department of the Environment
A458 from Shrewsbury, direction Much Wenlock;
turn right at Cross Houses for Pitchford and Acton Burnell

Acton Burnell is not the easiest castle to find; though only 4 miles (6·5 km) from Shrewsbury, it is tucked away south of the Shrewsbury/Bridgnorth road (but clearly marked on the Ordnance Survey map of the region). It is well worth the effort, however: one of the earliest fortified manor houses in England, and one of the most intact, it stands, beautifully kept, amid lawns and overshadowed by a giant cedar. It is a charming, red sandstone building with a tower at each end, and only the roof missing. Try to pick a sunny day, when the sandstone is seen to best advantage.

Acton Burnell owes its second name ('Acton' means a forest clearing) to Roger Burnell, a favourite clerical civil servant of Edward I who became first Chancellor of England and later Bishop of Bath and Wells. Though Edward I failed to negotiate Burnell's appointment as Archbishop of Canterbury (perhaps this was just as well, given the tragic experience of Henry II and *his* friend Becket in the previous century) he did grant him this

Acton Burnell, one of the earliest English fortified manors, shaded by a giant cedar tree.

Shropshire manor in 1284. A lucrative perquisite accompanying the grant was permission to cut timber in the royal forests of Shropshire. The house was completed in 1293 and remained in the Bishop's family until 1420, when it was abandoned.

The courtyard of Acton Burnell, rebuilt as a residence for Bishop Burnell in the reign of Edward I, showing generous windows and capacious chambers.

STOKESAY, SHROPSHIRE

Privately owned
A49, Ludlow/Shrewsbury; 6 miles (9·6 km) NW of Ludlow

Stokesay ranks with Acton Burnell as one of the earliest English fortified manor houses, being of late thirteenth-century vintage. Its unique appearance makes it one of the best-known smaller English castles, but its supreme value is that it offers a perfect example of what the long-vanished domestic interiors of larger castles would have looked like 600 years ago.

The castle was begun by the Say family in about 1240, but was bought in 1280 by Laurence de Ludlow, a rich wool merchant, who received Edward I's licence to crenellate about ten years later. Laurence completed the hall with its two squat flanking towers, adding a curtain wall and encircling moat. The Ludlow family retained the castle for 300 years before selling it in the early sixteenth century, and later owners added the splendid timbered gatehouse into the courtyard.

Stokesay is a chameleon: it looks completely different from the changing viewpoints as you walk round it. From the north, the walls and tower at the far end look formidable; from the west, the half-timbered residential upper storeys look welcoming and comfortable. Stokesay is indeed the epitome of the *domus defensabilis*, the 'defensible home'. It has a pitched and tiled roof, and amazingly large windows for so early a fortification. The fine solar chamber above the Great Hall can only be reached by an outside staircase, giving the solar's inhabitants complete privacy from the bustle in the hall below – which, however, they could observe at will through

Rich carving on the timbers of the Elizabethan tower gatehouse which commands the courtyard.

'squint' windows on either side of the magnificent fireplace. A half-timbered upper storey, sprouting from the north tower, provided the family and their guests with additional accommodation. At the other end of the castle, the south tower, reached by a drawbridge connecting it with the solar, was clearly Stokesay's 'survival shelter' for extreme emergency.

In the Civil War Stokesay's owner, Lord Craven, garrisoned the castle as a northern outpost for Ludlow, but happily Stokesay surrendered without firing a shot – and so was saved from Parliamentarian slighting. Thus was preserved one of the most attractive of all 'time-capsules' of medieval castle life. (*See also p. 167*)

The finely timbered Great Hall at Stokesay: on the right is the doorway to the courtyard, and the stairs at the far end lead to the half-timbered north tower chamber.

Stokesay from the north, with the incongruous but appealing half-timbered chamber projecting from the north tower.

LUDLOW, SHROPSHIRE

Borough of Ludlow
A4117 from Kidderminster;
A44/A49 from Worcester via Leominster;
A49 from Hereford, Shrewsbury

During the extensive reconstruction of about 1330 this four-storey tower crowned with a hexagonal turret was built into the angle of the outer wall.

Fifteen miles (24·1 km) south-west of Bridgnorth, Ludlow was one of England's greatest fighting castles and the most impressive stronghold on the Welsh March. Like nearly all its fellow castles on the Welsh frontier, Ludlow boasts extensive stone defences dating from the eleventh century, the period of the first curtain-wall defences in English castle-building. The castle was founded in 1085 by Roger de Lacy, on rising ground enclosed by the junction of the Corve and Teme rivers.

The layout chosen by de Lacy for his new castle was both audacious and novel. The audacity was the sheer size of it: the outer bailey could comfortably accommodate a cricket match, while the inner bailey annually houses both actors and audience for the Shakespearian productions of the Ludlow Summer Festival. The novelty was his modification of traditional castle design. Ludlow's layout derived from the familiar interlock of inner and outer baileys, with the inner bailey in the north-west corner of the outer perimeter; but there was no distinct keep as such, either on a motte or in the form of a great tower. The nearest equivalent at Ludlow is the square tower guarding the entrance to the inner bailey – clearly a forerunner of the great tower gatehouses of the coming two centuries. As at

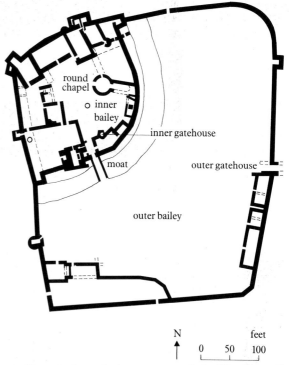

smaller castles of the same period, like Peveril, Ludlow's outer wall is studded with projecting square towers.

Another startling novelty, unique to Ludlow, is the chapel projecting into the inner bailey, anchored to the bailey wall. The west end of the chapel's nave swells into a cylindrical tower, another potential addition to the castle's innermost defences.

Ludlow's role was never restricted to that of a military stronghold: it was a centre of royal administration, the seat not only of the Mortimer Earls of March and subsequently of the House of York, but also of the Lords President of the Council of the Marches – an office which endured until its abolition by Oliver Cromwell. For the latter reason alone, quite apart from the natural capacity of the castle precincts, Ludlow received a steady succession of residential buildings, culminating in the sixteenth-century Great Hall – the evolution of a Norman stronghold into a Tudor palace.

Unlike most other English castles, Ludlow played an active part in both the Wars of the Roses and the Civil War. In the former it was a Yorkist stronghold, and from Ludlow in 1483 the young Edward V was conducted to London – ostensibly for his coronation, in reality to meet an unknown fate with his younger brother in the Tower. Though subjected to slighting for its adherence to the Royalist cause in the Civil War, Ludlow's defences were far too massive to be razed.

This is one of the foremost English castles: a superb and inspiring specimen of medieval military architecture, built to secure a conquest, and developed as a seat of government.

Zig-zag ornamentation crowning the Norman doorway to the round chapel at Ludlow.

The fortifications of Ludlow, built by Roger de Lacy to a novel and audacious design.

The inner bailey at Ludlow, showing the round

chapel and extensive range of apartments beyond.

Shropshire's answer to the Leaning Tower of Pisa: the tower wall of Bridgnorth Castle, which defied Parliamentarian slighting after its Civil War siege.

BRIDGNORTH, SHROPSHIRE

Borough of Bridgnorth
A454 from Wolverhampton; A422 from Telford;
A458 from Shrewsbury; A442 from Kidderminster

Standing 100 feet (30 m) above the river Severn, Bridgnorth is perhaps most famous for being one of Britain's three noted 'leaning tower' castles: a giant section of early medieval masonry has been leaning at an apparently impossible angle ever since the Parliamentarians slighted the castle after the Civil War. The other two are Caerphilly in Wales and Bramber in Sussex.

Bridgnorth commands one of the most strategic crossings on the upper Severn; there had been a Saxon *burh* there since 912. The castle was built in 1101 by the notorious Earl of Shrewsbury, Robert de Bellême, whose extensive holdings in England and Normandy included Arundel, as he was the Montgomery heir. Earl Robert has the unenviable reputation of having been the worst of the Norman barons: a vicious sadist who would much rather torture prisoners than ransom them, and whose wife (married, of course, for her lands) spent most of her married life in a dungeon at Bellême. He rebelled against Henry I in 1102, but the King promptly took the field and captured all of Earl Robert's castles, including Arundel and Bridgnorth. Henry finally imprisoned Earl Robert for life in 1112.

Troublesome subject though he was, Earl Robert was nevertheless a fine military architect whose keep at Bridgnorth was generally regarded as impossible to take except by blockade and starvation. It served England well as a 'frontier castle' on the Welsh March throughout the twelfth and thirteenth centuries, and again in the Glendower revolt of the early fourteenth. Its last siege was against the Parliamentarians in the Civil War, when it remained defiant even after the extensive slighting of 1646. The 30-foot (9·1-m) slab of the tower which refused to collapse has remained ever since at an almost incredible angle of 17 degrees from the vertical – over three times the 'lean' of the leaning tower of Pisa.

OTHER CASTLES TO VISIT

Astley, Warwickshire
Sixteenth-century fortified manor with twelfth-century moat and outer walls. Lady Jane Grey lived here. Serves today as a noted restaurant.

Kenilworth, Warwickshire
Glorious Tudor castle-into-mansion, with twelfth-century keep and fourteenth-century Great Hall.

Thornbury, Gloucestershire
One of the last defensible manor houses built in England, by the Duke of Buckingham in 1511. Now a fine restaurant (advance bookings required).

Broughton, Oxfordshire
Tudor mansion rebuilt from fourteenth-century fortified manor, with early fifteenth-century gatehouse and wide moat. Superb Tudor plaster ceiling in original Great Hall.

Belvoir (pron. 'Beever'), Leicestershire
Famous castle-mansion of original eleventh-century foundation, repeatedly rebuilt. Present appearance mostly from eighteenth- and nineteenth-century reconstructions. (*See also p. 284*)

Kirby Muxloe, Leicestershire
Moated brick fortified manor house of late fifteenth century (1480–4), begun by the Lord Hastings executed by Richard III. Appropriately lies about 8 miles (12·9 km) from the battlefield of Bosworth where Richard III was killed.

Nottingham, Nottinghamshire
City museum and art gallery, housed in seventeenth- and eighteenth-century rebuilding of renowned castle originally founded by William Peveril in 1070. Castle Rock is honeycombed with tunnels and passages, most notably 'Mortimer's Hole', reputedly used for the *coup d'état* which overthrew Edward II's murderer in 1329.

Dalton, Lancashire
Good example of rectangular fourteenth-century peel tower.

Lancaster, Lancashire
Fine twelfth-century keep, with (heavily reconstructed) King John's Hadrian's Tower and gatehouse. *Note:* Public access limited to times when castle is not being used as a court-house.

THE NORTH COUNTRY

CONISBROUGH, SOUTH YORKSHIRE

Department of the Environment
A630 from Doncaster, Rotherham

Conisbrough Castle stands on high ground looking down to the river Don, with its 90-foot (27·4-m) white tower keep visible for miles against the surrounding green. It is slightly later than the similar keep at Orford (p. 85), having been built by Hameline de Warenne in about 1185. And whereas Orford keep now stands alone, considerable sections of Conisbrough's outer defences remain.

The main difference between Conisbrough and Orford keeps, both superb examples of their period, is that Conisbrough has six external buttresses to Orford's much thicker three. Again, Conisbrough keep is cylindrical within and without, while the exterior of Orford is polygonal. Apart from the intact keep and sections of the curtain wall, the most impressive surviving part of Conisbrough's defences is the lower section of the gatehouse. The narrow barbican outside is designed with a double angle to deny attackers a direct approach to the gate.

Conisbrough, like Ashby-de-la-Zouch, has connections with *Ivanhoe*, namely the small chapel built into the buttress on the third storey. The roof is still a superb viewpoint, even if some visitors find the modern industrial vista less than inspiring.

The six intact flanking towers of Conisbrough's white stone tower stand in stark contrast to the ruined outerworks.

BOLTON, NORTH YORKSHIRE

Privately owned
4 miles (6·4 km) NW of Middleham,
A6108/A684 via Leyburn

Though Castle Bolton is not the most accessible of North Yorkshire villages, the castle which gave the village its name is worth the trip, and so is its view of Wensleydale.

Bolton is a fortified manor house which has belonged to the Scrope family for 600 years. The first Lord Scrope obtained his licence to crenellate in 1379, the second year of Richard II's reign, and rather than reconstruct his existing manor house (the usual practice) he built an entirely new one. Only half of this is in use today, the other half having been ruined in the Civil War.

The new castle placed the emphasis firmly on domesticity and comfort, as is apparent from the size of the rooms, and of the windows and fireplaces. The building of chimneys to avoid smoky rooms (part and parcel of domestic life since the Dark Ages) was still a novelty in the late fourteenth century. The castle's four corner towers were used as domestic quarters, with other accommodation grouped round the courtyard. One of the corner towers collapsed in a storm in 1761.

The comfort and space of Bolton was considered fit for the imprisoned Mary, Queen of Scots, in 1568–9. She was confined at Bolton for six months at the start of her 19-year imprisonment in England. The castle's defences, however, were still strong enough to require its garrison to be starved out in the Civil War.

A notable attraction at Bolton is the Wensleydale folk museum in the Great Chamber, and there is also a restaurant.

Bolton Castle, a fine example of a late fourteenth-century fortified manor house, with three of its corner towers still standing.

RICHMOND, NORTH YORKSHIRE

Department of the Environment
A1/A6108 from Darlington via Scotch Corner;
A684/A1/A6136 from Northallerton

Richmond Castle is remarkable for the high proportion of its stone defences dating from the first 20 years after the Norman Conquest, when it was built by a Breton baron, Alan de Ponthièvre. Like many castles in the Midlands and North Country, it was never an earthwork motte-and-bailey, but instead was built from the abundant local stone to exploit a suitable platform of high ground. Such sites naturally dictated the outline of the defences, whether circular, oval or rectangular, but Richmond is a decided novelty: an equilateral triangle, with the castle's fine tower keep and main gateway at the north-eastern apex. Richmond also boasts the oldest castle Great Hall in England (Scolland's Hall, at the southern apex).

The expansion of the original castle began under Henry II in the later twelfth century with the building of the imposing 100-foot (30·5-m) tower keep, entered in the usual fashion by a staircase leading to the first storey. The battlements were repaired (fairly accurately it would seem from other towers of similar type) in the eighteenth century; and the corner turrets have two storeys. But attempts of the same date to provide Richmond with outer defences reveal the limitations of twelfth-century defence works, which concentrated on

A view of Richmond's slighted curtain wall from the south-west,
across the river Swale.

The unique triangular plan of Richmond Castle, with the tower keep at the northern apex and the clumsy outer bailey tacked on at right.

strengthening the corners of the original structure. This could not work with a triangular inner perimeter, because the resulting outerworks extended away from each other instead of meshing together. A barbican was built to protect the main entrance beside the keep, and a truncated oval outer ward, the Cock Pit, was extended outward from the southern or Gold Hole Tower. The result was a yawning gap between the barbican's east wall and the eastern angle of the Cock Pit. A clumsy attempt was made to seal this gap with an outer curtain wall, which would have been virtually impossible to defend.

It may seem surprising that a castle as impressive as Richmond had such an uneventful history. Richmond lay well away from the principal lines of communication in medieval times: it commands little but the entrance to Swaledale, which evidently was quite enough for Alan de Ponthièvre.

A thirteenth-century manuscript illustration shows Richmond's battlements flaunting heraldic banners, with the keep and barbican shown clearly on the right.

SCARBOROUGH, NORTH YORKSHIRE

Department of the Environment

Seen from the town and harbour, Scarborough Castle looks truly impregnable: a mighty curtain wall studded with eight towers running across the entire horizon of Castle Hill, with the summit of a great tower rising beyond. From each extremity of this daunting barrier, outer walls and defence-works snake menacingly down from the heights.

Nor is this impression deceptive. Though many times besieged, and no less vulnerable to blockade and starvation than any other castle, Scarborough was only once captured by force: in 1645, during the first of two desperate sieges in the English Civil War.

No trace has survived of the first castle built at Scarborough, an adulterine castle, built by William le Gros during the Anarchy of King Stephen's reign in the early twelfth century. Henry II pulled this down and replaced it with a tower keep enclosed by a small bailey. The breathtaking long curtain wall running clean across the headland may have been begun by King John in the early thirteenth century but was certainly completed, with its barbican, under Henry III and Edward I.

As might be expected of a castle on such an

The eastern wall of Scarborough Castle keep : the only wall left intact after the terrible battering taken by the defences in the two sieges of the English Civil War.

exposed site, Scarborough was expensive to maintain. Repair estimates for the year 1619 were for a minimum of £4,000. Its position made it a key strongpoint of the North, however, vital to both sides in the Civil War. At the outset Scarborough was garrisoned for Parliament with a regiment of foot recruited and commanded by a local Member of Parliament, Sir Hugh Cholmley. Always unhappy with the legality of taking up arms against the King, he abandoned the Parliamentarian cause after the first big Royalist victory at Edgehill (October 1642), offering his men the choice either of leaving or of staying as a Royalist garrison. Nearly all stayed for the inevitable Parliamentarian siege, which finally came after the Royalist defeat at Marston Moor in July 1644.

With Parliamentarian outposts only 6 miles away, Cholmley spun out sham surrender negotiations for the next five months, enabling him to get in local supplies and fortify Scarborough town and harbour, on which his chances of receiving seaborne replenishment ultimately depended. When the attack finally began in January 1645 it was made by Parliament's allied Scottish troops, 3,000 in all against Cholmley's 200. By February the Scots had forced the garrison back into the castle and begun an intense bombardment which finally brought down the west side of the keep. Desperate fighting ensued for possession of the gatehouse, in which the Scottish commander was killed; but the attack was renewed under Sir Matthew Boynton, and by July Cholmley's position was hopeless. Those of his men able to walk marched out with the full honours of war on 25 July. Instead of slighting the castle, Parliament voted a day of thanksgiving and £5,000 to repair it. But the victors reckoned without the renewed outbreak of hostilities in 1648, and were always in arrears for payment of their troops. Boynton's son Matthew was now Governor of Scarborough, and he followed Cholmley's example and defected to the Royalist cause. The result was a second siege, hardly less intense than the first, lasting from September to December 1648. Fortunately, the Commonwealth's order for the destruction of the surviving defences of this fine castle was never carried out.

Scarborough's ruined barbican (foreground), with the curtain wall snaking away across the headland to the right and the keep's shattered interior on the skyline.

SKIPTON. NORTH YORKSHIRE

Skipton Castle Ltd
A650/A629 from Bradford via Keighley;
A65 from Leeds via Ilkley;
A56/A59 from Burnley via Nelson and Barrowford;
A59 from Harrogate

There are few more pleasant gateways to the Yorkshire Dales than Skipton, one of the happiest marriages between an unusually attractive country town and the Industrial Revolution. The town's development did not erase the original close association of the castle and Holy Trinity Church as the main focal points at the upper end of the High Street; there are few better examples of a modern town still dominated by its medieval castle.

Only one gateway has survived of the original castle, built in the twelfth century by Robert de Romille to command this valley junction on the upper Aire. The castle passed to the Clifford family in the fourteenth century and was completely rebuilt, receiving a fine curtain wall with rounded towers and a magnificent gatehouse.

What you see today is an object lesson in castle preservation, individual and corporate, dating back over three centuries. Skipton is one of the very few castles to have had the scars of Civil War damage promptly erased after the Restoration of 1660. After serving as a rallying-point for the Royalist forces beaten at Marston Moor in July 1644, Skipton's garrison under Colonel Sir John Mallory fought off its Parliamentarian besiegers until December 1645, and was heavily damaged in the process. Returning to her inheritance after the war, Lady Anne Clifford completely restored not only the castle but also Holy Trinity Church. Lady Anne signed her work by building the family motto into the balustrade over the gatehouse: DESORMAIS – 'Henceforth'. Today the castle is maintained by Skipton Castle Trust, and has an excellent illustrated guide.

Skipton Castle gatehouse with the Clifford family motto, DESORMAIS, built into the balustrade.

PICKERING, NORTH YORKSHIRE

Department of the Environment
A170 from Scarborough; A64/A169 from York via Malton;
A169 from Whitby

*The motte and keep of Pickering Castle, seen from the
'wrap-around' outer bailey which served
as a barbican.*

In total contrast to Helmsley, Pickering is a late eleventh-century motte-and-bailey castle, with stone defences added over the ensuing three centuries. Pickering is a 'two-bailey' castle with a northern inner ward, the shell keep on its motte in the middle, and a southern or outer ward enclosing keep and motte. When the outer ward was given its curtain wall in the fourteenth century, the resulting enclosure served as an enormous encircling barbican for the rest of the castle.

The date of the first castle built at Pickering is obscure, but it seems to have been in the reign of Henry I, early in the twelfth century. It was certainly a royal castle by the latter years of Henry II's reign, when the inner ward's stone curtain wall was built, together with the square Coleman Tower beside the entrance. The castle seems to have suffered heavily in the civil war of 1216–17, because an official enquiry was ordered in 1220 to determine the extent of the damage. The sequel to this enquiry was the rebuilding of the keep as a shell early in the reign of Henry III.

The conversion of the outer ward dates from late in the reign of Edward II and was prompted by a Scottish invasion of the North in the autumn of 1322. The following year Edward visited Pickering and detailed orders were issued for the rebuilding of the outer ward as a stone barbican. This seems to have been completed, with the square flanking towers – Mill Tower, Diate Hill Tower and Rosamund's Tower – by 1326, when Pickering passed to the Duchy of Lancaster.

From the later fourteenth century Pickering's story was one of rising repair and maintenance costs which failed to keep pace with the castle's evident decay. It played no active part in the Wars of the Roses, and by the outbreak of the Civil War in 1642 it was too far gone to be of use to either side; a survey of 1651 recorded that the chapel was the only roofed building left. Happily, the castle's down-at-heel and overgrown condition seems to have saved it from the extensive demolition which was certainly planned during the republican Commonwealth; and this most interesting motte-and-bailey development survived to be preserved in the present century.

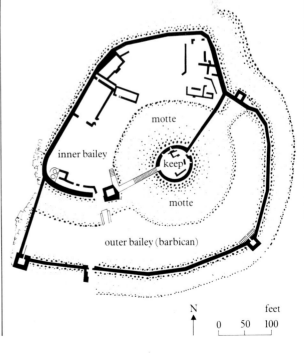

CLIFFORD'S TOWER, YORK

Department of the Environment

Clifford's Tower owes its name to Lord Robert Clifford, who was hanged in chains from the tower in 1322 after being captured by Edward II (one of the rare effective performances of that hapless monarch) after supporting the rebellion of Thomas, Earl of Lancaster. The tower is the keep of York Castle and should therefore be compared with the White Tower at London, for York was in medieval times – as it had been during the Roman occupation – the capital of the North. Just like the Tower of London, Clifford's Tower and its adjoining castle complex have served as royal fortress and palace, as a prison, and as a judicial and administrative centre. (As if to complete the comparison, York castle precincts even housed tame deer and a raven in the eighteenth century.) But there the parallels end, for

York Castle precincts, with Clifford's Tower at the centre, and the last remaining corner flanking tower and section of curtain wall to the right.

The North Country's most elegant shell keep : a thirteenth-century reconstruction on the original Norman motte.

the castles of London and York were otherwise entirely different. The Tower of London was a great keep, subsequently encased in concentric walls, while York's castle was a motte-and-bailey which never received concentric defences; and Clifford's Tower survives as one of the finest, most unorthodox shell keeps in the land.

After William I's original motte-and-bailey was restored during the crushing of the Northern Rebellion in 1069, York Castle was left with earthwork-and-palisade defences for over 170 years, until Henry III ordered its reconstruction in stone (1244). During the twelfth century, when nearly every other castle of similar importance at least began the conversion to stone defences, York was denied even the simplest of stone shell keeps. That no more ambitious defences were needed at York during these decades is a grim reminder of William's devastation of the North in 1069–70 and its long-lived effects. But it meant that the great Norman motte at York was never crowned with a simple cylindrical stone keep, as at Arundel or Windsor. Instead, York Castle's reconstruction in 1244–64 centred on a shell keep of an entirely novel design, reflecting the new ideas that transformed castle defences in the thirteenth century.

The new keep was not cylindrical, but *quadrilobate* – formed by four interlocking circles with their centres at the points of a square. No other English castle – not even the south coastal 'cloverleafs' of Deal and Walmer built by Henry VIII 300 years later – has this quadrilobate plan. The result was a neat combination of the advantages of flanking towers with the capacious circular courtyard of more orthodox shell keeps.

Clifford's Tower was not enclosed by the new bailey defences built at the same time, but rather connected to them by a ramp and drawbridge. They consisted of a curtain wall with round towers, with water defences to the north side provided by the damming of the river Foss. This bailey wall survived the siege of York in the Civil War, of which the medieval city walls bore the brunt, but only the southern angle remains today. The rest was removed during the eighteenth and nineteenth centuries, when the bailey was developed as a judicial and penal centre, with Assize Courts, a female prison and a debtors' prison.

HELMSLEY, NORTH YORKSHIRE

Department of the Environment
A170 from Thirsk, Pickering

Helmsley is a good example of a castle at the transitional stage between tower keep and concentric plan. It is an unusually symmetrical keep-and-bailey castle of the late twelfth century, with a curtain wall and flanking corner towers, and a barbican and concentric outer banks and ditches added in the thirteenth century. The castle stood only one recorded siege, in the English Civil War, and paid for it with a thorough slighting which levelled the curtain wall and left only half the keep standing. But there is plenty still to see.

The castle stands on a table of rock which seems to have dictated the rectangular defence perimeter from the start; no trace of a motte has been found. Helmsley was originally granted by William I to Robert of Mortain, the noted castle-builder responsible for Pevensey, who almost certainly built some form of palisade and wooden hall on the site; but the oldest stone buildings were the work of Robert de Roos (1186–1227). Though it was destroyed in the slighting, the outer face of the keep was originally given a most unusual rounded shape, with the keep's inner walls angled to conform with the outer curve. Here we have a late tower keep designed to double as a round flanking tower – a sophisticated stage in the evolution of the 'keepless' concentric castle.

The grandson of Robert de Roos, of the same name, added nicely to the family fortunes by marrying Isabel Daubeny, the rich heiress of Belvoir in Leicestershire; and it is a reasonable assumption that he used the proceeds to transform

Helmsley Castle, showing the curtain wall, moat and levelled corner tower, with the half-destroyed keep in the background.

Helmsley's defences during his tenure of the castle (1258–85). Two fully-concentric ditches and banks were added, together with an unusually large barbican of which only the outer face and gatehouse have survived. No trace of masonry walls has been found on the outer banks, but they could well have been crowned with palisades. These additions were followed by the square west tower, from which were extended the sixteenth-century domestic apartments of the west range. Tracing the later buildings at Helmsley is made easier because they are of brown sandstone, standing out clearly against the white limestone of earlier work.

Helmsley has been in continuous ownership since

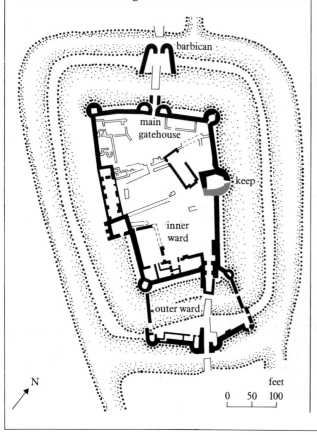

barbican

main gatehouse

keep

inner ward

outer ward

N

feet
0 50 100

*A besieger's-eye view of
Helmsley keep.*

its foundation, the present owners being the Earls of Feversham. The owner at the time of the English Civil War was the second Duke of Buckingham, but he was not in residence in 1644 when Sir Jordan Crosland defended Helmsley for Charles I against Sir Thomas Fairfax. When Crosland surrendered after a three-months' siege (November 1644) Fairfax levelled the curtain walls, barbican and inner keep. Ironically, when Buckingham returned to his ruined inheritance in 1657 he married Mary Fairfax – daughter of the man who had done all the damage 13 years before.

DURHAM

University of Durham

Durham Castle and the towering mass of the Norman Cathedral form the centrepiece of one of the most visually dramatic of all English cities. They stand on a high sandstone bluff ringed by a tight bend of the river Wear, and dominate the city from every viewpoint.

From the Norman Conquest of 1066 until 1836, the tight partnership of Durham Castle and Dur-

The imposing Tunstall Chapel : a reminder that Durham Castle was the palace as well as the stronghold of the prince-bishops of the Palatinate.

ham Cathedral symbolized a unique blend of Church and lay authorities. When Earl Waltheof was executed for treason by William I in 1074, the prince-bishops of the Palatinate of Durham took over the civil and military powers formerly wielded by the Old English earls, and before them the kings, of Northumbria. The powers of the bishops of Durham were unique: they were lay rulers as well as princes of the Church, and the Durham Palatinate

could mint its own coins, flaunt its own nobility in its own courts – even call out its own army. Durham Castle was, from its foundation, the bishop's palace as well as the key strongpoint of the city's defences.

The last Count Palatine of Durham, Bishop van Mildert, presented the castle to the new University of Durham in 1836, and it remains part of the University today. Because of this, visitors to Durham are best able to see the castle in the first three weeks of April and in the summer vacation – July to September – when the castle is open both morning and afternoon. For the rest of the year it is open only in the afternoon.

Durham Castle's old fighting ditch is now filled in, but apart from its many fine paintings and armour displays there is much to see, including the Norman crypt chapel, the late thirteenth-century Great Hall, and the splendid fifteenth-century kitchens.

Durham Castle's beautiful Norman chapel.

Arguably the most spectacular castle site in the whole of Britain : Durham Castle standing next to the Cathedral on its high sandstone bluff above the Wear.

BARNARD CASTLE, DURHAM

Department of the Environment
A67 from Darlington; A688 from Bishop Auckland;
A66/A67 from Penrith

Barnard Castle marks the old frontier between England and Scotland in the 1150s, when Northumbria, Cumbria and Westmorland were still under Scottish rule. It was built in about 1155 by Bernard de Bailleul on a dominant site on a low cliff above the river Tees. The Bailleuls or Balliols were a powerful Anglo-Scottish family with extensive lands in Galloway as well as northern England, and Barnard Castle was their English seat. This was the family which, having founded Balliol College at Oxford in 1263, provided John de Balliol as the puppet ruler whom Edward I unsuccessfully tried to establish as King of Scotland in the 1290s.

It is easy to see that in its heyday Barnard Castle compared favourably in size with other large northern castles such as Alnwick, Bamburgh and Dunstanburgh. The ruins cover no less than 6½ acres (2·6 hectares), and the castle is remarkable for having been screened by four baileys – another early, twelfth-century instance, like Ludlow and Richmond, of the move towards fully concentric castle defences. The splendid view from the fourteenth-century Round Tower helped to inspire Sir Walter Scott to write *Rokeby*. This was a staunchly Yorkist castle, which passed to Richard III on his marriage to Lady Anne Neville.

There is a treat in store for art lovers at Barnard Castle: another, much later 'castle', the Bowes Museum, a nineteenth-century imitation French chateau which houses one of the North Country's most famous collections of paintings, ceramics and furniture.

The twelfth-century curtain wall and square towers of Barnard Castle, with the later circular keep on the left.

The domestic face of Barnard Castle : the view across the fine surrounding countryside towards the chapel and great hall.

BROUGH, CUMBRIA

Department of the Environment
A66 from Penrith;
A67/A66 from Darlington via Barnard Castle

Brough is another very early Norman castle, like Peveril and Richmond, with a stone curtain wall dating from the late eleventh century. The castle is sited to command the upper reaches of Edendale, where the old Roman road (the modern A66) begins the long climb over Stainmore to the east. Brough's site makes it a 'hermit-crab' castle: the northern sector of the Roman fort of *Veterae*, built in the first century AD to keep the warrior tribesmen of the northern Brigantes penned in their hills.

The castle's development followed the standard pattern: an orthodox keep was added around 1175–1200, followed by a curtain wall with a prominent south-east round tower in the early reign of Henry III. As with Skipton, the excellent condition of Brough Castle today is due to the reconstruction ordered by Lady Anne Clifford, that remarkable and sadly unique castle-restorer of the late seventeenth century.

The impressive site of Brough Castle in Cumbria, commanding the upper reaches of Edendale.

The thirteenth-century round tower and curtain wall. Their deterioration was halted by the restoration work of Lady Anne Clifford after the English Civil War.

BROUGHAM, CUMBRIA

Department of the Environment
A66, 1½ miles (2·4 km) E of Penrith

Like Brough, the castle of Brougham occupies the site of an important Roman fort, *Brocavum*, which commanded the river crossing over the Eamont and stood at the junction of two of the key Roman roads piercing the Cumbrian hinterland. The outlines of the Roman fort can still be seen outside the castle walls.

A later castle than Brough by a century, Brougham accordingly developed along different lines: first the keep was built, around 1170–80, and then the thirteenth-century curtain wall and towers. Brougham was yet another castle of the Clifford family, which held most of the former county of Westmorland; but here the reconstruction achieved by the indefatigable Lady Anne Clifford after the Civil War was largely undone by her indigent vandal of a grandson. He saw Brougham as a convenient money-making stone quarry, and used it accordingly.

The view from Brougham Castle keep of the courtyard, the thirteenth-century corner turret and surviving curtain wall, and the outer ditch and bank.

The Eamont river crossing commanded by Brougham Castle.

CARLISLE, CUMBRIA

Borough of Carlisle

Carlisle was Roman *Luguvallium*, the western anchor of Hadrian's Wall against the Picts and Scots; and the town kept its role as a frontier bastion against Scottish invasions until the southward march of 'Bonnie Prince Charlie' in 1745. Like the other no-man's-land town of the Anglo-Scottish conflict, Berwick on the east coast, Carlisle was a frontier outpost which frequently passed from English to Scottish hands and back, whenever the Scots pressed their long-standing claim to the northern English counties of Northumbria, Cumbria, and Westmorland. Between the Norman Conquest of England in 1066 and the settlement of the Anglo-Scottish frontier in 1237, Carlisle changed hands no fewer than five times: Scottish until its conquest by William II in 1092; English until its seizure by David I of Scotland in 1035, profiting by the death of Henry I; recovered by Henry II in 1157; conquered again in 1216 when Alexander II of Scotland invaded the English North on behalf of

Stronghold against the Scots: the twelfth-century keep of Carlisle Castle, which over the centuries has seen more action than most other English castles.

Prince Louis of France; and recovered again, this time for good, when the English royalists triumphed and Prince Louis went home.

Given Carlisle's strategic importance – equal to Dover's, as the bastion of the north-west frontier at the other end of the country – one might expect to find a castle of exceptional size and strength there; but this is not the case. During the formative twelfth century, in which more southerly city castles like the Tower of London or Lincoln were steadily expanded, there was no unbroken continuity of occupation at Carlisle. Henry II added a keep to the castle begun on the north side of the town by William II in 1092, but the resulting combination was only embellished rather than transformed by Henry III and Edward I. Both these great castle-building kings concentrated on expensive priorities further south.

In a way, Carlisle Castle suffered architecturally from being in the wrong hands at the wrong time. When Edward I began his war to subdue Scotland in 1295, Carlisle was his western base camp – not a key enemy objective to be captured and made secure with a concentric giant castle like those he built in Wales. Nevertheless, the castle's fourteenth-century main gate has survived as a reminder of its stout defence after the English humiliation at Bannockburn in 1314, when the victorious Scots raided as far south as Richmond in Yorkshire.

Carlisle Castle always suffered from a common complaint of city castles: it was too hemmed in by the town, and so was an indifferent citadel. In 1540–3 Henry VIII ordered an entirely new citadel to be built in the town and it was this building, not the old castle, which was fully maintained and eventually reconstructed in 1807.

The fact remains that Carlisle Castle has seen more action than most English castles: in the medieval Scottish sieges of 1174, 1216 and 1314–18; in the Civil War siege of 1644–5, when it was attacked by the Presbyterian Scots fighting as Parliament's allies; it fell for the last time in its history to the Jacobites of Prince Charles Edward Stuart in 1745. Today, Carlisle Castle most appropriately houses the museum of the King's Own Border Regiment.

NEWCASTLE-UPON-TYNE, NORTHUMBERLAND

Borough of Newcastle

The 'new castle' of Newcastle's name was the earthwork-and-timber fortification built under William I in 1080, to command the Tyne crossing at the eastern end of Hadrian's Wall. The enormous rectangular stone keep, with walls 16 feet (4.8 metres) thick, was built under Henry II in 1171–5. When completed in its new form it was the strongest fortress in the north – its equivalents in Henry II's castle-building programme being Nottingham in the Midlands, Orford in East Anglia and Dover on the Channel coast.

The deterrent effect of Henry II's new castle on the Tyne was immediately demonstrated during the Scottish invasion led by King William 'The Lion' in 1174. William considered Newcastle impregnable and left it strictly alone, confining his efforts to Carlisle and the weaker castles of the north. In the later thirteenth century Newcastle was Edward I's main base in the north-east for operations against Scotland. It was at Newcastle that Edward's chosen puppet-king of Scotland, John de Balliol – after swearing fealty at Norham and being enthroned at Scone – did homage to Edward for his new realm in December 1296.

The battlemented roof of the keep at Newcastle has been restored; it offers impressive if hardly beautiful views of the Tyne. As with Newcastle's western counterpart, Carlisle, the keep's outermost defences consisted of the town walls, built primarily to take the first shock of Scottish attacks. Newcastle's walls, part of which can still be seen in Bath Lane, were begun in 1280. When completed they were 2 miles (3.2 km) in circumference. At the same time, the keep's main entrance was given extra protection with the building of the Black Gate.

Both the keep and the Black Gate house museum collections today. That of the keep covers the castle's history from 1171; that of the Black Gate is a decided rarity, a bagpipe museum! Together they make this unusually complete town citadel of the twelfth and thirteenth centuries of special interest to visitors.

The restored battlements of the keep at Newcastle, built in the 1170s on Henry II's orders to be the strongest castle in the North Country.

ALNWICK, NORTHUMBERLAND

Privately owned
AI or A189/A1068 from Newcastle; AI from Berwick-upon-Tweed

Alnwick is the Arundel of the North Country. It is a triumph of nineteenth-century internal and external preservation and reconstruction, converting one of medieval England's most embattled castles into a princely residence. Alnwick is still the seat of the Dukes of Northumberland: the functioning heart of a great English estate. The dukedom is a comparatively recent one. It was conferred in 1766 on the husband of the latest female descendant of the family which had held Alnwick Castle since its great days in the fourteenth and fifteenth centuries: the Percys of Northumbria.

Alnwick's founders, and first owners until the male line died out in 1297, were the de Vesceys. The first of the castle's many moments of glory came about 35 years after its foundation in Stephen's reign: the capture of King William 'The Lion' of Scotland in 1174, which abruptly cut short a Scottish invasion that had already recoiled from Carlisle and turned east in hopes of easier prey. (The Scottish King was captured in a surprise attack, having incautiously ridden too close to the castle in foggy weather.) On the death of the last de Vescey in 1297, Alnwick was held in trust by the bishopric of Durham until its sale to Henry Percy in 1309. During the castle's first century in Percy hands, it was extensively rebuilt with a curtain wall, round towers and a barbican, becoming more or less the fighting shell that the visitor sees today.

Alnwick Castle's domination of its surroundings was enhanced by extensive landscape-gardening in the eighteenth and nineteenth centuries. One of the most impressive viewpoints is from the north, across the River Aln, with the castle looming starkly

Alnwick's barbican, with its battlements manned by decoy 'defenders' to encourage the waste of enemy arrows.

The superb view across the river Alne of the fighting profile of Alnwick Castle, stronghold of the Percys.

One of the decoy garrison manning the barbican at Alnwick, poised to hurl a rock on the heads of attackers.

against the sky – the profile which Alnwick presented to many generations of Scottish invaders and marauding bands of Douglases, blood enemies of the Percys. The entrance is on the south side, guarded by a fine barbican. The barbican is a distinct novelty because its battlements are 'guarded' by sentries of stone (most of them, admittedly, restored in the eighteenth century, but a few dating from the fourteenth). These statues were no mere decorative whim: they were decoy targets, to encourage besieging marksmen to waste their arrows. From the barbican a bridge leads over the moat (recently excavated) which once joined the Alne, and into the outer bailey.

There are many splendid attractions awaiting the visitor inside Alnwick – the enormous library, the Grand Staircase, the armoury in the Constable's Tower, and the fine museum of British and Roman antiquities housed in the Postern Tower. All are open to the public at advertised times – remember that this is a home, not a museum. Alnwick town makes a pleasant visit in its own right; anglers will not need reminding that this is where the famous Hardy fly rods come from. Altogether, Alnwick makes a splendid day out. *(See also p. 278)*

BAMBURGH, NORTHUMBERLAND

Privately owned
AI/BI342 from Berwick-upon-Tweed via Belford;
AI/BI341 from Newcastle via Alnwick and Adderstone

Bamburgh is one of the oldest sites in English history, being the earliest recorded stronghold built by the invading Anglo-Saxons in the sixth century AD. The *Anglo-Saxon Chronicle* records that King Ida of Bernicia (northernmost of the two sub-kingdoms which made up the later Anglo-Saxon kingdom of Northumbria) fortified the rock of Bamburgh in 547. The name derives from Bebba, queen of Ida's grandson Ethelfrith: *Bebbanburh*, or 'Bebba's Town'. In the ninth century, when North-umbria went down in ruin to the Great Army of the Danes, the last free Englishmen of the North held on at Bamburgh, with no English king left to whom they could give their allegiance but Alfred the Great in the south. Two hundred years later, therefore, the Normans inherited both a superb natural castle site and a fighting tradition second to none.

The present castle stands on the headland of Bamburgh, protected to seaward by a 150-foot (45·7-m) sheer precipice. In 1095 the first Norman

Bamburgh Castle from the foreshore, with a fine view of the rectangular keep added by Henry II in the later twelfth century.

Bamburgh Castle on its headland, commanding one of the oldest natural defensive sites in northern England.

castle held out against William II in the revolt by Robert de Mowbray, Earl of Northumberland, and proved impossible to take even when Earl Robert was captured. His wife continued to resist, and the siege dragged on. It was only ended by means of blackmail, Countess Matilda surrendering on the King's threat that her husband would be blinded if she did not. Once Henry II had added the rectangular keep in the following century, Bamburgh's strength remained unassailable until the advent of cannon in the fifteenth century.

Bamburgh featured prominently in the Wars of the Roses, as one of the strongest Percy castles in the North Country. After the first coronation of the Yorkist Edward IV in 1461, the refugee King Henry VI and his Queen Margaret began an attempted Lancastrian comeback by returning to Bamburgh with Scottish help. For nine months (autumn 1463–May 1464) the illusion of Lancastrian rule was maintained from behind Bamburgh's walls; and when Warwick 'The Kingmaker' led a Yorkist army to recover the Lancastrian castles of the North, Bamburgh was, true to tradition, the last to hold out. Warwick thereupon made an end with artillery, his gunners breaching the walls and enabling the castle to be taken by assault: the first time that the capture of an English castle had been preceded by a cannon bombardment.

None of the extensive reconstructions in the eighteenth and nineteenth centuries have managed to detract from the grandeur of Bamburgh, still one of the most impressive castles of the North Country: a defiant mass of red sandstone on its ancient headland.

One of the strongest of the North Country Percy castles, Bamburgh remained

virtually impregnable until the advent of cannon in the fifteenth century.

DUNSTANBURGH, NORTHUMBERLAND

Department of the Environment
1½ miles (2·4 km) N of Craster, 2 miles (3·2 km) ESE of Embleton;
buses to both villages from Alnwick

From whichever direction you approach, and however close you may manage to park, the only way to reach Dunstanburgh today is on foot. This makes it advisable to visit it in dry weather, because the shortest walk is well over a mile; but this is not a castle to miss. For at its full splendour in the mid-fifteenth century, before its ruinous downfall in the Wars of the Roses, Dunstanburgh was one of the biggest and most beautiful castles in all England, with a mighty sweep of curtain wall enclosing a defended area of 10 acres (4 hectares) in extent. Though Yorkist cannon and slighting parties reduced it to splintered pinnacles 500 years ago, the ruins of Dunstanburgh still proclaim the glory of castles before the age of cannon.

Unlike Alnwick and Bamburgh, its partners in the Northumbrian 'big three', Dunstanburgh was not an ancient fortified site, or even a development of an eleventh- or twelfth-century castle. It was begun in 1313 by Thomas, Earl of Lancaster, the first stage being a long moat to enclose the headland, and a tower gatehouse. The granting of a licence to wall and crenellate by Edward II in August 1316 seems to have been a royal attempt to save face, for by then the castle's curtain wall was already virtually complete.

One of the most interesting modifications to Dunstanburgh's original defences was made in 1380 by John of Gaunt, Duke of Lancaster. He ordered the conversion of the twin-tower gatehouse into a fully enclosed keep. An inner square tower, connected to the outer curtain, was built behind the eastern gatehouse tower; and a new entrance was made outside this newly-created inner ward, screened by

An aerial view of Dunstanburgh from the north-east, showing the enormous circuit of the curtain wall and the massive keep at the right centre.

Dunstanburgh's north-eastern flank was guarded by the square Lilburn Tower, a postern gate for unleashing counter-attacks against besiegers.

a long barbican. Ingenious though it was, however, this reconstruction did little more than re-state the old obsession with converting the castle's weakest point (the main gateway) into its strongest point (the tower gatehouse). Neither Gaunt nor his successors added platforms or ports for the mounting of defensive artillery, without which enemy siege guns could be brought up with impunity to batter the walls at close range. This preoccupation with outdated techniques spelled Dunstanburgh's ruin during the repeated Yorkist sieges in 1462–4.

A series of Tudor surveys assessing the cost of repairing Dunstanburgh throughout the sixteenth century indicate that the keep, large stretches of the curtain wall, and the flanking towers remained in surprisingly good repair until about 1580, by which time the timbers of the roofs and floors had gone. In 1603, however, James VI of Scotland became James I of England, and Dunstanburgh lost its original role as a barrier against Scottish invasions. The unsupported stonework was left to degenerate into the splendid ruins the visitor sees today. There was no conceivable role for Dunstanburgh as a coastal-defence fortress; like Scarborough, it stood with its back to the sea. Dunstanburgh's real problem, however, was that it also faced back towards the past.

Battered by five centuries of North Sea gales: the weathered stones of Dunstanburgh, with arrow-slit and garderobe shoot.

WARKWORTH, NORTHUMBERLAND

Department of the Environment
A1068 from Alnwick;
A1068 from Newcastle via Newbiggin-by-the-Sea

Lying only 6 miles (9·6 km) south-east of Alnwick, Warkworth is, predictably, another of the great Percy castles of the North Country. In many ways, it is a more impressive castle than Alnwick, for it is the North Country's finest specimen of a 'growth' castle, carrying the stamp of consistent development from the eleventh to the fourteenth centuries.

Warkworth is also that considerable rarity, a castle with a fourteenth-century great tower on an earth motte, as at Dudley and York.

The first castle built at Warkworth, in a bend of the river Coquet, may have been of late eleventh-century vintage, but a motte-and-bailey was certainly established there by 1139. It escaped the

The Coquet river at Warkworth, commanded by the great tower residence of the Percys – one of the very few great towers built on an earlier motte.

destruction of adulterine (unlicensed) castles of similar date early in the reign of Henry II, and a rectangular curtain wall was added in the following century. The real transformation, however, was wrought under Percy management in the late four-teenth and early fifteenth centuries: the building of the great tower on the motte. This is of a plan unique in England, that of a 'Greek cross': a square tower with projecting flanking towers formed by the arms of a cross. Warkworth's tower is, however, nothing like the solid mass of Clifford's Tower at York: it was unmistakably built for residential comfort just as much as for defensibility, with a lavish allocation of windows.

The tower escaped the worst damage inflicted by repeated sieges, of which it endured two in the English Civil War – by the Scots in the Marston Moor campaign of 1644 and by the Parliamen-tarians in 1648, who slighted it when they withdrew. In 1672, Warkworth's bailey defences suffered their worst-ever damage when the castle was 'canni-balized' for building materials; but the great tower still stands proudly on its motte, one of the most prized ornaments of the Percy family for nearly 500 years.

Family residence as well as fighting stronghold: the chapel at Warkworth, looking towards the altar.

The unique feature of Warkworth Castle is its great tower, completed in the early fifteenth century in the shape of a Greek cross.

NORHAM, NORTHUMBERLAND

Department of the Environment
A698/B6470 from Berwick-upon-Tweed

The road from Berwick, 8 miles (12·9 km) to the north-east, runs through the filled-in moat of what was once one of the strongest border fortresses in England. This magnificent rectangular keep (90 ft high × 84 ft × 60 ft/27·4 × 25·6 × 18·3 m) was built in the 1160s to safeguard the three northern counties after their recovery by Henry II from Scottish rule. Norham was not, however, a royal castle (though it often reverted to royal control in succeeding centuries). It was built by the formidable Hugh de Puiset, Bishop of Durham, and should be seen as a symbol of the raw power wielded by the prince-bishops of the Durham palatinate. Bishop Hugh's splendid keep was a massive replacement for the earlier castle built at Norham in Stephen's reign (1121) and destroyed by the Scots.

The new castle's first adventure came in 1173–4, when Bishop Hugh, collaborating with the very menace which Norham had been built to check – a Scottish invasion – joined the rebellion against Henry II. When this ended so unexpectedly with the surprise capture of William 'the Lion' under the walls of Alnwick (*see* p. 136) the discomfited Bishop was obliged to surrender Norham to the King with his other castles. It was at Norham, in November 1292, that John de Balliol swore fealty to Edward I as vassal King of Scotland, before his temporary instalment on the Scottish throne – the first step, for the English, on the road to their defeat at Bannockburn 22 years later. In the Wars of the Roses, Norham surrendered to Warwick's army after the fall of Alnwick, thus preserving largely intact one of the finest and most imposing of England's many twelfth-century 'great keeps'.

Broad-backed twelfth-century vaulting supports the mass of the keep.

The huge keep of Norham Castle, built after 1160 to secure the northern counties after their recovery from Scottish rule.

OTHER CASTLES TO VISIT

Knaresborough, South Yorkshire
Keep, fourteenth-century gatehouse, curtain wall and towers added to original Norman foundations. Museum contains armour worn at Marston Moor in Civil War.

Middleham, North Yorkshire
Fine keep of late twelfth century, though outer curtain demolished and ditch filled in.

Muncaster, Cumbria
Privately-owned nineteenth-century reconstructed mansion (by Anthony Salvin) incorporating twelfth-century square tower. *(See also p. 279)*

Sizergh, Cumbria
Fourteenth-century peel tower with Tudor Great Hall; further seventeenth- and eighteenth-century additions.

Lumley, Durham
Fourteenth-century fortified manor, with palatial eighteenth-century reconstruction by Vanbrugh. Today a luxury hotel noted for 'medieval banquets'.

Raby, Durham
Famous Neville stronghold of fourteenth and fifteenth centuries, with nine distinctive towers. Still superb despite removal of outer curtain walls and draining of moat.

GLOSSARY

adulterine castles Unlicensed castles, built without Crown permission during the prolonged civil wars or 'Anarchy' of King Stephen's reign (1135–54). Most were pulled down by his successor Henry II (1154–89).

bailey Enclosed area screening castle's main defences.

barbican Outer tower or walled area blocking direct approach to main gate of castle.

bastion Platform or low tower projecting from main walls to increase effective defensive fire. Originally of rounded shape; usually pointed from 1540s on.

battering Sloping a wall inward from a wider base for greater strength.

concentric castles Castles with two or more lines of defence, one inside the other with the innermost higher than the outer, creating a web studded with mutually supporting strongpoints.

crenellations, crenellate Fighting battlements consisting of stone *merlons* interspersed with *embrasures* which permitted defensive fire. 'Licence to crenellate' was the Crown's permission to fortify an existing manor house or build a new castle.

curtain wall Perimeter wall surrounding *bailey* or *keep*. Usually studded with *flanking towers*.

donjon Medieval name for *keep*; originally the wooden tower built on the *motte*.

drawbridge Wooden bridge across ditch or *moat*, raised to complete circuit of outer defences and prevent direct attack on gate. Would be raised at night.

embrasure Gap between *merlons* to permit defensive fire (archery or other missiles) against attackers below.

enceinte Fortified enclosure, usually referring to circuit of outer ramparts with bastions for the emplacing of guns.

flanking towers Towers projecting from corners of *keep* or main stretch of *curtain wall*, both to strengthen the structure and bring foot of wall under defensive fire.

garderobe Wardrobe, also containing privy.

gatehouse Defences protecting main castle entrance, often the strongest point of the castle.

hoard *also* **brattice** Wooden platform rigged outside battlements to allow missiles to be dropped on attackers below. From fourteenth century, supplanted by permanent stone *machicolation*.

keep Later word for *donjon*: the castle's stronghold, usually a tower.

linear castles Castles with *baileys* or *wards* arranged in a chain, instead of one inside the other as with *concentric castles*. The usual development of castles sited on ridges of high ground.

machicolation Stone platform extending out from top of battlements, supported on small arches; fulfilled role of earlier wooden *hoards*.

merlon Stone section of battlements, interspersed by *embrasures*. Often pierced for additional defensive fire.

mine Tunnel driven by besiegers under castle defences, to bring down a tower, corner of *keep*, or key stretch of wall in order to create a breach for a decisive assault.

moat Water-filled ditch, often linked to nearby river or stream.

motte Shaped natural hill, or wholly artificial mound, on which *donjon* was built. Strongpoint of early castle defences.

murder hole (also *meurtrière*) Opening in *gatehouse* porch ceiling and/or wall to allow attackers, trying to force gate or *portcullis*, to be attacked without means of retaliation.

peel or **pele tower** Tower stronghold without outer defences, for defence against Border raids.

portcullis Heavy wooden gate shod with iron, mounted in grooves, which could be dropped to block a key gateway or passage. Attackers thus trapped could then be attacked through *murder holes*.

slighted Deliberately rendered indefensible by being wholly or partly demolished.

solar Upper-storey private room offering privacy to lord and family. Often accessible only by outside staircase.

ward Enclosed defensive area; later word for *bailey*.

Bamburgh Castle

Callaly Castle

Alnwick Castle

Seaton Delaval

Meldon Park

Raby Castle

Muncaster Castle

Constable Burton

Norton Conyers

Sutton Park

Ripley Castle

Burton Constable

Chatsworth

Little Moreton Hall

Hardwick Hall

Haddon Hall

Holkham Hall

Belvoir Castle

Burghley House

Houghton Hall

Blickling Hall

Stokesay Castle

Deene Park

Broughton Castle

Woburn Abbey

Layer Marney Tower

Eastnor Castle

Blenheim Palace

Gorhambury House

Hatfield House

Berkeley Castle

Cliveden House

Hughenden Manor

Mapledurham House

Clandon Park

Knole

Ightham Mote

Longleat House

Sutton Place

Loseley House

Hever Castle

Great Dixter

Wilton House

Purse Caundle Manor

Petworth House

Penshurst Place

Beaulieu Palace House

Castle Drogo

Arundel Castle

St Michael's Mount

GREAT
ENGLISH
HOUSES

Russell Chamberlin

A Nobleman's Levee, c. 1730, by Marcellus Laroon, a revealing appraisal of the role of the great English house at its apogee.

INTRODUCTION

ABOUT the year 1730 Marcellus Laroon, a not otherwise particularly distinguished artist, painted a picture – *A Nobleman's Levee* – which exactly summed up the role of the great house at its apogee. In the mid-ground the nobleman, coldly indifferent to the press of petitioners awaiting him, is leisurely putting the finishing touches to his attire. On the walls in the background is evidence of his family's lineage, wealth and power in the form of portraits, paintings and tapestries. The faces and characters of those awaiting his lordship's pleasure are all strongly individual. In the left foreground an elderly gentleman, swelling with indignation at his cavalier treatment, is being calmed by a flunkey. Next to him a young fop, accustomed to being kept waiting, is offering snuff to a fellow sufferer. Beside them, a swaggering braggadocio is glaring across at the cause of their humiliation. Resignation, or anger are the predominant reactions to their indifferent reception. What Laroon has presented us with is an exact, though singularly unattractive view of life: the great house, after it had ceased to be a fortress, became a reservoir of wealth, and in order to allow that wealth to be redistributed throughout society, it was necessary to engage the attention, and the goodwill, of its owner.

Currently, each of the handsome guidebooks to Woburn, Longleat and Beaulieu – leaders in the 'stately homes industry' – bears a personal message from the house's owner. Each message is a variant on the theme that, without the public, the house could not continue to exist in its traditional form, if at all. At Longleat, the Marquess of Bath records: 'In these days of heavy taxation it would be impossible to maintain [the house] in the condition in which you see it but for your contributions.' At Beaulieu: 'Your visit helps to preserve a vital part of our national heritage.' At Woburn, the Marquess of Tavistock says unequivocally: 'We have become custodians, no longer the owners.'

The difference between the subject of Laroon's painting and these sentiments, the shift in emphasis from the crowd appealing to the single figure, to the single figure appealing to the crowd, measures the scale of the enormous, though bloodless revolution that has taken place in the interim in the United Kingdom. Until the 1880s, the majority of those who did not live in one of the chartered towns or cities, lived on one of the estates of the nobility contributing, willy-nilly, to the upkeep of the great house that formed the ganglion. The introduction of estate duty in 1894, coupled with the agricultural depression, began the great change. It accelerated in the between-war years (it has been calculated that about a quarter of the land changed hands between 1918 and 1922) and again immediately after World War II. On an estate of £1 million, some four-fifths could be demanded in death duties, unless the family successfully exploited a macabre guessing game. Duties could be avoided if the estate was passed over to the heir a fixed period (currently five years) before the death of the donor. In 1946, the Duke of Devonshire unexpectedly died just four months before the period expired, and the estate was taxed at eighty per cent. One arm of the government frequently defeats the intention of the other. In 1983, at a time when official concern was being expressed at the break-up of art collections, Customs and Excise threatened to levy Value Added Tax on the proposed 'sale' of Kedlestone Hall to the nation for a nominal £2 million, arguing that the contents were being used to attract a fee-paying public.

The ambivalent manner in which the British regard this segment of their national heritage is well illustrated by the fact that they have no adequate name for this class of building, unlike their continental equivalents – 'schloss', 'palazzo', or 'château'. The term 'country house' manages at once to be imprecise and misleading: imprecise, because any rurally situated house must obviously be a country house; misleading, because it conveys a limited, Victorian atmosphere of expensive cigars, leather upholstery and political intrigue. The currently fashionable term 'stately home', derived from Noel Coward's satirical ballad, has an air of wry self-mockery – partly envious – that faithfully reflects a period of social fragmentation and unease. 'Great house' as used in this book, has obvious limitations, but it does convey both the sense of relative size (the phrase 'the big house' is still used in rural communities when referring to the building that was once the centre of social activity) and the sense of history that imbues these houses.

The vague terminology applied to the class of house contrasts with the precise description of the

Chatsworth – the epitome of a great English country house.

house itself, which also places it at some point in history. 'Palace' is rare – very rare apart from royal and episcopal buildings. 'Castle' is a survival from the Middle Ages: Arundel, Berkeley and Alnwick are all genuinely military structures which have, almost absent-mindedly, become homes. 'Manor' describes a once vital function – the great house as a generator and reservoir of rural wealth; it was only later, in the eighteenth century, that its role as a consumer and dispenser of wealth dominated its other functions. 'Hall' is simply the description of a form or structure – the barn-like building which once served as a kind of tribal meeting place, then became a nucleus and finally a fossil. 'Abbey' or 'Priory' indicates the great plunder of the sixteenth century that accompanied the dissolution of the monasteries. 'House', like the non-use of 'palace', marks that prudent English tendency to play down possession so that the rich man will use the same term for his vast mansion as the poor man uses for his hovel. Many a manor house has upgraded itself to castle status (Stokesay and Broughton are cases in point) and many a castle is a nineteenth-century confection. But the labels do serve to give some historical orientation.

England had established its basic unit, the manor, long before the Norman Conquest, giving William an easy means to reward his followers. Each manor could have only one lord, but a lord could have many manors. In the two centuries following the Conquest, the great house was either a castle, or a defended farmhouse. The owners of these farmhouses did not automatically fortify them: permission had to be sought from the monarch, who granted his licence only reluctantly, for each fortified building created a potential threat.

From the mid-thirteenth century, another role was added to the traditional functions of defence, and agricultural production and storage: the more wealthy owners began to treat their uncompromising structures as potential homes, and indulged in a little cautious decorating. The major advance, for the very wealthy, was the use of glass in windows, following the example of such magnates as Sir Walter Poultney, who inserted glass in the walls of Penshurst in 1340.

The Great Hall continued as the centre of all social life. The floor was commonly of beaten earth strewn with rushes and known, significantly, as the marsh. Even as late as the sixteenth century the fastidious Dutchman, Erasmus, described with dis-gust just what lay under the top layer of fresh rushes. At one end of the hall a screen cut off the entrance door and service quarters. The innately conservative English were to retain this screen long after the domestic arrangements had become more sophisticated, turning it into elaborately decorated stonework. At the other end of the hall was the raised dais for the master and his family.

The Battle of Bosworth in 1485, which brought the Wars of the Roses to an end, marked a moment of change in British history as precise as that of the Norman Conquest. The heroic period now lay in the past: the future would lie with statesmen, merchants and financiers rather than with soldiers. The new king, Henry VII, summed up the qualities of the new age in his own person – an avaricious, parsimonious man but also one imaginative enough to finance Cabot's explorations. The coming men resembled their monarch and suddenly a swarm of new families – Cavendish, Cecil, Russell, Thynne – were pushing aside the old nobility, making their fortunes through a skilful combination of commerce and political astuteness. And they began to build new houses, not simply adapting the old.

Glass windows now became a characteristic of the new type of house, evidence not only of private wealth but also the social stability that permitted domestic life to be carried out behind so frail a barrier. Battlements and gatehouses continued to be built, but as much from tradition as from necessity. The Great Hall sank in status, the family moving to more private but splendid rooms on the first floor. The introduction of flues to relieve smoke-filled rooms produced the towering fireplaces and the fantastic chimneys of Tudor England.

Architecture faithfully reflected the social changes of the mid-seventeenth century. The great Elizabethan and Jacobean mansions like Hardwick, Burghley and Knole, were by then old fashioned, though built less than a generation earlier by wealthy men and women to entertain and impress their monarch. Now rising prices, less capital and the emergence of a new middle class led imperceptibly to the building of less ostentatious houses, compensating for their loss of size with an increased opulence in interior decoration. Grinling Gibbons was among those craftsmen who gained fame and a modest fortune from this new emphasis. Confidence and arrogance came back with a flourish in the eighteenth century. The Enclosure Acts and West Indian sugar vastly increased the income of the country gentry at a time when it was fashionable to have aesthetic tastes. The injection of wealth not only resulted in a wave of rebuilding by the gentry, the medieval and Tudor houses of their ancestors making way for the latest style of brick boxes, but it also created a kind of megalomania where the greater the acreage tamed and covered, the more esteemed the architect and patron. The park now came into its own, and the names of gardeners like Capability Brown and Humphrey Repton rivalled those of architects.

Coincident with the rise of landscape gardening, 'stately home' visiting began on a large scale, unwittingly providing one of the means which was to allow the house to survive in the unimaginable twentieth century. The aristocracy had always expected, as a matter of course, to receive the hospitality of their equals while travelling, but now permission to enter and view almost any great house became widely available. Indeed, in 1778 William

Constable actually advertized that his splendidly refurbished house of Burton Constable was now open to the public, perhaps the first example of a now almost universal custom.

Uncritical admirers of the English country house are fond of claiming it as the supreme example of British architectural genius, ignoring such superb urban creations as the inns, cathedrals, guildhalls and assembly rooms which this rurally-orientated people have created. But the eighteenth century also succeeded in reducing far too many houses to a boring uniformity. Endless Red Drawing Rooms, Green Sitting Rooms and Bronze Dining Rooms took the place of chunky, differentiated, medieval and Tudor chambers. And the dreaded names of Capability Brown and Humphrey Repton, superb artists though they were, feature again and again as they dragoon the English landscape into a preconceived pattern of harmony. It is with a sense of relief and refreshment that the visitor comes to a place like

Gheeraerts' painting of Lady Sidney and her children, c. 1595, at Penshurst Place

Haddon Hall, Penshurst Place or Ightham Mote, all of which escaped that homogenizing blight and bear the marks of their centuries upon them.

It must be admitted, too, that many of the artefacts in the houses would be better displayed in a modern gallery or museum. At Knole, for instance, Reynolds' portraits of Samuel Johnson and Oliver Goldsmith are at a height and angle that makes it virtually impossible to study them. But they are placed there because that is where they were hung by the owner a year, a decade, or a century ago.

That, of course, is the supreme justification for the survival of the great house. It is not an art gallery; it is not a museum. It is a home, if on a titanic scale. The very haphazardness of the collections, the changes of fashion that dictate the enlargement of this room, the elimination of that, the introduction of this piece of domestic equipment or the elimination of that, are a precious record of the passage of time. And at the heart of the house is 'the family'. It is precisely this subtle link between the house and the same genetic group that has inhabited it for perhaps centuries, which saves the English country house from becoming a mausoleum, like so many of the châteaux of France. The Gowers Report, commissioned by the government in 1948 to study the problem of such houses, came to the conclusion that they were kept alive by the presence of their families, 'That the owner of the house is almost always the best person to preserve it. . . .'

But how to ensure the continuance of such a symbiosis? The Treasury of the British government was brought round to the realization that the country houses of the kingdom formed part of the national heritage – part indeed of its stock in trade in an era of increasing tourism – and that somebody, somewhere, has to pay for them. As early as 1910 the Inland Revenue was able to accept property in lieu of taxes; but it was not until 1946, under a Socialist government, that a Land Fund was set up which compensated the Treasury for lost taxes, and so allowed the nation itself to acquire control of houses while allowing the families to continue to live in them. In return, public access on a reasonable basis had to be allowed.

The National Trust was employed as the major piece of machinery to bring about the transfer. But the Trust provides only one way out of the dilemma, and in the eyes of many it is by no means an ideal solution. Superbly maintained though their houses might be, inevitably they become institutionalized.

Perhaps more effective in the long run is the action of the Historic Buildings Councils, set up by the Gowers Report. The Councils are empowered to make grants for essential repairs, in return for a minimum number of days of public access each year.

Increasingly, tourism is vital to the survival of these houses whether directly in terms of admission fees, or indirectly as a condition of government aid. There is, however, an increasingly healthy tendency for houses to draw on their own resources: Blenheim, Beaulieu and Knole have all established educational officers who, working with the local authority, are exploiting these houses' most priceless asset – their status as living history.

And over the past decade or so a hopeful new phenomenon has become apparent – the return to such houses of younger people, heirs of those who had abandoned or rented them a generation or more ago. The return is, perhaps, partly motivated by the rise in agricultural revenues which makes maintenance economically more possible. But it seems to be motivated too by that growing interest, amounting almost to an obsession, which our society has in preserving the past. These new owners face a formidable task. In most cases they have given up well paid careers; now new skills are demanded of them – that of accountant, hotelier, historian, caterer, and frequently farmer. The returns are mostly limited to the right to maintain genetic continuity, to live in the house where one's ancestors were born. In the best British manner we have established a compromise which is working, but only just – a kind of holding operation. The shape of the final solution is not yet visible, much less the means of acquiring it.

The houses in this book are arranged in chronological order of style. Although the living house changes its form century by century, or even decade by decade, certain dominant characteristics do remain which allow the house to be slotted into a particular period. It is these characteristics which determine their place in the present book. Thus Callaly Castle, though externally seventeenth century, is placed in the earlier period because of its possession of a pele tower, while Arundel Castle, though founded in the eleventh century, is here placed in the nineteenth century because of its interior decoration. By this means it is hoped to provide a bird's eye view of the development of the great house in England over some nine centuries.

THE MIDDLE AGES

BAMBURGH CASTLE, NORTHUMBERLAND

16 miles (25.7 km) N of Alnwick,
6 miles (9.6 km) from Belford,
3 miles (4.8 km) from Seahouses

BAMBURGH presents one of those extraordinary contrasts in which England excels. The meandering coastal road enters a tiny village that has been somewhat prettified, with mown verges, antique shops and teashops. But rearing up from the neat lawns is a vast castle of rose-coloured stone, like some mythological monster trapped in time. From its battlements you can see Lindisfarne, the Holy Island on which owners of the castle established a monastery that became a centre of learning while

The Cross Hall at Bamburgh Castle, with its rich panelling and fine Flemish tapestries.

England sank into darkness and chaos. Close to the castle gate is the Grace Darling museum, touchingly amateur, but for that very reason conveying with stark drama the story of elemental strife between land and sea that characterizes this wild coast.

The great rock to which the castle clings has been inhabited throughout history. The Romans, with a lively eye for a good military site, certainly used it: recent archaeological evidence shows that a beacon was established here. It enters recorded history in AD 547 when it became the seat of Ida, an Anglo-Saxon king, and it remained a royal stronghold for the next 1,000 years. The kings of Northumbria made it their seat until it was sacked by the Vikings. William the Conqueror lost no time in raising an enormous fortification on this rock that dominated the coastal route between England and Scotland – most of the existing external work is Norman. Many kings of England stayed here and John Baliol, the last king of Scotland, made his submission here.

During the Wars of the Roses Bamburgh succumbed to the artillery of Edward IV, the first castle in England to do so. The thunder of those guns marked the end of all castles as defensive sites. But the Crown still held on to Bamburgh, though it was allowed to fall into dilapidation. In the eighteenth century it passed into private hands and became the object of a remarkable social experiment – a kind of miniature welfare state run by the Archdeacon of Northumberland as a charity. But endowments proved inadequate; in 1894 the trustees sold the castle to the armaments millionaire Lord Armstrong, and he immediately put forward an immense programme of restoration and rebuilding.

Armstrong's work represented 'the acme of expenditure with the nadir of intelligent achievement'

The silhouette of Bamburgh Castle. This great rock has been guarded throughout history.

– the caustic judgement of an architectural historian. Certainly this romantic attempt to recreate a medieval fortress would be rejected by a modern archaeologist as inaccurate, but time has mellowed earlier criticisms. For this is the Victorian idea of a medieval castle, which is interesting to compare with Alnwick – the Victorian idea of a Renaissance palace, or Arundel – the Victorian idea of 'Gothic' Christianity.

The Great, or King's Hall at Bamburgh is an excellent example of the process adopted. The finish is Victorian, but the shape of the Hall itself is that which was revealed when the eighteenth-century additions were removed. The carved ceiling is entirely in the medieval spirit for it is the artistry of one man, Thomas Worsnop, who worked for years at Cragside, Lord Armstrong's seat. Armstrong's own portrait in the Hall sums up the man and his dream. Wearing peer's robes, he is pointing at a plan of the castle, a curious medley of the medieval and the modern but as true to its day as Pugin's Houses of Parliament were to the previous generation.

BERKELEY CASTLE, GLOUCESTERSHIRE

s of the town of Berkeley,
midway between Bristol and Gloucester, just off A38

ENGLISH history is replete with grisly political murders, but there can be few to equal that which took place in Berkeley Castle in 1327. The deposed king, Edward II, had been handed into the safekeeping of Thomas, Lord Berkeley – an honourable man but with no special love for the fallen monarch, and therefore deemed a good gaoler until the king's future was decided. But Edward's adulterous wife, the infamous Isabella, and her lover Mortimer wanted the impasse resolved. And so it was.

The centuries have changed the room in which Edward met his death – except for one detail. In a corner there is a deep and sinister hole. Well-attested accounts have it that corpses both of men and animals were thrown into the hole, breeding a pestilence that usually proved fatal to the prisoner. But Edward survived. Marlowe, who loved a gory tale, picked up the story in his tragedy *Edward II*, in which two turnkeys speculate on the reason for the king's survival. One says to the other:

> Yesternight, I opened but the door to throw
>   him meat
> And I almost stifled by the savour

Indirect methods failing, direct murder was decided upon. The account of the method varies: Marlowe has it that the wretched man was stamped to death beneath a table. John Trevisa, who was almost certainly resident in the castle at the time,

The main entrance to the castle, set in an octagonal tower in the inner courtyard.

declared that Edward was hideously murdered 'with a hoote broche [spike] put through the secret place posterialle'. The screams of the dying man, it was said, could be heard in the town – a manifest impossibility considering the thickness of the castle's walls and the distance of the town, but attesting to the horror that the story aroused. Lord Berkeley was not present at the time of the murder – a diplomatic absence, in all probability. Altogether, this was an uncharacteristically violent episode in the centuries-long history of a family whose name has usually been associated with peace, and whose members bore such soubriquets as the Wise, the Magnanimous and the Makepeace.

Certain family names have a popular significance

The wretched Edward II was imprisoned in this room, and was horribly murdered here in 1327.

quite irrelevant to their historical weight. Berkeley is such a name. Whether it is because of a London square immortalized in a sentimental song, an exclusive London hotel or, more likely, the famous hounds, the name sets up familiar echoes in an English ear. The family, in fact, is one of the few to bridge that violent discontinuity created by the Norman Conquest. Its direct founder, Robert Fitz-hardinge, was a grandson of one of Edward the Confessor's horse-thanes. He was wise enough to support Henry II against Stephen (the Berkeleys usually had the ability to spot the winner) and was granted the already massive castle in 1153. He probably rebuilt the keep immediately; it still dominates the structure, though there is a breach in it now, imposed by the Parliamentarians during the Civil War. It can be repaired only by express permission of Parliament, permission that has neither been sought nor granted, so that what was once a mark of disfavour is now a mark of historic distinction.

In certain lights the immense building seems to float on the green sea of its surrounding meadows. Those innocent fields, in fact, were part of its highly efficient defences for they could swiftly be flooded at need. Gertrude Jekyll, that eminently practical, literally down-to-earth gardener, launched into near poetry when describing the castle: 'When the day is coming to its close, and the light becomes a little dim and thin mist-films arise from the meadows, it might be an enchanted castle, for in some trick of evening light it cheats the eye into something ethereal, without substance, built up for the moment into towering masses of pearly vapour.' The beautiful colour of its stone, described as being that of potpourri, rose petals mixed with lavender, is a combination of pink sandstone and blue-grey tufa, which together give that ethereal quality.

The castle is, and always has been a living home, and each generation has made the changes thought necessary for comfort and ease. But no interior decorator has been unleashed upon the place, no Earl of Berkeley has returned from travels in Italy determined to transform his Gloucestershire castle into a Roman or Venetian palazzo. The dimensions of the rooms remain much as they were built: the Great Hall is a perfect example of early fourteenth-century architecture. Passages twist and wind, windows give sudden, unexpected views – the Middle Ages still remain upon the place. (See also p. 99)

Berkeley Castle – built to dominate the river Severn. The softly mottled colouring of the castle's stonework is produced by a combination of sandstone and tufa.

The Great Hall, built on the site of the original hall about 1340. The roof is contemporary,

but was repaired in 1497. The screen has 16th-century decorations.

STOKESAY CASTLE, SHROPSHIRE

8 miles (12.8 km) from Ludlow,
¾ mile (1.2 km) s of Craven Arms off A49

DESPITE its grandiose name, this is not a castle but a fortified manor house – and far more interesting for that very reason. Castles are common enough in England, but most of the earlier manor houses have been transformed out of all recognition, where they have not been demolished outright and rebuilt in the fashionable eighteenth-century idiom. Built in the late thirteenth century, abandoned in the early nineteenth century and sensitively restored in the late nineteenth century, Stokesay Castle is a survivor from a vanished world.

A family called Say had their 'stoke', or dairy farm here about 1115. The tower was built a century later, its lower two storeys being the oldest examples of stonework at the castle. Most of the building of the manor, however, was the work of Lawrence, a wool merchant, who made his fortune in nearby Ludlow, and decided about 1281 to put his money in the land. Stokesay later came into the hands of the first Lord Craven, and as a result was besieged during the Civil War, Craven being an ardent Royalist. But not ardent enough, it seems, to watch his home being destroyed for a lost cause, and it was surrendered hastily to Parliamentary forces in 1645. Following the normal practice of 'slighting', the massive curtain walls were reduced to less than a third of their original height.

Over the next century, frequent sub-leasing of the manor to local families caused it to become ever more dilapidated. By 1814, it was unequivocally described as 'abandoned to neglect and rapidly advancing to ruin'. In 1869 it was bought by John Darby Allcroft who, in a remarkably public-spirited manner, thoroughly restored it though without any intention of living in it. His descendants have also accepted responsibility for maintaining it although it remains empty, apart from the gatehouse.

The visitor receives two quite different impressions on entering the courtyard. Standing with one's back to the gatehouse and looking across what is now a green lawn, one sees an ecclesiastical-looking range of stone buildings flanked by towers. To the north is the original tower built by the Says while the other, known as the South Tower, was

Stokesay, seen across the flower-spangled churchyard, with its towers and contrasting Elizabethan gatehouse.

The solar to which the family withdrew for privacy. Begun about 1285, its contents date from the 17th century.

begun by Lawrence of Ludlow. The range in-between consists of the Great Hall and the Solar wing which form the heart of Stokesay, and was also mostly Lawrence's work.

But turning round, one is immediately transported forward several centuries, for the gatehouse is a comfortable half-timbered Elizabethan dwelling, and the encircling stone walls serve only as a demarcation between the courtyard and the rolling Shropshire hills. Before they were slighted they would have towered up to at least half the height of the original stone gatehouse, creating security but also a decidedly gloomy and claustrophobic courtyard.

To enter the Great Hall is to receive a sudden and dramatic correction to the popular idea of the romantic delights of medieval life. This is where the lord of the manor dined with his family and retainers, where they gathered to pass the endless hours in inclement weather. And it is simply a great barn. The roof timbers high overhead disappear into shadow even on a bright day, and the rafters in the centre are still blackened from the smoke of the

hearth below. There is no sign of a chimney. It needs little imagination to reconstruct the hall as it must have appeared on a winter's night – a great cavern, swept by icy draughts, choked with smoke. The lord and his lady were only too aware of those killing draughts: their high table was set as far as possible from the door.

The contrast between hall and solar could not be more marked. The solar, here as elsewhere, was the response to the growing desire of the family to have some privacy, some other, smaller chamber where it was possible to introduce an element of comfort. The undercroft of the solar block was used as cellarage and storage. The solar proper was on the second floor, reached by an external staircase outside the hall. The naked stone walls of the room were panelled in the seventeenth century but one can still look beyond this later refinement and see what this room would have offered those taking refuge from the Great Hall. The low ceiling creates at least an impression of snugness, and the large windows are designed to let in the sunshine which gives its name to this type of chamber (*solarium*). (*See also p. 110*)

BROUGHTON CASTLE, OXFORDSHIRE

2 miles (3.2 km) SW of Banbury
on the Shipton-on-Stour road (B4035)

AMONG the treasures of this friendly, moated manor house (which Henry James described as 'the most delightful home in England') are two unassuming little volumes, one of them bound in vellum. They constitute the original manuscript of that indefatigable young lady, Celia Fiennes, whose spirit of sheer curiosity took her the length and breadth of seventeenth-century England, accompanied only by a man servant. Her journal, with its breathless, high-spirited prose, provides a view into a vanished England – which, she says, with splendid xenophobia, 'will cure the evil itch of over-valuing foreign parts'.

Although born in Wiltshire, Celia Fiennes was related to the Fiennes family who owned Broughton Castle (and who, three centuries later, still do). She naturally stayed in the houses of her relatives and friends whenever possible, and her testimony provides priceless first-hand evidence of the social life of her day. What she has to say of Broughton Castle, her grandfather's seat, is not very flattering, expressed in her typically, unpunctuated style. 'It's an old house moted all round and a park and gardens but are much left to decay and ruin, when my brother came to it.'

The house (for house it is, despite its martial title) was a good 300 years old when she visited it, for it was begun in the late fourteenth century by a Sir John de Broughton. Although its moat is not as picturesque as those at Ightham and Hever, it is decidedly more impressive – a great sheet of water almost wide enough to be called a lake. The only

A typical fortified manor house. The gatehouse controlled the only access – the bridge across the moat.

The Star Chamber, with its hand-painted Chinese wallpaper.

access to the house is across a bridge and through a massive gatehouse. Most of the curtain wall that was built along the line of the moat in the early fifteenth century has been demolished, but one is most vividly aware of being at the heart of a defended complex that was well able to look after its own. The Fiennes acquired the house by marriage in 1451 and about a century later transformed it from a manor house, built for protection, into a family mansion. This is the appearance that it gives today, but the original medieval building is everywhere evident – most noticeably in the Great Hall.

In a modest little room on the upper floor of one of the towers, the course of English history was changed. There, between 1629 and 1640, William, Lord Saye, and others opposed to Charles I met to plan their campaign (under the pretext of being members of the Providence Island Company). Nicknamed Old Subtlety, William has had a bad press. Contemporary historians (mostly Cavalier) loathed him: for the great Clarendon he was 'proud, morose and of a sullen nature, one who had conversed much with books ... who lived sordidly in the country'. But though a Puritan, Lord Saye was no Leveller: it is more than likely that, like many a would-be reformer before him, he was overtaken by events – the man who started an avalanche by removing a pebble.

Broughton Castle has changed little over the years. It was saved from the worst excesses of nineteenth-century 'restoration' by the profligate young fifteenth Baron. In 1837 the castle was virtually stripped of its contents – even the swans on the moat were sold. The auctioneer's catalogue, with the prices realized, shows that objects were sold for pence rather than pounds. The art collec-

tion was dispersed for ridiculous sums. There may be room to doubt the authenticity of the Bruegel sold for £2 19s, but not the Knellers or the Lelys which went for a guinea each.

Subsequently, the house passed through the hands of various tenants before returning again to the family, who determined to make it support itself. The house is, in effect, divided into two. The private rooms are a delightful mixture of the casually intimate and the historic: the ceiling of the kitchen, is of bare thirteenth-century stone sheltering highly efficient twentieth-century equipment; and a newly-built circular staircase, traditional in shape but modern in substance, connects upper and lower floors. But there is no sense of a museum in either private or public section: children of the present Lord and Lady Saye were brought up in the Chinese Room with its rare and vulnerable wallpaper. The beautiful Long Gallery was recently restored by John Fowler, creating new wallpaper out of antique blocks, using a warm orange colour that echoes the Oxfordshire ploughland visible through the windows. And summing up the symbiosis of new and old is the immense new carpet in the Oak Room, paid for by a film company who used the castle as their setting.

The spectacular ceiling of the Great Parlour, dated 1599.

PENSHURST PLACE, KENT

In Penshurst village, 7 miles (11.2 km)
s of Sevenoaks-Tunbridge Wells road,
3½ miles (5.6 km) w of Tonbridge on B2176

'I AM the greengrocer. I live over my shop', the owner of Penshurst Place remarked, during a discussion about the problems of maintaining and living in a great country house in the last quarter of the twentieth century. One is tempted to paraphrase the wartime Churchillian phrase 'Some greengrocer! Some shop!' For the shopkeeper is Lord De L'Isle VC, KG, and the shop is his immense extended home – half country house, half castle – which centres on a medieval manor house still intact after more than six centuries.

Penshurst, the birth place of Sir Philip Sidney and still in the possession of the Sidney family, demonstrates that there is no one answer to the problem of conservation and survival. Lord De L'Isle refuses to accept government grants for repairs, arguing that this leads to loss of independence. And where other houses are tied closely to their estates, at Penshurst estate and house have been separated. Lord De L'Isle believes that house and garden must be run as a business, generating if possible its own income. 'An agricultural estate is, at best, no more than self-balancing economically and can easily be drained financially if it is too closely bound to a great house in a single management unit.'

There has been a garden at Penshurst for at least six centuries, its outward form undergoing many changes. But neither Capability Brown nor Humphrey Repton arrived here to put their bland, homogenizing touch on everything. The great protecting walls, begun in 1570, have survived. But the gardens, restored during the nineteenth century, deteriorated again during World War II and have been under course of restoration ever since. Now they form a great series of carefully planted hedges and walled enclosures – a renaissance of the formal English garden. Other attractions are an imaginative adventure playground for the young and a permanent exhibition of agricultural implements and machinery.

The house itself is a classic example of organic growth. The great Baron's Hall was built between

The Baron's Hall with its screen and minstrels' gallery.

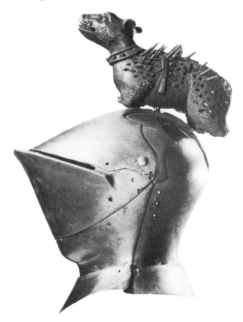

The helmet of Sir Philip Sidney.

The south front showing the original curtain wall, defensive Garden Tower (right) and central Great Hall.

1338 and 1349. Half a century later it was enclosed in a curtain wall that gives an outline as clear and exact as that of a child's fort. Over the next two centuries, more buildings budded off from the Baron's Hall, creeping towards the encircling wall. No longer required as defence it slowly disappeared in most places, though some of the towers were incorporated within the residential building.

But throughout all this, the Baron's Hall remained unchanged. It is different in degree, though not in kind, from Stokesay so that one can see here the last flowering of that great, primitive meeting place, the hall, which is at the heart of all medieval dwellings. The screen that masks the serving doors is still a simple wooden screen, though on an immense scale; the lord's dais still remains; the great hearth is still central. A fire of logs occasionally warms twentieth-century visitors as it warmed kings, princes and feudal lords as they dined at high table in the Middle Ages. And from the huge, naked but curiously friendly chamber great stone steps wind up to another civilization, for they lead to the dining room that appears, by contrast, to belong to our own time.

This gallery at Penshurst was added in the 1820s.

RABY CASTLE, DURHAM

1 mile (1.6 km) N of Staindrop village
on Barnard Castle-Bishop Auckland road (A688)

EVEN today, when time has mellowed the stone and set the whole in gentle parkland, the first and last impression of Raby is of an enormous, almost brutal strength. This is still a castle, despite the fact that centuries have passed since it last saw military action. The towers rear up, spiky with turrets, toothed with crenellations. There are nine of them altogether, each with its own identity and distinctive history, linked together by the curtain wall. Passing through the gateway, the visitor is immediately confronted by the massive Clifford's Tower; the biggest tower of all it was specifically designed to protect the gatehouse, or render it untenable if it was taken. Beyond is the oddly-shaped Bulmer's Tower; where all its neighbours are rectangular, this is leaf-shaped, or perhaps more appropriately, like a spear facing southward. Time has cast its

The richly decorated octagonal drawing room at Raby.

homogenizing mantle over it, but Bulmer's Tower is probably the oldest part of this ancient castle. Tradition claims that its bottom course is the work of no less a person than Canute – 'Emperor of the North' as he called himself – and certainly he had his seat at Raby.

The octagonal Kitchen Tower, curiously domestic in this range of military might, has not changed since it was first built in the fourteenth century. While state rooms and the family's lodgings may alter from century to century in accordance with the whim of fashion, domestic quarters change only slowly in great houses. Why change a kitchen or a brewery except to make it bigger or for better access?

Tracing a legendary descent from Canute's niece, the Nevills ruled here for nearly 400 years, until the fatal Great Rising of the North in 1569. On that occasion the Catholic barons decided to rebel in favour of Mary, Queen of Scots. Their plot – which was to cost most of them dear, above all, the last Nevill – was hatched in this very same castle. Wordsworth romanticized the occasion:

> Seven hundred knights, retainers all
> Of Nevill, at their master's call
> Had sate together in Raby's Hall

The Hall has changed considerably in appearance.

Part of the original medieval building, the Hall owes its present appearance to Carr's work of 1781.

Raby's many-towered skyline, each tower with a clear identity. The immense curtain wall is thirty feet high.

William Burn (1789–1870), the Victorian architect, gave it the fashionable neo-Gothic look together with a splendid new ceiling, and lengthened it by some seventy feet. But looking down this immense stretch is to realize that Wordsworth scarcely exaggerated. It was indeed quite likely that 700 men gathered here. They were by no means unanimous about the proposed rebellion against Queen Elizabeth, but the Lady of Raby goaded them on – and lost her estate for her pains. The Crown cannily held the castle for over fifty years until Sir Henry Vane bought it in 1626, and his descendants hold it today as the Lords Barnard.

The interior was much altered by John Carr of York in the 1780s. His work is to be found all over the north, but there is nothing to equal the extent of his alterations here, the most bizarre being the adaptation of the entrance hall. The inner court of Raby is surprisingly small, too small for a horse and carriage to turn around, so Carr altered the hall enabling a horse and carriage to pass *through* it. Most of the castle's furnishing is post-eighteenth century, the result of one of the blazing family rows that characterize so many great houses. The first Lord Barnard was so furious when his son married without his permission that, in 1741, he sold off everything moveable, chopped down all the trees in the park – and even contemplated demolishing the building. But the characteristic white-painted cottages of the estate remain; once they are out of sight, the visitor knows that he has left the lands of the Lord Barnard.

HADDON HALL, DERBYSHIRE

PARADOXICALLY, neglect preserved Haddon Hall unchanged for posterity. In the early eighteenth century its owners, the dukes of Rutland, abandoned it for their grander house – Belvoir Castle. Haddon, lost among its Derbyshire hills, dreamed on while the outside world went on its racketing way. When Celia Fiennes visited the house in 1697 she emphasized the remoteness of the countryside; certainly, only a tough and curious-minded traveller like herself would deliberately seek out such a place. 'You are forced to have guides: the common people know not above two or three miles from their home.' She thought Haddon not particularly remarkable – 'a good old house all built of stone but nothing very curious as the mode now is'.

That final phrase of hers – 'nothing very curious as the mode now is' – is the key to the interest that Haddon holds for us today. While other houses were going through the drastic rebuilding of the eighteenth century, or the no less drastic restorations of the nineteenth century, Haddon was left untouched except for maintenance. It was not until 1924 that the Marquis of Granby (later the ninth Duke of Rutland) moved to Haddon and made its restoration his life's work. Part of the building is used today as a hunting lodge or holiday home. But most of it is empty, giving the visitor an unrivalled opportunity to inspect a house which developed between the late eleventh and the early seventeenth centuries.

The history of Haddon Hall goes back to the beginning of English history, for William the Conqueror gave the original manor to an illegitimate son, William Peverel. His descendants lost the estate during the civil wars of the twelfth century,

Sir Henry Vernon built this room as his 'parlour' in 1500. The painted ceiling is contemporary, although carefully restored in 1926.

The chapel, with its Norman arches and font, contains several fifteenth-century murals including this fine portrayal of St Christopher striding through the river, and two of St Nicholas.

and it came into the hands of the Vernons who were to hold it for 400 years. According to legend, a daughter of the Vernons, Lady Dorothy, eloped with her lover, John Manners, during the wedding festivities of her sister in the Long Gallery. Whatever the truth of the story, Lady Dorothy Vernon did indeed marry John Manners, later Duke of Rutland. Thus, one of the great romances of the sixteenth century was instrumental in transmitting the estate to its present owners.

The house, in its idyllic setting, is reached over a seventeenth-century bridge across the rushing river Wye and then up a steep and winding lane, the very epitome of the approach to a medieval castle. Restoration has been done with extreme care and subtlety. What appears to be a perfectly carved runnel in the entrance porch, for example, is stone worn by centuries of footsteps. Beyond the gatehouse is the kind of physical evidence of the changing past that makes Haddon so fascinating, even to the layman. Where the south wall joins the gatehouse, it looks as though amateur masons, working without direction, have produced a hodgepodge of styles. The apparent confusion, however, is the result of trying to abut a new wall, running down a slope, to an existing wall. In most other houses, this kind of evidence has been smoothed away.

Haddon is thus a three-dimensional textbook of medieval architecture. In the tall, narrow chapel, the observant eye can find evidence of almost every century since it was begun by the Normans. Here, again, the paradox of neglect as a preservative is demonstrated. The Puritans, in their anxiety to shield the eyes of the faithful from ungodly images, whitewashed the exquisite medieval murals. They were thus protected until the whitewash was removed during twentieth-century restorations.

Haddon Hall is built on a hill, the 17th-century gardens descending by splendid stone terraces to the river.

All through the house is this sense of the past impinging on the present, most immediately and most poignantly perhaps in the kitchens. Carbon deposits from the rushlights can still be detected – by touch as well as sight – on the walls. The great bake ovens are of a kind that were still in use in Derbyshire well within living memory. Wood shapes the place: on one wall a vast baulk has been carved into two basins; in the centre of the floor is the starkly-named killing block – a massive piece of

The oak-panelled Long Gallery.

wood with a crude hole bored through it. A rope, passed through this, forced the animal's head down onto the block where it could be dispatched, as witnessed by the many deep grooves in the wood.

The Banqueting Hall retains the dais which allowed the lord and his family to be psychologically separate from, though sharing the same room with, their retainers. The splendid roof timbers are new, part of the 1924 restoration. Hidden in one of them is a leaden box giving precise details of the restorations for the benefit of posterity.

But it is in the Long Gallery that time has really been frozen. Dorothy Vernon would have known this room, for it was built by her father and has remained quite unchanged. Even on a dull day it is flooded with light: the curious distortions of the diamond window panes throughout the house are deliberate, an ingenious device to catch light at all angles. Over the centuries, idlers have scratched their initials and varying sentiments on the glass. Here, above all, the beauty of wood emerges in its own right, faded now to a beautiful silver-grey, and unobscured by pictures except the curiously moving landscape painted by Rex Whistler in 1933, showing the ninth Duke and his son looking down on this beautiful, lonely house.

BEAULIEU PALACE HOUSE, HAMPSHIRE

In Beaulieu 5 miles (8 km) SE of Lyndhurst

ST BERNARD of Clairvaux, the founder of the first Cistercian abbey in Burgundy in 1098, deliberately chose a remote and isolated site. He advised his followers to do likewise. 'Trust one who has tried it', he wrote. 'You will find more in words than in books.' The great abbey of Beaulieu, founded in 1204 under the patronage of King John, was established in an isolated corner of the New Forest, already known as Beau Lieu, or 'beautiful place'.

When the monastery was dissolved in 1538, it was bought by Thomas Wriothesley, later the first Earl of Southampton, for £1,350 6s 8d. Most of the buildings were demolished, and the stone was used to build castles to guard the Solent. But the monks' refectory became the parish church, whilst the Great Gatehouse was adapted as a manor house. It was altered again in the 1720s, and considerably enlarged in the 1870s by the architect Sir Reginald Blomfield for Lord Henry Scott, later first Baron Montagu of Beaulieu. Palace House today has the outward appearance of 'Scots baronial', but the interior is a remarkable mixture of the fourteenth and nineteenth centuries. In the Upper Drawing Room, for example, both a piscina and an aumbry still exist, while in the Dining Room there is a fourteenth-century bread cupboard, probably the oldest piece of furniture in the house. Thus the possessions of medieval abbots mingle with those of nineteenth-century lords of the manor.

Beaulieu is one of the great houses which has adopted tourism as a means of financial viability. The attractions of medieval abbey and of manor house were augmented in 1952 when Lord Montagu opened his collection of vintage cars to the public. This developed into the National Motor Museum, now owned by a trust.

Beaulieu Palace House, with the original Great Gatehouse of the abbey at the heart of a complex which took on its Victorian Gothic shape between 1870 and 1873.

An altar once stood in this Upper Drawing Room, immediately below the far east window. On the right is the piscina in which the priest washed the chalice.

Now the main Dining Room, this was originally the Inner Hall of the gatehouse. The 14th-century bread cupboard still survives.

At Beaulieu, museum, tourist and residential roles are all interlocked. An outstanding project has been the gradual excavation and restoration of the abbey ruins under professional direction, together with research into the life of the now vanished monastic community. Although Beaulieu may be part of the world of entertainment, it also has more serious functions. An education service was established in 1972, and countless school children are given an insight into living history. The house has been arranged as one large diorama, with the visitors somehow a part of it. In most of the rooms there are historic figures, from 1538 onwards, wearing appropriate costume, illustrating either some aspect of the house's history or furnishing in a series of tableaux.

If Longleat pioneered the idea of opening to the public, and Woburn took that to its logical conclusion, Beaulieu was probably the first to capitalize on the fact that education can be a profoundly absorbing activity, to be enjoyed rather than endured.

The ecclesiastical origins of Palace House.

ST MICHAEL'S MOUNT, CORNWALL

½ mile (0.80 km) from the shore at Marazion (A394),
connected by causeway; 3 miles (4.8 km) E Penzance
The National Trust

THE castle-capped island rears up from the waters of Mount's Bay like a vision from an Arthurian romance – but this island was colonized at least a millenium before Arthur was born. It is almost certainly, the island of Ictis, where continental traders picked up the Cornish tin bound for the Mediterranean. Writing about AD 20 Diodorus, the Greek historian, picked on the phenomenon which made the island particularly useful. 'During the ebb tide the intervening space [between island and coast] is left dry and they carry over to the island the tin in abundance in their wagons.'

At ebb tide now there is a handsome rough causeway, laid down about 1425 by the monks who erected the first permanent buildings on the island.

By carefully judging the time of arrival, the traveller can stroll across – and it is a decidedly curious experience to enter a port on foot from the seaward side. A path winds steeply upward, through banks of flowers, towards the massive steps, carved from the rock itself, by which the castle is entered. By the side of the path, roughly halfway up, is a deep well which figures in that enduring folk story – Jack the Giant Killer. The Mount was supposedly built by a giant called Cormoran, a great stealer of mainland cattle, until Jack dug a pit and enticed him into it.

The atmosphere of legend, of fairy tale, lingers throughout St Michael's Mount. Building has been in progress on the crest for over seven centuries, from 1135 when the first priory was built, to the

The Blue Drawing Room, converted c. 1740 from the 15th-century Lady Chapel and decorated in Gothic style.

The early morning sun outlines the building – part castle, part church, part home – an integral element of the Mount.

Victorian addition of 1878. But because the builders all used the same material – granite – and because they adopted similar solutions when faced with the same constructional problem – how to fit a building on to a crag – the whole seems one great structure.

St Michael's Mount was a daughter of that other island priory across the Channel, Mont St Michel. The problem of the dual loyalty of its monks was solved when, in 1424, control was handed over to Syon Abbey. At the dissolution, the Crown retained control of so important a military site, leasing it to carefully vetted governors. In 1647 a Parliamentary colonel, John St Aubyn, was nominated Governor and bought the island in 1659. Descendants of St Aubyn, enobled as Lords St Levan, continued to hold both the buildings and the island until 1954, when they gave St Michael's Mount to the National Trust with a substantial endowment, although the Lords St Levan still reside there.

This is no make-believe castle, despite its picturesque appearance. Its long history has been punctuated by sieges, rebellions and occupations. Perkin Warbeck, the Pretender to the throne, found refuge here with his beautiful 'queen', Catherine, in 1497. Sir Francis Bassett, the King's Governor, honourably defended it against Parliamentary forces in 1642. It was militarily active as late as 1812 when its guns dismasted a French frigate, and even in World War II it had a strong garrison, and was machine-gunned from the air.

The main entrance to the castle. Having made the steep ascent to the left, one enters by the low, solid door in the centre, with the rock falling away sheer behind.

The Chevy Chase Room. Originally the refectory of the monastery, the roof timbers are 15th century. The frieze of hunting scenes gives this room its name.

The great, rambling building began to be properly adapted to residential purposes in the mid-nineteenth century. An entire new wing was built in the 1870s, but in general the existing ancient building was preserved and modern comforts and interior decorations were imprinted upon it. The Chevy Chase Room which takes it name from the frieze of hunting scenes, is the original twelfth-century refectory whose fifteenth-century roof was restored in the nineteenth century. Most remarkable, perhaps is the conversion of the fifteenth-century Lady Chapel into a drawing room in the mid-eighteenth century. The views from it are superb, for it looks out immediately upon the north terrace on the very summit of the island. But, despite its elegance, it must, one feels, have been a cold and comfortless place.

IGHTHAM MOTE, KENT

2½ miles (4 km) S of Ightham off A227,
6 miles (9.6 km) E of Sevenoaks

THE meaning of the first part of this curious name is straightforward enough, for it is the name of the nearby village of Ightham. In the infuriating English manner, however, the house is actually in the village of Ivy Hatch. But does 'mote' mean a meeting place, as has been suggested? Or is it a more likely reference to the moat which surrounds this exquisite manor house? It is all of a piece with the uncertainty that hangs over much of its history.

Some houses change hands only rarely: at Ightham Mote there have been seven families in six centuries, three of them in the seventy years between 1521 and 1591. Its survival today is due to a remarkable act of disinterested generosity on the part of an American. The last owner of the house had died in 1950, and when it came on the market a group of local businessmen bought it to prevent it falling into the wrong hands. In 1953 Charles Henry Robinson, a businessman from Portland, Maine, made a bid for it. It is said that returning home by sea he changed his mind, and wrote a letter cancelling the bid – but forgot to post it. Although domiciled in America, he directed the restoration of the house over the following years and subsequently made arrangements for it to be left to the National Trust on his death.

Visiting ancient houses one after another, one is tempted to escalate superlatives, but Ightham Mote really is a jewel. It is difficult to find, although less than twenty-five miles from London, for it is tucked away in a private little valley down narrow Kentish lanes. Apart from the fourteenth-century gatehouse

The courtyard is a fascinating melange of periods and styles, from the 14th-century stone hall on the right to the 19th-century dog's kennel close by. The oriel window is 16th century, inserted in what was the solar.

The main entrance with its 15th-century doors.

The 14th-century Hall arches rest on carved corbels.

it does not pretend to be a castle, as do other moated manor houses, but is simply a large private house, surrounded by a walled moat that is the delight of neighbouring ducks. The first builder was Sir Thomas Cawne, whose armour-clad effigy is in the parish church. Over some thirty years, before his death in 1374, he had built perhaps half the existing

One of the stone figure corbels
in the Hall.

house, including the lower part of the gatehouse, the moat and the Great Hall. The latter was to undergo considerable changes, the last in 1872 when Norman Shaw was commissioned to make it habitable according to nineteenth-century standards. This was the period when a seated female skeleton was found walled up in a cupboard, her age, identity and the motive for the bizarre occurrence all being unknown.

Subsequent owners continued the building, gradually creating a delightful square courtyard dominated by the Tudor additions of Richard Clement in 1521. It was during this time that the house gained a most unusual, and today probably unique feature – the barrel vault of the chapel. The vault is made up of alternating wooden panels carrying various badges and motifs – the rose of York, the arrows of Aragon, the portcullis of Beaufort (now the arms of Westminster City Council) and others. They are now much faded, although an imaginative recreation of one section gives an idea of the colourful, not to say gaudy, impression of the original. Such ceilings were made for the elaborate temporary pavilions used during ceremonial outdoor events of which there were many, such as the Field of the Cloth of Gold, and this may well be a survivor.

The walled moat extends round the entire house, fed by a clear stream.

THE FIFTEENTH CENTURY

GREAT DIXTER, EAST SUSSEX

½ mile (0.80 km) N of Northiam, 8 miles (12.8 km) NW of Rye,
12 miles (19.3 km) N of Hastings, just off A28

IN a less dramatic fashion, this is as remarkable an exercise in historical restoration as was Hever Castle. The house was all but derelict when the architectural historian, Nathaniel Lloyd, bought it in 1910. Edwin Lutyens was given the job of restoring and enlarging it, and embarked on the task shortly before he undertook his massive commission of Castle Drogo.

Great Dixter is a delightful example of a timber-framed house, that solid yeoman's home built from the oak of the great Weald that once lapped all this region of south-east England. The first recorded reference to the manor is as early as 1220, but the oldest part of the present house, the Great Hall, dates from about 1450. Lutyens restored the hall to its original dignified proportions by boldly removing floors and partitions which had been inserted after the hall was built, but were of impressive antiquity when he came to tackle the task. He enlarged the house in two entirely different ways.

Lutyens' tile-hung addition on the left is in honest contrast to the timbered front of the original building, but both parts combine to make a satisfying whole.

The front was extended in a manner which, while within the vernacular tradition of the whole building, was honestly distinct from it. Lutyens achieved this by hanging it with tiles contrasting with the half-timbering of the original building. He extended the back in a manner that was startlingly innovatory then. He found an early sixteenth-century timbered cottage at Benenden, also in a derelict state, and transported it bodily to Great Dixter, incorporating it at the rear of the house. The technique is much used today to preserve small historic buildings – particularly those in the way of road development. The entire Weald and Downland Museum at Singleton, near Chichester, is made up of such salvaged buildings, but it needed an architect of Lutyens' confidence and sensitivity to achieve this success in 1910.

He also designed the gardens, retaining many of the original farm buildings. The oast house, for instance, was in use until 1939. Seventy years after completion a family link is still maintained, for the estate is run by Quentin Lloyd, and the now famous gardens by Christopher Lloyd, sons of the man who originally saved the house.

The Wealden house displayed: the Hall at Great Dixter.

The topiary garden is also Lutyens' work, the oast houses and farm buildings of the original complex being incorporated into the design.

NORTON CONYERS, NORTH YORKSHIRE

CHARLOTTE Brontë visited Norton Conyers whilst acting as governess to some unruly children near Harrogate in 1839. Upstairs in the attics was a room to which legend clung; sometime in the previous century, a mad woman was supposed to have been confined there. This strange story stayed in Charlotte's mind and later, through the alchemy of the artist, emerged in *Jane Eyre*, with the mad woman as Mrs Rochester, and Norton Conyers as Thornfield Hall.

Norton Conyers was originally a fortified manor house. It has been continuously occupied throughout its 500-year existence and has seen many changes. The unusual roughcast which covers the exterior is misleading; it was added in the eighteenth century to protect the late fifteenth-century brickwork. But here and there the exterior shows indications of its earlier appearance: an arrowslit and battlements remind one that even in the fifteenth century a Yorkshire farmer was well advised to provide means for his protection.

The house is named after two families who successively owned it. The Conyers were Norman, acquiring large areas of land in Yorkshire and Durham as their share of the loot after the Conquest. The Nortons acquired this part of their properties by marriage in the late fourteenth century, but being ill-advised enough to take the wrong

Roughcast conceals the early brickwork which dates from the 15th century, while the distinctive curved gables date from the 17th century.

The Hall. The 19th-century painting of the Quorn Hunt shows Bellingham Graham as master.

side in the Catholic rebellion of 1569, forfeited it to the Crown. The Grahams, a Scottish family, bought the house and lands in 1624 and their descendants remain there today.

The boundary walls of grey stone still survive, providing a lively picture of the cheapness of labour before the twentieth century. All great estates had these walls, whose total length must surpass the Great Wall of China. A narrow drive leads directly to the front of the house, which is separated from the surrounding parkland by a ha-ha, that ingenious device to divide the domestic area of a house from its grounds, yet allow the one to blend visually with the other. The park is landscaped, but without flamboyance, for Norton Conyers' role in history was not that of a castle, nor of a 'prodigy house' designed to impress the monarchy, but of a manor, the heart of an agricultural estate.

The same decent reticence pervades the house. This is a home, not a showplace. The front door leads directly into the hall, whose contents are the accretion of centuries. In the centre stands the

The gateway to Norton Conyers' garden of unusual plants.

house's greatest treasure, an exceedingly rare sixteenth-century inlaid table. At one end, under an enormous picture of the Quorn Hunt, painted by John Ferneley in 1822, is a long and ancient refectory table, its surface scored with grooves cut for the purpose of playing shove ha'penny. This was last used for its designed purpose seven years ago at a family wedding; the bride's dress is on display upstairs.

A superb wooden staircase sweeps up out of the hall. On one landing there is a curious horseshoe-shaped mark. According to legend, it was made by the horse which brought one of the Grahams home from the battle of Marston Moor in 1644, where he was wounded; it galloped so hard that its shoe was red-hot on arrival. It seems an improbable story; yet the piece of wood bearing the mark has been carefully moved to its present position in order to preserve it.

Certainly the legend of the mad woman is rooted in fact. But her name, her social standing – was she a servant, or a member of the family? – are now all forgotten.

The orangery, built about 1776.

CALLALY CASTLE, NORTHUMBERLAND

2 miles (3.2 km) w of Whittingham,
10 miles (16 km) w of Alnwick

THIS solid, grey house set among the Northumbrian hills perfectly demonstrates the near impossibility of giving an exact date to any country house. A casual glance classifies it as a late seventeenth-century classical mansion and this, so far as the externals are concerned, would be accurate enough.

But within the grounds of Callaly Castle are three ancient British tombs, British earthworks, part of a Roman road and the foundations of a Norman castle. A substantial part of the house itself is a pele tower, one of the fortifications unique to this once troubled border area. Originally, a pele was simply a palisade or stockade into which cattle were driven to protect them from raiders. In the course of time the palisade evolved into a solid stone tower with cattle housed on the ground floor and humans above. And when, in time, the rule of law made such massive fortifications quite unnecessary, the tower usually served as the starting point for a purely residential building.

This was what happened at Callaly. On the left of the south front is a massive, square wing – the original pele tower built in 1415. The Saxon owners of the manor continued to live here even after the

The south front. On the extreme left is the pele tower, built about 1415, the starting point of the whole complex.

191

Norman Conquest, paying thirty shillings a year in tribute, and delivering a fully grown oak to Callaly Castle every other day from Whitsun to August for the king's hearth. A Norman family called Clavering bought the manor in 1217 and were destined to live there for 600 years. They had a turbulent history: remaining Catholic like so many of their fellow northerners, they suffered considerable penalties as a result. They also took the side of the ill-fated King Charles during the Civil War and later were involved in the 1715 rebellion, for which they were penalized yet again. Nevertheless, they seem to have been a remarkably resilient family; it was not until 1876 that, with the failure of the male line, the castle was sold to Major Alexander Browne, whose descendants hold it today. In a thousand years of history, therefore, Callaly has changed hands only three times.

The apparent regularity imposed on the building's externals in the seventeenth century is belied by the maze of passages and rooms within, for building has continued from the fifteenth to the nineteenth century. An example of the complexity awaiting the visitor who wants to unravel Callaly's architectural history is vividly shown in the guidebook's attempt to explain the development of the north front. 'This is very difficult to follow,' the guidebook says with truth. 'The original outside North Wall is now the South Wall of the passage which runs inside the castle itself, parallel to the

Detail of the Drawing Room.

North Front. The west end of the inside wall was the outside wall of the great hall, built in 1619.' The entrance to the smoking room illustrates the ad hoc manner in which the house has grown. The entrance runs through what is virtually a tunnel seven feet long and is, in fact, the immensely thick wall of the pele tower, the smoking room occupying what would have been the cattle pens five centuries ago.

In 1757, part of the south wing was gutted to make way for the rococo Drawing Room, one of the best mid-eighteenth century rooms in this style in the north. The last major additions to the castle were made in the 1890s when the Brownes acquired it. The present music room is a remarkable adaptation of a once-open courtyard that is now a prime example of Victoriana. Prominently displayed in it is the exquisite marble head of a horse. Found at Ephesus on the site of the Temple of Diana, it was part of a superb collection of marbles and objets d'árt for which an entire museum wing was built in 1891. The British Museum bought most of the collection, but this sculpture – which St Paul might well have seen – remained to create one of those curious historical links that characterize the country house.

Marble horse's head, found at Ephesus in 1841. The rest of the collection was sold to the British Museum in 1899.

The Drawing Room is on the site of the original Great Hall immediately east of the pele tower. Its present form and decoration date from 1757.

PURSE CAUNDLE MANOR, DORSET

In Purse Caundle village,
4 miles (6.4 km) E of Sherborne

THERE are few semantic delights to equal the place names of the West Country. The meaning of many even now is conjectural. As late as 1963, when Arthur Oswald was researching Purse Caundle Manor for *Country Life*, he could remark 'No one knows the meaning of its delightfully improbable name, which might have come out of some old book of country receipts. If ever there was an inhabitant called Purse, he is unknown to history.' But in August 1978, a lady visiting the manor announced 'I am born a Purse.' So she was. Painstaking research slowly disclosed that, in 1065, somebody called Purse the Elder built cottages for 175 serfs in the village of Caundle, which became known thereafter as Purse Caundle.

The manor house itself, tucked into the heart of the village, was built at least 400 years later. In the late thirteenth century a certain John Alleyn lived in a house on the site with a duty 'to keep and lodge the king's sick or injured hounds at the king's cost', but the building of the present house did not commence for another two centuries. It is a stone building, grey and mellowed, blending in with its surroundings. From the village lane to the east, it seems little more than a cottage, though with an uncommonly handsome oriel window. But this is deceptive. Successive owners, working up to the seventeenth century, greatly extended the old house, producing some odd anomalies. Why is the ceremonial Great Chamber on the service side of the house? Where was the original kitchen? A rather dull, seemingly Victorian passageway proved on examination to be the original screens passage, for the old doorways that once connected buttery and pantry with the Great Hall had been covered with plasterwork. A considerable amount of restoration was undertaken in the early twentieth century by Lady Victoria Herbert, but architecturally, Purse Caundle Manor still poses as great a puzzle as the semantics of its place name.

The size and complexity of the house, seen from the south front; it was extended westward in the 17th century.

The screens passage, with the kitchen to the right.

The oriel window on the east end of the manor.

The 15th-century Hall with its later tiebeams.

THE SIXTEENTH CENTURY

LONGLEAT HOUSE, WILTSHIRE

4 miles (6.4 km) SW of Warminster,
4½ miles (7.2 km) SE of Frome
on A362 (between Bath and Salisbury)

HENRY Thynne, sixth Marquess of Bath, was the first owner of a great house to attempt to make it pay for itself. On the death of his father in 1946, he was faced with a bill of £700,000 in death duties. Money raised by selling land staved off that immediate threat. But by the end of the 1940s it was becoming increasingly apparent that very few country houses could maintain themselves in the traditional manner. In 1947, the Marquess decided to open Longleat to the public on a fee-paying basis. It was a decided gamble. The car-owning population was still small, petrol was rationed, and it was by no means certain that so unprecedented an idea would catch on in a country still suffering from austerity. But his family supported him. Household treasures were disinterred from lofts and stables and put on display; odds and ends of liveries were put together; the great State Coach repainted, and a ground floor bedroom turned into a souvenir shop. The house was opened to the public in April 1949 at an entrance fee of 2s 6d (12½p); by the end of the year, 135,000 people had visited it.

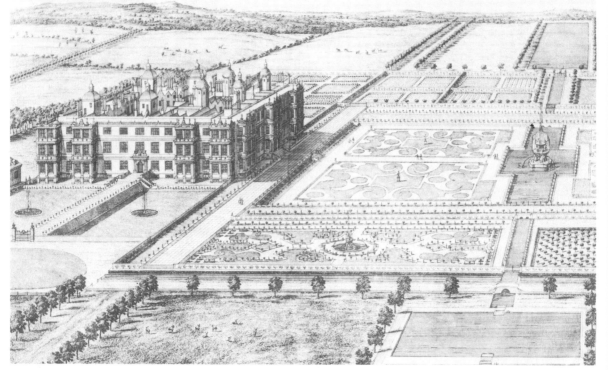

This engraving by Kip shows the formal gardens replaced by Capability Brown's landscaped parkland.

196

Apart from the fireplace and minstrels' gallery, the Great Hall is much as Thynne planned it in 1559.

Showmanship has continued to be the salvation of Longleat. In 1964 the impresario Jimmy Chipperfield suggested the establishment of a 'safari park', an unheard of proposal in its day. Despite opposition levied both locally and nationally (his peers sternly adjured him that a Wiltshireman should stick to cattle, sheep and deer) the Marquess adopted the idea with such success that 'The Lions of Longleat' became a household phrase. The stately home industry had been born in a slightly bewildered post-war world. Longleat has maintained an unabashedly populist approach, appealing to the well-known British tendency to love a lord. Lions, hippos and steam engines exist alongside this splendid Elizabethan-fronted house with its sumptuous interiors. The portrait of the Marquess shows him not only as owner but as enthusiastic promoter.

It is, perhaps, appropriate that Longleat should have been the first to blaze the tourist trail to solvency, for it was the first of the Elizabethan prodigy houses. Its builder was a Midlander, John Thynne, who was born in Shropshire of humble parentage. A self-educated, self-made man, hard and thrusting, his portrait at Longleat shows him characteristically clutching a sword. But though he

was undoubtedly physically courageous, gaining his knighthood on the battlefield of Pinkie in Scotland, it was not as a fighter that he made his money, but as a manipulator and fixer. He was steward to the first Duke of Somerset, Protector and virtually ruler of England during the minority of Edward VI. Thynne nearly shared Somerset's fate but where the master lost his head on Tower Hill, the steward was merely fined £2,000 – a fate which for Thynne was scarcely preferable to death.

His house became his central passion. In 1540 he had bought the remains of an Augustinian priory in Wiltshire for £53, and began building about seven years later. Work continued for twenty years, but scarcely had the house been completed when most of it was destroyed by fire. Doggedly, Thynne began again and produced one of the paradoxes of architectural history. Although he had two well-known architects on his pay-roll, the Englishman Robert Smythson and a Frenchman, Allen Maynard, the overall impress of the house emanated from him. And this brutal, unsubtle, penny-pinching parvenue, like Bess of Hardwick, transcended his day; influenced by the new tide of thought that was sweeping northward from Italy, he created one of the first truly Renaissance houses in England.

Externally, Thynne's house looked much as it does today, with its skyline of graceful little turrets, some of which are the intimate banqueting houses of

Longleat's ceilings are its great glory. A detail from the saloon, inspired by the Palazzo Massimo, Rome.

One of the earliest, and finest examples of the Elizabethan prodigy house, Longleat introduced the Italianate style into England.

the period. Inside, the Great Hall is also detectably his, from the flagstones to the roof. But elsewhere all is changed. In 1757 Capability Brown transformed the formal water gardens, created from the millstream of the priory – the original Long Leat – into a series of lakes. The story of the house followed that familiar graph of rise, fall and, occasional rise that characterizes the history of great houses. In the eighteenth century, Longleat was neglected for fifteen years. In the nineteenth century, its interior was totally altered by the fourth Marquess who, returning from his Grand Tour with a passion for all things Italian, and with his coffers full from the agricultural boom of the mid-century, threw himself into the task of redecorating without thought of cost. The ceiling of the State Dining Room is composed not simply of decorations of the Italian school, but actual Italian paintings painstakingly inserted into the ceiling. And despite its modest

name, the ceiling of the Breakfast Room is copied from the Doge's Palace in Venice, as, too, is the ceiling of the Lower Dining Room. The sumptuous style of decoration was carried out by Italian craftsmen under the direction of John Crace in the 1860s.

The twentieth century is reflected in the remarkable murals of Alexander Thynne, Lord Weymouth and heir to Longleat. Among much else, he has proclaimed the independent State of Wessex with Longleat as its capital, and announced his disapproval of hereditary titles. Having studied as an artist, he has covered the walls of his private apartments with enormous murals created out of sawdust and household paints. They include illustrations of the Kama Sutra and the Paranoia Murals. Not surprisingly, perhaps, they do not feature in the official guide, but a separate publication by Lord Weymouth, which also includes an account of his philosophy and artistic techniques, is available.

BURGHLEY HOUSE, NORTHAMPTONSHIRE

I mile (1.6 km) SE of Stamford, just off A1

WILLIAM Cecil, Lord Burghley, lies not far from his great house under an ornate tomb in the church of St Martin, Stamford, where he was laid to rest in 1598. The funeral ceremony was in Westminster Abbey but at his own request he was brought, without pomp, to his house and then buried in the town where he had started his career. That career was an object lesson in the fact that the best way to make money in Tudor England was to be a lawyer. Historians have had some harsh things to say about Burghley: the merciless manner in which he harried Roman Catholics; the cold skill with which he jockeyed Mary, Queen of Scots, to her death. But Queen Elizabeth used him as a staff to support and chastise. In his personal life he emerges as a warm human being, never so happy, it was said 'as when he could get his table set around with young little children. He was happy in most worldly things, but

The old-fashioned courtyard, showing its rather claustrophobic, but essentially private nature. The stone is in fine condition after four centuries.

most happy in his children'. There are worse epitaphs.

Cecil began building in 1556 on the remains of a monastery known as Burghe. Writing to his friend Sir Christopher Hatton, who was also engaged in building a vast house at Holdenby, Cecil gives some indication of the motivation behind these monstrous buildings that were springing up over England. They were designed to impress the queen, tempting her to a visit which, though financially expensive, was politically desirable. 'God send us both long to enjoy her,' Cecil wrote, 'for we both mean to expend our purse in these.' He succeeded in his purpose but poor Hatton did not: Elizabeth never came near Holdenby.

Cecil appears to have acted as his own architect, and the house was largely finished by his death in 1598. Daniel Defoe's description of its external appearance in 1722 holds good today. 'It was more like a town than a house,' he thought. 'The towers and the pinnacles, so high and placed at such a distance from one another, look like so many distant parish churches in a town.' But the interior had already changed greatly. Cecil's descendant, the fifth Earl of Exeter, was a dedicated traveller and a passionate admirer of Italian culture, and in 1680 began to turn the austere Elizabethan rooms into the modish Baroque. The fashionable Neapolitan painter, Antonio Verrio, was installed – and proved to be an expensive burden. For ten years he lived sumptuously and autocratically, bringing in his own servants, relatives and friends to form a miniature court and his patron was heartily glad to see the back of him. But he brought fame to the house.

Celia Fiennes visited it shortly before Defoe, giving a more detailed picture of the interior, in particular of Verrio's recently completed murals. Although impressed, as a strong-minded Puritan lady she deplored the large visible expanses of opulent female flesh. Burghley 'was very fine in pictures, but they were all without Garments or very little that was the only fault the immodesty of the pictures especially in my lord's apartment'. But she was fascinated with everything else, the great gate by Tijou in particular. 'The door you enter is of iron carved the finest I ever saw, all sorts of leaves

The Heaven Room, not only Verrio's undoubted masterpiece, but probably the finest painted room in England, completed in 1694.

Burghley's splendid roofscape. Tijou's gate, which so fascinated Celia Fiennes, is in the centre of the range.

flowers figures birds beasts wheate in the Carving', and she calculated that it took at least two hours to see the house, much the same as it does today.

Verrio's work is the showpiece of the house, in particular the extraordinary Heaven Room. Although three walls and the ceiling are totally covered with mythological figures (some of which stride out disconcertingly, or peer over the spectator's shoulder at eye level) the room is bright and welcoming, largely because the fourth wall is almost entirely glass. Verrio put himself in the picture, a plump, balding man looking decidedly pleased with himself, as well he might considering how agreeably he lived while creating this fantasy.

In the early 1980s Burghley House encountered the crisis only too common among these great houses. The Marquess of Exeter died in October 1981 (the title going to a brother in Canada) and his wife died the following June. There was no-one to take responsibility for the house. The Trustees then approached Lady Victoria Leatham, the Marquess's daughter by his second marriage. She and her husband were living elsewhere, pursuing demanding, full-time careers. A building of this nature makes voracious demands on time; although it was in good condition – indeed, to stand in the courtyard is to be amazed by the quality of the stonework – parts of it were undeniably shabby and the logistics of the whole formidable. The kitchen is 200 yards from the living quarters! But they decided in favour, moved in at the end of 1982 and began the task of adapting the vast treasure chest to its present dual role of family house and public heritage.

For it is a treasure house. In April 1983 a remarkable exhibition of Oriental and European ceramics, comprising some 250 pieces, was put on display, all of which were found in the house – some pieces tucked away in long forgotten cupboards. They include rare Japanese ceramics acquired by the fifth Earl during his Grand Tour, and faithfully recorded by his private secretary, Culpepper Tanner, in a detailed inventory. The inventory not only survives, but proved vital in tracking down and assembling the items in the exhibition.

MAPLEDURHAM HOUSE, OXFORDSHIRE

4 miles NW of Reading
off Caversham-Woodcote road (A4074)

IF Mapledurham House seems oddly familiar to devotees of *The Wind in the Willows*, there is a simple explanation. E.H. Shepherd, the most successful illustrator of this children's classic, probably used the house as his model for Toad Hall. Kenneth Grahame, the author, lived just across the river at Pangbourne and knew this stretch of the Thames intimately.

Mapledurham is more than a house; it is a tiny working model of a complete feudal estate, with almshouses, mill, church, Big House and estate cottages, miraculously surviving in unspoiled Oxfordshire hills almost on the fringes of the ugly sprawl of Reading. Access to Mapledurham is either over Caversham Bridge, or by boat, or the long way round through Pangbourne, across the toll-bridge into Whitchurch and then down a long rough road. Nobody casually passes through the tiny village – one makes a pilgrimage to it.

On approaching the house from this land side, it is noticeable that one of the little window gables seems to be glistening even on a dull day. For it is covered with oyster shells, the once secret sign that this was a safe house for Roman Catholics. It has always been a Catholic house, holding fast to the Old Faith even during the fiercest years of persecution.

The house seems to be turning its back to the visitor. Sir Michael Blount, who built it in the year of the Armada, deliberately turned it to face the east, bearing in mind the warning of the fashionable physician, Andrew Boorde: 'the south wynde doth corrupt and doth make evyl vapours'. Like all living houses, Mapledurham has adjusted, adapted and fidgeted itself into comfort over the centuries, but it is still a late Elizabethan house. The modern entrance is through what used to be the Great Hall, remodelled in 1828 to make an entrance hall but still with the dignity of its origins. A delightful feature is a series of carved animal heads, some of them portraying a proverb or fable like the extraordinary

The east front of Mapledurham, probably the model for E. H. Shepherd's Toad Hall in The Wind in the Willows.

The family built their chapel in 1797, taking advantage of the Catholic Relief Act which had been passed in 1791.

four-eared, four-eyed creature illustrating Aesop's story of the wolf in sheep's clothing. Flanking the fireplace are two deer, carved from a single tree.

Visitors are usually taken next into the Library where there are portraits of Teresa and Martha Blount, the close friends of Alexander Pope. He penned for Teresa a teasing little poem, commiserating with her on leaving the bustling life of town for the dullness of the countryside:

> To morning walks and prayers three hours a day
> To muse and spill her solitary Tea
> Or o'er cold coffee trifle with a spoon
> Count the clock slow and dine exact at noon.

Nevertheless Pope himself was a frequent visitor to the house between 1707 and 1715, and his portrait by Kneller and some of his possessions are preserved upstairs in the boudoir.

Mapledurham experienced the common fate of so many country houses, passing into the hands of a collateral branch of the family, declining almost into extinction and then slowly being brought to life again by a devoted owner. After World War II it was all but derelict when John Eyston, the present owner, in 1960 persuaded the Historic Buildings Councils to make a grant and so began a long, slow programme of restoration.

The restoration was not limited to the house. Close by is the beautiful watermill, 100 years older than the house itself, and which was actually working until 1947 when it became totally derelict. Now in working order, it is possible to buy flour from one of the very last working watermills in the country.

The entrance hall was built in 1828, incorporating the Tudor Great Hall.

LAYER MARNEY TOWER, ESSEX

3 miles (6.4 km) from Tiptree,
1 mile (1.6 km) s of B1022 Colchester-Maldon road

In terms of modern skyscrapers – or even of medieval cathedrals – Layer Marney Tower is not particularly high, being little over eighty feet. But its total unexpectedness in the flat Essex countryside, and the fact that it is flanked by relatively low domestic buildings gives it a presence out of all proportion to its actual size.

Henry, first Lord Marney, who built the tower about 1520, doubtless intended it to be simply the gatehouse to a far grander edifice than now exists. But with his death in 1523, and that of his son two years later, the short-lived barony became extinct.

Lord Marney had been a Privy Councillor to Henry VIII and almost certainly accompanied him to the fabulous Field of the Cloth of Gold. Like his contemporary, Sir Richard Weston of Sutton Place, he was undoubtedly influenced by the new Italian style of architecture that was entering France. Terracotta was one of the features of this style and, again like Sir Richard, he used it when designing his own house. The windows, in particular, of Layer Marney and Sutton Place bear a family resemblance.

The lavish use of glass on the tower betrays its purpose: it was built for prestige, not defence. A number of these tower houses were springing up all over England during the fifteenth and early sixteenth centuries, East Anglia being particularly rich in them. Sir Henry was almost certainly seeking to outdo his son-in-law, Sir Edmond Bedingfield, whose great gatehouse tower at Oxburgh was one of the wonders of Norfolk, and Sir Henry succeeded.

The terracotta tiles at Layer Marney illustrate its affinity with Sutton Place.

The hall, looking much as it would have done at the time of Lord Marney's death in 1523.

The outstanding size of the gatehouse implies that Lord Marney intended the house itself to be a far larger building.

LOSELEY HOUSE, SURREY

2½ miles (4 km) SW of Guildford,
1½ miles (2.1 km) N of Godalming (off A3100)

LOSELEY House came into being indirectly as a result of that great sixteenth-century act of plunder, the dissolution of the monasteries. When, in 1562, Sir William More decided to rebuild his old manor house in a style fit to welcome his pernickety queen, Elizabeth I, he found in the abandoned Cistercian monastery of Waverley Abbey a ready-made source of worked stone. The blocks which his masons carted away were at least 450 years old, so his house was mellow with age even as it rose. They used clunch to dress the corners, obtaining it from the vast chalk quarries of Guildford some three miles away. This soft, indigenous material was also used with great effect for interior decoration. The extra-

ordinary chimney-piece in the Drawing Room now looks as pristine as the day it was carved from a single block of chalk four centuries ago.

The Mores were not often in the dangerous mainstream of history. For over 400 years the family quietly farmed their rich fields and meadows – no sequesterings, no assassinations, no beheadings, only the occasional domestic tempest. The family records, now in the county muniments, survive to give substance to their story. In them, Lord Burghley warns his friend Sir Christopher More that the Queen is intent on visiting Loseley and the entertainment had better be up to standard. The Earl of Southampton, a 'suspected Papist', is tem-

Most of the building materials for Loseley came from the ruins of Waverley Abbey, near Farnham, giving the house an instantly mature appearance.

The chimney piece in the drawing room is unique, carved out of a single block of chalk to a Holbein design. The ceiling was decorated for the visit of James I.

porarily placed in the custody of Sir William More with consequent dislocation of family life. Anne, the daughter of Sir George More, secretly marries John Donne and her infuriated father throws the presumptious poet into the Fleet prison for his pains.

In 1689 the house passed by marriage to the Molyneux family, now called More-Molyneux but still living in the same house as country gentlemen and farmers. The twentieth century took its toll. When the present owner, James More-Molyneux, inherited it in 1945, he and his wife faced an all but impossible task. The roof leaked; the windows were broken; horses were grazing on the once velvet lawns and grass now grew up to the windowsills.

But Loseley sought, and eventually found its twentieth-century salvation in the oldest of all sources of wealth – the land. A herd of Jersey cows was built up, and the estate almost accidentally developed a flourishing business in dairy produce. 'The farm secretary at the estate office said it was a pity to throw all the skimmed milk away. Couldn't we make cottage cheese? So we did. Then yoghurt.' Eventually the estate entered into an association with an expanding chain of health-food shops. They have also created a successful trade making prefabricated houses, which began with the casting of concrete blocks for the estate. Today their houses are sold throughout the world.

The estate consists of 1,000 acres comprised of six farms all busily working in an area often pejoratively dismissed as 'commuter country'. Farm tours now form one of its many attractions, and in season, fruit picking attracts hundreds of visitors. But Loseley House is still essentially a family home, little changed over the centuries. No great access of wealth in the eighteenth or nineteenth centuries tempted its owners to pull down and rebuild in the fashionable style. Passing through the doorway with its welcoming motto, *Invidiae claudor, pateo sed semper amico* (Closed to envy, always open to a friend) is to become aware of a present maintaining close contact with its past.

HATFIELD HOUSE, HERTFORDSHIRE

TWENTIETH-CENTURY town planning – in particular, the creation of an immense new road system – has buried Hatfield in a vast, anonymous urban development. It is only too easy to go speeding past, unaware of the delightful little market town that still exists, attached to this enormous palace that covers almost as great an area. But it is worth threading a way through the modern overlay and entering Hatfield House from the town side rather than by the great ceremonial drive, for that way one proceeds chronologically from the older to the newer part of the building. 'New' here is of course relative, for the house was built in 1611 by the son of the same Lord Burghley who built Burghley House in Northamptonshire.

Climbing a steep hill, lined with elegant Georgian houses, one enters a massive gatehouse. Immediately opposite is a great red brick building, the remains of a palace built by Cardinal Morton in 1497. It became the childhood home – and subsequently the prison – of the young princess who became known to history as Elizabeth I. Her half-sister, Mary, had also known the house as a prison. Legend has it that she hastened to the top of the tower to see her father, Henry VIII, ride by and called out to him but he did not acknowledge her presence by the flicker of an eyebrow.

The tower remains, and so does the Great Hall, but everything else was demolished by Robert Cecil. Hatfield was, in effect, forced upon him. His father, that great builder, was also the founder of a house called Theobalds in Hertfordshire and left it to him in his will. James I much admired it, and 'suggested' to Cecil that he should exchange it for one of the King's own mansions at Hatfield, not far away. Emanating from such a source this proposal was tantamount to a command and Cecil, with what grace he could muster, took over Morton's old mansion in 1607. He demolished most of it, using the bricks to build his own house. He apparently

The south front of Hatfield House. Built to the formal E plan, it was the work of Robert Cecil, in 1611.

Much of the chapel was remodelled in the 19th century but these windows are those installed by Robert Cecil.

The Marble Hall at Hatfield is the last and most elaborate version of the medieval Great Hall.

The 1st Marchioness of Salisbury by Sir Joshua Reynolds.

The Grand Staircase, with its 'dog gates', is the English version, in oak, of the fashionable Renaissance style.

acted as architect himself, though Inigo Jones laid out the splendid stone forecourt and a young carpenter, Robert Lyminge, was to learn enough of his trade here to emerge as architect at Blickling eight years later.

The enormous building had one primary function – to entice the monarch to a visit. Built in the newly fashionable 'compact' form, that is, without a court-yard, its two great wings were designed to act as lodgings for the king and queen, the king to the east, the queen to the west. The rest of the Cecil household was tucked away in lesser quarters. An inventory of 1611 among the Hatfield papers makes it clear that two sets of furniture were provided for the royal lodgings, one for use by the king and queen and a less valuable set for use in their absence. Ironically, James I never visited Hatfield in full state.

LITTLE MORETON HALL, CHESHIRE

4 miles SW of Congleton, off A34
The National Trust

THE first sight of this dramatic black and white building is doubly misleading. It seems remarkably unstable, with the upper storey leaning over at all angles, and looks as though it was built all at the same period. But wood, its primary material, has a trick of settling in on itself, of moving in dozens of ways to snug itself down for the centuries. And the building of Moreton Hall spanned well over 120 years but, because the same beautiful material was used throughout, it seems homogenous.

The only approach to the house is the bridge over the moat that completely surrounds it. Here, one encounters immediately one of those profound differences of value that separate one historical period from another. Immediately to the left of this unique and ceremonial entrance is the point of discharge of two major privies – an unthinkable arrangement in a twentieth-century building, but accepted quite casually by the sixteenth century.

The house grew in a clockwise manner, creating a courtyard at its heart. The oldest part is the northern range, opposite the gatehouse. Here is the Great Hall – literally so, for when it was built in 1480 it completely dominated the rest of the house, which then appeared simply as an appendage to it. A century later, this towering chamber lost its attraction to the family and it was divided horizontally. But some time before 1807, when John Sell Cotman sketched the Hall much as it appears today, the floor was removed – part of the restless adapting, and readapting which marks all living houses. The ghostly outlines of the doors that were made in the

The courtyard of Little Moreton Hall. The lantern windows were added to the earlier north wing in 1559.

The proud boast of Richard Dale who 'made thies windovs by the grac of God' in 1559.

upper half of the walls are still visible under the whitewash.

Some sixty years after the Great Hall was built, bays were added to it and the neighbouring withdrawing room, initiating a period of expansion that was to continue until 1600. A succession of buildings crept down the eastern side, and then turned west to create the gatehouse range. And it was on this range that the family seems to have been touched by megalomania. No Elizabethan gentleman's house could be deemed complete without its Long Gallery, where he could stroll during inclement weather and, perhaps, hang a few portraits of his ancestors. John Moreton decided that the only place for this fashionable addition was balanced on the top of the southern, or gatehouse range. The nature of the architectural problems posed is vividly demonstrated by the great beams of

the gallery's roof: they are quite evidently holding the walls together like great clamps.

Apart from the black and white woodwork, the most characteristic feature of Little Moreton Hall is its glass windows. Glass was no longer quite the luxury it had been a century before when cautious owners took their glass windows with them from manor to manor. By 1559 when Richard Dale, a carpenter, put up a series of windows and proudly recorded the fact on the lintel, there were over a dozen glass factories working in England. What is unusual is the variety of patterns used throughout the house.

The impression carried away from the Hall, unlike that conveyed by so many houses of the period, is of an interior flooded with light. The Long Gallery is particularly favoured with windows along the length of every wall. The house is almost completely empty today, which enables the visitor

The north front, dating from the fifteenth century, faces the Elizabethan-style garden laid out in recent years.

Placed precariously above the south wing, the Long Gallery is clamped together by the roof beams.

The south wing of Little Moreton Hall, seen across the moat. The Long Gallery runs behind the strip window on the top floor.

to appreciate to the full the virtuosity of three or four generations of carpenters. But the emptiness does not detract from the feeling that this was once a home: to the contrary, there is an almost eerie sensation of having arrived at an interim period, that one family has moved out and another is just about to move in.

The Moretons (who took their name from a local farmstead) were associated with the place from the thirteenth to the twentieth century. The last private owner, Bishop Thomas Abraham, was a cousin of the family who inherited it in 1913. He left a vivid description of the house as he first saw it in 1892. 'I remember taking a day off at Lichfield to run down and see what she [his cousin, Elizabeth Moreton] had left me and shall not forget the thrill as I topped the rise after Scholar Green, walking from Kidsgrive Station, and saw the front of the old black and white house in spring sunshine confronting me. It has been in my heart and dreams ever since.' Bishop Moreton did much to preserve the Hall before giving it to the National Trust in 1937.

HEVER CASTLE, KENT

3 miles (4.8 km) SE of Edenbridge off B2026

HEVER has three totally different claims to historic interest. It was here, sometime in the 1520s, that Henry VIII met Anne Boleyn, and the course of English history began to change. In 1903, the American millionaire, William Waldorf Astor, bought the decrepit building and created one of the most brilliant of architectural restorations. But in 1982 the present Lord Astor, descendant of William, decided that life in the castle, shared with a quarter of a million visitors, was insupportable, and placed it on the open market. A property company acquired it and, after breaking up the vast estate, turned the ancient edifice into a purely tourist attraction.

After the Boleyns, or Bullens, had died out, the castle deteriorated and by the late nineteenth century was simply a farmhouse. Built in the mid-fourteenth century, the very nature of the exquisite building dictated the remarkable solution which Astor adopted in order to make it a family home again. The castle is entirely surrounded by a moat and, as with most buildings of its type, the accommodation available was scarcely up to modern standards – certainly not the standards of a millionaire with a vast staff and wide social contacts. To have extended the actual castle would have been to destroy the very characteristics which attracted Astor – in particular, the moat. He therefore decided simply to restore the castle itself, and build a totally separate structure for domestic purposes. That separate structure took the form of a Tudor 'village'. From a distance, particularly when viewed from the castle, its variegated materials and skylines have all the appearance of a village that has evolved over the

The 'village' to the left of the castle – Astor's imaginative solution to the accommodation problem – is in fact one huge interconnected building.

The castle set in its moat. Apart from access to the village, the only entrance is still by medieval drawbridge.

centuries. But though it appears to be composed of a dozen or more separate elements it is, in fact, one vast building, all of whose parts are connected, and joined to the castle itself by a bridge. Over a thousand men worked for four years on this creation, laying out the beautiful gardens, and restoring the castle.

The standard of restoration and workmanship would have been outstanding even for the 1980s; for its day it is little less than extraordinary. The attention to detail can perhaps best be illustrated by Henry VIII's lock, an elaborate mechanism that always travelled with the monarch, and was placed on the door of every room in which he slept. Astor not only acquired it, but had an exact copy made, the two being used for the doors in the sombre dining room. It takes an expert of great skill to detect which is the original and which is the copy.

The castle was stripped bare when Astor acquired it, giving him a free hand not only to restore and decorate according to sixteenth-century taste but also to hang paintings and tapestries that illuminate its major period, Tudor. This careful choice of objects seem now to belong to this building and no other: Holbein's portraits of Anne Boleyn and her royal murderer; the poignant layette for Queen Mary's baby that was never born and Gheeraerts' portrait of an acidic Queen Elizabeth are among the treasures that add a priceless dimension to this ancient castle.

King Henry VIII's lock.

HARDWICK HALL, DERBYSHIRE

2 miles (3.2 km) s of Chesterfield-Mansfield road (A617),
6½ miles (10.4 km) NW of Mansfield
and 9½ miles (13.6 km) SE of Chesterfield
The National Trust

BESS of Hardwick lies alone on her splendid tomb in Derby cathedral, crowned with a coronet, an altogether appropriate monument. Which of her four husbands could be chosen to lie in effigy beside her, and who could doubt her right to that circlet of sovreignty, queen as she was over a sizeable area of Derbyshire? Her portrait as an old woman in Hardwick Hall itself gives further substance to her character. One is immediately reminded of that other Bess, her contemporary Elizabeth, Queen of England – except that Bess of Hardwick is, if anything, rather more regal. The great beaked nose, the firm mouth with compressed lips, the cold, dark eyes under supercilious brows all attest to the character of a woman who, in her seventies, expressed her will in brick and stone in the form of one of the most extraordinary of Tudor houses.

The splendid staircase which leads to the equally impressive High Great Chamber, Bess's 'presence chamber'.

The year of her birth is uncertain, but was probably around 1520. Her family was solid, rather than distinguished, owning a manor house among the Derbyshire hills. Her first marriage, at the age of fifteen, was to a local squire named Barlow, who died soon afterwards, leaving her a sizeable fortune. Her own mistress now, and no longer simply the matrimonial pawn of her parents, she could afford to wait nearly fifteen years for her second husband. Sir William Cavendish was a great catch, for he was a man who was not only in the confidence of the king but, as Treasurer of the Chamber, had access to that vast flood of wealth brought about by the dissolution of the monasteries. His political strength lay in the south (the Cavendishes originated in Suffolk) but Bess wanted to remain on her own ground.

Even today, Derbyshire is a little England of its own: in winter, snowfalls can cut off entire towns for days. In the sixteenth century it was as remote as Scotland. Nevertheless, Cavendish acquiesced in his bride's wishes. They bought a manor house called Chatsworth and immediately began rebuilding it in a grander manner. Cavendish died, leaving Bess in possession of his vast properties, including the now splendid Chatsworth. One more marriage, to an otherwise unknown man called William St Loe who died in 1565 (leaving her yet more estates) prepared her for the biggest catch of all. In 1568 she married George Talbot, sixth Earl of Shrewsbury, one of the most powerful men in England. Dynastic marriages were not often happy but this one proved unusually acrimonious – a fact which led directly to the creation of Hardwick Hall. Before long, the quarrels between Earl and Countess were so violent that she moved out of Chatsworth, back to the family home. But what had been adequate for young Bess of Hardwick was decidedly not good enough for the Countess of Shrewsbury. Talbot's death left her in sole possession of an enormous fortune and, at the age of seventy, she threw herself into creating the biggest house of its day.

Although Bess employed an architect, Robert Smythson, one may be certain that this is, in every

Bess of Hardwick's initials flamboyantly crown her towering house with its remarkable range of windows – 'more glass than wall'.

sense, her house. Like her contemporary, Thynne, at Longleat, this not particularly imaginative woman managed to transcend her day, leaving fashion behind to create what must have seemed a startling innovation. In place of the courtyard, that dull claustrophobic space that was derived from the cloisters, she used the modern H formula, creating a solid compact building. The hall, instead of running parallel to the front in the medieval manner, is at right angles to it and towers up through two storeys. But it was in her use of glass that she set her impress upon the house. The main west front, crowned with the proud initials ES and a coronet, is a glitter of reflection, the stonework used simply as a frame for windows. She, or her architect, cheated: anxious for symmetry at all costs the windows ignore the position of the rooms behind and in some cases the floor actually bisects the windows.

For the visitor, the attraction of the house lies largely in the fact that it looks exactly as it did when its formidable creator breathed her last here at the age of eighty-eight. Her descendants preferred Chatsworth, over the following centuries transforming it from an Elizabethan house to that which we see today. Hardwick they left alone; but it remained in the family and was maintained in good condition. Even Bess's furniture remained *in situ*, as can be seen from the inventory she drew up in her own hand at the age of eighty-four. In 1959, the Duke of Devonshire, inheritor of both Chatsworth

and Hardwick, passed the latter over to the Treasury as part payment of death duties. The 400-year-old link was broken, but the future of the house assured for it was given to the National Trust.

Of all places in the house, Bess of Hardwick lives on in that splendidly named room, the High Great Chamber, used purely for ceremonial purposes. Placed on the second floor, the chamber provided the pretext for a grand ceremonial staircase. And Bess grasped that pretext. The great stone stairs at Hardwick seem like a frozen cascade. It was in the High Great Chamber that Bess held those masques and entertainments beloved of the Elizabethans. Given so bizarre a character, one might expect the room to be a blaze of gaudy colour but the overall effect is of muted browns and greys. The room was built around the tapestries that cover the walls for they were bought in 1587, four years before the house was begun: they fit just below, and are echoed by the painted plasterwork frieze. The room is austerely furnished: Farthingale chairs stand stiffly around the wall in the Elizabethan manner, and there is a walnut table that sums up Bess of Hardwick's marital career for it carries the arms of Hardwick, Cavendish and Talbot.

Bess of Hardwick in her widowhood.

The Long Gallery, some 166 feet in length, was probably designed to take

the Flemish tapestry. Bess's portrait still hangs here where she placed it.

RIPLEY CASTLE, NORTH YORKSHIRE

In Ripley; 3½ miles (5.6 km) N of Harrogate,
7½ miles (12.1 km) from Ripon

IN 1784, Sir John Ingilby of Ripley Castle was faced with a problem common to his class and time: his old manor house was decidedly the worse for wear after some 300 years of continuous occupation. His solution was decidedly uncommon. Where his contemporaries would have happily razed the old house and built completely anew, he recognized the past as something valuable in its own right. As he wrote to a friend, 'I was determined upon preserving as much as possible of the old place and by that means have spoiled my plan in the opinion of some people – but notwithstanding the inconveniences of our Ancestors' buildings I prefer them to the modern structures.' He then added, in a spirit which seems of the twentieth rather than of the eighteenth century, 'Any man who has money can build a house, but few can show the same house his family has lived in for so many years.'

Ripley Castle today is a mosaic of periods, the worn-out swept away and entirely rebuilt (it is now thought by the architect, William Bellwood) but the rest refurbished. The oldest part of the house is the gatehouse, built in 1418. The Crown was most reluctant to allow private citizens the right to build fortifications and the Ingilbys received their permission to do so only because of the threat from the Scots, and those under General 'Black' Douglas in particular.

Ripley Castle seen from the park: an example of a fortified manor house transformed into an elegant residence.

The old tower of 1555 also survives. The ground floor houses the Library and it was here, on a July night in 1644, that the redoubtable Lady Ingilby sat guard over the 'rebel' Oliver Cromwell while armed with two pistols. The battle of Marston Moor had just been fought; her husband Sir William was in hiding near the battlefield when Cromwell arrived at the castle requesting lodging for the night. She agreed reluctantly and led the way to the Library 'where, sitting on a sopha, these two extraordinary personages equally jealous of the other's intention, passed the whole night'. Asked later why she had two pistols, Lady Ingilby answered simply 'I might have missed with the first.' Altogether, it is an episode that does equal honour to the lady and the 'rebel'.

In this same room is a portrait of a member of the family who is currently a candidate for canonization – Francis Ingilby, a Jesuit priest who was hanged, drawn and quartered in 1586. Upstairs in the Knight's Chamber is a tiny priest's hole which Francis probably used while evading capture for nearly four years. So well constructed and hidden is it that it was not discovered until 1964 when repairs were being made to the room. This Knight's Chamber has its original sixteenth-century panelling and with the low ceiling conveys the dark, rather claustrophobic nature that characterizes so much of the domestic architecture of this period. The beautiful Tower Room has a splendid ceiling, especially made to commemorate the visit of James I in 1603, and a curious modern story. During renovations in 1930 the present fireplace at the far end of the room was detected behind the panelling.

The sixteenth-century Tower Room – venue of a poltergeist?

In order to protect the discovery, the room was locked for the night. On being opened in the morning a scene of utter confusion was disclosed, the massive furniture having been tossed around like so much matchwood. The cause is unknown – it has never happened again.

The village attached to the castle is an intriguing example of idiosyncratic town planning. By the early nineteenth century the cottages were in an advanced state of decay and the decision was made to demolish them all and rebuild. The current Ingilby was a decided Francophile and instead of building the village in the vernacular he modelled it on one in Alsace-Lorraine. It is for this reason that the village hall, a solidly built structure, boasts the name 'Hotel de Ville'. The little village does, in fact, have the indefinable air of a township.

And, as a corollary to Sir John Ingilby's devotion to the old house in the eighteenth century, it is worth recording the dedication of the current owner, Sir Thomas. When he came of age he was offered the choice of selling up or shouldering the increasing burden of maintaining the place. He chose the latter, and over the past few years more and more means have been explored to allow the house to contribute to its own maintenance. The use of fuel from the estate for the modern wood-burning equipment that now heats the castle, shows how even the traditional has been redirected to serve new needs.

The Library, where Cromwell was 'entertained'.

SUTTON PLACE, SURREY

2 miles (3.2 km) NW of Guildford, off A1

SUTTON Place gained a certain element of fame in the 1960s and 1970s when it became the home of Paul Getty. He acquired it for the most prosaic of reasons: it was cheaper to buy a 450-year-old house which, though beautiful, nobody wanted, than to pay for hotels. Sutton Place became both his home, and the European headquarters of Getty Oil. It was opened, somewhat grudgingly, to the public on severely limited occasions – the gardens eight times a year and the house itself for a couple of hours on a Sunday afternoon. Two thousand people and more would form an immense crocodile and shuffle through the three principal rooms, though their interest probably lay less in the Tudor mansion than the fact that it was the home of the richest man in the world – and sometimes it was possible to get a glimpse of that fabulous being as he peered out from the gallery.

Getty's death in 1976, and the oil company's subsequent decision to sell the house, posed for Sutton Place the problem that faces so many historic houses. Few private individuals could possibly pay

Francis Bacon's paintings in the sober Great Hall sum up Sutton Place's role as a centre for the arts.

for its upkeep. The State, in the form of local planning officers, resolutely opposed any alterations – yet no large institution could use the house without making drastic alterations to its interior. The Getty regime, by treating the house as a kind of super-luxury hotel for their globe-trotting executives, had provided an answer of sorts. What would happen now that its founder was dead? In due course, a new solution was found.

Sutton Place provides a microcosm of English history. William the Conqueror personally acquired the estate. It was fought over so viciously and damaged so extensively, that in 1353 royal appraisers dismissed it as being virtually valueless. In 1521 Henry VIII gave it to Sir Richard Weston, one of his favourite councillors. Sir Richard may be fairly described as a professional survivor. Despite the fact that his son was beheaded for cuckolding the king (or, to be exact, for contemplating it, the lady in question being Anne Boleyn) Sir Richard remained in high favour. He began to build his house in the mid 1520s.

The archives have been lost and its early history has to be deduced from its appearance. A very early example of the undefended manor house, it is evidence of the builder's confidence in the strength of the monarchy, and the relative tranquility of southern England. (The builders of Norton Conyers, just forty years before, were careful to provide it with good fortifications.) Sutton Place's most obvious characteristic is its Renaissance balance and grace. Weston had spent much time in France (he was among those who accompanied the young Henry to the Field of the Cloth of Gold in 1520) and had been much impressed with the new Italianate chateaux on the Loire.

He built his splendid new house in brick, but liberally ornamented it with terracotta tiles, creating an exotic effect among the Surrey water meadows. They allowed the unknown architect a remarkable degree of precision and plasticity while providing a clue to the parentage of the house: their design is Italian, but their usage English.

The house was originally a quadrangle but fire destroyed one of the ranges. In 1782 the owner, John Webbe-Weston conceived the unnerving idea

The Italianate Loire chateaux may have influenced Sir William Weston when he built Sutton Place.

of cladding the entire fabric of the house in the fashionable stucco classicisms and gothicisms of the period. Fortunately, he was dissuaded. Sutton Place is a testimony to the fact that the best safeguard for a historic building is a decent penury. The family who occupied it never grew rich enough to be able to 'improve' it, and today it is basically the same building as envisaged by Sir Richard Weston.

History repeated itself for Sutton Place. After Getty's death, it was bought in 1979 by the Anglo-Texan Oil Company, who leased it to Stanley J. Seeger. His first intention was to use it as a private home, but gradually the idea evolved of creating a trust, under whose aegis would be attempted the renaissance of an English country house. It was an idea that only a millionaire – and a philanthropic millionaire – could have carried out.

With a paying public limited to around forty at a time, the house and grounds continue to be the main attraction, but in addition there is the permanent Seeger Collection of paintings as well as concerts and visiting exhibitions. Over some eighteen months, 300 people worked on the place at an overall cost of some £5 million. The project for the house was largely restorative, but the development of the garden was entirely creative, the work of Sir Geoffrey Jellicoe, and on a scale unknown since the gardens were designed at Chatsworth. Those who

had wondered how Repton or Capability Brown were able to look into the future and plan their slow-growing miracles could gain an insight by visiting Sutton Place during this formative period. One of the features planned has been a ceremonial avenue of oak trees, which will not achieve maturity for at least another 100 years. A vast lake has been created, together with 'surrealist' gardens where perspective has been doctored. One was inspired by Magritte, another by Miro and a third acts as the setting for Ben Nicolson's vast sculptured wall. This formal garden is perhaps most memorable of all, only the immaturity of the slower-growing plants betraying the fact that it is a recent creation. It looks as though the house had been waiting four and half centuries for this to complete it.

A detail of the outstanding terracotta tiles. Other designs include a visual pun on the name 'Weston'.

DEENE PARK, NORTHAMPTONSHIRE

8 miles (12.8 km) NW of Oundle,
6 miles (9.6 km) NE of Corby on A43

WHEN James Thomas Brudenell, seventh Earl of Cardigan, began the canter that developed into the Charge of the Light Brigade at Balaclava, he was heard to mutter to himself, 'Well, here goes the last of the Brudenells.' Time proved him wrong: 130 years later Brudenells still live in the large house from which he set out on the road to the Crimea, as they have done for the past four centuries or so.

Deene Park perfectly illustrates the English love of understatement, their preference for imprecision of language, for in any European country this 'house' would be classed as a palace. Sir Robert Brudenell, Chief Justice of England, bought it in 1514. He had to pay a ground rent of £18 a year to Westminster Abbey. (And so did his successors. They had to pay that same £18 a year until 1970 when the Church Commissioners sold it to them outright!) A lawyer with the right connections was in a good position for making money, and arranging good marriages for his children. Sir Robert did both, laying the foundation of the Brudenell fortune.

His grandson, Sir Edmund, married an heiress and with her money began building on a grand scale. Legend has it that her life was made so miserable over demands for funds that Sir Edmund's

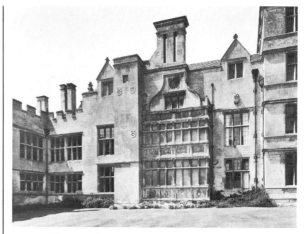

The complex east front, most interesting of all as it probably incorporates the main building of the medieval manor.

conscience-stricken ghost haunts their bedroom. Sir Edmund, in effect, began a building programme that was to continue for nearly 300 years: the last major addition was built in 1810, and as late as 1919 the beautiful little Oak Parlour was enriched with seventeenth-century oak panelling taken from a house on the family's Yorkshire estate.

But Deene Park, like so many of its peers, soon seemed bound for extinction. In World War II it was commandeered for troops and was all but derelict by the end of the 1940s. The family grimly held on in a house with little plumbing, no heating or electricity, a leaking roof, and a kitchen so far from the living area that Mrs Brudenell used a bicycle to reach it. But a generation's devoted work has since restored the house to a living home.

Although the architecture of Deene Park covers nearly three centuries, the visitor is immediately plunged into the Elizabethan heart of the place. The entrance is through a beautiful, dignified courtyard, on one side of which is Sir Edmund's Great Hall, built in 1572, a chamber which combines majesty and homeliness to a remarkable degree. The complex ceiling of carved chestnut soars high up into the gloom, but warmly upholstered couches by the great fireplace show that this is a family house. Next to them is a sixteenth-century refectory table and

The architecture of Deene Park spans nearly three centuries. This beautiful courtyard shows the original Elizabethan hall range, which was built in 1572.

View of the house from across the canal. The bridge was built in the 18th century from the balusters of a 17th-century garden terrace.

bench which, though antique (they have been in the hall since it was built) look as though they were used that morning.

Family portraits are scattered throughout the house, together with those of long-serving members of the staff painted by Richard Foster in 1970. It is impossible to escape the family's most famous, or, at least, most notorious and certainly vainest member, Lord Cardigan. In the Dining Room is de Prades' great painting of him leading the Charge at Balaclava on his chestnut horse, Ronald – Ronald's head and tail are preserved in a case along with the Earl's gaudy uniform. Nearby is James Sant's painting of Lord Cardigan describing the battle to the Royal family. It is said that Queen Victoria was once part of the portrait, but indignantly had herself removed on hearing of Cardigan's private life. An x-ray examination has, alas, punctured another good story, for no trace remains.

The Great Hall, built by Sir Edmund Brudenell in 1572.

THE SEVENTEENTH CENTURY

WILTON HOUSE, WILTSHIRE

In Wilton, 2½ miles (4 km) w of Salisbury on
Exeter road (A30)

At least one detail of Wilton House will be known by name to most visitors, and that is the splendid Double Cube room, designed by Inigo Jones and completed by John Webb about 1653. At once majestic and elegant with its high, rich ceiling, and white painted walls with gilded decorations, it was planned as a setting for Van Dyke's superb series of family portraits. Improbably, this most famous of English seventeenth-century interiors was the oper-ations room for Army Southern Command during World War II. One can only postulate the decision of an anti-Arts Minister to create so bizarre a set of circumstances. But the room and the house both survived, and Wilton House today holds probably the richest art collection still in private hands.

William Herbert, first Earl of Pembroke, founded the family fortune. This voluble Welshman was already high in royal favour when he married Anne

The sober, almost austere exterior does little to prepare the visitor for the interior richness of colour.

The Double Cube Room, perhaps the most famous feature of the house. Designed by Inigo Jones and completed by Webb about 1653, it appears today exactly as it was when built.

The Colonnade Room, formerly the State Bedroom, decorated in white and gold. Completed in the early 17th century, most of the furniture is 18th century, by William Kent.

The Library, 'ungothicised' by Reginald, 15th Earl of Pembroke, who succeeded to the title in 1913.

Palladian Bridge, built in 1737 by Henry, 9th Earl and Roger Morris.

Parr, sister of Henry VIII's sixth and last wife, in 1534. Henry, with his customary generosity with other people's property, gave him the abbey of Wilton in 1544 and he immediately began to build the present Tudor house. Tradition has it that he sought the advice of the King's brilliant painter, Hans Holbein.

It was in his son's day that Wilton House became a celebrated centre of politics and the arts, somewhat resembling the role that Cliveden was to play three centuries later. Henry, second Earl of Pembroke, was married to Mary Sidney, brother of the poet and soldier Sir Philip Sidney. 'In her time', said the gossip John Aubrey 'Wilton House was like a college, there were so many learned and ingeniose persons. She was the greatest patroness of wit and learning of her time.' Among those who thronged her court were naturally her brother Philip (scenes from his *Arcadia* are to be found in the Single Cube Room) Ben Jonson, Edmund Spenser, and Philip Massinger, and there is a strong, though unsubstantiated tradition that Shakespeare, with his company, gave a first performance at Wilton of one of his comedies – possibly *As You Like It*.

BLICKLING HALL, NORFOLK

1½ miles (2.4 km) NW of Aylsham on N side of B1354,
15 miles (24 km) N of Norwich
The National Trust

ON the anniversary of her execution, a coach and horses carrying Anne Boleyn's headless ghost is said to rattle through the park of Blickling Hall. On her wooden statue, placed next to that of her daughter Elizabeth on the great staircase, two centuries after her death, is carved the unequivocal claim *Hic nata*. Whatever the truth about the ghostly coach, the claim that she was born here is easily disproved for her family seat was at Hever in Kent. Her father did own the old manor house, built about 1390, which preceded the present building and that is probably the basis of the legend; it seems all the odder considering that the coach was not invented until a century after her death. What is historically certain is that Blickling was the first house to come to the

Thomas Ivory almost entirely rebuilt the Great Hall in 1767, adapting and extending the staircase to match. The figures of Anne Boleyn and her daughter Queen Elizabeth neither of whom had any real connection with Blickling, are nevertheless prominent on the staircase walls.

National Trust under the Country House scheme. Lord Lothian, its last owner and a staunch supporter of the Scheme left it to the Trust when he died in 1940. No members of the family live there now, and the former estate offices serve as the National Trust's headquarters for East Anglia.

Connoisseurs of country houses will immediately spot the affinity between Hatfield and Blickling: Blickling's architect, Robert Lyminge, also worked at Hatfield. Sir Henry Hobart, James I's Lord Chief Justice, bought the old manor at Blickling in 1616 and three years later commissioned Lyminge to build a new house. Lyminge was doubtless influenced by the success of Robert Cecil's great house, but there could not be a greater difference between the settings of Hatfield and Blickling. At Hatfield, the visitor has to work his way round to the main front, gaining the impression of that splendid façade only cumulatively whereas at Blickling the whole façade comes suddenly and dramatically into view. Unlike most of its peers, Blickling is not buried deep in its estate; the winding road from the little market town of Aylsham passes through a wood and then alongside a great sweep of lawn, bordered by two immense yew hedges, that runs up to the house. At night, the effect is particularly striking for the National Trust floodlights the front and the whole looks like a stage setting, framed by the darkness of the nearby woods.

The yew hedges are considerably older than the house itself and so, too, is the dry moat in front, now a delightful sunken flower garden. The moat probably guarded the first manor house on the site, built by Sir Nicholas Dagworth, who bought the manor from Sir John Fastolf, the Norfolk magnate who was later to be immortalized as Falstaff. The dimensions of the old house influenced the shape of the new. Lyminge, for instance, did not adopt the then fashionable E or H shape, as was done at Hatfield, but created instead the relatively old-fashioned internal courtyards. The entrance hall was subsequently rebuilt by the local architect Thomas Ivory. It was Ivory who created a worthy setting for Blickling's famous feature, the great oak

The most spectacular room in a remarkable house, the Long Gallery became a library in the 18th century.

staircase with its guardian figures. Originally, the stairs ascended round the walls of a small well; Ivory boldly cantilevered the entire structure out from the walls so that it seems almost weightless.

The other great feature of Blickling is its superb Jacobean ceilings, in particular that in the Long Gallery. The creator of this remarkable work – some 123 feet in length and divided into thirty-one major panels – has only recently been identified as Edward Stanyan. His bill, dated 10 December 1620, showed that he was paid £38 6s for 'the architrave freese and cornish round about the gallery' and £50 16s for the 'freat seeling'. The Long Gallery also contains the Library which, while it cannot rival that of Holkham, contains an impressive range of treasures, including incunabula amongst its 12,000 volumes. The bookcases and the curious painted frieze are the work of the nineteenth-century artist John Hungerford Pollen. An associate of the Pre-Raphaelites, he was fascinated by Celtic art but much of the elaborate symbolism of his ornamental frieze defies interpretation.

Edward Stanyan's elaborate Jacobean ceiling.

The proportions of the 17th-century house were determined by the original

14th-century building. The affinity with Hatfield is evident in this garden front.

PETWORTH HOUSE, WEST SUSSEX

In the centre of Petworth, 5½ miles (8.8 km) E of Midhurst (A272/A283)
The National Trust

PETWORTH, like Hatfield, is unusual in its proximity to a town. One could almost describe the town as a development of the house, they are so close together. Writing in 1823 William Cobbett, the professional John Bull who had no particular love for the gentry, nevertheless admired Petworth while commenting on its size. 'Lord Egremont's house is close to the town and with its outbuildings, walls and other erections is perhaps nearly as big as the town, though the town is not a small one.'

There has been a house on this site since the early fourteenth century, but the present building is largely the creation of that extraordinary and unloveable man Charles Seymour, sixth Duke of Somerset. Nicknamed the Proud Duke, legend has it that on his journey from London to Petworth

outriders went ahead to clear peasants from his path so that their glances would not defile him. He expected to be served on bended knee and even his children were supposed to stand up when speaking to him. The house came to him by marriage – or, to be exact, the money with which to build it. Petworth was part of the vast estates of the Duke of Northumberland and in 1670 the only claimant to this wealth was a three-year-old child, Elizabeth. The unfortunate girl was married off three times before she was sixteen, her third marriage in 1682 being to Somerset. As soon as she came of age, he laid hands on her fortune to build this jewel of a house.

It is typical of the man that he built for show. The back of the house is a hodgepodge of sizes, shapes and periods, traces of the original manor house that

The west front of the house, seen from the park. The town lies behind and actually adjacent to the house.

After the fire of 1714, Louis Laguerre was commissioned to decorate a new staircase in his grandiose style.

The Marble Hall, the only major architectural feature of the 17th-century interior to survive both the fire and the later 19th-century alterations.

had grown over the centuries and which Somerset now left as good enough for domestic offices. The undercroft of the Great Hall also survives, as does the chapel. But the grandiose west front is all his, as is the Marble Hall. It lacks Clandon's icy grandeur and the friendly beauty of Houghton, but is still a masterpiece and is the only major internal feature of Somerset's day to survive a disastrous fire in 1714 and the restless alterations of the mid-nineteenth century.

For Somerset's work only provided a platform for his successors. A century later, the third Earl created the Carved Room. Here are now displayed Grinling Gibbons' superb limewood carvings, emphasizing in particular the portraits of the Proud Duke and his wife. In creating the frames for the pictures, Gibbons virtually created sculpture, so deep is his carving, all but detaching his distinctive

fruit and flowers from their background. Horace Walpole, no casual bestower of compliments, thought that this room displayed 'the most superb monument of his skill'. Next to the Carved Room is a shrine to perhaps England's greatest painter, J.M.W. Turner. His friend and patron, the third Earl, gave him a room as a studio and he came to love Petworth, visiting it again and again in the 1830s, leaving among much else that marvellous evocation of sunlit calm, *The Drawing Room at Petworth*.

'Capability' Brown, designer of Petworth's landscape.

In 1751, three years after the Proud Duke's death, Capability Brown was commissioned to lay out the gardens. Out of many designs, one was chosen in 1752 and in successive contracts over the next five years the gradual development of this enormous project can be traced. Brown's goal of a 'natural landscape' was achieved so successfully that it took in even William Cobbett. Visiting this entirely artificial development seventy years after it was completed, Cobbett, practical farmer and connoisseur of landscapes though he was, described the park as 'very fine . . . consists of a parcel of hills and dells which Nature formed when she was in one of her most sportive moods'. It would have amused and delighted Capability Brown to have been mistaken for Mother Nature.

Petworth is particularly rich in Grinling Gibbons' work.

KNOLE, KENT

At Tonbridge end of Sevenoaks, just E of A225,
25 miles (40.2 km) from London
The National Trust

DID Mervyn Peake ever visit Knole, one wonders? For this vast, rambling house seems the ideal model for that phantasmagoric castle Gormenghast, with its endless Earls of Groan, which is central to his trilogy. Certainly the house provided the background for one of the odder pieces of English literature, Virginia Woolf's *Orlando*, the story of the immortal boy/girl who changes sex through the centuries, symbolic of a family's transmission of identity. Virginia Woolf gave the manuscript to her friend Vita Sackville-West, and it now lies in a place of honour in the house. Vita Sackville-West herself left a lively portrait of the house in *Knole and the Sackvilles* which conveys the spirit of a great house as experienced by one who was born in it.

The core of Knole was built sometime in the late fifteenth century by Thomas Bourchier, Archbishop of Canterbury. Queen Elizabeth I gave the house to her cousin, Thomas Sackville, later Earl of Dorset. Sackville has some literary merit as the author of *Gorbuduc*, reputedly the first tragedy in English (and probably the least read); but he made his money as a politician under Elizabeth and James I, pouring his wealth into extending and decorating Knole.

Apart from its great size, what is most striking

The size of the house is vast, its variegated roofscape resembling that of a village or small town.

Built between 1605 and 1608, the staircase was a decided novelty for its day.

about the house is its interior gloom. This is partly the result of its architecture, but it is also the deliberate policy of the National Trust. Although the family of the present Lord Sackville continues to live in the house, maintaining the four-century link, Knole passed into the possession of the Trust in 1946. It was faced with the problem of conserving one of the richest and rarest collections of historic fabrics in Europe. As Lords Chamberlain to the monarch, the Sackvilles had a valuable perquisite – the right to discarded royal furniture – in particular the rich hangings and upholsteries. To protect these priceless fabrics, some now in their third century, light is reduced to a minimum. Attendants are armed with torches to illuminate details for visitors with a more than casual interest – an altogether odd experience, but one which was shared by others in the past. Horace Walpole, that indefatigable visitor of country houses said of Knole 'I worship all its faded splendour, and enjoy its preservation'.

One of the striking illustrations of this 'faded splendour' is the great staircase. It was an innovation in its time. People were accustomed to stairways that disappeared upwards from view and this splendidly balustraded creation, seemingly

The Green Court. The gatehouse is known as Bourchier's Tower, after Thomas Bourchier who began building Knole.

hanging in space and visible over all its length, must have been startling. This effect was increased still further by the *trompe l'oeil* decorations on the walls enclosing the staircase. Today the whole has faded, decorations on walls and on three-dimensional elements alike, and in the underwater gloom the eye is deceived for a moment into accepting the entire structure as a painted decoration.

The Cartoon Gallery, with its six copies of Raphael's cartoons, probably from the studio of Daniel Mytens.

CHATSWORTH, DERBYSHIRE

½ mile (0.8 km) E of village of Edensor off A623,
4 miles (6.4 km) E of Bakewell,
10 miles (16 km) W of Chesterfield

THIS enormous house achieved its final form in an almost absent-minded fashion. The original Elizabethan manor (built by Bess of Hardwick and her husband William Cavendish, about 1552) remained largely unchanged until 1686. This was the house which Mary, Queen of Scots, would have known, for it formed one of her many prisons. The restored Mary's Bower is a relic of this period.

Then, in 1686, the fourth Earl – created Duke of Devonshire for his support of William of Orange – began to pull down the south front. It would seem that, initially, he intended to do little more than put up a fashionable façade. But as many a rich man before him had found, the temptation to put his own impress on his day through the medium of bricks and mortar proved overwhelming. Gradually, one front after another was demolished and built in the

current style, the whole operation being finished just before his death in 1707. It was a curious process. The actual ground plan remained unchanged and it was as though the building was shedding one skin to grow another. The exquisite model of the house now on display in the north entrance hall illustrates what is not obvious in the house itself. The ad hoc approach to building resulted in a grave miscalculation with the east front some nine feet longer than the west. This would have resulted in a curiously slanting front had not the architect resolved the dilemma by building a bow to hide the fact.

The next great stage of building was that undertaken by the Bachelor Duke – William, sixth Duke of Devonshire (1790–1858). The wealth of the Cavendishes, already vast, was augmented by skil-

The west front, probably designed by Thomas Archer, with the personal aid of the 1st Duke.

240

The State Drawing Room. The ceiling is by Laguerre and the tapestries, based on Raphael's cartoons, were woven at Mortlake.

ful marriages, and drawing on this fortune the Bachelor Duke initiated a programme which was to last nineteen years. Among much else, he brought into being the enormous north wing, very nearly as big as the original house. Particularly valuable from the historian's point of view is the record he made of his work, in the form of a series of letters to his sister. In a relaxed, fluent, amiable manner he takes the visitor round from room to room, pointing out not only what was already there, but the changes he had made. He had some salty things to say about the grandiloquent work of some of his predecessors. The Duke's handbook remained unpublished for nearly 150 years until the present Duchess incorporated large sections of it in her own account of the house. Between these two records, both informal but well informed, the reader obtains an unusual insight into the running of, and the alterations made in a great house over a climacteric period.

Chatsworth thus has two essentially different parts: the stiffly formal seventeenth-century building and the still grand, but more humane nineteenth-century wing. The State Rooms lie on the upper floor. Regarding this range of vast rooms, the Bachelor Duke was sorely tempted. 'The State Dining Room was never dined in that I know of – the first room of this great unappropriated apartment which consumes in useless display the best habitable part of the house. What bedrooms might have been made here, with the South sun and beautiful views! I was much tempted – but finished conservatively by repairing the sinking floors and threatened ceilings.'

Displayed in these rooms is the whole function of a great house as an instrument of prestige. The eye is at first dazzled by the sheer wealth and detail of decoration – the gold leaf and stamped leather, the rich tapestries which cover the walls. But looking beyond and behind them is to see that these vast rooms are simply empty cubes with little or no clues as to how they were used socially. How, where and when did their occupants conduct their more intimate affairs – eating, dressing, washing – when not engaged in public display?

The incredible wealth of treasures at Chatsworth produces a kind of numbness (the house takes two hours for the visitor to see). One takes away a kaleidoscope of rich impressions. The extraordinary Oak Room, a whim on the part of the Bachelor Duke, who bought the carved oak panel-

William Spencer Cavendish, 6th Duke of Devonshire (1790–1858).

ling of a German monastery on impulse, and then built a room around them for which successive owners have rather desperately tried to find a use. The superb Chapel, built between 1688 and 1693 and totally unchanged. The chilly splendour of the sculpture gallery, filled mostly with nineteenth-century examples. The incredible Library, superlative in appearance and superlative in its collection. The nineteenth-century Dining Room with its curious ceiling which, the Bachelor Duke observed, gives the room the appearance of a cabin trunk's interior, and the modern sculptures and paintings, including Lucien Freud's disturbing 'Large Interior W.9'. However, two images remain: a small, cheap photograph of a smiling young woman holding a cockerel and, beside it, the large portrait of a handsome young man in uniform. The young man was the Marquess of Hartington, heir to the house, but killed in action in 1944. The woman is his wife, born Kathleen Kennedy, sister of the man who later became President of the USA, and who was herself killed in an accident in 1948, leaving as a record only this hasty snapshot, now placed among the portraits of the 500-year line of Cavendishes.

Louis Laguerre painted the upper part of this splendid hall, with scenes from the life of Julius Caesar, from 1692, since when it has not been changed. The ceiling was discovered to be sagging in 1936 and required two years work to make it safe.

WOBURN ABBEY, BEDFORDSHIRE

In Woburn; 8½ miles (13.6 km) NW of Dunstable on A50,
42 miles (67.5 km) from London off M1, exit 12

THE Marquess of Bath was undoubtedly the first owner of a great house to try and make it pay for itself. But equally undoubtedly John, thirteenth Duke of Bedford, was the first to carry the idea to its logical conclusion and turn his house into an entertainment industry. In consequence, Woburn Abbey is again and again cited in horror by purists as the fate worse than extinction awaiting great English houses. One wonders whether the more vociferous critics have ever visited the place. On approaching the house from the village of Woburn there is no evidence whatsoever of the notorious fairground or its ancillaries. Humphrey Repton did his work well nearly 200 years ago, the gently undulating hills and carefully sited copses masking a wide range of tourist activities which would have astonished him.

The reception area of the house is low key. A much thumbed copy of the Department of Employment's *Hours and Conditions of Work* hangs beneath stern portraits of the Russell family, but there is little else to show that one has entered an organization which employs 250 people, spends at least £1 million a year in maintenance and has to cater for about a million visitors each year. Behind that velvet front is a very steely business. The house, with its fantastically rich collections, is only one of many attractions. There is a complete gallery of antique shops, as well as craft shops, a restaurant and a zoo – each contributing its portion to the

The grotto – a delightful fantasy, built 1619–41 and possibly designed by Inigo Jones, then working for the 4th Earl.

The 4th Duke commissioned these views of Venice by Canaletto, which have hung in the room designed for them since 1800.

upkeep of this massive, grey, Palladian mansion.

Woburn Abbey, as its name indicates, was part of the great monastic plunder of the sixteenth century. It stands on the site of a Cistercian monastery; the abbot was incautious enough to make an uncomplimentary remark about Anne Boleyn and after his execution, the abbey and lands were given to John, first Earl of Bedford. Already well supplied with fat estates in the West Country, Bedford did nothing with his gift; nor did his descendants until, in the early seventeenth century, the fourth Earl moved from London to avoid the plague. Woburn was convenient for the capital, and successive members of the Russell family engaged in the English aristocrat's traditional pastime of tearing down and rebuilding. The main front of the house as it appears today is largely the work of Henry Flitcroft, who was commissioned in 1747 to transform the old monastic buildings into a modern residence. Following the shape of the Cistercian cloister, the house was built around a quadrangle – a shape it retained

until 1950 when the entire eastern range was demolished because of dry rot.

The Russell family has always been at, or near, the centre of political activity, sometimes profitably – as in the case of the first Earl – and sometimes decidedly unprofitably. William, Lord Russell, for instance, died on the scaffold 'a martyr to the Romish fury'. It has also bred its share of eccentrics like the twelfth Duke, who pulled down nearly half the house and who lived like a viceroy 'isolated from the outside world by a mass of sycophants, servants and an eleven-mile wall'. With his accidental death in 1953 it seemed as though Woburn had come to the end of its life as a family home, for the Russells now incurred death duties of £5 million. It was to pay off that enormous debt that the thirteenth, and present Duke of Bedford in effect founded the stately home industry.

In his minority the Duke had suffered decidedly from the Russell eccentricity. He describes in his autobiography how he was well into his teens before

Queen Victoria's dressing room, named after her visit to Woburn. Today it contains Dutch and Flemish paintings.

he even saw Woburn, much less realized he was a possible heir. He was working abroad successfully as a fruit farmer when he learned he had succeeded to both the title and the estate. Apart from the incredible tax due, the house itself was in an appalling condition with priceless art treasures jumbled with piles of junk in dusty rooms. Running the place as a home seemed to be out of the question. 'Although there would be a substantial income available to the family, there seemed to be no way of devizing any arrangement which would permit the furbishing and upkeep of Woburn, which to me was the only object worth preserving in the whole estate.'

There was, in fact, one possible way of doing so, but it had to be done wholeheartedly. 'I paid a couple of incognito visits to houses open to the public. However, they were all doing it on the theory that the sooner the visitors were in, the sooner they would be gone, the quicker you got the money and goodbye. That was not the way I intended to do it. I wanted to make people enjoy themselves, give them service and value for money and make sure they would come back again. If this enabled me to live in my ancestral home, everyone would be satisfied.'

In the event, everyone *was* satisfied: the public, who found a fascinating new venue; the taxman, who eventually collected his £5 million and the

Originally built by Holland as a conservatory, this sculpture gallery was created by the 6th Duke.

Russells, who again had a family home – even though they share it with a million or so people every year. In 1974, the Duke retired and his son, the Marquess of Tavistock, inherited the great building together with its problems.

The Marquess is a businessman – a stockbroker – who runs Woburn, too, as a business. His office, once the ballroom of the Abbey, is now its administrative nerve centre combining comfort, efficiency and historic interest in equal degree. (In it are two enormous desks pushed back to back, for the Marchioness takes a prominent part in the running of the machine.) He emphasizes his acceptance of, and his pride in the remarkable tactics used by his father to save his ancestral home. Public opening is essential to the survival of the building. And anyway, as he has said 'What could I do with fourteen sitting rooms, half a dozen galleries and the rest? It was different in the past. They used to have endless country house parties, with people moving in flocks from one to the other. Today, most of us are working.'

The English art of compromise has resulted in the salvation of Woburn.

The little Chinese dairy, built by Henry Holland during extensive rebuilding of the house in 1787.

THE EIGHTEENTH CENTURY

SEATON DELAVAL, NORTHUMBERLAND

½ mile (0.8 km) from the coast at Seaton Sluice,
between Blyth and Whitley Bay (A190)

THERE can scarcely be a more prosaic piece of real estate than the flat lands a few miles north of Newcastle. Tynemouth to the south, and Blyth to the north, extend industrial pincer movements towards the cold North Sea. But between the arms of these pincers, scarcely a mile from the coast, lies Sir John Vanbrugh's great house. It has a quality of eeriness due partly, no doubt, to the fact that for nearly 150 years this house – the seat of the 'gay Delavals' – was empty save for the ghostly memories of past revels. An immense fire gutted the interior in 1822 and it remained boarded up and shuttered until 1950 when its owner, Lord Hastings, partially restored it.

But it also has a quality of fantasy which arises from the nature of the building itself. Here, one

In front of one of the wings, partly facing the other, with the vast courtyard stretching away to the right.

The sense of a stage setting is carried strongly into the great hall, still marked by the fire of 1822.

The south front portico, less sombre than the overwhelming ceremonial approach of the north front.

feels, as at Blenheim, Vanbrugh was as much playwright as architect, in his mind's eye seeing some titanic stage set. Admiral George Delaval invited him north, after buying the estate from a cousin in 1717, to design a house 'for the entertainment of our old age' and, despite its great size, this element of entertainment seems to dominate all else. To get the full flavour one should approach the great north front on foot. The vast wings on each side of the equally vast court rise slowly to encompass the walker, until the steps leading up to the main entrance are reached. One feels a bar or two of *Parsifal* should be played as one enters the hall. Splendid as it must have been at the height of its glory, today it has an additional poignancy for the stone walls and statues are still marked by that great fire over a century and a half ago.

Admiral Delaval never saw his house completed for he died in a fall from his horse in 1723. The house in due course passed to a collateral branch of the family whose descendant, the twenty-second Lord Hastings, initiated the massive work of restoration, with the help of grants from the Historic Buildings Councils. The family established itself in the west wing where, Lord Hastings records: 'My son was born in 1960, the first time Delaval Hall had known such an event since my ancestress Rhoda Delaval gave birth to a son in the West Wing in 1757!'

HOLKHAM HALL, NORFOLK

2 miles (3.2 km) w of Wells,
s of Wells-Hunstanton road (A149)

A wartime aerial photograph, taken about 1943, tells the story of Holkham Hall in starkly dramatic terms. Immediately below lies the ordered mass of the great building, beyond it a dark belt of trees, a lighter belt of sand-dunes, and then the sea. The trees protect house and estate from the almost ceaseless north wind that roars in off the North Sea, while the house itself is in almost arrogant control of its environment, classical perfection set down among the bleak salt marshes. Indeed, at the time it was being built, a contemporary described the estate as 'a desert where two rabbits fight for one blade of grass'. Yet in due course this 'desert' became the laboratory for one of the most influential of all agricultural experiments, that initiated by 'Coke of Norfolk' in the early nineteenth century.

Thomas Coke, later Earl of Leicester, conceived the idea of the house while on the Grand Tour in Italy in 1713. He met William Kent and they determined to transport Rome to England, to build the perfect Palladian house in Norfolk, but it was not until 1734 that the foundations were actually laid. Coke died in 1759 before the interior was completed, but his imprint is firmly upon the house.

Holkham is a cerebral building, with every tiny detail planned for overall effect. The result from the outside, particularly viewed from the north, is cold and somewhat repellent. For the locally made bricks that were used have weathered little over the years and what might very well appear as a warm yellow-brown under a brilliant Italian sky seems stark and sombre under the steely light of East Anglia.

The impact is all the greater when one enters the

The south front with its fountain tableau, and the formal gardens, created by Nessfield in the 1850s.

The Marble Hall, understandably Holkham's most famous feature, with its fluted columns of Derbyshire alabaster.

State Rooms. The superb Marble Hall is a triumph. Kent used the rich alabaster of Derbyshire, in hues of ivory, purple and green for his material and drew upon the temple of Fortuna Virilis for his inspiration. This is no pastiche or copy, but rather a subtle transmutation of ideas. An 1830s guidebook remarked 'When the Person who shews this house is engaged, the company is conducted into the Vestibule. The curious visitor will not regret the time while contemplating the various subjects in the room.' The twentieth-century visitor will be as well rewarded.

Financially, Holkham has suffered less than many of its peers, largely because of the extraordinary richness of its library. The collection of books was originally made by the first Earl of Leicester on his Italian tour. From time to time, it allowed the Cokes to pay off a hungry Chancellor like so much Danegeld. Almost every sale made headlines in the national, and sometimes the international press. The most outstanding was the recent sale of the Leonardo da Vinci codex, which realized £2.2 million, to pay off death duties. An American bought this manuscript outbidding representatives from both Florence and Milan, but the British Museum was able to purchase the fourteenth-century Holkham Picture Bible so this, at least, remains in England. But the library is still one of the richest in the country. In 1947 the current Earl introduced was was then a revolutionary new idea, that of selling slides of the library's treasures in what the librarian, W.O. Hassall, somewhat fulsomely described as 'a miracle of cultural democracy'.

Thomas Coke, the agriculturalist, was a son of the

The north dining room is in the form of a cube, with a central apse for the serving table.

The saloon, the principal State Room, with its original wall covering of Genoa velvet.

builder and succeeded on his father's death. The Great Barn, designed for him in 1790 by Samuel Wyatt, is still a main feature of the grounds. It was here that Coke entertained his neighbours during the annual sheep shearings, when they discussed those new agricultural techniques that quietly revolutionized European farming. There was, in fact, a sheep shearing here in 1978. Appropriately enough, the estate has made a special collection of farming implements for the interest of visitors. And continuing that very Norfolk vein of practicality is the Holkham Pottery. Started by Elizabeth, Countess of Leicester, in 1957, it is now a flourishing industry, employing many local people.

HOUGHTON HALL, NORFOLK

13 miles (20.9 km) E of King's Lynn,
10 miles (16 km) W of Fakenham (A148)

THE position of Houghton Hall near the coast of Norfolk perfectly illustrates that concept of the 'country house' as an essentially urban structure in rural surroundings that typifies the eighteenth century. Coming through the forbidding pine forests around Sandringham, one arrives at a little cluster of white-painted estate houses grouped before an elegant wrought iron gate, the whole resembling something from one of the Grimm fairy tales. The approach to the house lies down a narrow lane, and there, rearing up from a great stretch of lawn is a building that would not look out of place in Paris. The paradox continues: the house is set in extensive parkland but the oaks, though formally planted, seem to melt into their agricultural background.

For such a perfectly designed, symmetric house, it is odd to find that it is the work of three architects. Colen Campbell was the main figure, but Thomas Ripley and perhaps James Gibbs had a hand in it between 1722 and 1735. But behind them all lay the forceful, unifying mind of England's first prime minister, Robert Walpole. His portrait by John Wootton hangs in the Stone Hall. Wootton has placed him in a rural setting (despite the incongruity of lavish gold braid on his coat) conveying the impression that Walpole wanted to make – that of a

Houghton – an outstanding example of Palladian architecture – is an urban house in a rural setting, for it is surrounded by its working Norfolk agricultural estate.

The Marble Parlour, with chairs of Genoa silk velvet and Chinese armorial plates; Rysbrack carved the overmantel.

bluff, no-nonsense Norfolk squire. But behind that heavy, rather complacent face was a shrewd mind and a highly cultured spirit. Improbably enough, the core of the great art collection of the Hermitage in Leningrad was assembled here among the Norfolk turnips by Walpole himself. His grandson, the third Earl of Orford, was eccentric to the point of insanity and, running the estate deep into debt, sold off the collection to Catherine the Great. Her portrait, too, hangs in the house – a miniscule return for such a great loss.

The Green Velvet Bedchamber is the work of William Kent, who designed the bed and painted the ceiling. The tapestries are from the Brussels workshop.

This was the only major depredation of the contents, and the house and furnishings today continue to reflect a subtle blend of solidity and elegance, itself an expression of Robert Walpole. Unlike his neighbour Coke at Holkham, he had no use for the brick that is the indigenous building material of Norfolk. It was good enough for the core of a wall but for its shell he wanted stone and obtained it from Yorkshire. Fortunately, Houghton was only a few miles from the bustling little port of King's Lynn: the hundreds of tons of Aislaby sandstone required were cheaply floated down from Whitby and carried by expensive oxcart only over the last short lap.

The interior of the house is all of a piece, for William Kent was not only responsible for the decorations, but made most of the furniture and the marble fireplaces. The stuccoist, Artari, was brought in to carve the moulding of the Stone Hall (see frontispiece), and the sculptor, Michael Rysbrack, created the fireplace. Both men worked on the similar Marble Hall at Clandon, but that great chamber is cold and uninviting, compared to Houghton's Stone Hall. This certainly does not lack majesty, but partly through its proportions, and partly through use of the warm Yorkshire sandstone, one feels this is a room that can be lived in as well as looked at.

The house has been open to the public only since 1976 and, like other owners, the Marquess of Cholmondeley has sought to create some additional attraction for the public. Here, the choice has been not lions or giraffes or other exotica but the shirehorses which created the agricultural wealth of Norfolk. Joe Green, who started as a stableboy at Houghton in 1926, returned in 1972 as head groom with the heartfelt remark 'It's like coming back to life again.' The great, gentle creatures browsing in the paddocks give their own air of solidity, of the permanent relationship between house and land.

The Great Staircase is in mahogany, one of the first uses of the wood in England. The murals are the work of Kent.

BURTON CONSTABLE, HUMBERSIDE

In Burton Constable, 1½ miles (2.4 km) N of Sproatley,
7½ miles (12 km) NE of Hull (A165)

IT is singularly appropriate that among the ghosts reputedly thronging Burton Constable (including an entire Roman legion clanking its way through the woods by the drive) should be that of William Constable, a benign presence in the Gold Bedroom. For the interior of the house as it now appears is very largely his work. Born in 1721, William Constable was possessed of a lively, enquiring mind – a type which, coupled with great wealth, did so much to advance the cause of science in the eighteenth century. He was a fellow of the Royal Society, for which he was proposed by no less a person than Banks, its formidable president. He was a member of the Lunar Society, a friend and patron of Joseph Priestley and a correspondent of Jean-Jacques Rousseau. In the Museum Rooms (originally a theatre) are displayed some of the objects which reflect his manifold interests – the interests of an aristocratic, scientific dilettante which, in due course, would provide a stimulus for the Industrial Revolution and all that came afterwards. There is the travelling medicine chest which he used on his long foreign trips, from which he brought back yet more ideas for the embellishment of his home. In the Muniment Room are displayed drawings by the craftsmen he employed in the massive programme of modernization that he embarked upon – sketches and plans by Robert Adam, James Wyatt, Capability Brown and Thomas Chippendale. All are of intrinsic interest, but even that is increased by the fact they are related to the building around them. One can enter the Drawing Room on the west front and see there the chairs Chippendale designed. Similarly, one can turn from Capability Brown's sketches and see in the gardens the actual lakes and bridges that he planned.

It is not known for certain when, or by whom, this massive house was built. It was probably the work of Sir Henry Constable, who died in 1606. His portrait in the Great Hall shows the house in the background, giving substance to this theory. But he was almost certainly building on, or near, a much older house. The Constables acquired the manor of Burton in the early twelfth century, and the oldest

The Long Gallery, built by Cuthbert Constable in 1736 ; the frieze is derived from the Bodleian Library, Oxford.

In contrast with much of the interior, the exterior remains an early 17th-century building.

It was William Constable (b. 1721) who transformed the interior of the Stuart house of his ancestors into 18th-century elegance, exemplified by the Yellow Drawing Room

surviving part of the existing house, Stephen's Tower, dates from this period. Externally, however, the house is one of the many portentous, red brick buildings which reflected the power and wealth of newly rich Elizabethan magnates.

William Constable, either through a fine feeling for history, or a preference for expending energy in decoration rather than construction, left all this untouched. His father, Cuthbert, began the work of change by creating the Long Gallery, as late as 1740 (and curiously old-fashioned he must have seemed to his contemporaries in doing so). William took up the task in the 1750s, which continued for the next twenty years. The last of his work was the Great Ballroom, which Wyatt built between 1775 and 1776, the plasterwork for which was carried out by an Italian, Giuseppe Cortese. Chippendale designed the furniture specifically for this room, charging £1,000 for it. So proud was William Constable of his newly furbished home that, in 1778 when Chippendale finished his work, he had notices printed saying that the house would be open to the public.

CONSTABLE BURTON, NORTH YORKSHIRE

On A684 between Leyburn and Bedale on A1

ARCHITECTURALLY, Constable Burton has had a decidedly odd history. Although the Wyvills have been established here for centuries, the building is purely Georgian, supposedly the result of a mistake. In 1762 Sir Marmaduke Wyvill commissioned John Carr to make certain alterations to the existing Elizabethan manor, agreed a sum of £1,500 for the work, and sensibly went away while it was being done. In his absence, however, Carr demolished almost the entire building, a single room surviving to greet the owner on his return. Wyvill seems to have been a remarkably tolerant man for Carr, instead of being driven off with contumely, was actually commissioned to build an entirely new house – at a cost of £10,000. Presumably, this was his original intention but in any event he did well by his client, creating this faultlessly Palladian villa.

But if Constable Burton is an almost textbook example of the eighteenth-century classical revival (so much so, that its elegant bridge and loggia might have come from the hand of Palladio himself) the means whereby it was brought back to life in the 1970s is itself a classic illustration of the problems facing the owners of country houses, and the solutions available. As with so many of its peers, the house was rented out between the two World Wars. On the death of the tenant, the Wyvills decided to take up residence and restore the house. Although the garden had been well cared for, the house had been less well maintained. 'For six months we lived in the Oak Room [its panelling was all that survived from the Elizabethan mansion]. No heating. No water. Nothing!' Over the following years, room after room was brought back into habitable condition. Furniture was unearthed after having been stored for more than forty years. In the interim, the boom in antique prices had given much of it very considerable value. 'But it belonged to the house – that was the whole point of the operation.' Restored, it now completes the whole.

The house, as a listed building, was eligible for a grant for repairs but, in return, had to be open to the

Constable Burton, showing John Carr's perfect Palladian front. The double stair leads over a bridge to the loggia.

The Drawing Room, with its distinctive chimney piece and plaster ceiling in Adam style.

public for the statutory minimum of thirty days a year. Unlike great houses of the order of Blenheim or Woburn, where visitors can be channelled through the State Rooms away from private quarters, smaller houses have literally to be open throughout. But the owners feel it is a fair return.

Although some 400 people visited Constable Burton in 1981, their combined entrance fee is only a drop in the ocean. How, then, is the place funded? The estate consists of 3,000 acres so the traditional industry of farming underpins the whole. The letting of shooting rights and accommodation also contributes greatly to the upkeep of the house. Between August and January the house is full; but it also entails a great deal of unglamorous hard work, the Wyvills necessarily adding the skills of hoteliers

to that of traditional hosts. These funds are channelled into the house, evident from its superb condition. It would be an interesting actuarial exercise to calculate what it would cost the State to keep it in equivalent condition.

The gardens are a major attraction – currently, there are eighty-two varieties of daffodil alone – and are frequently visited by horticultural enthusiasts. The neglected vegetable garden has been brought back to life. Labour costs today make it uneconomical – it is almost certainly cheaper to buy vegetables in the superb local markets than to pay for labour to grow them. But, like the antique furniture that has been given new life in an old setting, the restored vegetable garden is part of the whole vision of Constable Burton.

BLENHEIM PALACE, OXFORDSHIRE

THERE are two main approaches to Blenheim Palace from the beautiful little town of Woodstock, the Hensington Gate and the Triumphal Gate. The first-time visitor should unhesitatingly take the Triumphal Gate entrance. The high street leads into a stone quadrangle surrounded by a high wall. There is no indication whatsoever of the stupendous vista which instantly opens up as the visitor passes through the gate. In one swift glance one is aware of Capability Brown's landscaped park, green slopes running down to a great lake, a bridge and in the distance the spires, triumphal arches and swagger-ing turrets of what seems to be a township. The vista resolves itself into a carefully planned theatrical setting, touched with fantasy, the perfect framework for the biggest drama of all, Vanbrugh's Blenheim Palace.

This, the only non-royal, non-episcopal palace among the hundreds of great houses in England, also challenges two basic English predilections: their dislike of monumental buildings and their suspicion of military heroes. A statue, perhaps, or a plaque is usually considered more than adequate. It is doubtful if many of the thousands who visit Blenheim each year are aware of its significance. For this great Baroque palace is a token of the nation's sense of pride and relief after the victory of Blenheim in 1704, sufficient to make it forget its normal thriftiness.

Built at royal Woodstock, it was the gift of Queen Anne to her triumphant general, the first Duke of Marlborough. No contract was drawn up – it scarcely seemed necessary, for were not the Queen and Sarah, Duchess of Marlborough, the best of friends, confiding in each other as Mrs Morley and Mrs Freeman? But the friends fell out, and bitter arguments later developed as to who owed whom for what, and a second battle of Blenheim ensued, which David Green has brilliantly chronicled in his history of the house.

Vanbrugh lost this battle. He also had his differences with the Duchess, and her continual criticism of his work brought the matter to a head. The finest talents of the day were employed in the embellishment of Blenheim – masons, and carvers such as Grinling Gibbons – but funds were curtailed and work remained unfinished. Vanbrugh resigned in a rage in 1716, and Hawksmoor was left to complete it. When the Duke died, Sarah was left with a vast sum of money and power 'to spoil Blenheim in her own way' as Vanbrugh put it bitterly. She was involved in lawsuits with over 400 people connected with the building of Blenheim, and by the end of her life had spent £300,000 on the palace, three times Vanbrugh's estimate. But she finished this enormous building, the most splendid relic of its age.

This is the ceremonial fulcrum of the palace for, standing with one's back to the great portico, one looks across the Grand Bridge towards the Column of Victory. Capability Brown, with a certain insensitivity, grassed over the forecourt, but the 9th Duke repaved it between 1900 and 1910. The finest talents of the day were used at Blenheim.

The State Dining Room. The ceiling and murals were painted by Louis Laguerre; some of the figures peering over the balustrades are imaginary, others are caricatures and others, again, portraits – among them Laguerre's own, much as Verrio included himself in the Heaven Room at Burghley.

Vanbrugh's massive Baroque palace, built to commemorate Marlborough's victory in 1704.

This aerial view of Blenheim captures the stupendous scale of the concept.

GORHAMBURY HOUSE. HERTFORDSHIRE

$2\frac{3}{4}$ miles (4.4 km) W of St Albans, off A414

THE visitor to Gorhambury sees a relatively modern house, actually built in 1777 but seemingly new for it has recently been refaced in sparkling Portland stone. But behind that calm front is a tide of English history and great names: Ethelred the Unready; Verulamium; Bacon and Skakespeare; Elizabeth I and Henry VIII. The original manor belonged to King Ethelred who gave it to the Abbot of St Albans. The name derives from Geoffrey de Gorham who built the first known house about 1130, doubtless using materials from the nearby Roman ruins of Verulamium. After the dissolution, it was bought by Sir Nicholas Bacon, father of the great writer, who promptly built a more splendid house higher up the hill. Elizabeth visited him there, and twitted him about its small size, where-

The formal façade of Gorhambury has changed little since Robert Taylor completed it in 1784.

Most of the paintings in the Yellow Drawing Room are contemporary with the house, and include Joshua Reynolds' group portrait of the four children of James, 2nd Viscount Grimston.

The Library, with its white marble mantelpiece by Piranesi. The books were catalogued on Francis Bacon's system.

upon he expanded it in time for her next visit. The cost of the royal reception is recorded in the accounts as £577 6s 7¼d for barely four days.

In due course the old manor house came to Francis Bacon. When not conducting affairs of state (he was Lord Chancellor under James I) writing his *Essays* and, according to his devoted band of disciples, penning the plays of Shakespeare, Bacon devoted much time to the house. He had no children, and when he died the house was bought in 1652 by the improbably named Sir Harbottle Grimston, a successful lawyer. The family flourished, and in 1777 the third Viscount Grimston followed the fashion of his class and day and built the present Palladian house. The old Tudor home was abandoned, though its ruins remain and its history pervades the later house. Here is the earliest-known, documented portrait of an Englishman, that of Edward Grimston, dated 1446. Gorhambury also contains an extensive collection of family portraits, running from the fifteenth to the twentieth century, together with enamelled glass windows from the old mansion and mementos of Francis Bacon.

He lives on in the Library which is catalogued according to his epochal divisions of knowledge, and it was here that seven of Shakespeare's plays were discovered. The oldest in private possession, they are now on permanent loan to the Bodleian Library, Oxford, but photographic copies are kept in the house to maintain the link between Francis Bacon (Lord Verulam) and the enigmatic playwright from Stratford-on-Avon.

Ruins of the original 16th-century manor, built by Sir Nicholas Bacon and preserved in the park.

SUTTON PARK, NORTH YORKSHIRE

HANGING in the entrance hall of this trim, early Georgian house is the engraving of a building with a tantalizingly familiar appearance and name – Buckingham House. The central block is, in fact, the precursor of Buckingham Palace and a previous owner of this house, the late Major Sheffield, was the descendant of that Duke of Buckingham whose London home was to become the monarch's palace. The Sheffield seat was at Normanby Park in Lincolnshire but the size of that house, together with the ravages created by open-cast mining in the park, caused the purchase of this house when it came on the market in 1963. The family had originated large properties in Lincolnshire and in Yorkshire, so the move was historically satisfying.

Sutton Park is built on the edge of the little village of Sutton-on-the Forest – as neat as the house itself and built of the same clamp-fired, rose-coloured bricks. Probably built by Thomas Atkinson in 1720 on the site of an Elizabethan mansion, it was

The Tea Room with its collection of Imari porcelain.

This exotic domed structure is, in fact, an ice-box, double-shelled and mostly underground for coolness.

Sutton Park's garden front. This modest, yet impressive, early Georgian classical brick mansion was built on the site of an Elizabethan manor in the 1720s, to which two elegant wings were added in the mid-18th century.

extended by two graceful wings in 1760 but has since remained unchanged. All the furnishings were brought from Normanby Park, including the elegant bookcases designed by Smirke especially for that house, and the series of family portraits, both maintaining continuity and giving the house an unexpected weight. The rooms have an easy eclecticism: the splendid Chinese Room (with rare wallpaper dated about 1760) boasts an Adam fireplace, also from Normanby Park, and the Dining Room has been completely recreated.

The gardens come as a complete surprise. The casual eye would assume they were contemporary with the house, but they have been designed entirely since 1963. The first year was spent uprooting neglected evergreens, reducing the number of gravel paths, taking in a large piece of the park which included a fine cedar tree – this gave the new garden an instantly mature look. An outstanding discovery was the splendid brick ice-house, one of the finest of its kind still in existence. Now restored, this circular pit, eighteen feet deep with a double-domed brick roof, despite its prosaic function, conveys a deeply mysterious atmosphere. Had its domestic use been unknown, one wonders to what religious purpose it would have been assigned.

CLANDON PARK, SURREY

At West Clandon 3 miles (4.8 km) E of Guildford on A247
The National Trust

IF Blickling was the first country house to come to the National Trust under the Country House Scheme, Clandon was the object of the Trust's first great restoration project when, over a period of two years, some £200,000 was spent. That sum has long been surpassed at Erdigg but Clandon established the precedent.

The Earls of Onslow bought the land in 1542 and erected a handsome manor house upon it. In the eighteenth century an Onslow married a wealthy heiress and promptly invested her money by building, about 1730, a house more in keeping with the times. It was a massive, square, red brick building designed by the Venetian Giacomo Leoni, in grounds laid out by the ubiquitous Capability Brown. The third Earl abandoned the place in the nineteenth century and for over forty years it went to ruin, its gardens overgrown and chimneys blocked solid by birds' nests. When the fourth Earl succeeded to the title in 1870, he recorded 'I was the first person who for many years was allowed to enter the house. It was almost bare of furniture and all blinds and curtains had perished.' The house temporarily returned to its former splendid life at the end of the Edwardian era, but was again virtually abandoned during the 1930s. Immediately after World War II the sixth Earl and his wife made a courageous attempt to bring Clandon back to life: one of the showpieces of the house are the dyed US army blankets out of which Lady Onslow made curtains for the huge windows. But the attempt was hopeless and in 1956 the house was given to the National Trust.

The immense work of restoration was put in hand. Between 1927 and 1945 much of the interior decoration had disappeared under a thick coat of whitewash, beneath which lay even more layers of paint smothering the original. John Fowler, the interior decorator who was entrusted with this delicate work, remarked: 'In a house of this age it is usual to discover in the State Rooms five or six layers of paint, and in the more domestic parts as many as twenty or thirty.' A major feature of Clandon is the remarkable Marble Hall where

Leoni's austere façade, to which was added the clumsy porch and porte cochère in the 19th century.

The original colours of the saloon ceiling – blue, pink and yellow – survived the ubiquitous whitewash.

plasterwork by the Italian stuccoists, Artari and Bagutti, had been worked to imitate marble. Under the whitewash that liberally covered this, Fowler discovered that two distinct kinds of plaster had been used – 'icing sugar' for the ceiling, and a rougher plaster for the walls – allowing a subtle distinction that had been eliminated by the whitewash brush. The 'coldest house in England' lived up to its reputation when cold water used for cleaning off the whitewash froze in sheets to the walls.

There have been at least a dozen changes in fashion since the house was first decorated, and it was decided to choose the early eighteenth century as the period to which the body of decoration should be related. The house is probably unique in that the much of the colour scheme for this time is known, and the work was faithfully and skilfully carried out by local craftsmen, repeating what their predecessors had executed two centuries before.

The subtle, intangible but vital link with the family is still maintained. The present Earl and his family live in the old Home Farm, itself an Elizabethan farmhouse only a few hundred yards from the house, and on the site of the original manor.

Clandon's splendid Marble Hall, patiently restored.

THE NINETEENTH CENTURY

ARUNDEL CASTLE, WEST SUSSEX

In Arundel, 9 miles (14.5 km) w of Worthing,
10 miles (16 km) E of Chichester

THE perils and prizes of high office could not be better illustrated than by the brilliant, bloody, turbulent history of the Fitzalan Howards, lords of Arundel Castle. Three of them were beheaded; one was probably poisoned (he was canonized in 1970 as St Philip Howard); two nieces, Anne Boleyn and Catherine Howard, finished up on the block, and their unscrupulous uncle Thomas, the third Duke, would have followed them had not death taken off his ferocious master, Henry VIII, the day before his own execution was scheduled.

And through all this, the family kept its hold on the building which was begun by Roger de Montgomery about 1067. It was probably Montgomery who built the castle's most distinctive feature, the motte and bailey, and from a distance Arundel Castle looks like a child's vision of what a castle should be like, with the Duke's standard flying

The Library. Ecclesiastical motifs are strong : even the chimney pieces resemble chantries.

Arundel Castle stands dramatically on its chalk spur above the river Arun.

proudly from the bailey when he is in residence. In the latter part of the eighteenth century, however, and throughout the nineteenth, the entire interior underwent a remarkable transformation. In 1777, plans were made to restore the half-ruined building into a worthy ducal seat. Successive dukes, sharing the Victorian belief that they knew far more about medieval buildings than people who lived in the Middle Ages, turned Arundel Castle into the romantic Victorian idea of a medieval castle.

Henry, the fifteenth Duke, brought the vast programme to a conclusion in 1910, and not content with 'restoring' the castle, he built the enormous Catholic churches in Arundel and Norwich, capital of his titular county. For, by one of the engaging ironies of English history, the premier English duke who traditionally arranges the great state ceremonies for the sovereign – who, by law, must be Protestant – is a Roman Catholic. Everywhere in the castle is evidence of this long compact with the Old Faith, and deep preoccupation with religion. The great library resembles the interior of a Gothic church – even its fireplaces are in the form of Perpendicular chantries – and one of its exhibits is a portable altar. The library contains one of the richest collections of books on Catholicism in

England. In the so-called Victoria Room there is a portrait of Cardinal Newman by Millais. The eleventh Duke rebelled against the prevailing religiosity and turned the private chapel into a splendid but unwelcoming dining room about 1795. The fifteenth Duke restored the status quo by building a new private chapel in what has been described as the most perfect expression of the nineteenth-century Catholic revival. The third Duke, who sent Catherine Howard to her death, peers out sourly from among the group of family portraits in the Picture Gallery while in the East Drawing Room are the mementos of Mary, Queen of Scots – a prayer book and gold rosary which she bequeathed at her execution to her fellow Catholics.

It is in the Fitzalan Chapel in the parish church, however, that the paradox of a Catholic duke in a hostile Protestant country is brought home. Built in 1380 (and desecrated in 1643) it can only be entered from the castle and, with the tombs of its dukes from the fifteenth to the twentieth centuries, is quite different in atmosphere from the body of the church. (See also p. 45)

The much restored Norman keep and barbican.

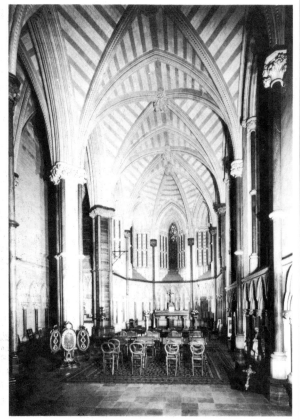

The Private Chapel: its stained glass, by John Hardman Powell, is inspired by that of Canterbury Cathedral.

Illuminated prayerbook and rosary carried by Mary, Queen of Scots, at her execution and bequeathed to the Howards.

CLIVEDEN HOUSE, BUCKINGHAMSHIRE

3 miles (4.8 km) from Maidenhead,
2 miles (3.2 km) N of Taplow on B476
The National Trust

CLIVEDEN House has entered political mythology as one of the great centres of manipulation – of 'fixing it' – between the two World Wars. Whether or not the so-called 'Cliveden Set' really did alter the course of affairs in the 1930s or whether, in Byron's words, its members 'thought they were running the world because they went to bed late', is still a matter of debate. But this great house, on its terrace high above the Thames, really was a magnet for the powerful as well as the merely fashionable, the gifted as well as the idle. Churchill, Henry James, Balfour and Rudyard Kipling were among those who joined the house parties presided over by the remarkable Nancy, Lady Astor.

The two previous houses on this site were both almost totally destroyed by fire. George Villiers, second Duke of Buckingham, built the first house, creating the vast terrace which his successors were to utilize. A baroque character –

> A man so various that he seemed to be
> Not one but all mankind's epitome

he killed the man he was cuckolding while the man's wife calmly looked on. (The shape of a duel sword, cut in the turf near the house, commemorates the event though the duel took place miles away near Putney.) His house was destroyed in 1795 and its successor in 1849. The present house was built by Sir Charles Barry (co-architect of the Houses of Parliament) in 1850 and was bought by the

The south front, overlooking the immense parterre and the river beyond, with the Borghese balustrade. Sir Charles Barry built this beautiful Renaissance house in 1850 for the Duke of Sutherland.

The Gothic Drawing Room, originally designed by Sir Charles Barry.

American millionaire, William Waldorf Astor, in 1893.

Although American by birth Astor, his son, and in particular his son's wife Nancy, became more English than the English – so much so that Nancy Astor became the first woman to enter the House of Commons as an MP. Astor senior spent vast sums improving the work of his predecessor, and remained true to the tycoon's creed that money really could buy anything. He cast his eye on the balustrade of the Villa Borghese in Rome and bought it for his splendid new house. The Italian government took the Borghese family to court for alienating a national work of art and received the Solomonic judgement that while the statues on the balcony were 'important antiques' the balcony itself was simply a 'decorative object'. Visitors to Cliveden may therefore lean on stonework which may once have been leaned on by Pauline Bonaparte.

Nothing prepares the visitor for the stupendous view from Cliveden's terrace. Entering from the Taplow Road, one is immediately confronted by a statuary group that almost achieves the level of kitsch – the vast Fountain of Love, created by an American sculptor living in Rome, depicting young maidens, in various stages of undress, reeling from the effects of Love. Astor commissioned this group specifically, which does raise doubts as to his aesthetic taste.

Beyond the fountain, the house becomes visible, compact and solid; and beyond that is the upper terrace with its startling view over the Thames which drew a gasp of admiration from John Evelyn, that connoisseur of vistas. It reminded him of

Thomas Story's Fountain of Love.

The stunning view overlooking the river Thames.

Frascati. The huge parterre, or formal garden, below does indeed seem designed for confidential political murmurings. It would be quite impossible to eavesdrop on those acres of lawn. The surrounding gardens are all heavily wooded – though carefully framing and not obscuring the vista – and from the opposite bank of the Thames the whole looks natural. But as with so much of the English landscape, what seems natural is of most careful construction. A visitor to Cliveden in 1793 described how the newly-planted trees were all anchored by ropes 'otherwise the Winds would tear 'em down'.

Astor's preference for classical antiquities are evident throughout the garden: Roman sarcophagi lined up dramatically against a dark yew hedge; the great Queen Anne's vase; the exquisite little Blenheim Pavilion and Octagon Temple. The interior of the house reflects the pastiche of the garden. Visitors to Cliveden may perhaps be startled by what appear to be copies of the Blenheim tapestries, commissioned by the Duke of Marlborough to commemorate the War of the Spanish Succession. Other, very similar tapestries were also to be found at Stowe and Stanmer, as well as a number of German schlosses. The canny Brussels weavers turned out a number of these tapestries, altering details to suit the buyers – and selling them to both sides.

Lord Astor left the house to the National Trust in 1942, and the Trust leased it in 1966 to Stanford University, California, honouring the Astors' wishes that Cliveden should be used 'to bring about a better understanding between the English-speaking peoples'.

ALNWICK CASTLE, NORTHUMBERLAND

In Alnwick, 30 miles (48.3 km) N of Newcastle, off A1

LOOMING up from the buttercup-strewn meadows along the river Alne, the exterior of Alnwick Castle is all that a medieval castle should be. There are even alert watchmen on the battlements, eighteenth-century copies of much earlier figures. But the interior is the Victorian idea of an Italian Renaissance palace. This contrast is the work of the fourth Duke of Northumberland. Like so many of his fellow aristocrats, he embarked on the Grand Tour of Italy in the early nineteenth century, and was much taken by the distinction between the exterior of most Italian palaces with their stark, uncompromising strength, and their luxurious interiors. He determined to create the same effect in Northumberland; it cost him more than a quarter of a million pounds in the 1850s, but he succeeded.

There has been a castle at this vital spot at least since the time of the Norman Conquest. In the early fourteenth century the Percy family, father and son, built most of the exterior which now stands. The first major changes took place during the eighteenth century when the first Duke of Northumberland transformed it from a castle into a residence. Canaletto's painting of the castle, now hanging in the Music Room, shows it shortly before these alterations. The greatest change is in the land itself, for the crags and crevices between castle and river, so evident in Canaletto's painting, have since been smoothed out by the busy Capability Brown, advancing the cause of civilization into the Northumberland wilds.

The great barbican or main gateway is unchanged, an entrance so important that it is virtually a little castle in its own right. Looking down through the gaps between the timber baulks of the bridge which it guards, one can see part of the recently excavated moat far below: once, it would have connected with the river. Through the less dramatic

The castle viewed across the river Alne. The bridge to the town, protected by the castle, lies to the right.

The utilitarian Guard Chamber transformed into a Renaissance interior. The pavement is of Venetian mosaic.

carriageway to the right, the visitor emerges from the shadow of the walls to see a great expanse of turf – the outer bailey – and rearing up from it the keep and the main mass of the castle. It is here that the Renaissance begins. The entrance hall of the keep is modest enough but it leads to the splendid Grand Staircase, each of whose treads is a single block of stone, twelve feet in length, from the nearby Rothbury quarries. The walls are lined with coloured Italian marble, and Venetian mosaic covers the floor of the Guard Chamber into which the staircase

The barbican, built about 1440, in effect a small independent fortress with its own garrison astride a moat.

The Grand Staircase, begun in 1861.

leads. Carved, gilded ceilings replaced Adam's designs. Time has a disconcerting habit of revealing truth in architecture as in everything else. To the fond eye of the fourth Duke and his Italian advisers, Staircase and Guard Chamber would have seemed perfect Renaissance structures but to the modern eye they are unmistakably nineteenth century, beautiful though they may be. The two great statues of Britannia and Justice in the Guard Chamber could be the product only of Victorian England.

There is an ordered richness throughout, cul-minating in the superb Red Drawing Room. The casual visitor will simply accept that order as though it were organic: the architect's drawings tell another story. The ceiling of the Drawing Room is composed of polygonal panels, but the room itself is irregularly shaped, having been altered to fit the design of the ceiling – a Procrustean solution that sums up the confidence and wealth of architect and patron.

The vast castle is no museum. Not only is it a family residence but it is also the heart of a huge working estate, including 6,000 acres of woodland and 160 farms. Tucked onto it, almost as an extension of it, is the little town of Alnwick. A large proportion of the local people earn their living, in one way or another, directly from the castle, and living here is rather like living in a garrison town where everyone is aware of the status of everyone else. The Percy lion, with its extraordinary tail sticking out like a poker, still guards the bridge that used to be the only access to the town from the north – the access that takes the traveller immediately under the walls of the barbican and its watchful statues. (*See also p. 139*)

MUNCASTER CASTLE, CUMBRIA

1 mile (1.6 km) SE of Ravenglass village on A595

THE name of Muncaster gives us a clue to its origin, for 'caster' is an indication of the Roman fort that once existed here, on the height which simultaneously defends the entrance to the Esk valley, and the little port of Ravenglass below. Today, Ravenglass is a quiet place, but as the Roman town of Glannoventa it was a vital link with the sea road that lapped Britain's coast.

Approaching Muncaster from the south is like driving over the edge of the world. It is necessary to go further and further south, before being able to turn north around the great mass of Furness Fells. Even today, the most direct route is from west to east along the Esk valley, and there is small wonder that the Romans took care to police this approach. (There are the ruins of another solid castle at Hardknott pass, about half way along the valley.) The remains of the fort are probably buried deep below the present castle, for coins of around AD 300 have been found.

The locations of military sites give a spectacular bonus: it was important to see the enemy at a distance and to have a clear expanse for retaliation. Muncaster enjoys such a bonus, and the views from the terrace can only be described as breathtaking. Edward VII, who prided himself on being widely travelled, proclaimed this the best view in Europe, and Ruskin impulsively described it as the 'gateway to Paradise'.

The castle went through a familiar cycle of change. The first post-Roman fort would have been built about 1260 by the Pennington family, to whom the lands had been granted half a century earlier. The massive pele tower – still a conspicuous feature of the garden front – was part of the considerable enlargement undertaken in 1325. During the Wars of the Roses Sir John Pennington gave shelter to Henry VI. According to legend, the King was wandering lost after the battle of Towton and was brought to the castle by a shepherd. Among the treasures shown at Muncaster is a fragile glass dish of indisputable age, known as the Luck of Mun-

The garden front of the house, as redesigned by Anthony Salvin, in pink granite.

The octagonal library, built in 1780 on the site of the medieval kitchen, with some alterations by Salvin in 1862.

The famous view from the terrace which led Ruskin to describe Muncaster as 'the gateway to Paradise'.

caster, supposedly given by the monarch to Sir John. It raises many questions. Why did the King express his thanks in so inexpensive a manner? How did the legend arise that the family's luck would hold good only as long as the bowl is intact?

Apart from the pele tower, little remains visually of the original building. Muncaster began its transformation into a purely residential building in the eighteenth century and then, in the nineteenth century, was 'medievalized' by Anthony Salvin. His patron, the young fourth Earl of Muncaster, Gamel Pennington, gave Salvin a very wide brief but died in 1862, at the early age of thirty-one, before the work was carried out. The Trustees of the estate, less enamoured with Gothick and shocked at the proposed expense, trimmed down Salvin's design to the benefit of the old building. Built in pink granite, Muncaster is still very much Salvin's work but without the flamboyance of Alnwick, remaining firmly within the vernacular tradition.

The Trustees' restraint, or Salvin's innate good sense, saved the beautiful octagonal library, built about 1780 on the site of the medieval kitchen. Salvin made a few interior alterations, but contented himself mostly with disguising the external shape. Much of the house's contents reflect the taste of an individual connoisseur, Sir John Ramsden, the sixth Baronet, who built up the collection between the two World Wars. But the drawing room, built on the site of a courtyard in 1861, contains one of the most complete collections of a family's portraits in England. Among them is one of the unfortunate Protector, first Duke of Somerset, father of Jane Seymour and thus grandfather of the short-lived Edward VI. The fifth Baronet married a descendant of Somerset – hence his portrait here.

HUGHENDON MANOR, BUCKINGHAMSHIRE

ONE of the problems for houses in the care of the National Trust is that, although they are well maintained and their future assured, inevitably they become museums as the families drift away. This is by no means the case at Hughenden Manor for although no member of the family lives there, it is pervaded throughout with the spirit of Benjamin Disraeli who bought it in 1848, spent his happy marriage here, and also died here in 1881.

Dizzy loved the place with a deep, personal, abiding love. But its acquisition was something of a contradiction in his nature. This Italian Jew with the affected manner, the ringlets and the dandified clothing, made his mark on the ultra-conservative British, not by playing down his mannerisms but by exaggerating them. The acquisition of that quint-essentially English institution, the 'country house', was doubtless initially a political gesture, the means whereby he showed the Commons, as he moved towards the leadership of the Tory party, that he too had his stake in the country. But, once established in it, his home ranked second in affection only to his beloved wife.

The house is pleasant and interesting, rather than distinguished, and were it not for that vibrant presence, it probably would not rank high on the

Francis Grant's portrait of Disraeli, 1852.

tourist circuit. It began life as a farm house, a 'house in the country', and was converted into a 'country house' (a distinction very real to the British) in 1738. John Norris, the antiquary, then acquired it, favouring the fashionable Gothick style beloved by the Disraelis.

The house cost Disraeli £35,000, most of it obtained on loan. Politics kept him in London, and much of the work of modernizing the house and laying out the garden fell on his wife, Mary Anne Disraeli. But husband and wife thought as one in all such things, and the garden is a perfect expression of them both. Sadly, Mrs Disraeli did not live to see the moment of the house's greatest splendour, and the almost unprecedented honour done to her husband when Queen Victoria visited the house in 1877. It was an informal affair – as much as Victoria's visits ever were informal – and she graciously planted a tree in her favourite's beautiful garden.

There are no great works of art at Hughenden,

Hughendon Manor – the entrance front. Disraeli's nephew, Coninsby, made some later alterations to the house.

The Library : in Disraeli's day this was the drawing room.

but the house is filled with mementos which throw a sudden, intimate light on some large historical canvas. In the so-called Berlin Congress Room is the cherry-wood fan, signed by all the statesmen who attended the Congress. Disraeli called the hall his Gallery of Friendship, for along it are hung portraits of the friends and allies he made through a long and active life. There are two portraits of Lord George Bentinck – that great 'swell', sportsman, politician and dandy – who generously came forward at the necessary moment and lent Disraeli a large sum to help buy the house.

Room uses have been switched around since Disraeli's time: what was the drawing room, with its distinctive Gothick arches, is now the library and vice versa. But Disraeli's study, which he called his workshop, is exactly as he left it. Victoria made a return visit to the house after his death, almost, one feels, as a pilgrimage and spent a long time in this comfortable but modest room. One of the pictures displayed is that famous cartoon in *Punch* that is a

key to the relationship between these two so very different people. In 1876 Disraeli secured for her the title of Empress of India and Tenniel's witty cartoon, *New Crowns for Old*, shows Disraeli as an exotic Oriental pedlar proffering the splendid crown of India to his queen.

Disraeli called his study 'my workshop'.

BELVOIR CASTLE, LEICESTERSHIRE

7 miles (11.3 km) WSW of Grantham between A607
(to Melton Mowbray) and A52 (to Nottingham)

ITS superb site, high on a dramatic ridge above the Vale of Belvoir gives this castle its name. William the Conqueror granted the land to his gallant standard bearer Robert de Todeni, who built the first castle, and whose massive stone coffin still resides here. But the castle itself has dizzily changed its form at least four times. The original Norman motte and bailey evolved into a crenellated fort, and in this form it came into the Manners family (later Earls and Dukes of Rutland) by marriage. Totally slighted after the Civil War it had been rebuilt by 1668, only to be demolished in the late eighteenth century as part of a massive rebuilding programme. Work began again in 1801, to Wyatt's design, and was all but completed when a great fire broke out on the morning of 16 October 1816. By the time it was brought under control, it had destroyed the entire north-east and north-west fronts, the great staircase and – far worse from an art history point of view – a number of great paintings, including Titians and Van Dykes.

The architects for much of the present building could best be described as talented amateurs, for they were a clergyman, the Reverend Sir John

Belvoir (pronounced 'beaver'), a magnificent martial building with many neo-Gothic features, is the romantic 19th-century concept of a medieval castle.

This aerial view of Belvoir castle shows its dominant position overlooking the Vale. This wooded hill-top has been a stronghold since the Norman conquest, for the first castle on this site was built by William the Conqueror's standard bearer.

The Elizabeth Saloon, named after the 5th Duchess.

The Elizabeth Saloon : detail of the painted ceiling.

Thoroton, and the Duchess of Rutland herself. Between them, this unlikely pair created a Gothic fantasy. The castle looks best either from a distance, when its multiple turrets do indeed seem lifted from a medieval illumination, or seen from inside. The details within are superb, from the Guardroom at the entrance, with its sweeping arches and stairways, to the richly worked Elizabethan Saloon, which started a new fashion for Louis XIV taste. Some

The Grand Staircase, with its portraits of the 5th Duke, and his wife Elizabeth, who played an important role in the creation of this Regency castle.

idea of the loss of paintings in that fire can be gained by the quality of the collection which survives, including works by Holbein, Teniers and Gainsborough. Altogether it is a curious coincidence that this castle, the ultimate in mannered reconstruction, should belong to the same family that owns Haddon Hall, an untouched survivor from the Middle Ages.

MELDON PARK, NORTHUMBERLAND

6½ miles (9.6 km) w of Morpeth off B6343

ON 17 October 1832, a flint glass box containing a newly minted sovereign of the reign of William IV was sunk in the turf of a plateau above the little Wansbeck river in Northumberland. Above this box, a massive two-ton block of honey-coloured stone was carefully lowered and the home of Isaac Cookson was begun.

The architect, John Dobson, would undoubtedly have been nearby. He had walked the grounds for an entire month, scrambling down the steep slope to the river and up again many times, looking for the perfect site. The fifty-year-old cedar tree planted then flourishes still, presenting something of a chronological problem to those unaware of the early nineteenth-century skill in horticulture. Dobson was then in his forty-fifth year and with a solid reputation behind him. He had done for his native Newcastle what Nash had done for London, creating a series of elegant streets whose design, though classical, was within the idiom of their day. After designing Meldon Park he built Newcastle Railway Station, establishing the archetypal railway station whose influence was to be felt around the world. On this October day, however, he was initiating the kind of work for which he now tends to be better known – building a home for a gentleman of substance.

Surely there can be no other period like the nineteenth century for an efflorescence of architectural styles. One tends to associate the entire century with the Gothick flamboyance which characterizes

Meldon Park, with Dobson's Ionic entrance porch.

its later stage. But here, in Northumberland, four years before the young Princess Victoria came to the throne, Dobson created for his patron a restrained, elegant, classical building – a perfect example of the Greek Revival.

Meldon Park is deceptively simple, a square building whose only external decorations are the severe Ionic columns of the porch. But this simplicity is the result of immense care. None of the features which disfigure houses from this date onwards – drainpipes, sewage pipes and the like – are visible: all are carefully tucked away behind that mellow stone. Even the gutterings are hidden by an elegant balustrade.

Inside, the house has the same indifference to its rural environment as Houghton. This is not so much a country house as a house in the country. The great rooms overlooking the secluded valley are not simply urban but metropolitan in feeling. The doors of the library are carefully disguised by false bookends, a device which tends to disconcert bibliophiles. But Meldon Park is very much a home, a fact to be put squarely to Dobson's account. In the words of the owner (a descendant of the Isaac Cookson for whom it was built), 'The house is easy to live in and very domestic: there is no oppression caused by grand scale for although the rooms are spacious they remain private, intimate.' The great vegetable gardens are slowly being brought back to life, one of its features being an enormous hollow wall which could be heated. As at Constable Burton, it forms a traditional part of a living country house.

The Library; the double doors are disguised as bookcases.

EASTNOR CASTLE, HEREFORD & WORCESTER

5 miles (8 km) from M50 (exit 2),
2 miles (3.2 km) E of Ledbury
on Hereford–Tewkesbury road (A438)

IT seems scarcely possible that the classical façade of the British Museum in London and the Gothic extravaganza of Eastnor could have come from the same hand. But the architect in both cases was Robert Smirke. The British Museum façade more closely approximates to the original inspiration than does Eastnor: no one could possibly mistake this for anything but the nineteenth-century whim of a rich man. But it is consistent throughout, even though its most characteristic feature, the great Gothic drawing room by Pugin, was not added until more than thirty years after Smirke had finished.

The work was commissioned by Lord Somers, who recorded in his detailed notebook on 23 June 1812, 'I laid this day the first ashlar ornamental stone, and placed under it a piece of money of Queen Elizabeth, my family having settled in Eastnor about that reign.' He provided some meticulous and interesting figures regarding its construction: 20,000 tons of stone and mortar were used in the first eighteen months, and 250 men were employed constantly over six years at a cost of £750 a week. The stone was brought from quarries in the Forest of Dean by barge and then ox-wagon at an overall

Pugin decorated the Drawing Room in 1849, drawing even more heavily on the 'Gothic' image than had Smirke.

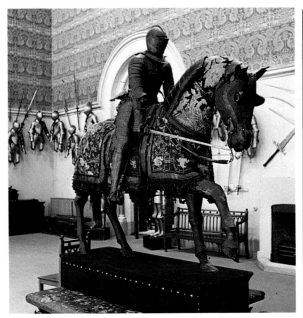

The equestrian armour is Italian, about 1640. The mural decoration may be derived from a Saracen banner.

The massive structure of the great towers as seen from the south front.

cost of £12,000. Shortage of timber, much of it swallowed up by the Napoleonic war, forced Smirke to improvize. He used cast iron stanchions for the roof trusses, their first known use in this manner, and they are still in good condition.

Eastnor is particularly interesting for its collection of art and armour. The third Earl Somers was an Italophile and brought back, among other treasures, tapestries from the Gonzaga palace in Mantua (originally woven for Catherine de' Medici) and a superb suit of armour belonging to the Visconti family of Milan.

Eastnor is also a refuge for the works of a Victorian painter who, immensely successful in his day, is undeservedly all but forgotten now. G.F. Watts was a friend of the third Countess and painted a number of frescoes for the Somers' London house at Carlton Terrace. The existence of five of these was reported to the Crown Commissioners in 1927 and in 1938 Joachim von Ribbentrop, the German ambassador then occupying the house as part of the German embassy, reported four more that had been boarded over. The frescoes were taken down in 1966 when the house was being drastically altered, and in 1976 were placed, on loan, in the Staircase Hall at Eastnor. Apart from the major collection now housed in the artist's home at Compton in Surrey, they form the biggest collection of the paintings of a man once known as 'England's Michelangelo'.

Eastnor, built in 1812 by Robert Smirke – the medieval castle as seen by a 19th-century romantic.

THE TWENTIETH CENTURY

CASTLE DROGO, DEVON

4 miles (3.2 km) NE of Chagford, 6 miles (1.6 km) S of A30
The National Trust

JULIUS Charles Drew, builder of Castle Drogo, was undoubtedly a nicer character than Sir William Thynne, builder of Longleat. But separated though they are by blood, time and customs, they nevertheless bear a curiously strong resemblance to each other. Both were self-made men, doggedly amassing a fortune. And both, having made that fortune,

The vast entrance with the motto Drogo Nomen Et Virtus Arma Dedit *(Drewe is the name and valour gave it arms).*

proceeded to spend a substantial part of it in creating a vast house. They also have another affinity, for one marks the beginning of a process and the other the end. Thynne's house was the first of the prodigy houses; Drew's house – one may fairly confidently predict – is likely to be the last castle built not only in England but in Europe.

Julius Drew, born in 1856, was very much a child of his time for he made his money out of the rapidly expanding British empire. Like so many young men of his day he 'went out East', to China, on behalf of his uncle Francis Peek in order to learn the mysteries of tea buying. Returning to England, he decided to set up business on his own. The result was the Home and Colonial Stores, its history exactly coinciding with the swift apogee and decline of the empire (it has now been absorbed into a well-known chain of stores). By the age of thirty-three Drew was so rich that he could retire and devote himself to his heart's desire. He had made his millions at about the same time, and in the same market, as Sainsbury and Lipton. Sainsbury stuck to business; Lipton threw his money into the sea in pursuit of yachting prizes, but Drew turned his money into stone.

His motives were common among self-made men from the time of classical Athens onward: having made his pile he wanted to backtrack and create, retrospectively, a dignity for it. This was the period when the would-be aristocrat did not simply buy land but also sought a title that would give a mellowness to his new-found wealth. Genealogists made a good living from that desire: a delighted Julius Drew was told that he was descended from the Drewes of Drewsteignton in Devon. They were descended, in their turn, from a certain Drogo or Dru who had 'come over with the Conqueror'.

The castle seen from below: the river Teigh lies behind and below, where the ground falls steeply away.

Given the ramifications of genealogy in a small, crowded and ancient island, there is no particular reason why the story should not be true. Julius Drew consulted a lawyer and, by deed poll, added that vital final 'e' to his name that made him of Norman descent. And as Julius Drewe of Drewsteignton he embarked upon the most ambitious of projects, the building of a castle to go with the name.

The construction of fake castles had become an obsession among the landed gentry during the nineteenth century. In 1857, Sir George Gilbert Scott had inveighed against what he called 'the monstrous practice of castle-building, unhappily not yet extinct. ... The largest and most carefully and learnedly executed Gothic mansion of the present day is not a sham fortress such as those of twenty years back, but it is a real and carefully constructed medieval fortress capable of standing a siege from an Edwardian army. Now this is the very height of masquerading.' Born just one year before Scott made his protest, Drewe would have grown to manhood at a time when 'the castle' most perfectly expressed the pretensions of power. And being essentially a conventional man, when he came to

Lutyens designed all the details at Castle Droga, even the furniture in the kitchen.

build his own house, he too thought in terms of something 'capable of standing a siege from an Edwardian army'. Nothing would be sham about it; from its granite foundations upward, everything must be real, everything must work as in a medieval fortress – even the portcullis over the main entrance to the castle.

He found the ideal architect in Edwin Lutyens. Behind him Lutyens already had some solidly successful commissions, while ahead of him lay the viceregal splendours of Delhi. It is a curious coincidence that this great architect should have built the last of the English castles and the last architectural expression of imperial power. Drewe and Lutyens admired each other, shared the same romantic but practical nature, had the same objective – and fought vigorously throughout the building of Castle Drogo, the tension between them proving creative, not destructive. As Lutyens said in one of his outbursts, 'I am very keen about your castle and must "fight" you when I know I am right.' The two of them made dozens of sketches through which it is possible to see the dream gradually becoming reality. At one stage Lutyens suggested cavity walls; Drewe insisted on authenticity throughout, even where it could not be seen. The walls were accordingly of solid granite with a necessary reduction in overall size.

The site was of pre-eminent importance: even in the twentieth century, a castle had to *look* as though capable of withstanding a siege. Drewe found it in the form of a great bluff above the gorge of the river Teigh. Even today the land that falls away from the castle is still wild – heather and pine-clad – with the stark moors rising on the other side of the gorge.

Work began in 1912. No one could have guessed that western civilization was plunging towards irrevocable change. But neither the cataclysm of World War I, nor the dizzily fragmenting society of the 1920s could halt the work. Drewe's eldest son was killed on the Western Front in 1917, but there were other heirs to ensure continuity and work went forward until 1930. After twenty years working upon his dream Julius Charles Drewe, descendant of Drogo the Norman, had exactly one year in which to enjoy his creation before he died in 1931. His son inherited it, and in due course his grandson who, while continuing to live there, gave the castle to the National Trust and so ensured the survival of Castle Drogo.

Lutyens' use of granite and oak to give a feeling of clean strength is shown in this corridor. Drewe's portrait hangs at the end of the passage.

Lutyens' genius has created a synthesis, not a pastiche. The overall external effect is undeniably house rather than castle, emphasized by the generous window spaces (simultaneously reminiscent of Hardwick Hall and Coventry Cathedral). But the internal details are those of a castle that has been modified to the comforts of twentieth-century life. Throughout, granite and wood are the media that speak of the past. There is a clean sparseness about the rooms which, flooded as they are with light, is curiously exhilarating. Lutyens panelled two rooms, the drawing room and the dining room, to soften the omnipresent granite. His genius extended to the smallest details: in the kitchen he designed not only the beautiful solid beech table, but also the pastry boards upon it – and even the draining boards by the sink. He placed the large portrait of Drewe on the landing of the splendid stairway so that the visitor ascends to it as to a shrine or memorial. But while this is Lutyens' design, it is Drewe's dream made substantial, one man working through the mind of another as always has been the case with the building of a great house.

GLOSSARY

aumbry Recess or cupboard in a church wall, originally for keeping sacred vessels, books etc.

banqueting house A small house in a garden, or small room in a house set aside for informal parties

bargeboard Endboard of a gable, usually decorated

Baroque Richly decorated style, originating in Italy *c.* 1600

battlements (also called crenellations). Regular openings in the parapet of a building for purposes of defence. Later (i.e. 18th and 19th centuries) used as decorative feature

belvedere Literally 'beautiful view'. Usually, a small detached building, built to command an attractive view

Brown, Lancelot 'Capability' (1715–83), architect and landscape gardener. His naturalizing style later became formalized

cantilever Projection (as in a staircase) supported at the wall end only

casement Window hinged on one side as opposed to sash

castellation See *battlements*

Chinoiserie Light-hearted imitation of Chinese motifs, usually 18th century

classical Style originating in, or derived from, ancient Greece or Rome

clerestory Windows along the upper part of a hall or church nave

corbel Projecting segment, or supporting block of a beam, usually decorated

crowsteps Stepped, or staggered, end of a gable, common in East Anglia due to its Netherlandish origin but rare elsewhere

cruck Primitive, massive form of timber-framing consisting of matched, curved timbers in an inverted v form

dissolution Technically, the 'resumption' into Crown hands of monastic properties, beginning with the Act of 1536 and completed by 1540

dais The raised platform at the end of a hall, separating the lord and his family from the household

Domesday book Census made for tax purposes in 1086

feudal system Pyramidical form of land tenure, based on relationship between lord and vassal. See also *manor*

friary House of mendicant, or preaching order, usually in or near urban locality (e.g. Dominicans at Blackfriars)

gable Triangular upper section of wall supporting a sloping roof

Gothic, Gothick Gothick was the first manifestation of the Gothic Revival, beginning *c.* 1750 and continuing into the early 19th century, relying largely on decoration. The Gothic Revival itself was based on greater archaeological knowledge and recreated medieval Gothic structurally. See also *Salvin, Smirke, Pugin*

Great Hall Main room of early medieval house

ha-ha Sunken fence, or ditch, designed to separate garden from park and so keep cattle out without visual boundary. Invented early 18th century

Kent, William (1684–17) Architect, sculptor, landscape gardener. Originated new style of landscape in England in contrast to formal, geometric gardens

Laguerre, Louis (1663–1721) He and his mentor Verrio (q.v.) covered acres of ceiling and walls with highly-coloured allegories, satirized by Pope. Came to England in 1683

lantern Turret, pierced with windows

Laroon, Marcellus (1679–1772) English-born genre painter

linenfold 16th-century panelling in form of hanging folds of linen

louvre (sometimes *louver*). Vent on roof or wall to allow smoke, cooking smells etc. to escape

manor Basic unit of territorial organization in feudal system

monastery House for enclosed order, as opposed to itinerant order, usually in remote areas (e.g. Benedictines)

neo-classicism Style, based on direct study of Greek and Roman originals, originating *c.* 1750

order The column (base, shaft, capital, entablature) in classical architecture: Doric – simplest and sturdiest form; Corinthian – ornamented with acanthus motif; Ionic – midway between Doric and Corinthian, i.e. more elegant than the former, less decorated than the latter

oriel Bay window

Palladian Of, or pertaining to the Italian architect Andreas Palladio (1518–80). Style introduced into early 17th-century England, revived a century later

pele tower Defensive tower, common in border countries from 13th to 15th centuries

piano nobile Literally 'noble floor'. In Italian palazzi, the first floor, reserved for the family; style later adopted in England

porte cochère Gateway and passage for vehicles through house into courtyard.

piscina Stone basin for water in a church

Pugin, Augustus (1812–52) Architect, ecclesiologist and writer, he believed that Christian religion was expressed only in Gothic art and no other

Repton, Humphrey (1752–1818) Landscape gardener, originally influenced by Capability Brown (q.v.)

Salvin, Anthony (1799–1881) Foremost 19th-century authority on medieval military architecture

screen Wooden, later stone, structure dividing service

area of Great Hall from the main area. The *screens passage* (between doors leading into service area and the screen) developed naturally from this

slighting The reduction, partially or wholly, by Parliamentary forces of a Royalist stronghold upon its capture

Smirke, Sir Robert (1781–1867) Architect. Although now best known for his classical work (e.g. the British Museum) his early career embraced the medieval (e.g. Eastnor Castle)

solar Derived from *solarium*. The 'sun room' on the upper floor of a medieval house. Used as family retiring room

Vanbrugh, Sir John (1664–1726) Dramatist and architect. His style was best suited to large-scale buildings, but he also designed a number of smaller houses

vernacular Of, or pertaining to, a region: not cosmopolitan

Verrio, Antonio (1639–1707) Charles II invited him to England to restore the Mortlake tapestries, but his first commission was at Windsor Castle. See also *Laguerre*

ENGLISH RIVERS & CANALS

Paul Atterbury

The river Severn near Buildwas, Shropshire. The upper reaches of the Severn are spectacular but this stretch of the river is unnavigable.

INTRODUCTION

England is patterned with thousands of waterways that have played their part in determining its landscape and history, and one of the best ways to enjoy the English countryside is to follow their routes. The great rivers, such as the Thames, the Avon and the Severn, and those with well-established tourist appeal, notably the rivers and streams that run through the Lake District, the Yorkshire Moors, the Derbyshire Dales, the Norfolk Broads or the Costwolds, are well known. However, for every waterway that is familiar, there are literally hundreds to be discovered anew. Among these are the man-made waterways, the network of canals that revolutionised industry in the eighteenth century but which later fell into disuse.

The shape of the English landscape was established during the Ice Age, when great glaciers carved out the broad river valleys. Later, forces of erosion, particularly wind and water, cut the deeper valleys, gorges and defiles that allow rivers and streams to drain the higher ground. The nature of the English landscape is sharply varied, a pattern that is clearly evident on the ground. The most dramatic scenery is in the north, where rivers have forced their way through solid rock, cutting narrow gorges and falling precipitously into steep valleys: Teesdale in Durham and Wensleydale in Yorkshire are typical examples of this spectacular landscape. Totally different are the placid rivers of the south coast, the Arun, the Ouse and the Cuckmere, which flow gently through wide valleys in a series of meandering curves. These meanders and the oxbow lakes they often create are the legacy of far more powerful rivers that carved out the wide deep valleys in which they flow. The Thames valley, for

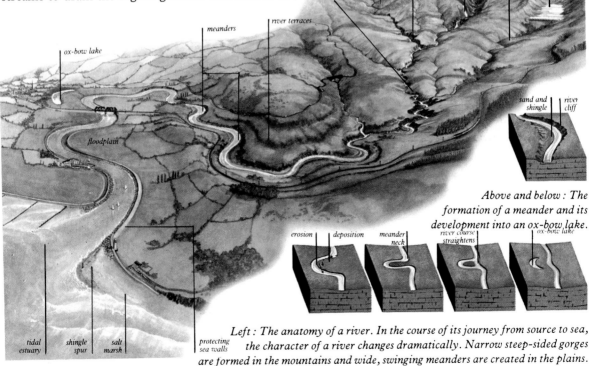

Above and below: The formation of a meander and its development into an ox-bow lake.

Left: The anatomy of a river. In the course of its journey from source to sea, the character of a river changes dramatically. Narrow steep-sided gorges are formed in the mountains and wide, swinging meanders are created in the plains.

The river Thames and the Pool of London from Tower Bridge, a view that includes some of London's most historic buildings.

example, is a wide stretch of low-lying land, flanked on the north by the Cotswolds and the Chilterns, and on the south by the Downs. Today the river, its flood plain and tributaries only fill a fraction of the huge valley that was formed in the Ice Age. From its source in the Cotswolds, the Thames falls steadily to its tidal estuary at sea level. Along its course are several large towns and cities, generally situated at important river junctions. Thus Oxford sits where the Cherwell joins the Thames, Reading surrounds the mouth of the Kennet, while London rests in a huge basin encircled by higher ground. London is situated there simply because it grew up as a settlement marking the last place where the river could be crossed before it joined the sea, and the highest point that boats could reasonably reach on the tide.

The course of a river can reflect the pattern of history over several centuries. Within a few miles its banks may reveal a Roman settlement, a medieval village, a cathedral, an eighteenth-century manor house with landscaped park, a corn mill, the wharves and warehouses of an inland port, a Victorian factory, a railway, a motorway and a modern housing estate. The river was for centuries the centre of village life, supplying water, food, power and sometimes transport, draining and irrigating the fields, supporting livestock and crops, supplying

entertainment and relaxation for the villagers and, by means of a bridge or ferry, giving the village strategic importance. A key building in any village was the mill which used water power to grind flour, the staple element in a rural diet. In the Middle Ages the mills, and thus the rivers too, were often controlled by the church, a reflection of the traditional position of the church as the source of wealth and power. Large and extravagant churches are still to be found in many riverside villages. During the gradual process of industrialisation mills and factories were built to exploit the river as a source of power, and locks and weirs were erected to make the river navigable and to allow boats to bring in raw materials for manufacturing processes and open up new markets for agricultural produce. From these small beginnings grew the Industrial Revolution, made possible by the ready availability of water power and water transport. Throughout the eighteenth century villages were turned into centres of industry, their growth encouraged by the spreading network of canals. Canal building became a mania and the most surprising and unlikely schemes were proposed. In the initial enthusiasm some of the wilder projects were actually built, plunging their backers into financial ruin. Many of these obscure canals can still be explored, picturesque memorials to misplaced optimism. Others, less obscure, are now being rescued from oblivion and restored for a new life of pleasure use.

The rivers have often played a role in the more turbulent periods of English history. The course of a waterway forms a natural barrier and for centuries boundaries have been drawn along the banks of rivers, separating countries, rival families, or regions in dispute. The routes of many rivers are marked by medieval castles built to guard a boundary or to control crossing points. Bridges, now purely objects of convenience, were originally of great strategic and economic importance, for the control of a bridge was effectively the control of the region. Today rivers still form the boundaries of a large number of counties; these may be simple administrative divisions but they are based on well-established historical precedents. Many important battles, from the Roman invasion to the Civil War, took place near rivers and their sites can be visited. Evidence of more recent military history is also hidden along the banks of the rivers and canals, notably the concrete block houses and defences hastily erected in 1940 when it appeared that every waterway would form a defensive line to hold up the German invasion.

A river is a means of draining the landscape and is thus a part of the rainwater cycle, and it is also a source of water supply. Although apparently random, this drainage pattern has been controlled by man for centuries. Certain parts of England have been radically altered by the control of water. The rich farmlands of the Fens were created from useless sodden salt marshes by the drainage schemes devised by Dutch engineers in the seventeenth century, while in the near future, the character of many major rivers could well be altered when tidal barriers turn seaways into pleasant waterways. Natural changes can also affect a river in a relatively short time. Some of the Cinque Ports of the south coast that were busy international seaports in the Middle Ages are now up to a mile inland, their harbours closed by silting.

Splendid churches in a timeless river landscape are one of the great delights of England's waterways. This fine church is at Fotheringhay, Northamptonshire.

George Cruikshank's eighteenth-century satire of a canal meeting, produced at a time when the enthusiasm for canals had become a veritable mania.

Today in England floods and droughts are rare, for water supply is controlled by a carefully balanced network of rivers, lakes and reservoirs that incorporates natural and man-made waterway courses. This network is the responsibility of a number of large regional water authorities. Apart from flood control, drainage, and domestic and industrial water supply, these authorities also deal with pollution, fishing and rights of navigation. The canals and some river navigations, such as the Weaver in Cheshire, are the responsibility of the British Waterways Board, which maintains the network, licenses pleasure boats, and looks after commercial transport and the interest of fishermen.

Increasing pollution has affected the role of the rivers during the last two centuries. Until the late eighteenth century rivers were the main source of fresh water; much of London's drinking water, for example, came from the Thames up to the early nineteenth century. The spread of industrialisation and rapid growth of towns and cities along the river banks turned the waterways into open sewers, however. Only in the last 30 years has any real progress been made in cleaning England's waterways but the strict controls now in force have brought salmon and trout back to rivers such as the Thames after a gap of over 150 years. Today the greatest problem is combating the pollution caused by farmers, whose pesticides and fertilisers are washed into small streams and make their way into larger rivers, affecting a wide range of plant and wildlife many miles away.

Fishing used to be an important part of the economic life of any tidal river but today the scale of the industry is such that most English rivers are simply too small to play a part in it. Commercial fishing survives in the oyster beds of East Anglia and the salmon rivers of the Welsh border, for example, and many small rivers have acquired a new economic significance with the spread of fish farming. However, in most areas, fishing has now become a weekend sport. Sport fishing is an increasingly popular hobby and its many practitioners can be seen lining the canal banks or enjoying the exclusive stretches of water reserved for game fishing.

The nature of boating has also undergone a radical change. Until the twentieth century the majority of boats on England's rivers and canals were involved with trade. The different characteristics of each waterway and the variety of trades plied upon them resulted in an astonishing range of strictly localised types of boat all built in a distinctive style for a specific purpose: the Humber keel, the Severn trow, the Thames barge, the Broadlands wherry, the canal narrowboat. The decline in water transport during this century has caused many of these boat types to become extinct, while others survive solely through careful preservation by enthusiasts. A trip to a river navigation or canal today will reveal a great range of boats but nearly all of these are for pleasure use; built in a universal style they are equally at home on the Ure or the Wey. Watching boats and ships is one of the greatest

A Humber keel sailing on the Stainforth and Keadby Canal in the late nineteenth century, when these boats were a familiar sight in the north-east.

Much loved by Constable, the meandering course of the river Stour in Essex is typical of the landscape that surrounds so many of England's smaller waterways.

pleasures of the waterways, whether they are the small skiffs, canoes or sailing dinghies common on the smaller rivers, or the great tankers and freighters sailing to and from the estuary ports.

Ports, harbours and docks are well worth exploring. England's waterways are full of reminders of the history of inland and coastal navigation from the Roman period onwards. Many towns and cities contain the remains of important, but often forgotten, river ports of the past. Norwich, Wisbech and King's Lynn reflect the maritime prosperity of the medieval period and the seventeenth century. Stourport, Bewdley and the other ports of the Severn reflect the Industrial Revolution of the eighteenth century. Liverpool, Manchester and the cities of the north-east look back to the wealth of the British Empire in the Victorian age. Felixstowe is a product of the modern container revolution. There are plenty of delightfully obscure little ports to be discovered too, for example, Winchelsea in Kent, or Morwellham in the West Country, fascinating ghosts of former maritime glory. Also interesting are the ports and harbours associated with military

history, notably the great naval dockyards that date back to the seventeenth century, such as Portsmouth and Chatham; the shipyards of the Tyne, the Wear, the Tees and the West Country where so many warships were built; and the small docks that grew in importance during the First and Second World Wars, for example the Channel ports and the river navigations of the south coast.

There are about 2000 miles of rivers and canals in England that are fully navigable and many hundreds of smaller waterways that can be explored by canoe or by some other type of portable boat. Navigable rivers and canals are usually well equipped with footpaths that follow the routes of former towing paths, and they can be explored just as well on foot. Smaller rivers and streams often flow through private land, however, and where this occurs walkers should make sure they keep to the official footpaths. England's waterways offer an extraordinary range of linear journeys, as the following pages reveal. All that is needed to enjoy them at first hand is a good map, plenty of time, a fresh eye, and a certain willingness to get out of the car and walk.

The rock-strewn and remote course of the East Okement river near Belstone provides a good introduction to the scenery of Dartmoor.

THE WEST COUNTRY

The landscape of the West Country has a wild and rugged quality, its age continuing to defy the smooth hand of civilisation. It is a dramatic landscape, rich in mystery, and one that reflects the region's spirit of independence. Over the centuries this spirit has survived successive invasions from the east and still retained its distinctive character. Even tourism, the greatest, and potentially the most damaging invasion of all, has not been able to alter radically the nature of the West Country.

To the west the landscape is rocky, thickly wooded in parts, and fringed by powerful cliffs and headlands. These features have determined the nature of the rivers which flow quickly through steep and twisting valleys before joining the sea in huge tidal estuaries that reach far inland. Further east, the rocks give way to hills that surround vast tracts of moorland. Bodmin Moor, Dartmoor and Exmoor are drained by numerous streams and rivers that flow away in all directions to wind their way to the sea. The south Devon estuaries retain the dramatic style of Cornwall, slightly softened by trees and the effects of years of cultivation, but in the north the coast and the estuaries become gradually wider and more generous, preparing for the transition to the rolling hills and flat marshlands of Somerset. These lands are riddled with waterways, many natural and many man-made for drainage purposes. Sedgemoor and the other moorlands of Somerset have a unique quality that has remained unaltered for centuries, which is why they have recently become the front line in the battle between agriculture and conservation.

The landscape has determined the development of the region. In Cornwall most major towns and cities have developed either on the coast, or in the sheltered corners of the river estuaries, a pattern that has not been changed by subsequent social or economic events. The traditional industries, fishing, boat-building and mining, are all dependent upon water, and the control of water. These industries encouraged the Cornish habit of self-reliance, an independence that has only been weakened in the last century, first by the coming of railways and road transport, and second by the gradual decline of the industries native to the region. For centuries the impact of mining has radically affected the landscape but with its gradual decay and the passage of time these effects have softened to become a major source of tourism. Only in the clay pits around St Austell is it still possible to imagine the appearance and feel of the West Country at the height of the Industrial Revolution.

Devon and Somerset are softer counties. Along the banks of their rivers, in their villages and towns, in their fine houses, parish churches and mills, in their rolling, well-ordered fields a more settled pattern of history is apparent. The rivers are longer, deeper and flow more gently, penetrating deep into the country and linking large inland towns and cities with the sea. There is a long history of river navigation, dating back to the sixteenth century and beyond, while the power of agriculture and industry in the eighteenth century inspired a most adventurous series of river and canal schemes, the relics of which can be explored throughout the region. One of the distinctive, and more confusing features of Devon and Somerset is the river names. There is an Otter and an Ottery, a Carey and a Cary, two Axes and an Exe, two Fromes and three Yeos, not to mention the Wolf, the Camel, the Deer, the Thrushel and the Parrett. It is all rather eccentric, and essentially English.

Lanhydrock House was built in the seventeenth century and has splendid formal and landscaped gardens. It stands overlooking the river Fowey in west Cornwall.

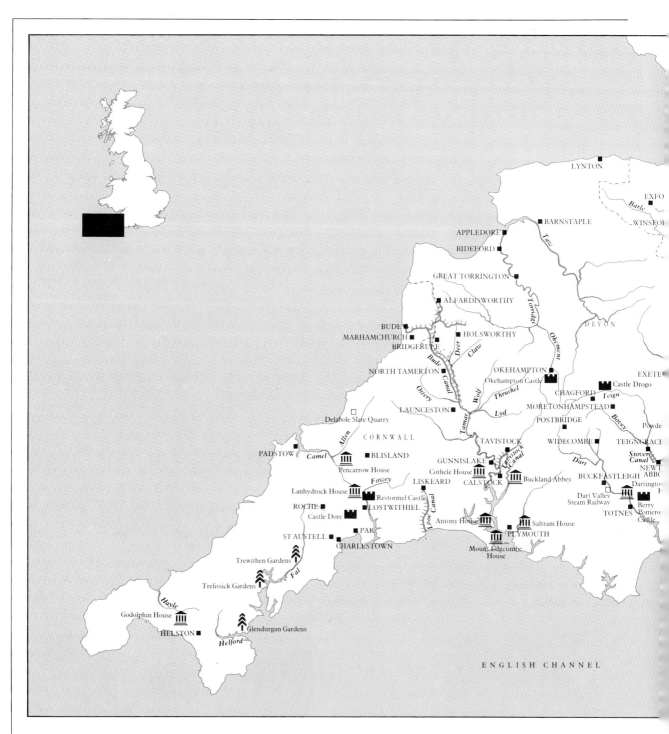

The rivers of west Cornwall

Dramatic tidal estuaries, long fingers of water, their steep sides thickly wooded, exploring the rocky landscape, leading to secret corners accessible only by water; these are the features of the west Cornish rivers.

The river **Hayle** rises in the hills near Godolphin House, built between the fifteenth and the seven-teenth centuries, and associated with the develop-ment of the Arabian horse in the eighteenth century. The course of the river is flanked by the remains of the Industrial Revolution, abandoned mines and quarries, the ruined engine houses and the mighty steam-powered beam engines that made the Revol-ution possible. The development of steam power was largely a Cornish activity, inspired by the need

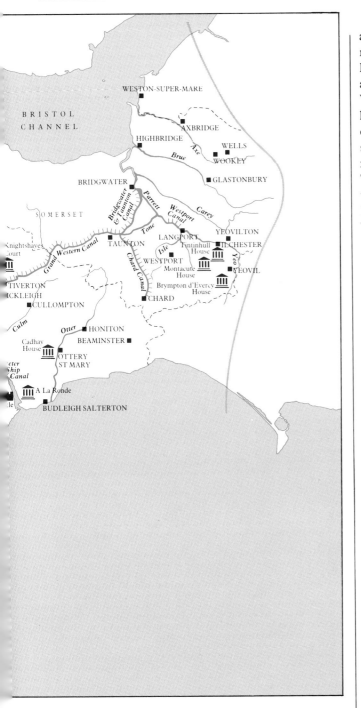

associations with Daphne du Maurier's novels. The river rises near Helston where there is a family leisure park that includes a Flambards village and an aircraft museum, while just to the north is the Wendron mining museum. The Helford estuary is known for its oysters and also for its gardens, many of which are semi-tropical because of the gulf stream. A good example is Glendurgan, at the mouth of the river. Other notable gardens, such as Trelissick and Trewithen, surround the **Fal** estuary, several miles of wandering tidal waterway linking the towns of Falmouth, Penryn and Truro. The Fal itself rises far inland, near the village of Roche with its unusual chapel, and then flows through a remote region dominated by the workings of the china clay industry before entering a wooded valley at Tregony.

The capital of the clay industry is St Austell, with its associated ports at Charleston, Par and Fowey. In the past Par was a centre for the export of the products of other industries, notably lead, tin and copper. A network of tramways and railways connected the mines with the port, and there were some small canals as well. Many of these were built by a notable mine owner, J. T. Treffry, and a suitable monument to him is a huge tramway viaduct, now isolated and forgotten in the thick woods that surround the valley of the **Par** river. To the east is the estuary of the **Fowey**, one of a number of rivers that drain Bodmin Moor. Its course is flanked by history: slate mines and subterranean caverns; the seventeenth-century splendour of Lanhydrock House with both formal and landscaped gardens; the ruins of the twelfth-century Restormel Castle; the town of Lostwithiel; while the estuary is overlooked by Castle Dore, a hillfort associated with the romantic legend of Tristan and Iseult.

Before leaving the south coast, it is worth making a slight detour to the **Looe** valley. The scenery is spectacular, a steep-sided valley cut through the rocks with at its base a fast-flowing river, a railway and a little road. At one time all methods of transport were represented here for in 1829 a canal was squeezed into the valley, linking Looe and Liskeard. Until the 1860s the canal was busy with boats full of agricultural produce, lime and, in particular, copper from the mines at Caradon Hill but the coming of the railway brought about its decline and it finally closed in 1909. Much of it has vanished, but old warehouses and the remains of some of the 25 locks can still be seen.

to drain the mines of flood waters, and Harveys of Hayle became one of the largest manufacturers of steam engines, exporting their products throughout the world from the ports of Cornwall. Having passed through the centre of Hayle, the river joins the sea in the wide sandy expanse of St Ives bay.

On the south coast is the thickly wooded estuary of the **Helford** river, noted for its seals and for its

On the north Cornish coast is the estuary of the river **Camel** which cuts its way inland to Wadebridge. The course of the river itself is a broad sweep from its source near Camelford, along the fringes of Bodmin Moor, through woodlands to the outskirts of Bodmin and then a sharp turn towards the sea. Near the river are gardens, an interesting church at Blisland, and the eighteenth-century elegance of Pencarrow House, while on the estuary are the seaside pleasures of Padstow. A tributary, the **Allen**, leads to Delabole, a slate quarry over 500 feet deep which has been worked continuously since the sixteeenth century. It is the largest man-made hole in England.

The Tamar and its tributaries

The **Tamar**, which rises near Youlstone just north of Bude on the north coast, almost cuts the West Country into two and is therefore an effective boundary between Devon and Cornwall. Its upper

The waterwheel at Morwellham, which was once a busy port and is now home to an industrial museum. The quays and warehousess can still be seen.

Tavistock in south Devon. The town takes its name from the river Tavy and was linked to Morwellham by the Tavistock Canal.

Morwellham. This featured locks, an aqueduct, inclined planes and a tunnel 2540 yards long. Morwellham became a major inland port, with wharfs able to handle 300 ton schooners. The reason for all this activity was the Devon Great Consols Mine, a group of copper mines on the east side of the Tamar that had grown up around the biggest lode of copper in Europe. They were at their peak during the first half of the nineteenth century and produced in all $3\frac{3}{4}$ million tons of copper, as well as arsenic, lead, tin and iron ore. In the late nineteenth century the industry slowly declined as the mines were exhausted and the canals closed, and gradually the whole area began to revert to its pre-industrial form. Morwellham became a ghost town, its quays overgrown, its buildings abandoned. Today, many of the remains of the Tamar's industrial boom are preserved and visitors to Morwellham can explore through them a chapter of West Country history that is hard to imagine now.

The maritime associations of the Tamar are, of course, far older, and have brought wealth to the river since the sixteenth century. The estuary is surrounded by fine houses, dating from the sixteenth to the eighteenth centuries: Buckland Abbey where Drake lived; Cothele House; Antony House; Saltram and Mount Edgcumbe. There were shipyards along the river, at Calstock and at Plymouth, a town associated with the Royal Navy since the sixteenth century, and still active as a naval base today.

reaches are remote and relatively inaccessible, to be seen only at quiet villages such as Alfardisworthy, Bridgerule and North Tamerton. It shares its seclusion with a number of tributaries that fan out in a great circle, the **Ottery**, the **Deer**, the **Claw**, the **Carey**, the **Wolf**, the **Thrushel**. These romantically named rivers can only be explored on foot. Villages are few, far between and pleasantly undeveloped, and the only town of any size is Holsworthy. At Launceston the Tamar emerges from its seclusion and then follows a winding wooded valley to Gunnislake. Along its route can be seen the achievements of both man and nature. There are many early bridges, there are fine houses, while on its tributary, the **Lyd**, there is a ruined castle, a dramatic gorge and a 90 foot waterfall. From Gunnislake southwards the Tamar is just as spectacular, but the achievements it records are of a different sort. The Tamar is tidal, and therefore navigable, from Morwellham to the sea but in the early nineteenth century boats could travel far further. The Tamar itself was extended northwards by the curiously named **Tamar Manure Navigation**, while the more significant **Tavistock Canal** was opened in 1817 to link Tavistock with

Brunel's Royal Albert Bridge crosses the river Tamar at Saltash. The river is still used as a safe anchorage by large ships that moor beneath the bridge.

The Bude Canal

Although there is little to be seen today, the north Cornwall port of Bude was, in the eighteenth century, seen as the starting point for a whole network of canals that were to run for 95 miles all round north Cornwall. At the same time the promoters of the Tamar Navigation conceived a canal along the line of the Tamar to Tamerton, north of Launceston, where it would link with the Bude Canal to create a complete cross-country waterway network. In the event these grand schemes came to nought, but the idea of the Bude Canal was revived in 1817. By 1825 over thirty-five miles of canals had been built, a main line and three branches, designed primarily to carry sea sand to inland farms where it was used as a fertiliser. A feature of the **Bude Canal** were the inclined planes, whereby boats were hauled up slopes by water or steam power, rising in the process up to 200 feet. The boats themselves were fitted with iron wheels so that they could be drawn up the rails of the inclined planes without being unloaded. West Country canal engineers tended to favour inclined planes rather than locks, as typified by the Bude Canal. This extraordinary network remained in operation until the late nineteenth century when it succumbed to railway competition, but much of its route can still be discovered by the enthusiastic explorer, including the sites of some of the inclined planes, notably at Marhamchurch, Hobbacott Down and Tamerton.

This short stretch of canal and a sea lock at Bude are relics of the Bude Canal, built in the nineteenth century to carry sea sand inland for use as fertiliser.

Decorative plasterwork is a major feature of Saltram House near Plymouth, designed by Robert Adam. Saltram is easily accessible from the river Tamar.

Dartmouth in Devon. A typical West Country port set in a wooded river valley, it has been used as a safe anchorage for centuries.

Through the efforts of the canal, Holsworthy became a port town, a description still used by some today. Some of the old wharves and warehouses can be seen outside the town.

The rivers of Dartmoor

A number of rivers flow southwards from Dartmoor to the south Devon coast, of which the most important are the Dart, the Teign and the Bovey. The **Dart** is a particularly attractive river, varied in character and easy to explore by car. Its two arms rise in the centre of Dartmoor, tumbling streams crossed by early clapper bridges as they cut their way through moor and woodland. A fine place to visit is Postbridge and nearby is Widecombe, with its famous fair in September. The arms come together at Dartmeet and it flows through a wooded valley to Buckfastleigh where there are a variety of attractions including an abbey, a museum of shells and the Dart Valley Steam Railway, which is the best way to enjoy the river. To the south is the Dartington Hall arts complex and then the river reaches Totnes and the limits of the tidal estuary. A tributary leads to the romantic ruins of Berry Pomeroy Castle, buried in the woods. The Dart estuary is thickly wooded and is best seen from one of the regular boats operating between Totnes and Dartmouth. Its mouth is guarded on each side by castles.

The **Teign** is tidal from Teignmouth to Newton Abbot and then turns northwards, flanking Dartmoor until it enters a wooded valley by Dunsford. Its upper reaches are surrounded by prehistory and overlooked by Castle Drogo, one of the last country houses to be built in England. Nearby is the attractive village of Chagford.

The **Bovey** is a tributary of the Teign, branching westwards between Newton Abbot and Bovey Tracey. It rises in the heart of Dartmoor, near Moretonhampstead, and then follows a wooded course through the moor. In the 1790s a short canal was built, from Teigngrace, north of Newton Abbot to the estuary. This, the **Stover Canal**, had a remarkably useful life and remained active until 1939. Its main traffic was clay, which was shipped in vast quantities from the Teign estuary to the Mersey, from whence it was carried to the Potteries in narrow boats along the Trent and Mersey Canal. The Stover Canal was also used to transport granite from the Haytor quarries, the stone used to build, among other things, the British Museum.

The Torridge and the Taw

The **Torridge** and the **Taw** share a common estuary on the north Devon coast, a long stretch of tidal water that links Bideford and Barnstaple. Both rise in Dartmoor, the Taw directly, the Torridge via its tributaries, and both flow northwards through typical Devon scenery to the sea. The Taw is easy to explore, flowing through a variety of small villages until it reaches Barnstaple, the first town of any significance, and its route is enjoyable, though predictable. The Torridge is more varied. It is linked to Okehampton by its tributary the **Okement**, a river overlooked by the ruins of Okehampton Castle, said to be haunted by Lady Howard, a blend of the Hound of the Baskervilles and Lady Macbeth, who each night runs from Okehampton to Tavistock in the form of a hound. The upper reaches of the Torridge are quiet and inaccessible, and inspired Henry Williamson to write *Tarka the Otter*. Great Torrington, a hilltop town of style, is approached through a wooded valley. For 50 years, until the 1870s, there was a canal between Torrington and Bideford. It is mainly represented today by an impressive five-arched aqueduct over the river

Great Torrington, a handsome and traditional market town, is one of the attractions of the river Torridge in north Devon.

Torridge which is now used to carry the drive to Beam House, north of Torrington. Below Torrington the river becomes tidal, and sweeps through Bideford and under the medieval bridge. Bideford, a handsome town and formerly a seaport of some significance, is ranged along the west bank. From here in the seventeenth century, ships that were probably built at Appledore on the mouth of the estuary, where there is still a busy shipyard, sailed for America, loaded with pilgrims and cargoes of locally made pottery.

The Exe

Devon's major river is the Exe. It rises in Exmoor, south of Lynton, and then flows across the moor, through Exford, Winsford and other small villages. It is joined by a number of tributaries, the most interesting of which is the Barle whose best feature is the 17-arch prehistoric clapper bridge at Tarr Steps. Between Exbridge and Tiverton the river is in a wooded valley, overlooked by the gardens of Knightshayes Court and the medieval Tiverton Castle. Between Tiverton and Exeter the landscape is more open and the main feature is the village of Bickleigh with its working water mill, medieval castle and farm museum. Exeter is an inland port of great antiquity. There has been a canal linking the city with the Exe estuary since 1566, and since the 1830s this has been a ship canal, allowing vessels up to 400 tons to enter the city. The canal follows the course of the Exe but is quite separate from it. Its terminal basin, near the city centre, is flanked by early Victorian warehouses, markets and the Custom House of 1681. The basin now houses the Exeter Maritime Museum with its collection of boats and ships of all periods and many countries;

The wild landscape of Exmoor, which is bisected by hundreds of small, fast-flowing streams. Its rolling moorland is the haunt of wild ponies and red deer.

The Exeter Maritime Museum, which has a collection of ships and boats from all over the world, is housed in the old warehouses of the Exeter Ship Canal.

included is one of the wheeled tub boats from the Bude Canal. Originally a Roman city, Exeter has a fine cathedral and interesting buildings dating from many periods. South of the city the Exe becomes a wide waterway, overlooked by the fifteenth-century Powderham Castle and A La Ronde, a unique sixteen sided house built in 1795, before it joins the sea at Exmouth.

A major tributary of the Exe is the **Culme**. It rises in the Blackdown Hills and flows through cider country to Cullompton where it is joined by the M5 motorway, whose continuing presence spoils what was an enjoyably quiet river. Further to the east along the coast is Budleigh Salterton, and the mouth of the **Otter**. This also rises in the Blackdown Hills but its course is more interesting, passing through Honiton and Ottery St Mary, and flanked by a number of fine houses and gardens, the best of which is the sixteenth-century Cadhay House.

The Somerset rivers and canals
East of the Quantocks the landscape changes, the rolling hills giving way to the low-lying marshlands of Somerset. These are drained by innumerable ditches and streams, many of which are man-made, as well as a number of major rivers. The most significant of these is the **Parrett**, once the centre of a chain of navigable rivers and canals that were originally conceived as an inland through route from Bristol to Exmouth. This ambitious project was never completed, but the remains and relics of its surviving components make a fascinating study for those keen to understand the 'canal mania' that gripped so many speculators during the late eighteenth and early nineteenth centuries. The course of the Parrett is from its mouth at Bridgwater Bay on the Bristol Channel, a remote area of mud flats that is now a nature reserve noted for its wildfowl, through the town of Bridgwater to Langport, the present limit of navigation. Until the 1870s, it was possible for boats to continue past Langport, whose elegant Georgian waterfront reveals its former importance, and then take either the river **Isle** and the **Westport Canal** to Westport or the river **Yeo** towards Ilchester. It is still possible to find the canal basin and its associated warehouses at Westport.

The Rolle Aqueduct, a spectacular memorial to a long abandoned waterway. It used to carry the Torrington Canal over the river Torridge in north Devon.

Tarr Steps, a prehistoric clapper bridge across the river Barle in Exmoor. A simple chain of stone slabs, the clapper bridge form is primitive but effective.

Although never navigable, the upper reaches of the Yeo are particularly rich in attractions. Around Yeovil there are a number of fine houses, including Montacute, Tintinhull and Brympton D'Evercy, while at Yeovilton there is the Fleet Air Arm Museum. Nearer Langport are the ruins of Muchelney Abbey.

Another tributary of the Parrett, the **Tone**, was made navigable from 1717, linking Taunton to Bridgwater and thus to the sea. Taunton in turn became an inland port of some significance and inspired the building of a number of other canals and waterways. The first of these was the **Grand Western Canal**, an undertaking planned to link Taunton with the river Exe south of Exeter. Work began in 1810 at Tiverton, but it was not until 1838 that it reached Taunton, and then it went no further.

Within ten years it was suffering from railway competition and by 1867 the Taunton half was closed. The Tiverton end fared better and remained in use until the 1920s, and then decayed quietly until 1971 when an ambitious restoration project began to bring it back to life. Today, it is possible to cruise along the restored section of the Grand Western Canal in a horse-drawn barge. The Taunton section of the canal must have been more dramatic as it featured seven vertical boat lifts and one inclined plane, but in most cases only the sites of these strange contrivances survive.

The second canal to reach Taunton was the **Bridgwater and Taunton**, opened in 1827 to provide a more direct route between the two towns. This survived in regular use until about 1907, and is still in good condition, although isolated from other waterways. The third was the **Chard Canal**, opened in 1842 between Taunton and Chard, and closed only 25 years later. This canal featured four inclined planes, three tunnels and a few aqueducts and, considering its short life, a surprising amount can still be seen. Although unconnected to the main Somerset network, another canal in this region that should not be forgotten, the **Glastonbury Canal**, was opened in 1833, linking Highbridge on the Brue estuary with Glastonbury. This survived for only 21 years, and few remains can be seen.

The Somerset rivers and canals have much to offer the visitor, including the distinctive marshland landscape with its interesting wildlife, the many small stone-built villages, the Battle of Sedgemoor and its dramatic effects, a choice of fine houses and the remains of an ambitious waterway network that once linked towns such as Taunton, Chard and Glastonbury to the sea.

An aerial view of Montacute House taken from the north-west. Montacute is one of a number of fine houses near the upper reaches of the river Yeo.

A horse-drawn passenger barge on the restored section of the Grand Western Canal near Tiverton. A popular attraction, it is the ideal way to enjoy the Canal.

The long Albert Street cutting which leads to Bridgwater docks, on the Bridgwater and Taunton Canal in Somerset.

The Axe

The river **Axe** marks the boundary between the moors and marshlands of Somerset and the Mendip Hills that rise sharply to the north. Rising, with its tributaries near Wells, it is a river of contrasts. In Wells the cathedral with its west front embellished with nearly 400 statues, its cathedral close and its bishop's palace provides a haven of quiet in a town badly affected by traffic. To the west lies the village of Wookey, famous for the series of caves through which the Axe flows, inhabited by Stone Age and Iron Age hunters as wall as later figures of legend such as the Witch of Wookey. More recently the underground waters of the Axe have been used for making paper. The limestone forming the western flank of the Mendips is riddled with caves, many formed by rivers which now flow underground, or disappear down small holes known as 'swallets'. The river continues to Axebridge, a handsome town built round a large central square with houses of all periods including a Tudor merchant's house known as King John's Hunting Lodge. To the west it curves round Bleadon Hill and then joins the tidal estuary that leads to Weston Bay and Weston-super-Mare.

Fairground horses at Wookey Hole Museum, which boasts a number of attractions apart from its celebrated series of caves.

*The old Cinque Port of Rye on the river Rother. Now nearly two miles from the sea, Rye was
a medieval port of some stature.*

THE SOUTH

It is the southern counties that flank the Channel which have witnessed the continuing pattern of social and economic change in England over the last 2000 years to the greatest extent. The rivers of the region have played a dominant part in the changes, and so anyone seeking to understand the history of Kent, Surrey, Sussex, Hampshire and Dorset should first look at the waterways that run through those counties.

When the Romans landed in Kent, their invasion forces were dependent upon water transport and so their beach heads were established around the mouths of the major rivers. Later, when Christianity was introduced into the country, its gradual spread followed a similar route, leaving a legacy of cathedrals, abbeys and small parish churches of a diversity probably unmatched elsewhere in England. Following the collapse of the Roman empire, waves of invading forces swept across England, all leaving their mark firmly on the southern counties. The last of these was the Norman invasion of 1066, the traces of which can be found throughout the region, in its architecture, in its place names, in the development of trade via the rivers, and in the links with France which are still very tangible today. In the early nineteenth century when the threat of invasion occurred, once more water was seen as the key to success or failure. River mouths were fortified, harbours were protected, and new waterways created to guard English ships from the threat of French guns. More recently the southern rivers have played their part again in safeguarding England's future, first by supplying the boats and the seamen that made possible the Dunkirk evacuation, and second by supporting the Normandy invasion of 1944.

Until the eighteenth century, this region had a very different appearance. In the east the wild and desolate marshlands of Kent gave way gradually to the dense oak forests that covered much of Surrey, Sussex and Hampshire, which in turn yielded to the rolling hills and plains of Dorset. During the seventeenth and eighteenth centuries most of the oak forests were felled to build ships and houses, and for the charcoal required for the smelting of iron. Both these industries were heavily dependent upon the rivers of the region. Later, as the wilder parts of Kent were brought under control, it became a centre for sheep and fruit farming and for brewing. Alongside agriculture, other industries developed, all making use of rivers and water power. During this period many of the rivers were made navigable, supplying a vital transport network that survived until the coming of the railways.

With the spread of industrialisation, the rivers became less important, reverting to their natural roles as controllers of the water supply and as adjuncts to agriculture. However, as the population of the region steadily increased, so the rivers acquired a new role, as centres of leisure and relaxation. Rivers were found to be an ideal relief from

Stained glass in Canterbury Cathedral showing pilgrims at Becket's tomb. Like many English cathedrals it has a riverside location, and stands on the river Stour.

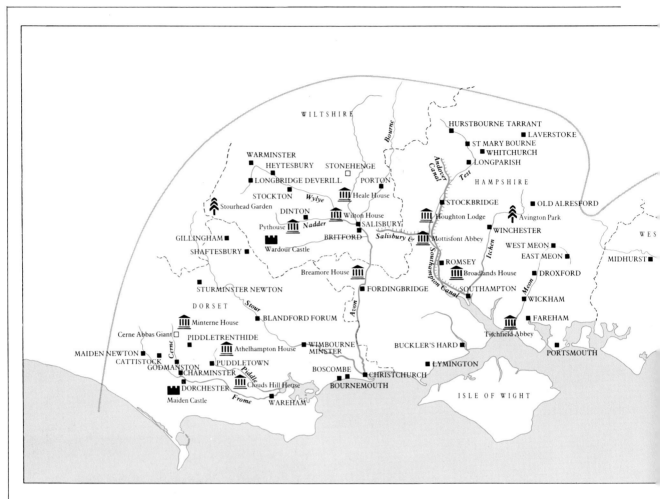

the pressures of suburban and commercial life, and the last 50 years have witnessed a great growth in activities such as fishing and boating. The rivers of southern England are becoming important again as their leisure potential is gradually realised.

The Stour

The **Stour**, which flows in a broad loop through Kent from the Downs above Folkestone to the sea at Pegwell Bay 20 or so miles along the coast, is a river that reflects much of the history of the region. Near its mouth is the great Roman fort of Richborough, one of the most exciting Roman buildings in England, and a vital defence for the Roman links between England and the European mainland. At the west gate of the fort, Watling Street started, an artery holding together the centres of Roman occupation. Nearby is the Cinque port of Sandwich, a town that is a port only in name for the continually changing course of the river has left it over a mile inland. From Sandwich the river meanders through the flat Kent marshlands to Canterbury, the tra-

ditional heart of Christianity in England whose roots were established by St Augustine in AD 597. Today the city is dominated by its cathedral, one of the four great cathedrals of southern England. Nearer its source, the Stour reveals other aspects of its past. The wealth of the area during the Jacobean period can be judged by the formal splendour of houses such as Chilham Castle and Godington Park, while the working water mill at Swanton underlines the importance of the river as a source of power prior to the Industrial Revolution. The tidal section of the river was navigable from the Middle Ages to the late nineteenth century, and for centuries Fordwich was a busy port for Canterbury, handling wool, timber and stone. However, the Stour played no part in more recent industrial activities. The railway town of Ashford straddles the river but makes nothing of it, as though expressing the dominant power of steam in the Victorian period, but nearby at Wye the river comes into its own as a source of water for the rich farmlands that have made Kent into the Garden of England.

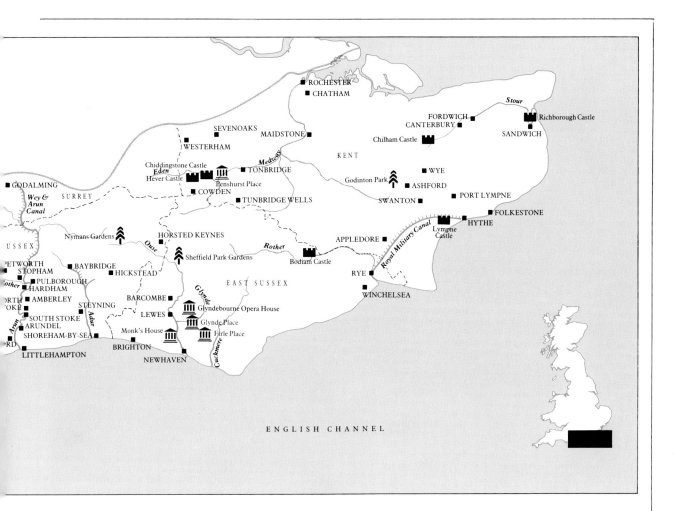

Lower Fittleworth Mill on the river Rother in West Sussex. The mill is one of many attractive buildings along the course of the river.

The Medway

The **Medway** is one of the forgotten rivers of England, yet it flows through attractive countryside, through towns and villages rich with history and, as a waterway navigable from Tonbridge to the Thames estuary, it has great potential for future development. It rises in the Weald and near its source at Cowden there is a furnace pond, one of the many visible reminders of the iron smelting industry of the seventeenth century. Although no longer wooded, the river retains the memory of this period until Tonbridge, a memory underlined by its tributary the **Eden** which links the great houses of Hever Castle, Chiddingstone Castle and Penshurst Place, all of which indicate the wealth of the region in Tudor and later periods. At Tonbridge the character of the Medway changes as it becomes a river navigation, one of the few survivors in this region. Locks, handsome bridges and riverside pubs now determine the nature of the river as it flows towards Maidstone, passing the oast houses at Beltring and other villages. The brewing industry originally

A peaceful rural scene at Teston in Kent, where a fine medieval bridge crosses the Medway, one of England's least known river navigations.

All Saints Church at Maidstone, viewed from the river Medway. The Medway remains tidal to just below Allington, where there is a sea lock.

came to Kent because of the Medway and its potential as a source of power and a means of transport. At Maidstone, the county town of Kent, the riverside is dominated by All Saints, one of the largest churches in the county, while to the north is Allington Castle, one of a number of castles built to defend the river. Others can be seen at Tonbridge and Rochester. Between Maidstone and Rochester are the obvious traces of the two great industries of the Medway, paper-making and cement, and the cathedral town of Rochester is full of interesting buildings and richly endowed with Dickensian associations. Beyond Rochester lies Chatham, until recently a naval base and garrison whose traditions go back to Henry VIII. Royal Navy ships are now no longer a regular part of the Medway scene, but there is still a great range of ships and boats to be seen, including tankers, freighters loaded with timber, pleasure boats and yachts, fishing boats and the traditional red-sailed Thames barges, preserved examples of which still sail in the Medway estuary from small harbours such as Hoo. A less visible part of the river's history is at Strood, formerly the terminus of the **Thames & Medway Canal** which ran from Gravesend to the Medway. Built to enable boats to avoid the dangerous passage round the North Foreland, the canal included in its route the second longest canal tunnel in England. The canal was closed in 1845 and few traces of it remain, except for the basin at Gravesend and the tunnel, now used by trains.

Royal Military Canal

Created between 1804 and 1806 during the invasion scares of the Napoleonic war, the **Royal Military Canal** is the only English waterway to have been built solely for defensive purposes. It formed a natural barrier against any invasion forces landing on the Romney Marshes, and allowed for the inland passage of small boats that might have been at risk at sea. The canal was later used commercially and remained in regular use until 1909. Even now it is still in reasonable condition and can be easily explored throughout much of its original length, by footpath or by minor road. The canal starts near the Cinque port of Hythe, leaving the town beside the northern terminus of the Romney, Hythe & Dymchurch Light Railway, another historical curiosity with its narrow gauge line and steam-hauled miniature trains. Surrounded by the strange scenery of the marshes, and against the backdrop of the former cliffs to the north, the canal makes its quiet way past Lympne Castle, Port Lympne with its zoo, wildlife

The Royal Military Canal. It was originally built to keep Napoleon at bay but such former glories now seem very distant.

park and gardens and the village of Appledore before joining the river Rother to the north of Rye. Another Cinque port now well inland, Rye is an interesting town that has suffered rather from tourism. Plenty of small boat activity maintains Rye's association with the sea, for the river Rother can be navigated north from Rye to Bodiam, where the fourteen-century moated castle is one of the best preserved, and most romantic examples of medieval military architecture. West of Rye the canal passes through Winchelsea before petering out near the sea at Cliff End. An exploration of this part of Kent reveals how the sea has steadily retreated over the last few centuries, leaving high and dry towns that grew up to serve the sea, including four of the five Cinque ports.

The Sussex river navigations

Along the Sussex coast, a number of rivers meet the sea in broad tidal estuaries, some of which are still active as ports. Before cutting their way through the Downs, these rivers drain the rich agricultural lands of north Sussex and Surrey, lands that in earlier centuries were thickly wooded. During the eighteenth and nineteenth centuries several of these rivers were made navigable for considerable distances through the building of locks and other engineering works. The greatest of these was the river **Ouse** which, from 1812 was navigable from the estuary at Newhaven to Upper Ryelands Bridge, 32 miles inland. Railway competition brought about the decline and final closure of the navigation in the 1860s, but a surprising amount still survives. Many

The oxbow bends of the Cuckmere River in East Sussex are a legacy of the great waterway that carved out

of the lock chambers can be found along the course of the river, while mills at Barcombe and elsewhere indicate that the river was busy in its heyday. It is worth exploring the upper reaches, to find these traces of history, to seek out the ponds that used to serve the iron smelting industry, to travel on the Bluebell steam railway at Horsted Keynes, and to enjoy the gardens at Nymans and Sheffield Park. From Lewes to the sea at Newhaven, the river was used commercially until the 1920s and still serves as an attractive link between two enjoyable, old-fashioned and lively towns. Nearby are Firle Place, and Monk's House, Rodmell, the latter the home of Virginia Woolf. A tributary, the **Glynde**, leads to Glynde Place and the Glyndebourne Opera House.

To the east is the river **Cuckmere**, a tidal river

Arundel Castle, the home of the Dukes of Norfolk for 500 years. The castle guards the gap made by the river Arun valley.

cutting its way through the Downs in a series of spectacular oxbow bends. Its upper reaches are now a centre for the English wine industry, with vineyards that can be visited. To the west lies Brighton, and beyond that Shoreham-by-Sea, a busy port on the mouth of the river **Adur**. This tidal river is still navigable for small boats through the Downs to Bines Bridge, near Steyning. During the middle of the nineteenth century the river navigation was extended to Baybridge by means of a canal with locks, the remains of which can still be found. Other features of interest along the river include Lancing College Chapel with its vast green tinted windows, and the All England Showjumping Course at Hickstead.

The most significant of the Sussex rivers is the **Arun**. It is still navigable for small boats from its estuary at Littlehampton to Arundel, a fine town clustered round the castle, the home of the Duke of Norfolk, while adventurous explorers in dinghies can follow the river northwards as far as Pallingham. Leaving Arundel the river passes the tiny villages of North and South Stoke before cutting through the Downs in a dramatic gorge at Houghton. To the east

the valley during the Ice Age.

lies Amberley, the Chalk Pits Museum of Industrial Archaeology and the fourteenth-century castle. By the village of Hardham, the Arun is joined by its tributary, the Sussex **Rother**, which flows through Midhurst, Cowdray Park and Petworth. To the north lies Pulborough, followed by the village of Stopham with its bridge of 1423, the finest medieval bridge in the region. At Pallingham, 25 miles from the sea, the navigable section ends, although the Arun continues northwards deep into the heart of Surrey. However, the Arun today is but a ghost of its former self, for in the early nineteenth century it was at the heart of a chain of navigable rivers and canals that linked London with Portsmouth and the English Channel. From the mid 1820s until 1871 boats could travel from London along the Thames to Weybridge, down the river Wey navigation to Shalford, near Guildford, along the Wey and Arun Junction Canal from Shalford to Pallingham, down the river Arun to Ford, halfway between Arundel and Littlehampton, and then to Portsmouth along the Portsmouth and Arundel Canal. This laborious and today inconceivable journey involved 116 miles of waterway, 52 locks and took at least four days. In addition, the river Rother was navigable from the Arun to Midhurst. This remarkable, and commercially unsuccessful series of waterways has been disused for over a century, and yet traces can still be found. The remains of many of the locks of the Arun and Rother navigations are still to be seen, and it is possible to follow the whole route of the **Wey and Arun Canal** on its meandering journey through some of the most attractive, and secluded, country in Sussex and Surrey. The river **Wey** is still navigable from Godalming to the Thames and so in the last ten years a Trust has been established to restore the Wey and Arun Canal to navigation. Work proceeds steadily, largely by volunteer labour, and so the dream of restoring 'London's lost route to the sea' may eventually become a reality. A century of quiet decay has been halted, but it will be many years before boats can once again travel from London to Littlehampton by the overland route.

The fishing rivers of Hampshire

As well as being the maritime heart of England, Southampton Water and its associated estuaries link the mouths of some of the prettiest, and at the same

The river Test, one of the great trout rivers of England. Here, a fly-fisherman tries his luck near Marshcourt, Hampshire.

The West Front of Winchester Cathedral. The cathedral was begun in 1079 and it is the longest in Europe, measuring 556 ft.

Buckler's Hard in Hampshire. Now a rather self-consciously preserved sailing village, it was a major ship-building centre until the eighteenth century.

time the most private rivers of southern England. To the east of the traditional ship building centres of Lymington, and Buckler's Hard on the Beaulieu river can be found the **Test**, the **Itchen** and the **Meon**. All three rivers are noted particularly for their fishing, the trout draws game fishermen to their banks from all round the world. Of these rivers the least known is probably the Meon, whose quiet valley is undisturbed by traditional riverside villages such as East Meon, West Meon and Droxford. At Wickham, a larger and more handsome town, there is a Regency watermill and a Victorian brewery. The river skirts to the west of Fareham, passing Titchfield Abbey, although by this time the peace has been shattered by motorways, railways and urban development. The Itchen is a very different river, although the countryside through which it passes is similar. At its heart lies Winchester, a city that has significantly affected the nature of the river since the twelfth century. Towards the end of that century the Bishop of Winchester, Godfrey de Lucy, built a reservoir and dredged the river to ensure an adequate water supply for his mills at Alresford and to make it navigable between Winchester and the sea. In the process he created one of the earliest river navigations in England, which survived until the fifteenth century. Restored again in 1710, the Itchen then remained in use as a navigation until the mid-nineteenth century. Exploration by car and on foot will reveal traces of several locks, and restoration of all or part of the navigation may one day be a possibility. The upper reaches are particularly attractive, with watercress beds, old mills, a steam railway, attractive but remote villages and the splendour of Avington Park, built in the Wren tradition. South of Winchester the river becomes less interesting as it approaches Southampton.

For fishermen, the most attractive river in the south of England is probably the Test, but there is far more to this river than trout. Although its banks are mostly private and therefore inaccessible, the Test is a particularly easy and rewarding river to explore by car. Rising in the Wiltshire Downs, it flows through attractive villages, Hurstbourne Tarrant, St Mary Bourne and Longparish for example, while its upper reaches are graced by two of the many unusual features that make the river so interesting. At Laverstoke is a mill that produces the paper used for banknotes, and at Whitchurch there is a silk mill. Watercress beds and thatched cottages

This sixteenth-century timber-framed fulling mill near Alresford, in Hampshire, reflects the long history of industrial use of the river Itchen.

accompany it to Stockbridge, an old coaching town. Further south the river valley is wooded and secluded, overlooked by the eighteenth-century Houghton Lodge and Mottisfont Abbey, a twelfth-century priory greatly expanded in the eighteenth century. The largest town on the Test is Romsey, dominated by its abbey, while to the south Broadlands, the former home of Lord Mountbatten, maintains the spirit of style and elegance that is characteristic of the river. Although the Test was never made navigable, its course was closely followed by the **Andover Canal**, an unrewarding venture that was in operation from 1794 to 1859. Today, little remains of the canal or its 24 locks.

The Hampshire Avon and its tributaries

The **Avon** rises in the Wiltshire Downs near Pewsey, crosses Salisbury Plain, cuts through the rolling hills of Hampshire in a wooded valley and then joins the sea at Christchurch. It is a long and remarkably varied river, matching the changing countryside through which it flows, and its salmon and trout make it attractive to fishermen. It is also a river that carries the memory of many centuries of English history, from the prehistoric mystery of Stonehenge and Woodhenge to the latest in military technology. Other centuries are represented by the Elizabethan manor house at Breamore, which also has a collection of carriages, and Heale House where King Charles was hidden for several days after the Battle of Worcester. Salisbury, with its cathedral and elegant seventeenth- and eighteenth-century architecture, reflects all the historical associations of the river. It is also a town that makes the most of its river, as can be seen in Constable's paintings. South of Salisbury is Fordingbridge, a good starting point for exploration of the New Forest, which flanks the Avon to the east. At Christchurch, a town that has spread all around the Avon estuary, there are all the pleasures of the seaside. The river Avon is unnavigable, but there were a number of attempts to link Salisbury with the sea. In the seventeenth and early eighteenth centuries the Avon was developed as a navigation and barges were able to reach Salisbury until about 1730. Apparently the Avon navigation was so fraught with difficulties that it was formally abandoned in 1772, and little trace remains today, except for an old lock near Britford. A later attempt, the **Salisbury and Southampton Canal**, which branched from the Andover Canal, was equally unsuccessful. It cost a vast amount of money to

Stonehenge is one of the better known attractions that can be discovered by exploring the remote rivers of Salisbury Plain.

build, was never completed and was only in operation for three years before being given up in 1808. Despite its short life, traces of this venture still survive but are best discovered on foot.

In spite of its lack of success in the field of navigation, Salisbury is still a waterway centre, for in and around the town the Avon is joined by a number of tributaries, the **Bourne**, the **Wylye** and the **Nadder**, all of which are worth exploring. The Bourne wanders across the Plain, through a number of small but attractive villages, as well as one or two with more sinister overtones, notably Porton and Boscombe. More interesting are the valleys of the Wylye and the Nadder. The former, which starts near Warminster, is characterised by a number of interesting churches, at Longbridge Deverill, at Heytesbury and at Stockton. The Nadder, which rises north of Shaftesbury, is a particularly well endowed river. Its valley is flanked by some fine houses, including the Palladian Pythouse, the classi-

cal style Phillips House completed in 1816, and the two Wardour Castles. One castle is the magnificent ruin of a fourteenth-century fortress embellished with Renaissance details in the sixteenth century, and the other, designed in 1768 by James Paine, is an extravagant but well-balanced mansion on a grand scale. Further to the east, by the junction of the Nadder and the Wylye, lies Wilton, traditionally the home of carpet making, and dominated by the seventeenth-century splendour of Wilton House, designed by Inigo Jones. Another feature of the Nadder is the distinctive cream coloured tufa stone used for the cottages in villages such as Dinton. This stone comes from the quarries at Chilmark, a mile to the north.

The Dorset Stour

The Dorset **Stour** has little in common with its Kentish namesake. It rises at Stourhead, one of the earliest of the eighteenth-century landscape gar-

Wilton House, home of the Earls of Pembroke for over four hundred years and one of the most splendid country houses in England.

dens, whose lakes, temples and wooded vistas anticipated the vogue for 'natural' gardens and landscapes that was to dominate the second half of the century. It flows south through Gillingham and the rolling countryside that characterises the region. By the time it reaches Sturminster Newton, a handsome and unspoilt town, the Stour has developed associations with Thomas Hardy, and in particular *Tess of the d'Urbervilles*, that are interwoven with the landscape, the villages and above all the rivers of the area. Fine towns and elegant buildings are a feature of the river, Blandford Forum, Crawford Bridge, Kingston Lacy and Wimborne Minster, as it wanders on its way to join the sea near Christchurch.

The Frome and its tributaries

The rivers of south Dorset are small and winding, but they link together many features of the county's past. Prehistory is represented by Maiden Castle, near the **Frome**, and the Cerne Abbas Giant, carved into the hills above the **Cerne**. There are abbeys, dark and romantic, such as the ruins of Bindon beside the Frome, and fine houses and gardens, notably Athelhampton on the **Piddle** and Minterne on the Cerne. There are churches, at Cattistock on the Frome, at Cerne Abbas and

Memories of Judge Jeffreys and the Monmouth Rising are never far away in Dorset. This sign hangs outside the Judge's lodgings in Dorchester.

Stourhead in Wiltshire is one of England's premier landscape gardens and it reflects the importance of water in eighteenth-century garden design.

Charminster on the Cerne and sad memorials, in Dorchester and elsewhere, of Judge Jeffrey's reign of terror following the Monmouth Rebellion. More recent history is reflected by the Tank Corps Museum at Bovington, overlooking the Frome valley. The Frome rises in the hills east of Beaminster, then flows in a steep valley through Maiden Newton to Dorchester and thence through more open country to the sea at Wareham. Its tributaries include the Cerne, which can claim, at Godmanstone, one of the smallest pubs in England, and the curiously named Piddle or Trent, with its string of even more curiously named villages: Piddletrenthide, Puddletown, Affpuddle and Briantspuddle. There is also Tolpuddle, whose fame stretches far beyond Dorset.

These rivers have strong literary connections. The spirit of Hardy is everywhere, from his birthplace at Higher Bockhampton above the Frome to the many settings that can readily be identified in his books. Less well-known is Dorset's association with T. E. Lawrence, 'Lawrence of Arabia'. His house, Cloud's Hill, on the hills above the Frome, can be visited, while in the fine Saxon church of St Martin's on the Wall at Wareham there is a fine monument, modelled by Eric Kennington.

The gentle flight of locks at Napton on the Oxford Canal show this rural English waterway at its best. At the summit is the attractive village of Napton-on-the-Hill.

THE THAMES

The Thames must be one of the most famous rivers in Europe. From its source near Cirencester to its mouth near Southend, it has been described, documented and dissected in all its aspects, and its virtues have been extolled by writers as varied as Charles Dickens, Jerome K Jerome and Kenneth Grahame. Its role in English history is so much a part of the education of successive generations of children that knowledge about the Thames is now almost instinctive. Since the invention of tourism itself, the Thames and its connections have been explored by an unceasing tide of visitors, on foot or horseback, by boat, bicycle or car. Despite all this, there are still many facets of this much-loved river that are not well known, and which warrant fresh voyages of discovery.

The Thames is a well connected river. It is blessed throughout its course by a great variety of tributaries and it has been linked by other canals and waterways to almost every corner of England. In the last 100 years a number of these links have been broken, but enough generally remains to make exploration enjoyable and worthwhile. The Thames is essentially a band drawn across England. It rises, with a number of its tributaries, in the Cotswolds which it drains to fertilize the rolling farmlands of Oxfordshire. It carves its way between the Chilterns and the Berkshire Downs, forming a wide valley

The river Thames winds its way through the heart of London, from Westminster Palace in the west to Tower Bridge and the docks in the east.

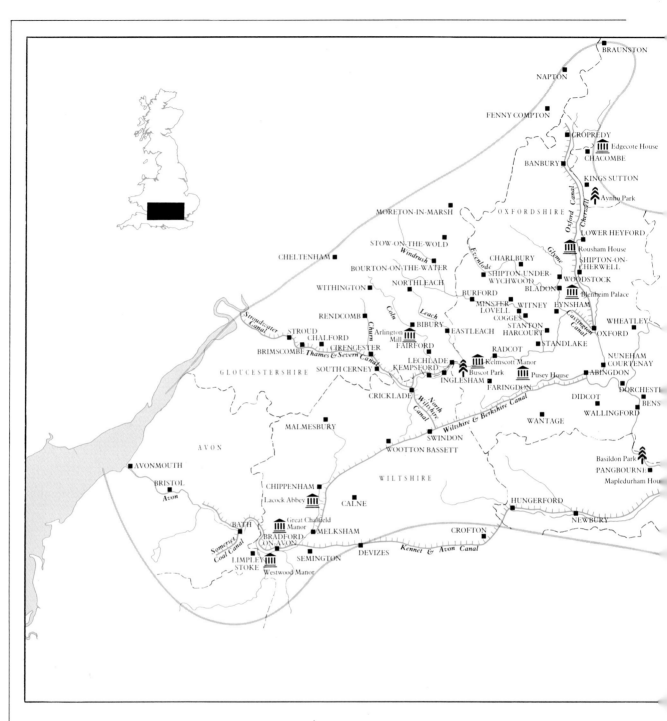

that leads it to the great basin in which London sits. From the high ground all around the basin further tributaries flow into the Thames, swelling its waters and driving them faster towards the estuary, flanked by the low-lying lands of Essex and north Kent. At its mouth the Thames is more than a mile wide. Over the centuries the river has been at the heart of English life, variously a valuable fishing river; a defensible boundary and the scene of many battles and campaigns; a transport artery bringing wealth to the towns and villages along its banks; a creator and supporter of industry; a source of fresh water; a sewer; the instigator of pageantry; and the background for leisure and relaxation.

The Thames

The **Thames** flows across the country from its source near Cirencester to its estuary by Southend,

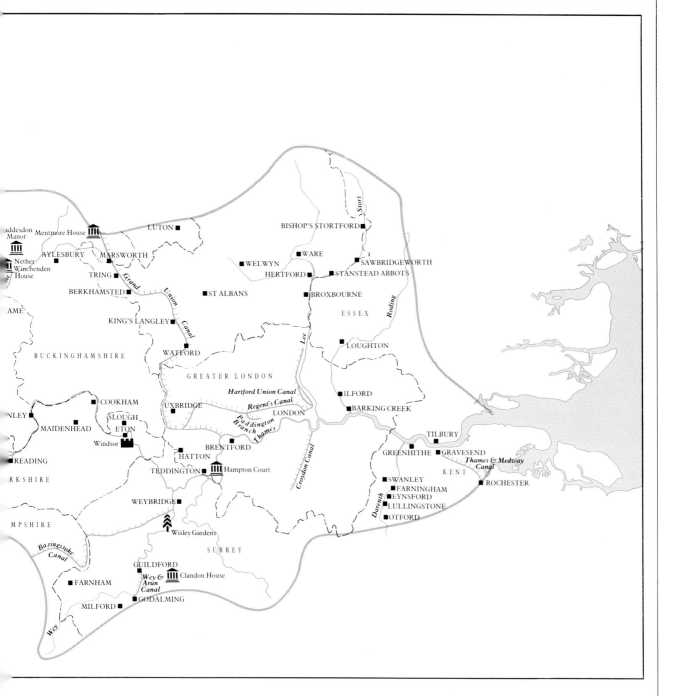

passing through towns and villages that have witnessed the making of English history. It has always been associated with boats, probably more so than any other river in England. The river has been navigable for much of its length since prehistory and today its smart locks with their decorative flower beds are a characteristic feature of one of England's most popular holiday regions. The heyday of the river was probably during the late nineteenth century when it was used by a great variety of boats. The upper reaches then were crowded with punts, camping skiffs, sailing dinghies and a surprising range of commercial canal barges. From Oxford to Teddington there were pleasure steamers, yachts, tugs and barges, while the tideway through London to the sea was always packed with fishing boats, sailing barges, coasters and larger merchant vessels. Today, exploring the Thames by boat is still a major holiday activity, although much of the river's commercial traffic has disappeared. The stretch from Teddington to the limit of navigation at Inglesham, just west of Lechlade, is always busy with pleasure boats of all sizes, a continuous stream of traffic

The pleasures of boating on the Thames, in its Edwardian heyday, graphically illustrated in Edward Gregory's Boulter's Lock–Sunday Afternoon.

making its way through the towns and villages that give the river its broad appeal.

The Thames can for convenience be divided into sections, each of which has a distinct character and contains specific features of interest. The least known section is the unnavigable stretch from the source to Inglesham, where the attractions include the source itself, marked by a statue in a field and strangely dry for most of the year; the Cotswold Water Sports Park near South Cerney; the little town of Cricklade with its eighteenth-century houses and fine Tudor church tower; Kempsford, once the home of the Plantagenets and Fairford, where some of the best early stained glass in

England is to be seen. Inglesham church is a treasure, a tiny thirteenth-century building complete with box pews. The river in this stretch is shallow, twisting and often inaccessible, but near Inglesham the towing path begins which then continues all the way to London.

The next stretch, from Lechlade to Oxford, is particularly attractive. The broad river valley is flanked on the south by the Berkshire Downs, the Ridgeway and the Vale of White Horse, and on the north by the Cotswolds. There are many interesting towns and villages; Burford, Witney, Faringdon, Stanton Harcourt; some fine houses and gardens; Buscot, Kelmscott and Pusey; and at Radcot and Newbridge, two of the oldest bridges on the river.

Between Oxford and Reading the Thames comes into its own as a major tourist river, easily explored both by boat and by car. The best feature of this stretch is the dramatic, steeply wooded valley cut through the Chilterns, but there are many other attractions. It is an area rich in archaeology and history. The Ridgeway crosses the Thames at Streatley. There are abbeys at Abingdon, Dorchester and Reading, a castle mound at Wallingford and fine houses at Basildon and Mapledurham. The nautical college at Pangbourne is worth a visit, as is the famous rose nursery at Nuneham Courtenay and there are some unusual museums, including the steam railway centre at Didcot and a vintage bicycle collection near Benson. There is even a vineyard near Reading.

From Reading to London the Thames pursues a familiar course, passing through the famous boating centres of Henley, Cookham and Maidenhead, and following a winding course along the wooded north side of the valley. This stretch reflects many aspects of English history, most notably at Eton, Windsor and Hampton Court. After passing through the elegant and decorative outer suburbs of western London, the Thames reaches Teddington, and the tideway begins.

The London tideway used to be a great commercial river, the root of the city's prosperity, but over the last 20 years commercial traffic has steadily declined as, one by one, the London docks have closed. Today London's river has a new future as a centre for leisure activities. East of London, all the former docklands are now facing redevelopment and so the nature of the river is bound to change. Even the tides can be controlled by the new Thames barrier at Woolwich. Tilbury in Essex is now the

Henley, a decorative riverside town that makes the most of the Thames. It really comes to life when the annual rowing regatta is in progress.

centre of commercial traffic, while many ships that would formerly have docked in the heart of London now sail no further than Felixstowe in Essex, the fastest growing dock complex in Britain. The wide tidal river east of London is predominantly industrial, but it is full of interest. Traces of England's maritime past can be found at Tilbury, Greenhithe and Gravesend while further east, on the Kent shore, is a wild and little known area of marshland that is full of wildlife, old castles and defence systems, and remote villages unchanged since the time of Dickens. The Thames joins the sea flanked by oil refineries, holiday camps and caravan parks and the seaside pleasures of Southend whose mile-long pier marks the effective end of the river.

The very familiarity of the Thames may limit its appeal for many people but there is far more to the river than a simple linear pleasure park. The greatest, and at the same time the least known aspect of the Thames is its role as the centre of a major network of rivers and waterways that linked many parts of southern England with the Midlands. Today this network is considerably smaller than it was in its heyday in the early nineteenth century, but it is still extensive and well worth exploring. Like the Thames itself, its connecting network of rivers and canals can be divided into a series of sections individually attractive to visitors.

The Cotswold rivers

The Cotswolds, a landscape of high, rolling hills, open grazing land and attractive stone villages, is drained by several rivers which flow rapidly down to join the Thames. These rivers are a natural way to explore the Cotswolds for they link many of the most interesting villages. First among these rivers is the **Churn**, whose seven springs were formerly considered a rival source for the Thames. Near Rendcombe, on the Churn, is one of the surviving habitats of the large edible snail introduced by the Romans. The **Coln**, rising east of Cheltenham, is a fast-flowing trout stream that connects remote villages such as Withington with the rich architecture of Bibury, Arlington Mill and Fairford, before joining the Thames near Inglesham. The **Leach**, a secretive river that flows underground for some of its course, rises near the handsome wool town of Northleach, the home of the Cotswold Countryside Museum, passes through the village of Eastleach with its two churches and clapper bridge and then joins the Thames near Kelmscott Manor. More dramatic is the **Windrush**, the most typical of the Cotswold rivers. This rises near Stow-on-the-Wold then winds slowly along a magnificent valley to link

A glimpse of a typical Cotswold cottage at Minster Lovell on the river Windrush, which winds through some of the most attractive Cotswold country.

some of the most attractive of the Cotswold towns and villages. These include Bourton-on-the-Water with its many bridges, model village and perfumery; Burford; Minster Lovell, where the romantic ruins of the hall overlook the river; Witney, the home of the blanket industry; and Cogges with its farm museum. Before joining the Thames near Standlake, the Windrush flows through an area of gravel

The model village at Bourton-on-the-Water, crossed by many bridges, echoes the attractions of its orginal and captures the spirit of the Cotswolds in miniature.

pits, now used for water sports. The last of the Cotswold rivers is the **Evenlode**, which rises south of Moreton-in-Marsh. Remote, unchanged villages and fine churches mark its course to Shipton-under-Wychwood. Wychwood forest, now 1500 acres of natural woodland and formerly one of the greatest of English forests is flanked by the Evenlode as it passes through Charlbury. A tributary, the **Glyme**, leads to Bladon, Woodstock and Blenheim Palace, where it was widened in the eighteenth century to form the great lake. The Evenlode joins the Thames near Cassington, the site of the **Cassington Canal**, cut to link Eynsham with the Thames and long disused. None of the Cotswold rivers are navigable, but the Windrush and the Evenlode can be explored by canoe, particularly the lower reaches.

The river Cherwell and the Oxford Canal

Rising above Charwelton in Northamptonshire, the **Cherwell** links the dark stone villages of the Midlands with the honey-coloured stone of the Cotswolds and Oxfordshire. It is a placid river flowing through watermeadows and flanked by pollarded willows, but its banks are adorned with many architectural treasures, including Edgecote House, Aynho Park, and Rousham, with its early eighteenth-century landscape garden by William Kent. There are fine churches at Chacombe, Kings Sutton and Shipton-on-Cherwell. Among its towns and villages, Banbury, Cropredy and Lower Heyford are interesting. The Cherwell's approach to Oxford is particularly attractive, dominated by the tower of Magdalen College and the eighteenth-century bridge. In Oxford the Cherwell is much used for punting.

From Cropredy southwards to Oxford the Cherwell runs closely beside the **Oxford Canal** and in a number of places river and canal merge. However, the Oxford Canal is a quite distinct waterway, not simply a canalisation of the Cherwell. Opened throughout in 1790 from Oxford to Hawkesbury, near Coventry, the Oxford Canal links the Thames with the Midlands, and was conceived as part of a grand eighteenth-century scheme to link the Thames, Severn, Trent and Mersey. Until 1805 the Oxford Canal was the only route linking London with Birmingham, Liverpool, Manchester, and the other industrial cities of the north. The main traffic on the canal was coal, a trade that continued until the 1950s. Now the Oxford Canal is entirely used by pleasure boats, and is one of the most popular cruising routes. It is above all a rural canal, its winding course following the contours of the landscape. The most notable engineering features are the flight of locks up to the summit at Napton and the long cutting at Fenny Compton. A variety of

The magnificent Gothic tower of Magdalen College in Oxford dominates the river Cherwell at Magdalen Bridge, where it joins the Thames.

stone and brick arched bridges, wooded locks, small aqueducts and characteristic wooden lift bridges, plus the visual attraction of the Cherwell valley make the Oxford Canal a pleasure to explore.

The Thame

Rising near Aylesbury, the **Thame** is one of the lesser-known of the Thames tributaries. Its source is surrounded by grand houses, ranging from the Tudor elegance of Nether Winchendon to the Victorian splendour of Waddesdon, but the Thame is predominantly a quiet rural river. The main town, from which it takes its name, is Thame, an attractive but strangely little-known place with a range of interesting buildings flanking a long main street. Near Wheatley is the Waterperry Horticultural Centre, after which the river makes its way through a rather remote landscape to Dorchester and its junction with the Thames.

The Thames and Severn Canal

One of the least known features of the Thames today is its former connections with the rivers of the west of England, and in particular with the Severn. At one time, there were three cross-country canal routes between the two rivers but none of these are navigable today. The first one to be built was the **Thames and Severn Canal**, opened in 1789 from the Thames near Lechlade to Stroud, where it connected with the **Stroudwater Canal**, an eight mile link between Stroud and the river Severn opened in 1779. Despite the obvious advantages of its route, the Thames and Severn never prospered. It suffered from shortage of water, it was poorly constructed and its locks were too small, making it impossible for the large trows, or barges, of the Severn to sail directly to the Thames. All cargoes had to be transhipped on to smaller barges at Brimscombe, where a major inland port grew up to serve the canal. The journey between the two rivers was slow and laborious, and so the Thames and Severn carried little traffic, particularly during the latter half of the nineteenth century. The last through journey was made in 1911, after which the canal gradually decayed until its final closure in 1933. The Stroudwater was closed a few years later,

The recently restored portal of the 3000 yard-long Sapperton Tunnel in Gloucestershire, the most impressive feature of the long-closed Thames and Severn Canal.

Hidden delights lie in store for those who take the trouble to explore England's abandoned canals, in this case the Thames and Severn near Cirencester.

in 1941. Although sections of the canal have disappeared, it is possible today to follow its route. Indeed, a Trust has been established to campaign for its reopening and already considerable progress has been made. An easy section to follow is between Stroud and Chalford, where there is a clear towpath and the remains of locks, mills and other canal structures. However, the most memorable features of the Thames and Severn are the 3800 yard long Sapperton Tunnel, whose ornamental portals are still to be seen, and the distinctive circular lock-keeper's houses, five of which survive. The most striking of these still stands guard over the abandoned lock chamber where the canal used to join the Thames, near Inglesham.

The Kennet and Avon Canal and its connections

The second of the great cross-country routes linking the Thames with the Severn was the **Kennet and Avon Canal**, which was completed in 1810. This was formed from three distinct waterways: the river Kennet navigation from Reading to Newbury, opened in 1723; the river Avon navigation from Bath to Hanham, near Bristol, opened four years later; and the canal built in 1810 to link the two.

The Kennet and Avon is a particularly attractive canal, engineered on a grand scale with wide locks and elegant aqueducts. It passes through a landscape of continual variation, its route linking many towns of great architectural interest, for example Bath, Bradford-on-Avon, Devizes, Hungerford and Newbury. Although successful in its early years, the canal later suffered from railway competition and

Restoration work on the Kennet and Avon Canal, where a massive flight of 29 locks at Devizes is slowly coming to life thanks to dedicated volunteers.

trade declined steadily through the latter part of the nineteenth century. Its condition also deteriorated, and the last through passage was made in 1951. Although never formally closed, the canal rapidly became derelict, until the Kennet and Avon Canal Trust was formed to campaign for its restoration. During the last 20 years remarkable progress has been made and much of the route is now open again, thanks largely to the volunteer efforts of the Trust and its members. Today only a few major obstacles remain, the mighty flight of 29 locks at Caen Hill, near Devizes, and a number of places where main roads cross the canal on the level. However, it is now clear that by the mid 1980s boats will once again be able to travel from the Thames to Bristol overland. Although parts of its route are remote, the Kennet and Avon is easy to explore as it has a good towing path throughout its length. It also has a number of remarkable features, including the Caen Hill flight, the aqueduct at Limpley Stoke, the steam pumping engine at Crofton and the tunnel beneath Savernake Forest, as well as a wealth of interesting buildings.

In its heyday the Kennet and Avon was itself part of a larger waterway network. At its western end, near the Dundas Aqueduct at Limpley Stoke, are the remains of the junction with the short **Somerset Coal Canal**. Opened in 1805, this was built to link the Somerset coalfield with the rest of the inland waterway network. It was a dramatic undertaking, with flights of locks, inclined planes, tunnels, aqueducts and other engineering features and during the 1830s and 1840s it carried over 100,000 tons of coal a year, from over 20 pits. It remained in use until the 1890s when much of its course was built over by railway companies. Today, its route can still be traced, and some of its main features, the Midford aqueduct and the locks at Combe Hay for example, can still be seen and are reminders not only of the canal, but also of a period when coal mining was a staple industry in Somerset.

The third cross-country waterway was the **Wiltshire and Berkshire Canal**, a long-forgotten canal that meandered from Abingdon on the Thames to its junction with the Kennet and Avon at Semington, west of Devizes. The Wiltshire and Berkshire Canal was opened in 1810, a remote, rural undertaking with no major engineering features, designed to supply an alternative route for the Somerset coal traffic to Oxford and the Midlands. Its route managed to avoid all major towns, although branches were built to Calne, Chippen-

Brunel's dramatic suspension bridge, which crosses the Avon gorge at Clifton, near Bristol, high above the river.

ham and Wantage. Surprisingly it remained quietly profitable until the 1870s but then it declined rapidly under the pressure of railway competition and was finally abandoned in 1914. Because its route was largely through undeveloped farmland, much of the canal can still be traced. A good place to start is Wootton Bassett where there are several old locks close together, while its course is quite distinct near Wantage. In 1819 the canal was linked to the Thames and Severn by a short branch, the **North Wiltshire Canal**, which helped to increase its traffic. Although long abandoned, this can also be traced, particularly around Cricklade, where there are the remains of two aqueducts, one over the Thames, and the old canal basin at Latton, where the canal joined the Thames and Severn. In all, there are over 65 miles of forgotten canals in Wiltshire and Berkshire, an interesting legacy of the 'canal mania' of the early nineteenth century.

The Bristol Avon

The **Avon** rises south of Malmesbury and flows southwards through Chippenham and Melksham in a typical Wiltshire landscape. It is an area rich in fine houses, including Lacock Abbey with its museum of photography, the moated Great Chalfield Manor

and Westwood Manor with its topiary garden. At Bradford-on-Avon the river swings westwards and is joined by the Kennet and Avon Canal which shares its valley course as far as Bath. From Bath to Bristol the Avon is a busy river navigation, passing through Bristol's floating harbour. Formerly one of Britain's major ports, Bristol sees little commercial traffic now, but Brunel's *Great Britain*, the first screw-driven transatlantic steamship, is preserved in the harbour as a fitting reminder of the city's maritime past. West of Bristol the river, now tidal, sweeps through the Clifton Gorge, far below Brunel's dramatic suspension bridge and then flows quickly through an industrial environment to Avonmouth docks, and the wide expanse of the Severn estuary. The river Avon represented the final link in the chain of navigations that enabled boats to travel from London across England to Bristol.

The Wey and its connections

The **Wey** has two sources, both of which drain the South Downs. One rises near Alton in Hampshire and flows through Farnham and past the ruins of Waverley Abbey to Milford, where it joins the other arm. This rises in Sussex, south of Frensham Ponds, some of the many ponds in this area formed originally to supply water power for the iron smelting industry of the sixteenth and seventeenth centuries. The Wey flows through typical Surrey countryside to Godalming, where it becomes navigable. Built originally by the Weston family of

A view of the Wey at Weybridge, the start of this attractive river navigation's rural route to Godalming in Surrey.

Winter on the Grand Union Canal in Buckinghamshire, a reminder of the days when commercial carrying by narrow boat was an all-year-round activity.

Stoke Bruerne in Northamptonshire. A traditional canal village, it is the home of the Waterways Museum, one of the most important canal museums in England.

Sutton Place, the Wey navigation was opened from Guildford to the junction with the Thames at Weybridge in 1653. Eighty years later it was extended to Godalming. The Wey is a pleasant, rural navigation, relatively unchanged since the nineteenth century with riverside mills, quiet villages and it retains an air of privacy even when surrounded by London's suburbia. Guildford is the only town of any size, and it makes the most of its river. Less appealing towns, Woking, Byfleet and Weybridge, for example, are conveniently avoided by the river. There are a number of attractions on or near the Wey: Tudor Sutton Place; eighteenth-century Clandon House; the Royal Horticultural Society gardens at Wisley; and the remains of the old Brooklands motor racing circuit. Its greatest appeal, however, is its unchanged quality. The Wey is still navigable, although commercial traffic ceased in the late 1960s. Now owned and operated by the National Trust, the Wey is a popular cruising river.

In the nineteenth century the Wey was even more important. It was the first part of a long and tortuous navigation that linked London with Portsmouth and the English Channel (for details see *The South*). It also connected Basingstoke with the Thames via the **Basingstoke Canal**. This derelict waterway joins the Wey at West Byfleet, having followed a rural and heavily locked route. Easily explored by car or on foot, the Basingstoke Canal is slowly being restored and will eventually be open to boats as far as Odiham. The original terminus at Basingstoke is permanently separated from the rest of the canal by the collapsed Greywell tunnel.

London's canals

Apart from the Thames, there are, or were a number of other waterways in London. Rivers such as the **Fleet** and the **Tyburn** have long since disappeared or been converted into underground sewers. Some canals have also vanished but not without trace. Much of the route of the optimistically named **Grand Surrey Canal** which ran from the Thames at Rotherhithe to Camberwell and Peckham can still be traced, for this was part of the Surrey Docks complex and was not finally closed until 1970. More obscure is the **Croydon Canal** which opened in 1803 to link Croydon with the Grand Surrey Canal at New Cross. The canal had 26 locks in 9 miles and it was closed in 1836 after an uneventful life. However, a length of this unlikely waterway can still be seen in Anerley, converted to a park.

London still has a number of active canals, mostly linking the Thames and the London docks with the **Grand Union Canal**. Conceived as a more direct route between London and the Midlands, the Grand Union, or rather Grand Junction Canal as it was originally called, was opened at the start of the nineteenth century. Its route was from Braunston, where it joined the Oxford Canal to Brentford in west London, where it joined the Thames. With its large-scale engineering and its more direct route linking major towns, the Grand Junction Canal was immediately successful, establishing a pattern of busy commercial carrying that continued until the 1960s. Today, the Grand Union is still the major waterway link between London and the Midlands and the North, but pleasure boats now make up its traffic. However, plenty of the old narrow boats survive and these can often be seen on the Grand Union, sometimes still in their old working formation of paired boats.

The Grand Union's route north from Brentford is predominantly suburban and industrial but once north of Uxbridge, having passed the branch to Slough, the environment improves. There are plenty of locks, some grouped in flights, often with convenient canalside pubs, as the canal climbs towards its summit level at Tring. The canal is particularly attractive in Watford, King's Langley and Berkhamstead, while Marsworth offers an old canal workshop, branches to Wendover and Aylesbury, and nearby a variety of unusual birds on Tring Reservoirs. Between Tring and Bletchley the canal passes through rolling, open countryside, flanked by attractive villages, and a number of grand houses, including Mentmore, Ascott and Woburn. North of Bletchley the canal is enjoying a new lease of life as part of Milton Keynes. At Cosgrove is the junction with the old branch to Buckingham. This was closed in 1910, but it is still possible to follow much of the

This aqueduct carrying the Paddington arm of the Grand Union Canal across the North Circular Road provides a dramatic lesson in transport history.

route on foot. A few miles further north is Stoke Bruerne, a traditional canal village and the home of the Waterways Museum which brings to life over 200 years of canal history. Nearby is Blisworth tunnel, over 3000 yards long and opened in 1805. It is just wide enough for two boats to pass, but there is no towing path in the tunnel. Just beyond the tunnel is Gayton, and the branch to Northampton, which is a vital link between the canal network and the river Nene, and thus with the rivers and waterways of eastern England. The canal then travels through a

The wide locks of the Grand Union Canal at Berkhampstead, which carry the waterway

up to its summit at Tring. The landscape is a blend of countryside and suburbia.

more remote landscape, crossing the town of Weedon on a huge embankment, and passing the junction with the Leicester canal, to the east Midlands and the Trent, before entering the 2000 yard Braunston Tunnel. Braunston itself is an unchanged canal village and a good place to see traditional canal boats. Shortly after the village the Grand Union meets the Oxford Canal, and then follows a varied route to Birmingham. It passes Warwick and Leamington; the dramatic flight of 21 locks at Hatton; Knowle; and the Birmingham suburbs, mostly hidden by the wooded sides of a deep cutting. This completes the direct route from London to the Midlands.

In order to expand its trade in London, and to avoid the problems caused by the tidal Thames, the Grand Junction company built a branch canal to Paddington which opened in 1801. This swings round western London in a broad curve to meet the **Regent's Canal** at Little Venice, a picturesque canal centre in the heart of London. The Regent's Canal was opened in 1820 to connect the Paddington Branch of the Grand Union with London's dockland and the Thames via the Limehouse Basin. This canal has many elegant and interesting features and is one of the least known pleasures of London. It passes through Regent's Park and the Zoo; Camden Town; round the back of St Pancras; under Islington in a long tunnel; through Hackney and on to London's East End. Much of the towing path has now been opened as an urban footpath and the best parts of the canal are easily accessible. In addition, there are a number of regular waterbus services. An interesting way to see London is by water, via the Thames, the Grand Union Canal, the Paddington Branch and the Regent's Canal.

The Lee and the Stort

The last of London's river navigations is the **Lee**. This rises near Luton and flows through St Albans, and Welwyn to Hertford, where it becomes navigable. The Lee is a river of great contrasts. Its upper reaches through rural Hertfordshire are attractive, linking interesting towns and villages, such as Ware, Stanstead Abbots, Broxbourne and Waltham Abbey. It then becomes a pleasantly suburban river, before plunging through the industrial and urban sprawl of north-east London. Much of the Lee valley is now being developed as a centre for sport and recreation and it is a rural lifeline into the centre of London. The Lee joins the Thames at Limehouse Basin, where it also connects with the Regent's Canal and the rest of the canal network. There is also a short branch, the Hartford Union Canal, which links the Lee directly with the Regent's Canal. The lower reaches of the Lee still see some commercial traffic, although the main users of the navigation are now pleasure boats.

The river **Stort** was made navigable in the 1760s, to link Bishop's Stortford with the river Lee, and thus with the Thames. Dependent for many years on agricultural traffic, the Stort is still one of the least developed and most attractive of the waterways of southern England. Its landscape has East Anglian qualities, and its route is marked by attractive villages and waterside mills, notably at Sawbridgeworth. The Stort bypasses much of Harlow New

Dramatic urban scenery on the Regent's Canal near Paddington in west London, where a short arm of the canal leads into Paddington Basin.

The elegant mill and maltings at Stratford on the river Lee, one of a number of stylish industrial buildings along the busy lower reaches of the Lee.

Town but its quiet and privacy may in future be affected by the expansion of Stanstead into London's third airport.

The Darenth and the Roding

Two of the least known and most attractive of the Thames tributaries are the **Darenth** and the **Roding**. Both are surprisingly remote and rural for much of their course, despite their proximity to London. The Darenth rises near Westerham in Kent, and flows along a pleasant wooded valley to Sevenoaks. It then turns north, passing Otford, Eynsford and Farningham on its way through the Downs. Despite its rural nature, it is a river of some history. There is a Roman villa at Lullingstone,

castles at Eynsford and Lullingstone, and the remains of a Bishop's Palace at Otford. North of Swanley the Darenth loses its rural quality, and flows through Dartford and the Erith marshes before joining the Thames. The Roding is in many ways the Essex equivalent of the Darenth. It is a quiet river, meandering for much of its course through attractive farmland and remote villages. Famous once for its eels, the river now adds a traditional flavour to London's outer suburbs. Mills, fine churches and farms accompany the Roding as far as Loughton, where it surrenders its privacy to the MII motorway and suburban development. At Ilford the Roding becomes tidal and then joins the Thames at Barking Creek.

For much of its course the river Wye flows quickly through a steep and wooded valley that is undoubtedly one of the finest in England. It is seen here near Symonds Yat.

THE SEVERN

The Severn is one of England's greatest rivers and it has determined for centuries the social and economic structure of its region. Effectively, its wide and fertile valley forms the border between England and Wales, providing a more powerful and permanent barrier than the castles and fortifications erected by man. Between the Roman period and the late eighteenth century the Severn was navigable far north of Shrewsbury and deep into Wales, and so it was the backbone for all development of the area. Its importance can be measured in many ways. Great cathedrals, abbeys and castles line its banks and a series of inland ports, Gloucester, Worcester, Stourport, Bewdley and Ironbridge, mark its route. Rich agricultural lands surround it and the industries associated with the river since the Middle Ages; coal, iron, milling, pottery and porcelain, boatbuilding and fishing; are all part of the Severn's history.

The importance of the river is also evident from its huge network of connecting waterways, many of which serve the inland ports along the Severn. Rivers which join the Severn include the Wye (to Hereford), the Teme (to Ludlow) and the Avon (to Stratford), while canals, built mostly during the late eighteenth century, connected many parts of the Severn with the English waterways network. Many of these canals can still be explored today and some of the inland ports, notably Sharpness and Gloucester, are still in commercial use. As a result, boats can use the Severn to visit many parts of western England and the Midlands.

The scenery of the Severn valley is very varied. Rolling farmland, orchards, steep wooded valleys

The imposing ruins of Buildwas Abbey in Shropshire. The church, built in the twelfth century, is the best preserved part of the abbey.

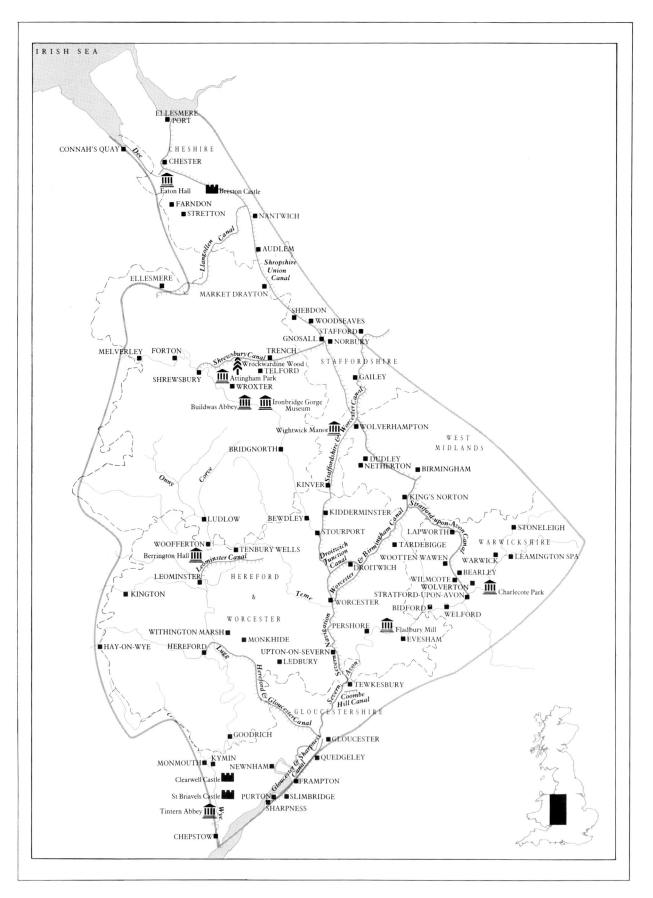

IRISH SEA

ELLESMERE PORT

CONNAH'S QUAY
Dee
CHESHIRE
CHESTER
Eaton Hall
Beeston Castle
FARNDON
STRETTON
NANTWICH

Llangollen Canal

AUDLEM
Shropshire Union Canal
ELLESMERE
MARKET DRAYTON
SHEBDON
WOODSEAVES
STAFFORD
GNOSALL
NORBURY
MELVERLEY
FORTON
TRENCH
Shrewsbury Canal
Wrockwardine Wood
TELFORD
STAFFORDSHIRE
GAILEY
SHREWSBURY
Attingham Park
WROXTER
Buildwas Abbey
Ironbridge Gorge Museum

Wightwick Manor
WOLVERHAMPTON
WEST MIDLANDS

BRIDGNORTH
Onny
Corve
DUDLEY
NETHERTON
BIRMINGHAM

KINVER
KING'S NORTON

LUDLOW
BEWDLEY
KIDDERMINSTER
STOURPORT
Stratford-upon-Avon Canal
STONELEIGH
WARWICKSHIRE
LAPWORTH
TARDEBIGGE
WOOTTEN WAWEN
WARWICK
LEAMINGTON SPA

WOOFFERTON
TENBURY WELLS
Leominster Canal
Berrington Hall
Droitwich Junction Canal
DROITWICH
WILMCOTE
WOLVERTON
BEARLEY

LEOMINSTER
HEREFORD
&
Teme
WORCESTER
STRATFORD-UPON-AVON
Charlecote Park

KINGTON
WORCESTER
BIDFORD
WELFORD

WITHINGTON MARSH
MONKHIDE
PERSHORE
Fladbury Mill

HAY-ON-WYE
HEREFORD
Lugg
UPTON-ON-SEVERN
LEDBURY
EVESHAM

Hereford & Gloucester Canal
TEWKESBURY
Severn
Avon
Coombe Hill Canal
GLOUCESTERSHIRE

GOODRICH
GLOUCESTER

KYMIN
MONMOUTH
NEWNHAM
QUEDGELEY
Gloucester & Sharpness Canal
Clearwell Castle
FRAMPTON
St Briavels Castle
PURTON
SLIMBRIDGE
Tintern Abbey
Wye
SHARPNESS

CHEPSTOW

354

The suspension bridge across the mighty estuary of the river Severn, a seemingly delicate but vital link between England and Wales.

and dramatic hills can all be found in close proximity. The towns and villages of the Severn valley exhibit interesting variations in regional architecture, from the timber-framed styles of Shropshire and Cheshire to the Georgian elegance of Shrewsbury and Upton. There are also fine churches, interesting country houses, and a rich legacy of industrial history that reflects the part played by the Severn in the development of the Industrial Revolution. The river's industrial history can be explored in areas such as the Forest of Dean, and particularly at Ironbridge, the cradle of modern industrialisation. The passage of time has softened these relics of industry and given them picturesque qualities. The region is now predominantly rural, although modern industry is never far away, with the Black Country and the Midlands spreading to the east. Here again history can be explored in an unusual way, however, for the Black Country still boasts over 100 miles of navigable canals, the remains of a huge network that was the lifeblood of the region during the nineteenth century. There are several connections between the Severn, and the canals of Birmingham and the Midlands. These little known waterways mark the contrast between the rural and the industrial landscapes and bring to life a vibrant era of English history.

To the north of the Severn lies Chester and the river Dee. Chester is one of England's finest small cities, endowed with a rich collection of typical Cheshire buildings. This area enjoys a varied landscape of farmland interspersed with the ponds and low-lying marshes that are the result of centuries of salt extraction. A number of traditional market towns are linked to the Severn by the Shropshire Union Canal. This, one of the last main line canals to be built in England, follows an attractive route from Wolverhampton to Ellesmere Port.

355

The Severn

The **Severn** rises in Wales, high in the Cambrian Mountains south of Machynlleth, and sweeps in a series of dramatic bends through Llandidloes and Newtown to Welshpool. From here it swings east towards Shrewsbury, crossing the border into England by the village of Melverley. Although hard to believe today, Welshpool was the limit of navigation early in the nineteenth century, when the typical

Abraham Darby's iron bridge over the Severn. Built in 1778, it was the first iron bridge in the world and underlines the importance of Coalbrookdale.

Severn sailing barges, or trows, regularly made the 128 mile journey upstream from Gloucester. During the last 150 years the navigable section of the river has steadily dwindled, and now only about 45 miles from Gloucester to Bewdley is accessible to other than small, portable boats.

The Severn is a wide and generous river contained by high banks, which winds its way through attractive, and sometimes dramatic scenery. Its long history as a navigation stretches back to the Roman period and probably beyond, and this ensured that a number of fine towns have grown up along its banks: Shrewsbury, Bridgnorth, Bewdley, Worcester, Upton-on-Severn, Tewkesbury and Gloucester. Not many rivers can boast two cathedrals and a major Norman abbey within a few miles. The Severn also connects with a number of other waterways, making it an important through route for cruising, and in its lower reaches, for commercial traffic. The character of the Severn is quite distinct. The first impression is one of size. Even the now unnavigable section between Bewdley and Welshpool seems wide and impressive, far more important-looking than the equivalent upper reaches of the Thames which, by comparison dwindles to a stream quite quickly above Lechlade.

It also seems relatively untamed. The high banks serve as permanent reminders of the power of the river when in flood, and the six locks on the navigable section are large and powerful structures, clearly built to handle small ships rather than boats or barges.

The route taken by the Severn is well worth exploring, for there is much to be discovered along its banks. Between the Welsh border and Shrewsbury the river is rather remote. Few roads approach its banks but the landscape is interesting, with distant views of the Long Mynd to the south. The Severn really comes to life when it reaches Shrewsbury, a town that makes the most of its river. Here, there are fine bridges, a castle, several good churches, timber-framed and Georgian buildings and museums, while to the east of the town are the twin attractions of eighteenth-century Attingham Park and Roman Wroxeter. Approaching Ironbridge, the Severn enters a steep wooded gorge, overlooked to the north by the Wrekin. It is hard today to realise that this area was one of the starting points for the Industrial Revolution. Here, at Coalbrookdale, Abraham Darby first smelted iron with coke, the revolutionary technique that was to make cast iron the raw material for industrialisation. In the eighteenth century the valley was filled with the smoke and flames of the furnaces, a scene depicted by many painters of the period as a vision of Hell. Today Coalbrookdale is a wooded valley filled with picturesque and overgrown ruins, memorials to England's industrial past, now all well cared for by the Ironbridge Gorge Museum Trust. There are furnaces and factories, railways and canals, porcelain and tile works, wharves and quays. In the centre is the great iron bridge itself, the first iron bridge in the world, crossing the river in the splendid steep arch that has stood since 1778. There are also many eighteenth- and nineteenth-century buildings of interest, while the ruins of Buildwas Abbey connect the area with the twelfth and thirteenth centuries.

The wooded valley of the Severn continues to Bridgnorth, a handsome town with a castle and, somewhat unexpectedly, a funicular railway. Bridgnorth has other railway connections, for it is the northern terminus of the Severn Valley Railway, which is one of the premier steam railways in England and a fine way to see the river between Bridgnorth and Bewdley. Although the trows and barges have long departed, Bewdley still has the

An enjoyable way to explore the river Severn is by steam train. The route of the Severn Valley Railway includes this iron viaduct over the river at Arley.

atmosphere of an eighteeenth-century inland port, with fine quays and warehouses, and a maze of narrow streets to be explored on foot. A similar but rather more down-to-earth atmosphere pervades Stourport, a town developed entirely in the late eighteenth century around the junction of the Severn and the Staffordshire and Worcestershire Canal. The large canal basins with their elegant buildings and bridges are an indication of the scale of traffic that formerly used this waterway route from Stafford via Wolverhampton and the Black Country to the Severn. Although still in a valley, the river is flanked by a more open landscape between Stourport and Worcester. Worcester is also an excellent river town, with a riverside dominated by the cathedral and the eighteenth-century stone bridge. Here, large locks lead from the Severn into the extensive network of basins that serve the Worcester and Birmingham Canal, another eighteenth-century link between the Severn and the Black Country.

An open landscape of meadows and woods follows the river south towards Tewkesbury and Gloucester, with distant views of the Malvern Hills to the west, and Bredon Hill and the Cotswolds to the east. Along the way is Upton, another fine Georgian town, its riverside dominated by the church with its curious copper dome. At Tewkesbury is the Norman abbey and the confluence of the Severn and the river Avon. This part of England is famous for its fruit, and the Severn is very much a cider river here, with a number of pubs along its banks specialising in the many different varieties and flavours. From Wainlode Hill, between Tewkesbury and Gloucester, there is a good view of the Severn, now a wide and mighty river winding its way through a landscape of rolling farmland. Nearby is the entrance to the disused **Coombe Hill Canal**, a relic of an eighteenth-century plan to build a canal from the Severn to Cheltenham. Only three miles, with two locks, were ever built and it was closed in 1876.

North of Gloucester the Severn divides into two channels. One leads to the old **Severn Navigation** that followed the original course of the river to Sharpness and the estuary. The other passes through Gloucester and its extensive docks and basins to meet the **Gloucester and Sharpness Canal**, a wide ship canal opened in 1826 to bypass the difficult stretch of the Severn. The old route, which is tidal throughout, follows a wild course through marshland, the river flowing steadily faster among sandbanks to its estuary. This is a remote area, noted for its wildlife. At Slimbridge the Wildfowl Trust has one of the largest reserves in the country. It is also a good place to see the Severn

Worcester Cathedral, with its magnificent fourteenth-century tower, dominates the river Severn. The city was granted its first royal charter in 1189.

Bore, a tidal wave that sweeps up the Severn from the Atlantic about 250 times a year. It is at its best during the high tides of spring and autumn, when waves up to nine feet high drive up the river, briefly reversing its natural flow. One of the best viewpoints is at Stonebench, west of Quedgeley. South of Sharpness the estuary rapidly widens as the Severn becomes a major seaway, passing Chepstow, the mouth of the Wye, the Severn road bridge and the huge docks complex at Avonmouth, the modern port of Brisol.

The 16 mile long ship canal follows a more sedate and rural route and is still used by a variety of ships and barges making their way from the Severn estuary to Gloucester's docks, and occasionally northwards to Worcester. All the bridges over the canal can be opened, allowing the passage of ships

up to 190 feet long and 29 feet wide. Timber and oil are the principle cargoes. The canal itself is not unattractive, but there are few towns or villages along its route. The most interesting features are at Sharpness, where there are the extensive and busy docks, at Purton, where the canal overlooks the Severn, and at Frampton, which claims to have the largest village green in England. Near Gloucester is Saul Junction, a former waterway crossroads, where the **Stroudwater Canal**, closed since 1954, crossed the Gloucester and Sharpness on its way to join the Thames and Severn Canal. Until the decline of the latter in the late 1920s, it was possible to travel from Lechlade on the Thames direct to the Severn via the Stroudwater Canal, or to Gloucester and the other Severn towns. Gloucester's docks are well worth exploring, as many of the original nineteenth-century wharves and warehouses still survive. Fine and elegant red-brick buildings, many of them are now either disused or converted to other purposes.

The Severn's surviving connections

In its heyday, the Severn was at the heart of a network of connecting waterways that linked the river with the Midlands, London, the South-West, South Wales, North Wales, Liverpool, Manchester, and ultimately with all the other inland waterways of England. A great many of these waterways have disappeared, but a number still survive that can easily be followed and the whole of the Severn region is well worth exploring. The connections that still survive are the **Worcester and Birmingham** and **Staffordshire and Worcestershire** Canals, and the river **Avon Navigation**. The Worcester and Birmingham Canal was opened in 1815, linking Gas Street Basin in the heart of Birmingham with the Severn at Worcester. The canal runs for most of its route through attractive countryside, but it is most notable for its engineering. Its 30 mile length includes 5 tunnels and 58 locks, of which 36 are grouped together in less than 3 miles, between Tardebigge and Stoke Prior. Nowhere in England is there a greater flight of locks. In addition, the flight starts at Tardebigge with the deepest lock (it has a 14 foot drop) in the English narrow canal network. Of the tunnels, the longest is King's Norton, just outside Birmingham, 2,726 yards of subterranean passage carved through Wast Hill. At King's Norton there is also a junction with the Stratford Canal.

Little used today, Gloucester docks are a splendid memorial to the Victorian period, and to the great days of the Severn as a commercial waterway.

The Staffordshire and Worcester Canal is a far older undertaking, and dates back to the 1770s, when it was planned by the engineer James Brindley as part of the original Grand Cross canal system to link the Thames, the Severn, the Trent and the Mersey. Despite its age, it remained in commercial use until the late 1950s. The canal runs for 43 miles from Stourport on the Severn to Great Haywood near Stafford, where it joins the Trent and Mersey Canal. It is a route that is still unusually attractive despite the proximity of the Midlands and the Black Country. A particularly old-fashioned canal, still largely unchanged since the eighteenth century, it has attractive bridges and locks, with tunnels and cuttings carved through red sandstone. The best features are the basins at Stourport, the route through the centre of Kidderminster and the remains of distinctive circular toll houses at Stewponey and Gailey. Also worth seeing are the flight of locks with their octagonal toll house at The Bratch, the village of Kinver and the dramatic Kinver Edge, Wightwick Manor with its William Morris associations and the Elizabethan gatehouse at Tixall,

overlooking a stretch of canal turned into an ornamental lake. At Stourton there is a junction with the Stourbridge Canal, which leads to Birmingham via the massive Dudley and Netherton tunnels, while a former branch, closed since the 1920s, linked the canal to Stafford.

The river Avon (not to be confused with the river that flows from Bath and Bristol to the Severn estuary at Avonmouth) links Tewkesbury on the Severn with Stratford-on-Avon. This 44-mile navigation represents one of the most remarkable achievements in recent waterway history. Rising near Stanford, south of Lutterworth, the Avon follows a meandering course through the Midlands. Passing north of Rugby and south of Coventry it avoids the main areas of industry, and manages to remain largely rural. Apart from Stoneleigh, the site of the annual Royal Agricultural show, the first place of interest is Leamington Spa. Nearby is Warwick, whose castle enjoys a splendid riverside site. The Avon is quite a substantial river, flowing through the town and under an elegant aqueduct which carries the Grand Union Canal. Between

Warwick and Stratford the Avon winds through farmland, passing the Elizabethan Charlecote Park. At Stratford, whose waterfront is dominated by the Shakespeare Memorial Theatre and Holy Trinity Church and where the river flows under two multi-arched stone bridges, the Avon Navigation starts.

The Avon was first made navigable during the late 1630s. In 1717, the river was separated into two navigations, the Upper and the Lower, which met at Evesham. Commercial traffic continued until 1873 when the river became impassable to boats larger than skiffs or canoes. The locks and weirs collapsed on the Upper river, but the Lower river remained in occasional use until the 1940s. In 1949 a Trust was formed to restore the Lower river to navigation, a task that was completed in 1965 when the river was reopened from Tewkesbury to Evesham. Work was carried out largely by voluntary labour and all the necessary finance was raised privately by the Trust. The success of this restoration scheme inspired, first a similar restoration of the Stratford Canal, from Lapworth to Stratford, and second the reopening of the Upper Avon. This was an astonishingly ambitious scheme, requiring the creation of nine new locks, numerous weirs and other works, the raising of several hundred thousand pounds and the extensive use of volunteer labour over a long period. Construction work started in 1969 and in 1974 the Avon Navigation was reopened, linking Stratford with the Severn for the first time for over a century, and making available to pleasure boats a cruising circle comprising the Avon, the Stratford Canal, the Worcester and Birmingham Canal and the Severn. The route of the Avon to Tewkesbury is attractive and rural. It winds its way through fields and between tree-lined banks from the crowded waterfront at Stratford, through Welford, Bidford with its fifteenth-century bridge, Evesham, Fladbury Mill, Pershore with its abbey and Georgian houses, and then round Bredon Hill, through Tewkesbury and on to the Severn, where both commercial barges and seagoing yachts can be seen.

The Great Parlour, Wightwick Manor. The house, extravagantly decorated by William Morris, stands beside the Staffordshire & Worcestershire Canal.

Fladbury Mill on the river Avon, one of the features that makes this recently reopened river navigation so appealing to visitors.

The Severn's lost connections

Its river and canal connections make the Severn one of the liveliest waterways in England, but a century ago it was far busier for a number of important connecting waterways have largely disappeared. These include the **Shrewsbury Canal** and the **Shropshire Canals**, the **Droitwich Canals**, the **Hereford and Gloucester Canal** and, although its connection with the Severn was never more than a dream, the **Leominster Canal**. Among the large-scale exhibits preserved by the Ironbridge Gorge Museum Trust are some short stretches of canal and an inclined plane, the remains of an extensive network of small tub-boat canals that grew up to serve the industries of Ironbridge and its region during the eighteenth century. Between 1768 and 1792 several short canals were built independently for the coal and iron traffic and in 1796 the Shrewsbury Canal was opened to link them together and to provide a connection with the Severn. These canals were small, but they required dramatic engineering. There were many locks, tunnels, and a number of inclined planes to connect the different levels and during the early nineteenth century the whole area must have been a hive of extraordinary activity. Parts of the system were closed in the nineteenth century, but much survived into this century, the network dying gradually from the 1900s as coal mines were exhausted or the ironworks abandoned. The last section to remain in commercial use was part of the Shrewsbury Canal, which was not finally closed until 1944, but the network

The inclined plane was much favoured by eighteenth-century engineers. None are in operation today but the Hay Incline, seen here, has been restored at the Ironbridge Gorge Museum.

had already been isolated by the closing in 1921 of the Trench inclined plane, the last to operate in England. The rapid expansion of this region since the formation of Telford new town has obliterated most of these canals, but traces still remain. The angled slopes of inclined planes can be found at Wrockwardine Wood and Trench, there is an aqueduct at Dawley and warehouses and other canal buildings at Wappenshall. However, the best way to understand this forgotten network is to visit Iron-bridge Gorge Museum. Here are preserved boats, sections of canal, a cast iron aqueduct that formerly carried the Shrewsbury Canal over the river Tern, and an inclined plane complete with track to show how the small tub boats or their cargoes were hauled from one level to another.

In 1771 a short canal, the **Droitwich Barge Canal**, was opened to link Droitwich with the river Severn. Nearly seven miles long and with a number of locks, the canal was built to serve the salt trade, which continued to flourish throughout the nineteenth century. In 1853 another short canal, the **Droitwich Junction Canal**, was opened to join Droitwich to the Worcester and Birmingham Canal at Hanbury Wharf, thus completing a small circuit of waterways. Little used during this century, the canals were abandoned in 1939. Although built over or filled up in places, the routes can still be followed, a process that will become steadily easier as the Trust formed in 1973 to reopen the canals works towards its goal of full restoration.

One of the more unlikely products of the 'canal mania' of the late eighteenth century was the **Hereford and Gloucester Canal**, a waterway that has been largely forgotten and whose remaining artefacts stand in splendid isolation in magnificent countryside, looking as remote today as the creations of some prehistoric civilisation. The canal was built in two sections; the first, from Gloucester to Ledbury opened in 1798; the second, from Ledbury to Hereford in 1845. By the time it was completed, the canal was already out of date and what little traffic it carried was already under threat from the railway. Despite this, it somehow managed to survive and boats continued to carry building materials, coal, grain and cider, from Hereford to and from the Severn. The last commercial cargo was carried in 1883. A railway was then built on the route of the canal from Ledbury to Gloucester and this in turn has vanished, leaving little trace of Hereford's association with the industrial revolution. However, many of the buildings and engineering features that were part of the canal between Hereford and Ledbury can still be found, silent witnesses to the misplaced enthusiasms of eighteenth-century speculators. There are wharf buildings at Withington Marsh, Kymin and elsewhere, there is a pretty canal bridge at Monkhide, and Ashperton Tunnel still stands in its deep cutting. Near Prior's Court there is an aqueduct over the river Leadon. However the most significant memorial to the canal is at Oxenhall, where the great tunnel, over 2000 yards long, still survives.

Even more inconceivable now is the **Leominster Canal**, a bizarre late eighteenth-century scheme to link rural Herefordshire with the Severn. The canal was planned to run from Kington to Stourport via Leominster, a route that involved 4 major tunnels, 2 large aqueducts, and over 60 locks. Only about 18 miles, from Leominster to Southnet Wharf, were ever built before the money ran out, leaving the canal isolated and virtually useless. Some form of trading on the canal continued until it was closed in 1859, but it was virtually dead from the moment it opened. A number of relics remain to interest the explorer, for example Putnal Field Tunnel, near Berrington Hall, locks and wharves at Woofferton and, nearby, an aqueduct over the river Teme. Near Newnham there is a small tunnel, a handsome brick aqueduct over the river Rea and fine buildings at Marlbrook Wharf. However, the most intriguing memorial to the canal is the 1,250 yards long Southnet Tunnel, which was never used commercially. It was completed in 1795 as part of the route from Southnet onwards towards Stourport, but collapsed shortly afterwards and was then abandoned.

The Stratford-upon-Avon Canal

Indirectly part of the river Severn network, the **Stratford Canal** was opened in 1816 to link the river Avon at Stratford with King's Norton, south of Birmingham, where it joined the Worcester and Birmingham Canal. A short branch at Lapworth connects with the Grand Union Canal. The canal was successful at first and saw considerable traffic between the Severn and Birmingham via the river Avon, but the closure of the Avon Navigation in 1873 brought about a rapid decline, particularly of the lower section from Stratford to Lapworth. Impassable since the 1930s, this lower section remained somehow in existence until 1958 when closure seemed imminent. At the last moment a restoration scheme was mounted, using volunteer labour, and in 1964 the canal was reopened to Stratford, the restoration having cost exactly half the estimated cost of closure. Since then, the southern section has been administered by the National Trust.

The Stratford is a particularly attractive rural canal, much of its course is through quiet farmland. There are distinctive bridges, some in cast iron and

Unusual features of the Stratford-on-Avon Canal are the barrel-roofed lock houses, and the iron footbridges that divide to allow the passage of the towing rope.

split in the centre to allow the passage of the towing rope, pretty lock cottages and, at Wootten Wawen and Bearley, large iron aqueducts carrying the canal over roads and a railway. The locks are grouped in flights at Lapworth and Wilmcote. After its rather private rural route, the canal comes to a splendid

The imposing ruins of Monmouth Castle on the river Wye. A fast-flowing border river, its historical importance is underlined by the number of castles built along its banks.

terminus in a basin surrounded by flowers beside the Shakespeare Memorial Theatre in the heart of Stratford, a terminus that is now connected once again with the restored Avon Navigation.

The rivers of the Border

One of the most attractive of English rivers is the Wye, its longstanding popularity based on the magnificent countryside that surrounds it and the diversity of towns, villages and buildings to be found on its banks. Rising in Wales, the river crosses the border at Hay-on-Wye, a town at the foot of the Black Mountains that houses the world's largest bookshop. Between Hay and Hereford small villages accompany the remote course of the river, but after Hereford its route becomes more dramatic, winding its way through a wooded valley. A number of pretty suspension bridges cross the river, adding to the almost Alpine flavour. There are plenty of castles to underline the historical importance of the Wye as a border river: Goodrich, Monmouth, Clearwell and St Briavels. The steep wooded banks contain memorials to many other centuries and there are prehistoric monuments, associations with King Arthur, sections of Offa's Dyke and a number of traces of the industrial history of the region, notably the iron industry that flourished in the Forest of Dean and along the banks of the Wye during the seventeenth and early eighteenth centuries. The most spectacular part of the Wye is

probably the stretch from Monmouth to Chepstow and the junction with the Severn estuary, a steep and twisting valley that is a suitably romantic setting for Tintern Abbey. Today the fast-flowing waters of the Wye attract only canoeists and fishermen in small dinghies, but until the middle of the nineteenth century it was possible for barges to reach Hereford. A traditional navigation dating from the thirteenth century, the Wye was greatly improved in the 1660s and by the eighteenth century boats could find their way to Hay, hauled on long ropes by gangs of men, a technique used also on the upper reaches of the Severn. Since the navigation was abandoned in the 1860s, the river has steadily silted up, and its fast-flowing and tortuous course today shows no trace of its commercial past.

A tributary of the Wye is the **Lugg**, which flows from its source in the Radnor Forest west of Presteigne to Leominster, and then to its junction with the Wye east of Hereford. The Lugg is an undramatic rural river, its course marked by several pretty villages, but it too was once a navigation. During the eighteenth century locks were built to enable barges to reach Leominster, a traffic that continued until the 1860s, but nothing remains today.

The third border river is the **Teme**, which, with its tributaries, links another stretch of splendid countryside to the Severn. A group of rivers, the Onny and the Corve and their associated streams flow from Wenlock Edge to join the Teme near Ludlow. The Teme, which rises in Wales west of Clun Forest, becomes a significant waterway in Ludlow, a splendid town whose castle overlooks the fast-flowing river. From Ludlow the Teme continues to Tenbury Wells and thence to its junction with the Severn south of Worcester, its course marked by wooded valleys, rolling farmland, hop and fruit fields and a series of quiet and undeveloped villages. Although not a classic waterway itself, the Teme adds Ludlow to the list of the fine towns of the Borders and the Severn valley that are linked by water.

The Dee

One of the great mountain rivers of north Wales, the **Dee** rises at Lake Bala, and then follows a tortuous and often violent course among rocks and rapids to Llangollen. As it approaches England, the river becomes more sedate, the mountains giving way to rolling farmland that forms a pleasant and decorative background to its twisting course. At Farndon, east of Wrexham the Dee becomes tidal and navigable as it flows under the fourteenth-century bridge. The pleasant rural course of the river continues to Chester, passing the grounds of Eaton Hall, after which it really comes to life. Chester is a handsome city with a complete city wall, a cathedral, a wealth of timber-framed, Georgian and Victorian buildings, and a pretty waterfront with a number of attractive bridges. It boasts a variety of boats, from canoes and skiffs to large passenger launches, as well as the occasional barge, for the Shropshire Union Canal also passes through Chester and there is a lock

The castle at Ludlow is one of the many attractions of this fine town built above the flowing waters of the river Teme.

to connect the canal to the Dee. West of Chester the character of the Dee changes dramatically as it becomes a fast-flowing tidal estuary, with sandbanks and other hazards to navigation. Low-lying marshland and, near Connah's Quay, industrial development dominate the banks.

The Shropshire Union Canal

The **Shropshire Union Canal** Company was formed in 1846 from the amalgamation of a number of smaller, independent canals, dating mostly from the eighteenth century. Despite considerable reduction through closures during the 1930s and 1940s the Shropshire Union network is still extensive. The main line runs from Autherley, on the Staffordshire and Worcestershire Canal north of Wolverhampton to Ellesmere Port on the Mersey estuary, where there is a connection with the Manchester Ship Canal. There are two branches: one runs from Nantwich to the Trent and Mersey Canal at Middlewich; the other climbs through spectacular scenery to Llangollen in north Wales. The main line was built in three sections, each of which has a quite distinctive character. The first section, from Nantwich to Chester, was opened in 1774. It is a wide canal whose original eighteenth-century elegance is still apparent. The second section, opened in 1796, runs from Chester northwards to Whitby on the Mersey, later renamed Ellesmere Port. The third, opened in 1835, goes from Nantwich southwards to Autherley. This last section, handsomely engineered by Thomas Telford, reflects the improved

This elegant iron aqueduct carries the Shropshire Union Canal over the A5 near Brewood. The road and canal were both engineered by Thomas Telford.

The Boat Museum at Ellesmere Port, housed in the old basins and warehouses that formed the northern terminus of the Shropshire Union Canal.

standards of its day, with its straight route, high embankments, deep cuttings, tall bridges and locks grouped in flights.

The directness of the route between Wolverhampton and the Black Country and the Mersey ports enabled the Shropshire Union to remain in commercial use until the 1960s. Despite this, it is an attractive, predominantly rural canal, its route marked by interesting canal architecture and engineering features. Particularly notable are the bridges, the buildings and wharves, especially those at Autherley, Norbury, Tyrley, Market Drayton, Nantwich and Chester; the lock flights at Tyrley and Audlem, and the dramatic cuttings and embankments at Gnosall, Woodseaves and Shebdon (that at Shebdon took six years to build). There are also fine aqueducts that carry the canal over the A5 at Stretton and Nantwich. The main towns, Market Drayton, Nantwich and Chester, all feature the black-and-white timbered architecture of the region and are well worth exploring. The course of the canal through Chester is particularly impressive, featuring a flight of locks cut from solid rock beneath the towering city walls. Chester Zoo is by the canal north of the city. Between Nantwich and Chester the canal winds through attractive and often dramatic scenery, dominated for several miles by the imposing ruins of Beeston Castle, perched high on a rocky and overgrown hilltop. North of Chester the most interesting feature is Ellesmere Port, currently being developed into a centre for living canal history. The surviving nineteenth-century wharves and warehouses there are now the home of the Boat Museum, a large and steadily growing collection of inland waterway craft and related relics, where the skills of the canal craftsmen are being preserved for posterity against the background of large vessels passing on the Manchester Ship Canal.

At Hurleston, just north of Nantwich, the branch leading to north Wales leaves the main line of the Shropshire Union. At first a rural, meandering canal, more like a river in character, the Llangollen arm becomes more dramatic as it approaches Wales. The strange and wild landscape of the peat bogs at Whixhall Moss gives way to the so-called 'lake district' of Ellesmere, a group of nine wooded lakes that surround the canal. Ellesmere, itself, is a pleasant country town with an attractive basin lined with original warehouses, at the end of a short arm.

At Welsh Frankton is the junction with the long Montgomery branch that runs southwards to Welshpool and Newtown, a beautiful canal derelict since the 1940s, but now slowly being restored and brought back to life. A few miles further on the canal crosses into Wales over Telford's great stone aqueduct at Chirk. Nearby, at Pontcysyllte, is one of the greatest wonders of the waterways, an astonishing iron aqueduct over 1000 feet-long that strides across the river Dee on great stone pillars, 120 feet up in the air. Designed by Telford and completed in 1805, this masterpiece should be admired both from the Dee valley below, framed by Welsh mountains, and from the precipitous towpath beside the canal on the aqueduct itself.

Until its closure in 1944 there was another branch canal that connected the main line at Norbury to the Shrewsbury Canal at Wappenshall. Opened in 1835, this 10 mile waterway with its 23 locks was a vital link between the canal system of Ironbridge and the Severn valley, and the main canal network. Little of the route now remains, but part of the lock flight at Norbury, further locks at Newport and a three-arch aqueduct at Forton can still be seen.

The Birmingham Canal Navigations

In order to understand the importance of the development of the English canal system in the eighteenth century, it is vital to visit Birmingham

The Black Delph flight of eight locks, which connects the Birmingham Canal Navigations with the Stourbridge Canal, in a landscape that is full of contrasts.

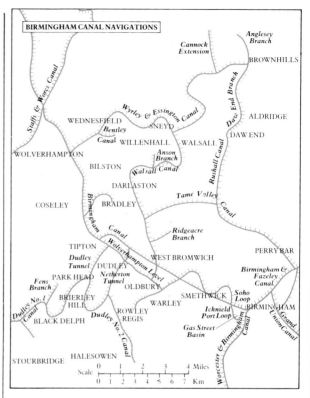

An unusual view of Spaghetti Junction from below, one of many strange sights to be seen along the hidden waterways of the Birmingham Canal Navigations.

which has an extraordinary network of predominantly urban canals. The **Birmingham Canal Navigations** grew up from 1769 to serve the new industries of Birmingham and the Black Country, and at its peak in the middle of the nineteenth century the network totalled over 160 miles. There were over 200 narrow locks, more than 500 private arms or basins connecting factories to the system, 3

Farmer's Bridge locks at the start of the Birmingham and Fazeley Canal. This was once a busy life line of the Birmingham Canal Navigations.

tunnels over a mile long, at Dudley, Netherton and Lappal, numerous aqueducts and bridges, and many branches connecting the network to other English canals. About 100 miles of the network still survives, allowing Birmingham to claim more miles of canal than Venice. To explore the Birmingham Canal Navigations (or BCN as it is commonly known) is to step back in time and enter a secret world, largely unchanged since the Victorian period. This exploration can only be made by boat or on foot, but the effort is worthwhile for it brings the history of the Industrial Revolution to life. Commercial use of the BCN continued until the early 1970s, but since then industry has gradually retreated, allowing much of the network to become both an unofficial museum of the Industrial Revolution and an unofficial wildlife park. It is a private world where flowers, butterflies and birds thrive among the overgrown ruins of industry and into which the twentieth century only occasionally intrudes. To travel by boat unseen beneath the concrete chaos of Spaghetti Junction, or to moor in a secret basin surrounded by traditional painted narrow boats, hidden in the heart of Birmingham are pleasures unique to BCN.

The heart of the BCN are the main lines from

Hidden in the centre of Birmingham and at the heart of the canal network, Gas Street Basin is the home of many traditionally painted narrow boats.

Birmingham's Gas Street Basin and its connections southwards with the Stratford and Worcester and Birmingham Canals to their northern connections near Wolverhampton with the Staffordshire and Worcestershire, and Shropshire Union Canals. Built between 1769 and the 1830s, these main lines encapsulate the history of the English canal system. Other BCN branches lead to the Grand Union Canal, for the south and London, to the Coventry Canal for the Midlands, and the Stourbridge Canal for the west and south-west. Notable among the parts of the BCN to have been lost is the **Wyrley and Essington Canal**. Closed during the 1950s and now only traceable in short sections, this meandering canal wound its way northwards through the Black Country to join the Coventry Canal near Lichfield.

Today the BCN is run down, occasionally depressing and often dirty. The only evidence of its frenetic life of 30 years ago is derelict and decaying buildings, overlooking gloomy waterways filled with rubbish. However, as industry retreats, so the BCN is slowly coming back to life, first as a secret and rarely disturbed natural wilderness, and second as a waterway network of great variety and interest, whose amenity potential is unrivalled in England. Redevelopment is under way, sometimes carried out with sympathy, as at Farmer's Bridge in Birmingham, and sometimes in a crude and mindless way as in the pointless removal of the Victorian warehouses that used to surround Gas Street Basin. There is a danger that the very qualities that make the BCN so unique will be swept away, but at the moment there is plenty of the eighteenth and nineteenth centuries still to be seen, a survival encouraged by the Black Country Museum at Dudley. Although they may not have a universal appeal, the unique attractions of the Birmingham Canal Navigations do deserve careful and sympathetic exploration.

The pretty flight of ten locks at Foxton on the Leicester Line of the Grand Union Canal, a busy and popular spot in the summer.

THE HEART OF ENGLAND

The river Trent flows through the heart of England in a great sweeping curve that effectively divides the Midlands from the North. With its connecting waterways the Trent forms a line from the Mersey to the Humber estuary. Although rarely explored, the Trent has considerable potential and interest. The surrounding landscape is predominantly farmland and woods, perhaps lacking in drama but attractively rural and typically English. The route of the Trent is full of history. Along its banks are Roman settlements, medieval castles and abbeys, fine Tudor and Georgian mansions, country villages, large cities and towns, the latter reflecting the rapid growth and expansion of the Victorian period. The Trent has been a river navigation for centuries, an important artery leading into the centre of England and today boats can still travel much of its length. The river is also the backbone of a waterway network that extends navigation in many directions, a radiating system built in the eighteenth century to bring the Industrial Revolution to some of the more remote corners of England. The landscape of the heart of England ranges from the bare hills, moorland and wooded valleys of the Peak District to the low-lying and desolate marshlands that flank the Trent's tidal estuary. In between are the miles of gently rolling farmlands that determine the character of the Midlands, a countryside whose subtle beauty deserves careful exploration. Rivers and canals offer the perfect way to discover and appreciate this style of countryside, and there is no shortage of pleasant, old-fashioned and meandering waterways to follow.

The same waterways reflect the impact of centuries of gradual development, making the history of the region and its sources of wealth easy to understand. In many areas the ridge and furrow of the medieval system of cultivation can still be seen, sometimes sharply divided by the line of an eighteenth-century canal. The sites of deserted medieval villages can be explored, as well as the great industrial cities of the Victorian period, whose growth was totally dependent upon the availability of navigable waterways. Stoke, Derby, Nottingham

The river Trent at Newark, a handsome town whose waterfront is dominated by the ruins of its twelfth-century castle.

and Leicester are typical creations of eighteenth-century industrialisation, cities whose considerable wealth was founded upon their staple industries, pottery, coal, engineering, textiles, and their ability to export their products via the waterways. Stafford, Newark, Grantham and Macclesfield reflect an earlier period of history and an earlier form of wealth, based largely on agriculture and land management. The rivers played their part in the development of these more traditional towns and cities, and there are still plenty of traces of pre-industrial England to be discovered. The wealth of the region can be measured by the great number of fine houses and country estates, the tangible relics of a powerful, land-owning class whose considerable wealth inspired the building of river navigations and canals. Canals came early to this part of England, and many still survive in a virtually unchanged eighteenth-century state. Complete with great tunnels and other dramatic feats of engineering, they are fitting memorials to the ambition and ingenuity of their builders. The canal age was effectively launched in 1776 by the building of the Trent and Mersey Canal, the first of the grand trunk canals designed to link together the major waterways and industrial centres of England. From this waterway grew the vast network that made possible the Industrial Revolution, a turbulent period whose history can still be traced along the rivers and canals by the discerning explorer.

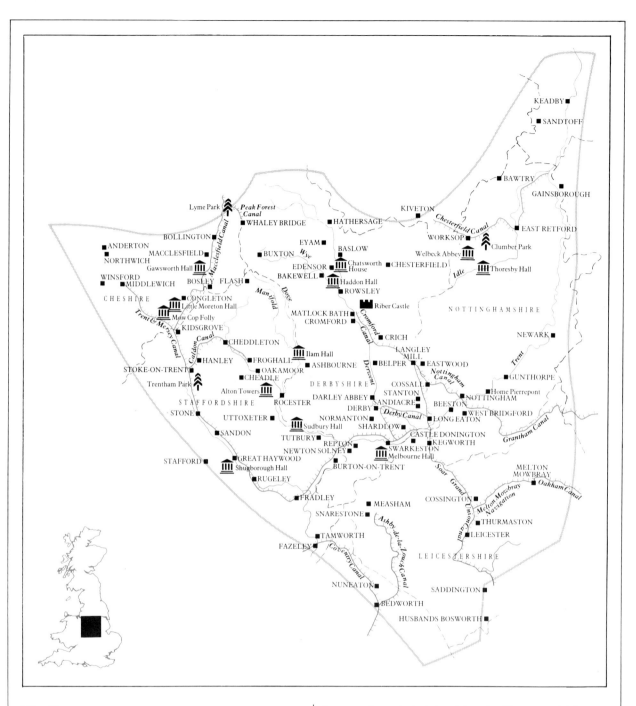

The Trent

The course of the **Trent**, which runs through Staffordshire and Nottinghamshire, falls into two distinct parts. The first stretch, from the Trent's source near Stoke to Shardlow, midway between Derby and Nottingham, winds along a varied but generally unexciting route, lined by farmland, willow trees and the occasional village or town. Leaving behind the potbanks and housing estates of Stoke, the Trent flows through Trentham Park towards Stone, where it is joined by the Trent and Mersey Canal. River and canal then share the same valley, passing Stafford and Rugeley, with Cannock Chase and Shugborough Hall to the south. From Rugeley to Burton the Trent follows its own route, although the canal is never far away. Burton, the brewing capital of England, grew up around the Trent which, during the seventeenth and eighteenth centuries, was navigable through the town. East of Burton the river moves briefly into Derbyshire.

The importance of the lower reaches of the river Trent for commercial traffic is underlined by this industrial scene at Torksey.

After Repton it flows under the medieval bridge near Swarkestone, passes Melbourne Hall and the racing car museum at Castle Donnington, and then it reaches Shardlow, the start of the Trent Navigation and the eastern terminus of the Trent and Mersey Canal.

The second part of the Trent, from Shardlow to Trent Falls where it joins the Humber estuary, is very different. Navigable for several centuries, and steadily improved since the eighteenth century, the Trent quickly becomes a major waterway, with 13 large locks to facilitate the passage of boats along the 95 mile route to the estuary. At first it follows an industrial course through Long Eaton, Beeston and Nottingham, curving round the castle mound and passing the Nottingham Canal Museum housed in an old Trent warehouse, but after the junctions with the Derwent and Soar, the river moves into a more open landscape filled with the lakes formed from old gravel workings. At Holme Pierrepont, one of these has become an international rowing and water sports centre. The Trent is not a pretty river, but there is plenty to see in the surrounding towns and villages and a variety of boats use the river. Some commercial traffic still survives, notably barges carrying stone, gravel and oil. Gunthorpe, the site of a Roman river crossing, is a good place to watch the boats. Small and rather isolated villages follow the river to Newark, a handsome town with a twelfth-century castle, a fine parish church with a huge spire, some good Georgian buildings and an interesting variety of traditional shops. North of Newark, at Cromwell Lock, the Trent becomes tidal and assumes the character of a wide, fast-flowing, powerful waterway requiring skill and experience to navigate. Its high banks and the low-lying landscape of the region limit the views of the river, which follows a winding course to Gainsborough, passing at Torksey the mouth of the Fossdyke Navigation which leads to Lincoln. Gainsborough is a pleasant small town that retains the atmosphere of a ninteenth-century inland port and is still busy with a variety of commercial traffic. North of Gainsborough the size and power of the Trent steadily increases and it becomes a daunting sight as it approaches the estuary. At West Stockwith the river passes the junction with the Chesterfield Canal and the river **Idle** (navigable since the seventeenth century to Bawtry but visually unexciting) and then the surroundings become more industrial as the Trent turns into a mighty seaway, navigable only by large ships. At Keadby is the junction with the Keadby and Stainforth Canal, a link with the canals and navigable rivers of South Yorkshire.

The river Derwent adds the all-important dimension of water to the magnificent gardens of Chatsworth House.

The Chesterfield Canal

Opened in 1777 to link Chesterfield with the river Trent, this 46 mile canal had 65 locks and one major tunnel. Despite its isolation from the rest of the English canal network, the **Chesterfield Canal** was a commercial success throughout the nineteenth century and until 1908 when the tunnel at Norwood collapsed. This disaster effectively sealed off the canal west of Worksop, leaving the western section to Chesterfield to fall into gradual decay, while the eastern section, from Worksop to the Trent at West Stockwith continued to carry commercial traffic until the 1950s. Since then the canal has been used increasingly by pleasure boats as it offers a rural solitude unequalled by many other English waterways. From West Stockwith to East Retford the canal follows a winding and rural route, flanked by small and pretty villages and then beyond Retford it enters an area known as the Dukeries, a wooded, rolling landscape richly decorated with country houses. Nearby are Clumber Park, Welbeck Abbey, Thoresby Hall, houses built on the fortunes made from the Nottinghamshire coal fields in the eighteenth century. The coal fields made the canal successful but brought about the collapse through subsidence of the tunnel. The present terminus of the canal is just beyond some impressive warehouses in Worksop, but the route to Chesterfield can easily be explored, to discover lock flights, the remains of the great Norwood Tunnel, which is over 3000 yards long, and the remote, wooded stretches of canal between Kiveton and Worksop.

The rivers of the Peaks

The Peak District, an oasis of wild and rugged country surrounded on most sides by urban and industrial development, can be enjoyably explored by following its rivers. The **Derwent**, the Dove, the **Manifold** and the **Churnet** all flow rapidly from their sources high in the Peaks towards the Trent, their routes marked by steep valleys, remote farms and villages and frequently spectacular scenery. The greatest of these rivers is the Derwent, which rises in the inaccessible moorlands above the Derwent Reservoir, overlooked by Kinder Scout, the Dark Peak and other hills that reach towards the 2000 foot level. From the reservoir southwards, the Derwent is accompanied by minor roads and so exploration is easy. With Sheffield only a few miles to the east, the Derwent is surprisingly undeveloped, its natural privacy protected by the inhospitable nature of the terrain. Typical Peak villages, Hathersage, Eyam and Baslow, cluster round the river in its valley, and then south of Baslow the landscape becomes more open as the Derwent flows through Edensor and the grounds of Chatsworth House. Water is an essential feature of Chatsworth, its classical bridges, mighty cascade and huge fountain all make a major contribution to the park. Still in a valley but now a substantial waterway, the Derwent continues to Matlock and Matlock Bath, dominated on the west by hills rich in prehistoric remains, and on the east by the nineteenth-century Riber Castle and its wildlife park, and the wooded Heights of Abraham. At Cromford there are the great mills established by the Arkwrights in the eighteenth century, mills that originally were dependent upon the Derwent for their power. This is another region where the remains of the Industrial Revolution can be explored and wondered at, the mills, the lead mines, the pumping engines, the ironworks, early railways and the Cromford Canal. To the south is another opportunity to discover a vanished aspect of English life, the Crich tramway museum. The Derwent flows through Belper, another mill town, before entering the outskirts of Derby, passing Darley Abbey. Derby does not make much of its river, and there is little to show that the Derwent was once a busy navigation that connected Derby to the Trent. The navigation was abandoned in the late eighteenth century, however, after the opening of the Derby Canal, which offered a more direct route. South of Derby the Derwent flows through unexciting country to join the Trent near Shardlow.

The Derwent has one tributary of importance, the river **Wye**. This rises north of Buxton, passes attractively through the town, and then enters the

The pleasures of tramway travel can be re-experienced at the Crich Tram Museum, a mecca for tram enthusiasts and time travellers.

Dovedale in Derbyshire, the most popular of the Peak District's limestone dales. It offers some remarkably varied scenery and strange rock formations.

dramatic valley of Miller's Dale. Inevitably popular among visitors to the Peaks, the Wye continues on through Bakewell to its junction with the Derwent at Rowsley. Old mills mark its route, while Haddon Hall overlooks its valley. The Dove and the Manifold are Peak rivers of similar attraction and interest, flowing along parallel valleys before joining near Ilam Hall. The Dove, which forms the border between Derbyshire and Staffordshire, rises near Flash, England's highest village. Its valley is remote, undeveloped and accessible only on foot for most of its route, but its splendid scenery, particularly through Dovedale, is well worth the effort. The Manifold is accessible from minor roads, and its valley is more dramatic: caves, swallow holes and precipices mark its route. South of its junction with the Manifold, the Dove is a more significant river, passing west of Ashbourne before entering the thickly wooded valley known as the Staffordshire Rhinelands. Nearby is Alton Towers, the only pleasure park in England that attempts to rival Disneyland. Leaving behind the attractions of the Peaks, the Dove becomes a gentle river. It winds its way through farmland, round the outskirts of Uttoxeter, through the grounds of seventeenth-century Sudbury Hall, past Tutbury with its castle and then to the junction with the Trent near Newton Solney.

The fourth of the Peak District rivers is the Churnet, which like the Manifold has its own distinct character despite being a tributary of the Dove. Rising north of Rudyard Reservoir, the river winds its way round Leek and then enters the attractively wooded Churnet valley, along a route which it shares with the Caldon Canal. At Cheddleton are the preserved mills where the flints for the pottery industry were ground by water power and nearby is the Churnet Valley Steam Railway. Froghall and Oakamoor are quiet towns in the Staffordshire moorlands, a region of rural isolation still unaffected by the proximity of Stoke-on-Trent and the Potteries, while to the south is Cheadle, with its magnificent church designed by Pugin. The Churnet then passes through the grounds of Alton Towers, flanked by wooded hills and, shortly after Rocester, it joins the Dove.

The canals of Derbyshire and Nottingham

The importance of the river Trent as a navigation inevitably encouraged the building of a number of canals during the eighteenth century designed to connect the new centres of industry to the river, and thus to the developing national waterway network. Some of these canals are still in existence today, but others have largely disappeared. Besides paying little attention to its river, the Derwent, Derby is one of the few major cities and centres of industry to have lost completely its connection with the canal system. Throughout the eighteenth century barges were able to reach Derby along the Derwent, but in 1796 this journey was made easier by the opening of the **Derby Canal** which ran from the Erewash Canal westwards to Derby, through the city, and then south to join the Trent and Mersey Canal at Swarkestone. Commercial traffic continued to use the canal until the early 1960s and it was closed finally in 1964. The owners of the Derby Canal somehow managed to escape the nationalisation of

Bottle ovens are now a rare canalside sight in Staffordshire. These examples are preserved at the Gladstone Pottery Museum, Stoke-on-Trent.

the rest of the canal system and so were able to sell off much of the course of the canal for development during the 1960s. As a result, there is very little of the Derby Canal to be seen today, and even the Holmes Aqueduct, the first cast iron aqueduct in the world, has been destroyed.

The earliest canal in this area is the **Erewash**. Opened in 1779 from Sawley on the river Trent to Langley Mill, 12 miles to the north, the Erewash was the backbone of a small waterway network serving the coal mines and ironworks of the region. Ironically it is the only part to remain navigable, all the later developments having been closed. Its route is not particularly exciting as it mostly runs through a mixture of urban and industrial surroundings, but there are some features of interest, notably the canalside lace mills at Long Eaton and Sandiacre (where there are also the remains of the junction with the Derby Canal), the Stanton ironworks, Eastwood, which was the birthplace of D.H. Lawrence and the recently restored Langley Mill Basin. A century ago Langley Mill was a bustling canal centre, for two other waterways came together here.

The first of these waterways, and by far the most interesting, is the **Cromford Canal**. Opened in 1794, the canal ran from Cromford on the river Derwent, the home of the Arkwright cotton mills, to Langley Mill where it joined the Erewash. It was a dramatic canal, cut along the steep Derwent valley and it had a number of unusual features, including several aqueducts and the 3000 yard Butterley Tunnel. Coal, stone, lead and iron were the staple cargoes on the canal, which thrived until 1900, when the tunnel collapsed, effectively cutting the canal into two parts. Decay was fairly rapid, particularly on the section between Cromford and Butterley, and the canal was quickly abandoned. However, that is not the end of the story, for part of the upper section of the Cromford Canal has recently been restored, largely by volunteers. Today, Cromford is once again a centre of canal activity. The extraordinary ingenuity that inspired the Industrial Revolution can be explored at Cromford Wharf, with its original warehouses; High Peak Wharf, where the trucks of the Cromford and High Peak Railway started their strange journey aross the hills and moorlands of Derbyshire to Whaley Bridge, by being hauled up the first of a series of inclined planes; the restored Leawood steam pumping engine, which lifts water from the Derwent into the canal; the handsome Wigwell aqueduct. There are boat trips along the restored section, which eventually will reach Whatstandwell and Ambergate. From Ambergate southwards much of the canal has disappeared including most of the locks and the Pinxton branch, but the daunting portals of Butterley Tunnel are still to be seen.

The second canal to join the Erewash at Langley Mill is the **Nottingham**. This ran from the Trent, near Trent Bridge, to Langley Mill, passing through the centre of Nottingham, and it was designed to allow traffic from the Cromford Canal, particularly coal and iron, a direct route to Nottingham and the Trent. Commercial traffic continued until the 1920s and the canal was closed in 1937. Much of the Nottingham Canal has now vanished but there are the remains of locks at Wollaton and an aqueduct at Cossall, and between Trowell and Cossall a stretch survives which still holds water. The Nottingham Canal deserves a better fate than the total obliteration that has been the lot of its neighbour, the Derby Canal, for although not particularly scenic, its remains are a tangible witness to the industrial development of the region in the late eighteenth century.

The Trent and Mersey Canal and its branches

One of the greatest of the English canals as regards both length and historical importance is the **Trent and Mersey** or, as it was called at first, the Grand Trunk Canal. It was planned originally as part of the great cross of canals designed to link the Mersey, the Trent, the Thames and the Severn, and it was the first of the waterways to link together the two coasts of England. James Brindley was the engineer and work started in 1766 on the 93 mile route. Among the promoters of the canal was the potter Josiah Wedgwood, who realised that the future development of the pottery industry in Staffordshire was dependent upon an improved system of transport between the factories in Stoke and the docks at Liverpool. As a result his new factory, built at Etruria during the 1760s, was situated beside the canal. The Trent and Mersey runs from Preston Brook, south of Runcorn, where it leaves the Bridgewater Canal to Shardlow in Derbyshire where it joins the Trent Navigation. Despite its industrial associations, the Trent and Mersey is a predominantly rural canal that enjoys a continuously changing landscape. It was a difficult and expensive canal to build and its completion was delayed by a number of engineering problems, notably the digging of the great tunnel through Harecastle Hill, north of Stoke. When it was finally fully opened in 1777, the canal was an immediate success and was directly responsible for the rapid growth of a number of towns and cities along its banks, in particular Northwich with its salt industry, Stoke and its potteries and Burton with its breweries. Commerical traffic continued to use the Trent and Mersey Canal until the 1960s, with pottery materials as the staple cargoes right up to the end.

The Trent and Mersey is an interesting and varied canal to explore, with 76 wide and narrow locks, including some in pairs, several tunnels and aqueducts and a variety of attractive bridges. At first the canal follows the wooded valley of the river Weaver but at a higher level so there are good views of the river and its shipping. At Anderton is another wonder of the waterways, the unique vertical lift that transports boats between the Trent and Mersey and the Weaver below. This extraordinary piece of Victorian engineering, built in 1875, consists of two great iron water tanks, in which boats are raised or lowered. From here onwards the landscape is dominated by the salt industry, with mines at Marston, Northwich and Middlewich. Continual subsidence has caused the canal to be raised high above the surrounding landscape. At Middlewich there is a junction with the branch from the Shropshire Union Canal to the west, and then a long flight of locks carries the canal round Sandbach and up to Kidsgrove and the Harecastle Tunnel. Just north of

Hazelhurst Locks on the Caldon Canal, which was reopened in 1974 after years of disuse. The branch to Leek leaves the main line here.

The vertical lift at Anderton, one of the wonders of the waterways. It transports boats from the Trent and Mersey Canal to the Weaver below.

the tunnel is the junction with the Macclesfield Canal, which leaves the Trent and Mersey on the south (crossing it on a fly-over aqueduct) after which the canal proceeds north towards Manchester. There are actually two Harecastle Tunnels. James Brindley's original bore was closed by subsidence over 50 years ago, leaving Thomas Telford's tunnel of 1827 as the only way through the hill. The mouths of the two tunnels still stand side by side and the passage through is a daunting experience as the roof is only six feet above the waterline. After Harecastle, the canal passes through the centre of Stoke, although most of the traditional canalside potteries with their characteristic bottle-shaped ovens have disappeared. Near the centre of Hanley, one of Arnold Bennett's 'Five Towns', is the

The northern portal of the narrow Harecastle Tunnel on the Trent and Mersey Canal

at Kidsgrove in Staffordshire. The canal water is stained red by underground mineral deposits.

Froghall Basin, the terminus of the Caldon Canal. The Basin features a warehouse and some giant lime kilns and is approached through a low, narrow tunnel.

junction with the Caldon Canal, while a number of smaller canals and branches, now mostly derelict or vanished, used to connect various pottery factories to the Trent and Mersey. All the great names of the industry – Wedgwood, Minton, Spode, Doulton – owed their success to the Trent and Mersey and its branches during the eighteenth and nineteenth centuries. South of Stoke the canal runs through pleasant rolling farmland, passing Stone, Sandon, Great Haywood and the junction with the Staffordshire and Worcestershire Canal, Shugborough Hall and Rugeley, a route shared with the river Trent. At Fradley there is a junction with the Coventry Canal and then, after a rural and rather remote section, the canal passes through Burton, following the line of the Roman Ryknild Street. An aqueduct carries the canal over the river Dove and at Swarkestone is the short arm that used to lead to the Derby Canal. The final village before the junction

with the Trent is Shardlow, a classic canal settlement complete with elegant warehouses and original wharves, richly ornamented with eighteenth century architectural details.

Although technically a branch of the Trent and Mersey, the **Caldon Canal** has its own distinctive personality. Seventeen miles long, the Caldon runs from the Trent and Mersey Canal at Etruria to Froghall. It was opened in 1779 and a short branch to Leek was added in 1802, followed by an extension from Froghall to Uttoxeter in 1811. The canal was built primarily for the transport of stone, which was brought from quarries at Cauldon Low to Froghall by a series of tramways. Never officially closed (with the exception of the Uttoxeter section which was converted into a railway in 1847), the Caldon survived in a rather derelict state until the early 1970s, when an ambitious restoration programme was launched. It was reopened to Froghall in 1974, along with much of the Leek branch. The Caldon is a canal of remarkable contrasts. It leaves Hanley and the potteries through a nineteenth-century industrial landscape, and then is suddenly in the heart of the countryside, surrounded by woods and moors, and overlooked by the hills of the Peak District. Between Cheddleton and Froghall the canal follows closely the valley of the Churnet, one of the most remote and beautiful stretches of canal in the country. At Froghall Basin there is a tiny tunnel, some warehouses and, almost buried in the woods, a dramatic series of lime kilns overlooking a sensitively planned picnic area.

The Macclesfield and Peak Forest Canals

The **Peak Forest** and **Macclesfield** Canals formed an important waterway route into Manchester from the south. The Peak Forest was the first to be built, running from Dukinfield on the Ashton Canal east of Manchester to Buxsworth Basin and Whaley Bridge, 14 miles to the south-east. Stone quarries, connected to Buxsworth by tramways, supplied most of the traffic and as late as the 1880s up to 30 boats a day were leaving the basin. However, this traffic died during the 1920s after which the Peak Forest began a slow decline and was impassable by the 1960s. Closure seemed inevitable but an ambitious restoration scheme using volunteer labour saved the canal, and brought about its reopening in 1974.

Once away from Manchester's suburbs, the Peak Forest quickly becomes a canal of great attraction, the section from Marple to Whaley Bridge is among the most dramatic in the country. At Marple there are 2 short tunnels and a magnificent stone aqueduct over the river Goyt with 3 huge arches that is over 100 feet high. A flight of 16 locks lifts the canal to an embankment built on to the side of the Goyt valley.

The Marple Aqueduct, a handsome three-arched stone aqueduct that carries the Peak Forest Canal over the river Goyt above a dramatic wooded valley.

Thickly wooded, with splendid views over the valley, this embankment continues to Whaley Bridge, passing the junction with the Macclesfield Canal. At Whaley Bridge there is a terminus basin with an original stone warehouse in which goods were transhipped from boats to railway waggons for the journey across the Peaks to Cromford, along the Cromford and High Peak Railway. Although long closed, the course of the railway can be followed on foot and the remains of its inclined planes explored. This is a worth while exercise as it clarifies the importance of this vital railway link between the canals of Derbyshire and the Midlands, and the canals of Manchester and the north-west.

Built comparatively late, the Macclesfield Canal formed an important link between the Peak Forest and the canals of Manchester and the Trent and Mersey. It is a handsome canal, built largely on the

One of the Macclesfield Canal's characteristic curving bridges, designed so that the towing horse could cross the canal without being unhitched.

The timber-framed extravagance of Little Moreton Hall, near the Macclesfield Canal.

500 foot contour and its route is marked by impressive embankments, notably at High Lane, Bollington and Bosley, which offer exciting views over the wooded river valleys and rolling farmland that mark the edge of the Cheshire Plain. Another intriguing feature of the canal are the elegant stone bridges that carry the towpath from one side to the other, designed so that the horse could be led across without having to be detached from the barge. The route of the canal is from Marple on the Peak Forest to Hall Green, near Harecastle on the Trent and Mersey, a route through Bollington, Macclesfield and Congelton. Besides the attractions of its landscape and architecture, the Macclesfield Canal also enjoys a variety of fine houses near its banks, including Lyme Park, Gawsworth Hall and the black-and-white splendour of Little Moreton Hall. There are several aqueducts and a flight of 12 locks in remote country near Bosley. Between Congelton and the junction with the Trent and Mersey, the canal is dominated by two great hills, The Cloud, and Mow Cop, the latter crowned by an eighteenth-century folly in the form of a ruined castle. Handsome, elegant, and built through a dramatic landscape, the Macclesfield Canal represents one of the final attempts by the great engineer Thomas Telford to hold the railway age at bay.

The Weaver

One of the lesser known of the English river navigations, the **Weaver** has continued to enjoy a busy commercial life, the result of steady improvement and development since 1732 when it was first made accessible to barges. The secret of the Weaver's success is the salt trade, for salt, and more recently chemicals, have always been the staple traffic. The Weaver rises south of Nantwich and then flows through a quiet landscape of farmland to Winsford, where the navigation begins. Large locks and swing bridges mean that boats up to 130 feet long and 35 feet wide can use the Weaver, and so there is always a variety of shipping to be seen, particularly in the section between Northwich and the Mersey. Despite its importance as a commercial waterway, the Weaver is still an attractive river. Some of the locks, at Dutton, Saltersford and Vale Royal, are set in attractive wooded countryside, still pleasantly remote despite the proximity of industry. Between Northwich and Frodsham the Trent and Mersey Canal flows beside the Weaver, but at a higher level, and the only link is via the vertical boat lift at Anderton. For the last four miles the Weaver is tidal, and so it has been bypassed by a canalised section that takes boats to Weston Point Docks, where there is a connection with the Manchester Ship Canal and the Mersey estuary.

The canals and rivers of the east Midlands

The east Midlands are served by two canal and river networks that enable boats to travel from the waterways of the south to those of the north. The first, formed largely by the **Coventry Canal**, connects the Grand Union and Oxford Canals from London and the south to the Trent and Mersey Canal and to the Birmingham Canals. The second, formed by a branch of the Grand Union and the river Soar, leads to the river Trent, and thus to the north-east.

Opened in 1790, the Coventry Canal runs from its terminus basin in the heart of Coventry to Fradley, where it joins the Trent and Mersey Canal. There are two other vital junctions on its route, first with the Oxford Canal at Hawkesbury, and second at Fazeley with the Birmingham and Fazeley Canal which leads to the Birmingham Canal Navigations. Traditionally a coal canal, the Coventry remained in commercial use until the 1960s, and coal mines, both active and long abandoned, still accompany the canal for much of its route. Despite this, it is not

The rolling farmlands of the Midlands provide an attractive setting for the Coventry Canal,
seen here near Polesworth.

unattractive, with long stretches running through woods and farmlands, passing a number of places of interest and some fine canal architecture. In Coventry itself the basin still has many of its original buildings and is well placed near the cathedral. Arriving in the city by boat is certainly more enjoyable than by car. Hawkesbury Junction is a traditional canal centre, retaining much of its nineteenth-century atmosphere and there is usually a good selection of working narrow boats to be seen. Leaving Hawkesbury the canal passes through largely urban surroundings to Nuneaton, and from there to Tamworth its route is enjoyably rural, with an attractive flight of locks through Atherstone. At Tamworth there is an aqueduct over the river Tame, overlooked by the castle. From Tamworth to Fradley the canal runs through a wooded landscape, its route bypassing Lichfield and marked only by small villages, including Huddlesford where there was a junction with the abandoned Wyrley and Essington Canal. Fradley Junction itself is a popular spot with an attractive pub and canal buildings.

There is one other aspect of the Coventry Canal that should not be overlooked, namely the two branch canals that join it. The first of these is the **Ashby-de-la-Zouch Canal**, which leaves the Coventry near Bedworth and then meanders northwards for 22 miles before coming to a stop in the middle of a field near Snarestone. Opened in 1794 to serve the coalfields of Leicestershire and south Derbyshire, the canal was remarkably successful and remained in commerical use until the late 1960s. Despite its name it never reached Ashby, although it used to have a more substantial terminus in Measham, the top few miles having been closed through subsidence. Today the Ashby is a totally rural and little used waterway, winding its way through the pretty villages of Leicestershire. It is rarely visited by boats because it does not really go anywhere, apart from passing the site of the Battle of Bosworth Field. River-like in quality, the Ashby is an idyll of peace and quiet in an overdeveloped region. Rather more unusual but largely vanished are the **Newdigate Canals**, a network of private canals built in and around his Arbury Hall estate by Sir Roger Newdigate between 1769 and 1796. The entrance to this network can still be seen north of Hawkesbury Junction but little else remains of the system that totalled over 8 miles and included 13 locks. Constructd to serve the coal mines around Arbury Hall and used for transport around the estate, the network declined during the early nineteenth century until eventually only the access waterway from the Coventry Canal remained in use. The remains of some locks and short sections of canal still survive in the estate and can be tracked down by energetic visitors to Arbury Hall.

The **Leicester** arm of the Grand Union Canal leaves the main line at Norton Junction, an area now overshadowed by the Watford Gap service station on the M1 motorway. A through route from the Grand union to the Trent, the Leicester arm was formed by the amalgamation of several small canal and river navigations, mostly dating from the late eighteenth century. A predominantly rural and rather meandering waterway, its commercial success was limited by the mixture of wide and narrow locks, which effectively prevented the larger boats on the Trent from penetrating further south than Leicester. Such restrictions do not affect pleasure boating and today the route is heavily used, particularly the remarkably attractive and remote section from Watford Gap to Leicester. There are few villages, but the canal enjoys good views over a rolling and wooded landscape, and there are a number of interesting tunnels, at Crick, Husbands Bosworth and Saddington. However the main feature of this section is the flight of ten locks at Foxton, an unusually pretty flight busy with boats during the summer. Nearby can be seen the remains of the extraordinary inclined plane, which raised and lowered fully laden narrow boats in huge tanks on rails. Powered by steam, and designed to replace the locks, this grandiose machine was only used between 1900 and about 1912. At the bottom of the Foxton flight is the branch leading to Market Harborough. The main line continues its wandering course towards Leicester, remaining rural and remote until the outskirts of Leicester itself. South of the city the canal joins the river **Soar Navigation**, which passes through the centre of Leicester in a handsome cutting. Unlike many Midlands towns

Despite its rural surroundings, the river Weaver in Cheshire is still a busy commercial waterway used by coasters carrying chemicals and salt.

Closed to boats in the 1950s, the Grantham Canal is typical of England's forgotten waterways and is one of the easiest to explore.

Originally built to carry coal, the rural Ashby Canal now follows a winding river-like course through miles of quiet Midland scenery.

and cities, Leicester seems proud of its waterway. North of Leicester the Soar widens into a major river, with fast-flowing weirs and large locks. The surroundings are still rural but a number of gravel pits accompany the river through a more open landscape. There are some pretty villages, Thurmaston, Barrow, Normanton and Kegworth, but as a rule buildings tend to stay well back from the river banks for the Soar is liable to sudden flooding. The Soar bypasses Loughborough (not an attractive town in any case) but nearby is the steam-hauled Great Central Railway. The Soar joins the Trent at Red Hill lock, in the shadow of the huge power station at Radcliffe. Although there is very little commercial traffic, the Soar is a popular waterway, much used by pleasure boats and easy to explore by road. Less known is its connection with the former **Melton Mowbray Navigation** and the **Oakham Canal**, a largely forgotten waterway whose junction with the Soar at Cossington can still be seen. This obscure waterway was opened in the late eighteenth century when the river Wreake was made navigable to Melton Mowbray. A few years later, in 1803, the 15 mile long Oakham Canal was built from Melton Mowbray to Oakham, making a total waterway of over 30 miles long with 31 locks. This rather unlikely system traded successfully for a number of

years but the Oakham Canal was closed in 1846 and the Melton Mowbray Navigation followed it 30 years later. Relatively easy to explore today, the waterway offers a number of attractions, including an attractively rural route, the remains of locks and wharves, some canal buildings and not least a golden opportunity to appreciate one of the more extraordinary schemes devised by eighteenth-century canal enthusiasts.

The Grantham Canal

One of the simplest of England's lost waterways to explore is the **Grantham Canal**. Opened in 1797, this 33 mile long rural canal ran from Grantham to the Trent at West Bridgford, its route wandering across the Vale of Belvoir. Boats continued to use the canal regularly until the 1930s and it was not totally closed until the 1950s, when locks were removed and bridges lowered. Since then, little has happened and the canal remains largely intact. It has water throughout much of its length and is easily explored on foot or by car with the help of a good map. More like a river than a canal, the Grantham has been the subject of various restoration schemes, but new coal mines planned for the Vale of Belvoir make any eventual reopening to boats more unlikely.

The parish church at Thaxted in Essex, one of the many attractions along the course of the river Chelmer.

THE EAST

The character of the eastern counties has been largely determined by the rivers and waterways. It has always been an isolated and self-contained area, and for centuries was dependent upon waterways for its links with the rest of the country. Roads were few and far between in a landscape composed of low-lying marshland prone to flooding and incursions by the sea. The marshland created natural barriers to isolate the region, an isolation encouraged by the great forests that used to cover the western part of Essex. Over the centuries the coast, with its miles of mud flats and tidal estuaries, has been created by the constant battle between sea and land. In some areas the sea has been driven back, in others it is still eroding the land. From Roman times the rivers have been exploited, for transport and as a means of draining the land and keeping the water level under control.

The rivers of eastern England fall into three distinct groups. First, there are the rural rivers of Essex and Suffolk, flowing through a rolling landscape of arable land and woodland, linking small villages and dominated by the spires and towers of innumerable churches. These rivers reach the sea via huge tidal estuaries surrounded by mud flats, the home for generations of fishermen and sailors. Individual and independent, these rivers are at the heart of the English tradition of landscape painting. Second, there are the rivers and Broads of Norfolk, a complex network of partly man-made and partly natural waterways that connect many of the major towns and villages of the region, and serve both for transport and drainage. Now, they are one of the great recreational waterways of England, frequently overcrowded, but still able to maintain their own distinctive quality. Third, there are the rivers and waterways of the Fens, a huge interconnected network of major rivers and drainage channels grouped round the Wash. This region was first tamed by the Dutch engineers of the seventeenth

The church at Hemingford Grey on the Great Ouse. The church spire was blown into the river during a storm in 1741.

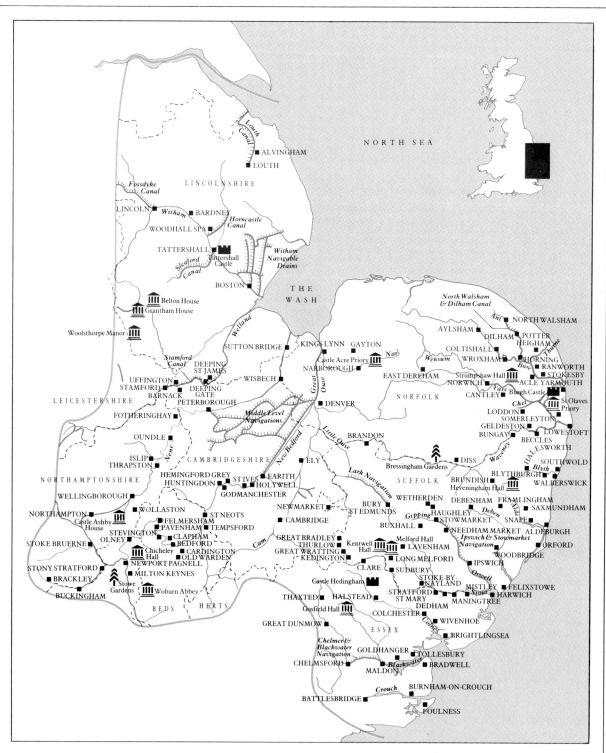

NORTH SEA

LINCOLNSHIRE

Louth Canal
ALVINGHAM
LOUTH

Fossdyke Canal
LINCOLN *Witham* BARDNEY
WOODHALL SPA
Horncastle Canal
TATTERSHALL
Tattershall Castle
Sleaford Canal
BOSTON
Witham Navigable Drains

THE WASH

Belton House
Grantham House

Woolsthorpe Manor

Welland
SUTTON BRIDGE
KINGS LYNN GAYTON
Castle Acre Priory *Nar*
NARBOROUGH

Stamford Canal
DEEPING ST JAMES
WISBECH
UFFINGTON
STAMFORD
BARNACK DEEPING GATE
PETERBOROUGH

EAST DEREHAM
NORFOLK

LEICESTERSHIRE

FOTHERINGHAY
Middle Level Navigations
DENVER

OUNDLE
Nene
BRANDON
New Bedford
Little Ouse
Great Ouse

North Walsham & Dilham Canal
Ant NORTH WALSHAM
AYLSHAM
DILHAM POTTER HEIGHAM
COLTISHALL
WROXHAM *Thurne*
HORNING
Wensum *Bure* RANWORTH
STOKESBY
Strumpshaw Hall ACLE YARMOUTH
NORWICH *Yare* Burgh Castle
CANTLEY
Chet St Olaves Priory
LODDON
SOMERLEYTON
GELDESTON
BUNGAY LOWESTOFT
BECCLES
HALESWORTH
Waveney
DISS SOUTHWOLD
Bressingham Gardens
BRUNDISH BLYTHBURGH *Blyth*
Heveningham Hall WALBERSWICK

ISLIP
THRAPSTON
NORTHAMPTONSHIRE
WELLINGBOROUGH

CAMBRIDGESHIRE
ELY
HEMINGFORD GREY
HUNTINGDON ST IVES EARITH
HOLYWELL
GODMANCHESTER
NEWMARKET

Lark Navigation
SUFFOLK
WETHERDEN DEBENHAM FRAMLINGHAM
BURY ST EDMUNDS HAUGHLEY SAXMUNDHAM
Gipping STOWMARKET *Deben*
BUXHALL NEEDHAM MARKET SNAPE
Ipswich & Stowmarket Navigation ALDEBURGH
Melford Hall ORFORD

NORTHAMPTON
Castle Ashby House
STEVINGTON
STOKE BRUERNE OLNEY
CLAPHAM
WOLLASTON
FELMERSHAM
PAVENHAM
ST NEOTS
TEMPSFORD
CAMBRIDGE
BEDFORD
Cam
Chicheley Hall
CARDINGTON
OLD WARDEN
NEWPORT PAGNELL
STONY STRATFORD
MILTON KEYNES
BRACKLEY
Stowe Gardens
BUCKINGHAM
Woburn Abbey
BEDS HERTS

GREAT BRADLEY
THURLOW
GREAT WRATTING
KEDINGTON
Kentwell Hall
LAVENHAM
LONG MELFORD
CLARE SUDBURY
WOODBRIDGE
IPSWICH
Orwell
STOKE-BY-NAYLAND
MISTLEY FELIXSTOWE
Stour HARWICH
STRATFORD ST MARY MANINGTREE
Castle Hedingham
DEDHAM
THAXTED HALSTEAD
Gosfield Hall
COLCHESTER
WIVENHOE
GREAT DUNMOW
Colne
BRIGHTLINGSEA
ESSEX
Chelmer & Blackwater Navigation
GOLDHANGER
TOLLESBURY
CHELMSFORD
Blackwater BRADWELL
MALDON
Crouch BURNHAM-ON-CROUCH
BATTLESBRIDGE
FOULNESS

century, whose legacy is miles of navigable waterway, some of the richest farmland in England, and
the remains of hundreds of windmills. Until the
early nineteenth century and the coming of steam,
over 700 wind-driven pumps kept the water levels
under control. This area stretches from the flat

landscape of the Fens to the Lincolnshire Wolds.
There are many reminders of the dramatic changes
that the region has witnessed since the seventeenth
century. Many towns and villages are built on low
hills, land that would formerly have been islands in a
great sea of impenetrable marsh. The remains of a

Burnham, on the tidal river Crouch in Essex. One of England's premier sailing centres, it attracts yachtsmen from far and wide.

number of abbeys and castles underline the feeling of isolation and independence that characterises the region. Yet, this is not a poor area. It benefited from successive waves of colonisation and there are traces to be found of the Romans, the Saxons and the Danes. More recently, the influx of Flemish weavers, builders and brewers helped to create the enormous wealth associated with the wool industry, from which came the magnificent churches to be found all over eastern England, including the four great cathedrals of Peterborough, Norwich, Ely and Lincoln. The final impetus came from Holland, which supplied the men who built the ports, controlled the rivers and drained the land. All these groups left their mark, on the buildings, on the roads, on the names, creating layer by layer a part of England that is distinctive, individual and highly cultured. Centuries of development have still left many areas of natural wilderness. The mud flats of the estuaries and parts of the Broads and Fens contain a great wealth of birds, plants and insects, which can be enjoyed by the visitor in addition to the variety of rivers, the changing landscape, and the special quality of light that can only be found in a region where the horizons are generally low.

The Essex sailing rivers

The Essex coastline has been formed by the continual battle between the sea and the land and so much of it is composed of marshland and mud flats broken up by the long fingers of tidal river estuaries. It is an isolated coastline, rich in bird life, with many areas only accessible by boat. For centuries the rivers have been used for trade, for fishing and for smuggling, allowing a number of inland towns and villages to develop as ports of some significance. Today the emphasis has shifted and while there are probably more boats than ever using the Essex rivers, most are there for leisure purposes. The river **Crouch**, which is navigable for 17 miles from Battlesbridge to its estuary at Foulness, is now one of the great sailing rivers of England. There are many yacht clubs, including some of the grandest in the country in and around Burnham-on-Crouch, which is a good place to watch sailing both amateur and professional. An even greater variety of boats can be seen on the river **Blackwater**, a wide tidal estuary navigable as far as Maldon. This is still a river for fishing boats, oyster beds and the traditional Thames sailing barges. Many of the villages, Tollesbury, Bradwell and Goldhanger for example, were formerly centres of local trade, and reveal traditions that are sometimes centuries old. There is a Saxon chapel near Bradwell, while Maldon, still a busy sailing centre, has a range of interesting buildings dating from the sixteenth to the nineteenth centuries. Maldon is also the terminus of the **Chelmer and Blackwater Navigation**, a canal opened in 1797 to link Chelmsford with the sea. This quiet and pastoral waterway remained in commercial use until the 1970s. It was used mainly by timber barges and now is largely recreational. The river **Chelmer** continues beyond Chelmsford, a rural stream flowing through the cornfields of Essex and linking towns such as Great Dunmow and Thaxted, where good examples of timber-framed and brick-built Tudor houses can be seen, as well as fine churches, Georgian streets and a preserved windmill.

To the north of Mersea Island, famous for its oyster beds, is the estuary of the river **Colne**. This rises near the Suffolk border, flows through Castle Hedingham, overlooked by the keep of the Norman castle, and the traditional market town of Halstead, then, passing near Gosfield Hall, the finest Tudor mansion in the county, it continues to the Roman town of Colchester, the scene of Boadicea's triumphs over the Roman army. Today, Colchester, with its Roman walls, Norman castle and priory, and range of buildings of later periods, is still a busy inland port. Small coasters sail up the Colne to the town quays on the tide, even though at low water the river is no more than a trickle. Between Colchester and the sea the river passes Wivenhoe, formerly a centre of boat building, and the fishing village of Brightlingsea.

The Stour

The **Stour**, which for much of its course marks the boundary between Essex and Suffolk, is a river firmly established in the English consciousness by the paintings of Constable. The Stour valley and its villages of Flatford, Dedham, Stratford St Mary and Stoke-by-Nayland must be one of the most familiar stretches of waterway in England, and yet there is far more to the Stour than this short section. In 1821 Constable wrote: 'I associate my careless boyhood to all that lies on the banks of the Stour.' Today, an exploration of the river can be just as rewarding, even if some of the banks have changed.

The Stour rises in the low-lying farmlands south of Newmarket and flows through villages of unchanged and unchanging quality, Great Bradley, Thurlow, Great Wratting, Kedington, on to Clare, a handsome town dominated by the ruined castle and priory. Nearby the river is flanked by vineyards, a revival of an industry that flourished in the Roman

Wivenhoe in Essex. An old fishing village on the tidal river Colne, it is now enjoying a new lease of life as a holiday and leisure centre.

Constable's The Leaping Horse, *a typical nineteenth-century Stour valley scene.*

period. This is an area rich in fine houses, and even finer churches, the latter reflecting the former wealth of the wool merchants. Traditional timber framed buildings can be seen in Long Melford and Lavenham, while Kentwell Hall and Melford Hall reflect the glories of Elizabethan brickwork. Sudbury, an old fashioned market town, is the birthplace of Gainsborough, and establishes the Stour as an artist's river. Sudbury also used to be the limit of navigation. From about 1705 to 1916 the Stour was used commercially between Sudbury and the estuary, and traffic survived on the lower reaches until the 1930s. Today, some of the Stour locks are being restored, and so boats may well one day return to Sudbury, to bring back to life the old quay warehouse. Many of the characteristic features of the Stour navigation are preserved in Constable's paintings, notably the meandering and rural course of the river, its distinctive locks, the locally built barges, the barge horses leaping the fences built across the towing path, and being ferried across on the barge when the path changes sides. These typical scenes may have gone, but it is still possible to identify the location of many of Constable's paintings, particularly those around Dedham and Flatford Mill.

At Manningtree the river became a wide estuary, bordered by mud flats, mills and small village quays. The river is now permanently separated from the estuary by a tide barrier, but the Stour estuary and connecting Orwell estuary are widely used by boats of all types. Manningtree and Mistley are visited by sailing barges, small coasters and all types of pleasure craft, while Harwich, at the mouth of the river, is traditionally a naval base, and a port for North Sea ferries and freighters. Across the river is Felixstowe, fast becoming the largest container port in England, and rapidly taking the place of Tilbury and the traditional docks of London.

The Orwell and the Gipping
The estuary of the **Orwell** still carries a wide range of boats and ships to Ipswich docks, which give the

town a traditional bustle and variety that is always lacking in those inland port towns and cities that have lost their association with the sea. However, until the 1920s there was another dimension to Ipswich that carried its maritime associations far inland to Stowmarket. The river **Gipping** rises in the rolling Suffolk countryside among the traditional villages of Haughley, Wetherden and Buxhall but it does not achieve any significance until it reaches Stowmarket. The **Ipswich and Stowmarket Navigation** was opened in 1793, allowing a regular traffic to develop along the Gipping through its 15 locks. For well over a 100 years this quiet and undramatic river carried cargoes of agricultural produce, lime, timber, building materials and even explosives between the two towns. Today, the best way to explore the Gipping is on foot as a towpath exists throughout its 17 miles. The remains of many of the locks can be seen, as well as the quays of pleasant towns and villages such as Needham Market. There are also mills and lime kilns, reflections of the navigation's *raison d'être*.

The Suffolk sailing rivers

The Suffolk coastline has three major tidal estuaries that have been associated with boats and sailing for centuries. It is a coastline of mud flats and wild birds, with a strong sense of isolation, and it has witnessed a few major changes in the last 100 years. Sailing for pleasure is the rule instead of sailing for a livelihood, but the essential nature of the area is unaltered.

A detail of a richly-worked purse-lid from the Anglo-Saxon Sutton Hoo Ship Burial. The Sutton Hoo treasures are now in the British Museum.

The **Deben** estuary runs inland through a wooded landscape to Woodbridge, a pretty town built on a low hill where sailing and boats are the major interest. The harbour, which like all Suffolk ports dries out at low tide, is dominated by the restored tide mill. Beyond Woodbridge, the Deben continues through quiet Suffolk villages to its source near Debenham. It was in the Deben marshes near Woodbridge that the Anglo-Saxon Sutton Hoo ship burial was discovered. A few miles along the coast is the mouth of the **Alde**, an eccentric river whose long estuary flows parallel to the coast for some distance. The strip of marshland that separates the river and the sea is a bird sanctuary. Just inland is Orford, whose ruined castle dominates the landscape, and whose oysters dominate the diet of both locals and visitors. At Aldeburgh, formerly a fortified town with a Martello tower still standing on the beach, and now an old fashioned sailing centre, the river turns sharply inland, to pass through woods to Snape, the limit of navigation. By the riverside at Snape is the Maltings, a concert hall and the focal point for the annual Aldeburgh festival established by Benjamin Britten in 1948. Inland the Alde continues to its source near Brundish, passing between the towns of Saxmundham and Framlingham, through a landscape that is the essence of Suffolk.

The third Suffolk river is the short **Blyth**, which rises near Heveningham Hall, one of the finest neo-classical mansions in England. It flows through the traditional market town of Halesworth, meeting the tidal estuary and surrounding mud flats at Blythburgh. From here the estuary can be sailed to its narrow mouth which is flanked by Walberswick and Southwold, the one famous for its associations with the painter Steer, the other renowned, among other things, for its brewery. Although it is hard to believe today, in 1761 the river Blyth Navigation was opened between Halesworth and Southwold and remained in use until the end of the nineteenth century. Many local trading boats used the navigation, aided by its four locks, but in the end the continued silting of Southwold harbour brought about its demise.

The Norfolk rivers and navigations

Although the Norfolk Broads must be generally familiar to everyone, few are aware that the Broads are simply part of a far larger network of over 127 miles of navigable rivers that link many of the major

The entrance hall at Heveningham Hall, one of the loveliest Palladian houses in England. The interior decoration is by James Wyatt.

towns of east Norfolk. This largely natural and self-contained system is without equal in England and for centuries it operated as a vital transport network, linking towns and villages that had no adequate road connections. A special type of sailing barge, the wherry, was developed, capable of reaching the narrowest and most isolated areas. In the nineteenth century hundreds of black-sailed Norfolk wherries could be seen, carrying every type of cargo, but today only one survives in sailing condition. This, the *Albion*, preserved by the Norfolk Wherry Trust, can be seen sailing the Norfolk rivers and Broads during the summer. Remarkably, the network is nearly as extensive as in the nineteenth century, and many areas are still only accessible by water.

Most southerly of the Broads rivers is the **Waveney**, which rises in Thetford Forest where there is a watershed between the Norfolk rivers and those of the Fens. Forming the boundary between Norfolk and Suffolk, the Waveney flows through Bressingham Gardens and Steam Museum, through Diss and a succession of little villages to Bungay, formerly the limit of navigation. Today the limit is Geldeston, whose derelict and isolated lock is guarded by one of the most unusual pubs in England, which as recently as the 1970s had no

Horstead Mill on the river Bure, one of the many attractions along this popular river in the northern section of the Norfolk Broads.

A windy day on the river Thurne, showing a typical Norfolk Broads combination of yacht, cruiser and restored wind pump.

running water or electricity. A pleasantly rural stretch of river leads to Beccles, a largely eighteenth-century town with one of the many large and unusual churches that are a feature of Norfolk, and then to the wide Oulton Broad which connects the river with Lowestoft, and thus with the sea. The Waveney then turns inland, passing the swinging railway bridge at Somerleyton, the ruined priory at St Olaves and the remains of the Roman fort at Burgh Castle, before joining the river Yare at Breydon Water, a huge lake that leads to Yarmouth.

The **Yare** is probably the most important of the Norfolk rivers, for it links Norwich with the sea at Yarmouth. Despite being nearly 30 miles inland, Norwich is still visited by a variety of commercial craft and so the winding course of the Yare is often decorated by coasters and cargo ships, as well as the many types of pleasure boats and sailing cruisers. The combination of a low-lying landscape and a twisting river results in the spectacle of large ships apparently sailing through the middle of fields.

Between Breydon Water and Norwich there are a number of more conventional sights to be seen, including windmills, the twisting course of the river Chet which leads to Lodden, an old market town, the sugar beet plant at Cantley and at Strumpshaw Hall a steam museum. Just outside Norwich the Yare swings away to the south, to continue its unnavigable course to Thetford Forest, and the navigation continues into the city centre on the river **Wensum**. Docks and warehouses, a variety of bridges, the remains of the city wall and the distant view of the cathedral herald the city itself. The navigation ends within sight of a number of Norwich's 32 medieval churches, a suitable place to begin an exploration of one of the finest of England's provincial cities. The Wensum continues its course through the city, and then it meanders in a wide arc through rural Norfolk to its source near East Dereham.

The best known of the Norfolk rivers is probably the **Bure**, which is linked to the rest of the network

Potter Heigham on the river Thurne. Potter Heigham is one of the great boating centres of the Norfolk Broads and its low bridge is a notorious tight squeeze.

by Breydon Water. It has become a pleasure river on a national scale, and many of its villages are devoted to the holiday trade. Boatyards proliferate, and in some areas the banks are lined by summer houses, bungalows and chalets. At the same time the river continues to express the traditional qualities of Norfolk, the reed-lined banks, the succession of Broads linked by river channels, the windmills and windpumps, the attractive and still isolated villages dominated by a rich variety of churches, the birds and wildlife that still survive despite the overcrowding during the holiday season, the waterside pubs and a constantly changing landscape. The most interesting villages along the Bure are Stokesby, Acle, Ranworth, Horning, Wroxham and Coltishall which is the limit of navigation. In the nineteenth century it was possible to continue for a few more miles to Aylsham. The Bure has two tributaries, which expand the navigable network eastwards. The **Thurne** leaves the Bure beneath the sails of a preserved pumping mill, and passes through the holiday and boating village of Potter Heigham to

link some of the most attractive Broads to the network, noted for their wildlife. The limit of navigation is Martham Broad, at which point the sea is less than a mile away. The **Ant** is a narrow and twisting river, flanked by isolated villages, interesting houses, the inevitable boatyards, and the reed beds that still supply many thatchers with their raw materials. Dilham is now the limit of navigation but in 1826 a canal was opened from Dilham to North Walsham. It has been disused since 1935 and is derelict, but the remains of its locks and warehouses can be explored.

The Great Ouse and its connections

Eastern England is blessed by two great river navigations, the **Ouse** and the Nene that not only connect with each other, but with the rest of the English waterways network, and with the North Sea via the Wash. The Great Ouse rises near Brackley in Northamptonshire, and its upper reaches are well worth exploring. An attractive river, twisting its way through the heart of England, it passes Buck-

Ranworth Broad, one of the most remote and least developed part of Norfolk's network of lakes and rivers. It is closed to powered craft.

The church and mill at Olney, Buckinghamshire. Famous for its pancake race, Olney is one of the many attractions along the Great Ouse.

ingham, with the gardens of Stowe nearby; Stony Stratford; the railway town of Wolverton, where it is crossed by the Grand Union Canal in an iron aqueduct; Newport Pagnell and Chicheley Hall, one of the most original early eighteenth-century houses in the country. The river continues past Olney, famous for its pancake race, some fine churches at Felmersham, Pavenham and Clapham and Stevington windmill before it reaches Bedford. The Great Ouse gives added interest to Bedford for here is the head of navigation. From Bedford to Huntingdon the river is pleasantly rural, passing through the market town of St Neots, but from Huntingdon onwards the scenery dramatically improves. A fourteenth-century stone bridge links Huntingdon with Godmanchester, a town of Roman origins, and both have buildings of interest. Houghton Mill is followed by Hemingford Grey, with its fine waterside church and twelfth-century manor house, while at St Ives the fifteenth-century bridge has a chapel in the centre. At Holywell the Ferry Boat Inn claims to have been established in 980. It also boasts its own ghost, a lady who rises from the floor every year on 17 March. At this point the landscape changes, and from here to the sea the Ouse flows through the flat Fenlands, rich farmlands reclaimed from the sea by the flood prevention schemes of the Dutchman Cornelius Vermuyden in the mid-seventeenth century. Vermuyden was also responsible for creating many of the navigations that can still be enjoyed today. One of these is the Bedford river, a straight canal from Earith to Denver, near Downham Market, that shortens the journey but offers little of interest for the visitor. The old course of the Great Ouse curves round to Ely, via Stretham where a steam pumping engine is preserved, a reminder that the water levels through this part of England have to be strictly controlled to avoid flooding. In some areas the land has sunk 15 feet during the last few centuries, and is still sinking. In this flat landscape, Ely cathedral can be seen for miles. Like Norwich, it is an attractive city when approached by water. From Ely to Kings Lynn the river is broad, fast flowing and of limited appeal, but Kings Lynn itself should not be missed. It is a town of great age and interest, built round a huge market square, and still busy as a port despite the Victorian quality of the docks.

The Great Ouse is also the backbone of a number of other navigations, but those that survive today are only a fragment of the system in its heyday. The **Ivel** is a small river that joins the Great Ouse at Tempsford, just east of Bedford, but in 1823 it was made navigable as far as Shefford, a navigation that survived until the 1870s. Little remains today but the Ivel has a number of aeronautical associations. Near its mouth are the huge airship hangers at Cardington, while during the Second World War the airfield at Tempsford was the base from which

agents were flown into France and other occupied countries on secret missions. A few miles to the south is the Shuttleworth Collection of historical aircraft, at Old Warden. The most important tributary is the **Cam** which links Cambridge, a splendid city to see by water, to the Great Ouse near Ely. North of Ely are three other tributaries but in their present shortened form they offer little of interest. The **Lark Navigation** now comes to a stop in a tiny village, New Row, but until the 1890s it was navigable to Bury St Edmunds. The Navigation had a chequered history which dates back to the 1700s but most of the surviving remains date from the 1890s when an attempt was made to revive it. As late as the 1920s steam tugs could be seen hauling lighters on some stretches. To the north is the **Little Ouse**, or **Brandon** river which was made navigable to Thetford in the late seventeenth century and survived in commercial use until about 1914. Today the limit of navigation is near Brandon, but the upper reaches are worth exploring through Thetford Forest as the river shares a common source with the Waveney and therefore provides a theoret-

The decorative 'Chinese' footbridge at Godmanchester on the Great Ouse, built in 1827. Godmanchester also boasts a fine fourteenth-century stone bridge.

ical link between the Norfolk rivers and Broads and the rest of the English waterway network. Near Kings Lynn the Great Ouse is joined by the **Nar**, a minor waterway rising near Castle Acre Priory. From the mid-eighteenth century to the 1880s this rather unlikely river was also navigable as far as Narborough, and even today the remains of the warehouses and quays can be seen.

The most significant of the waterways linking with the Great Ouse is a series of mostly man-made navigable drainage channels known collectively as the **Middle Level Navigations**. These are remote, low-lying and only visited by the more enthusiastic explorers but they are a hidden part of England that has a quality all its own. More important, they include two routes that link the Great Ouse with the river Nene, and thus with the whole of the English navigable waterway network.

The Nene

The second great river navigation of eastern England is the **Nene**. It rises near Weedon, as far from the sea as it is possible to be in England, and flows through rolling farmland to Northampton, where it becomes navigable. In Northampton the Nene is met by a branch of the Grand Union Canal and is thus linked to the English canal system. The river was first made navigable during the reign of Queen Anne but throughout the eighteenth and nineteenth centuries passage was often erratic and sometimes impossible. In the 1920s the navigation was taken in hand and a whole new series of locks were created, featuring the typical vertically rising guillotine gates. Today it is an enjoyable and easy river to travel along, and is somehow the essence of England as it winds its way among water meadows, and manages to avoid many of the towns and villages en route. It is totally rural, with more cows to be seen than people along the banks. For the same reason, it is a difficult river to explore by car, but local sights include Castle Ashby House, near Cogenhoe, mills at Doddington and Wollaston, near Wellingborough, and the medieval bridge that links Thrapston with Islip. Many of the villages are small and undeveloped, and enjoy fine churches. Near Oundle, a handsome stone town, the Nene begins a series of broad sweeping loops which carry it towards Peterborough. Riverside villages are now

Mepal in Cambridgeshire. Its distinctive waterways and rich variety of wildlife make it a good place to enjoy the landscape of the Fens.

Wisbech, one of the East Anglia's traditonal inland ports, has a waterfront of rare quality.
The seventeenth-century houses reflect a Dutch influence.

more frequent and include Fotheringhay, whose former castle witnessed the execution of Mary Queen of Scots. Near Peterborough is the Nene Valley Steam Railway, which crosses the river twice. Peterborough looks at its best from the river. The old parts of the town, including the cathedral and guildhall are by the river, and the quays are attractive. Leaving the city, the Nene passes the connection with the Middle Level Navigations which lead to the Great Ouse and then the character of the river changes. It becomes a wide waterway flowing through a flat landscape, with a tidal flow that increases as it approaches the Wash. The last town of any significance is Wisbech, an active inland port with one of the most interesting and attractive waterfronts in England. The quays are lined with fine mansions and warehouses, many of which are eighteenth century or earlier. From Wisbech the Nene races along its tidal estuary to the sea, across a landscape that used to be under the sea. Near Sutton Bridge, King John lost the crown jewels.

The Welland
The **Welland** is an isolated river that traverses a region devoted to bulb growing. Navigable now from Deeping St James to its estuary in the Wash, it was in the nineteenth century navigable as far as Stamford via the Stamford Canal which was cut in the 1660s and ran parallel to the river, with 12 locks. Traces of this very early canal can be found at Uffington and at Deeping Gate. South of Stamford is Barnack, the site of quarries which supplied the stone from which many of England's cathedrals and abbeys were built. In the Middle Ages, this stone was transported along the Welland, across the Wash and then to its various destinations via the early river navigations that were the only means of transport until the seventeenth century.

The Witham
The **Witham** and its associated waterways is probably the oldest river navigation in England still in use. It was first developed by the Romans for

Boston Stump on the river Witham. Standing more than 270 feet above the river, it dominates the flat Lincolnshire landscape for miles around.

drainage and navigation, and was then greatly improved during the eighteenth century. The Witham actually rises miles to the south near Melton Mowbray. It flows north, passing Woolsthorpe Manor, the birthplace of Sir Isaac Newton, Grantham House and Belton House, approaches the Trent at Newark and then swings away to Lincoln, where the navigation starts. Like most cities of eastern England, Lincoln makes the most of its river. The Witham passes through a narrow channel flanked by a range of interesting buildings, and the city climbs away to the north, a great slope of stone, brick and timber crowned by the cathedral. East of Lincoln the river is straight and predictable, with high banks hiding much of the landscape but there are features of interest, for example the remains of abbeys near Bardney and Tattershall, Tattershall Castle, and the little town of Woodhall Spa, one of the least known of English spas. In the distance can be seen the so-called Boston Stump, the tower of St Botolph's church which dominates the landscape for miles around. Boston is a fine town and an interesting port, its quays lined with eighteenth- and nineteenth-century buildings. It is a port of considerable antiquity, for the *Mayflower* sailed from here in 1620. There is much to attract the diligent traveller, including a windmill and, nearby, a tractor museum. The Witham estuary beyond Boston links with the Wash, and thus with the other great rivers of eastern England.

Although its best features are the towns along its admittedly unexciting course, the Witham is a river with some interesting connections. A lock in Boston marks the entrance to the **Witham Navigable Drains**, over 50 miles of navigable waterways whose primary function is to maintain the water levels in the surrounding land. This is probably the least known navigable waterway network in Britain, and worth seeing for that reason alone, although the appeal of a flat and isolated landscape, bisected by a series of secret waterways that seem deliberately to avoid all villages, is not universal. More interesting perhaps is the **Fossdyke Canal**, which connects the Witham at Lincoln and with the river Trent near Torksey. This canal, dug by the Romans in about 120 AD, is the oldest man-made waterway still in use, having been improved during the eighteenth century. It provides a vital connection between the Witham and the rest of the English inland waterway network. Until the 1870s there were two other navigations connected with the Witham, the

Lincoln is served by two waterways, the Fossdyke Canal and the river Witham. The Witham has a tortuous passage through the city and under the 'Glory Hole'.

Sleaford and the **Horncastle Canals**. Both opened in 1802, and were planned as part of the same development of the region. Although long closed, their routes can still be traced and the remains of locks discovered. Sleaford and Horncastle are both interesting little-known towns. Traces of the former canal basins can still be found in each, and in Sleaford, the canal company offices survive.

The Louth Canal

One of the least known of the Lincolnshire waterways, the **Louth Canal** was opened in 1770. Like others in the county, its construction was inspired by the constant transport difficulties posed by bad roads and the low-lying marshlands of the region. The canal, with its eight locks, linked Louth on the edge of the Lincolnshire Wolds, with the Humber estuary near Tetney, south of Cleethorpes. In a quiet way the canal prospered and remained in commercial use until the First World War. Although long abandoned, it is still in reasonable condition and its route can be explored. There are locks and warehouses to be seen, and a mill at Alvingham. Louth is an old market town where Lord Tennyson was educated. It has a good church with a tall spire, a rich selection of eighteenth- and early nineteenth-century buildings, and the local museum displays carpets made in the town.

Durham from the air, showing how the city is enclosed by the great sweep of the river Wear. The Cathedral is an outstanding example of Romanesque architecture.

THE NORTH-EAST

The north-east of England is in many ways the most secret part of the country, yet potentially it is the most exciting to explore. The region is formed of contrasting bands, wild and rugged scenery interspersed with thin strips of heavy industry. Each band is full of interest but demands in return a spirit of dedication and adventurousness from its visitors.

The most northerly band is formed by the Scottish borderlands bounded by the Cheviots, the river Tweed and the North Sea, a wild and remote region, filled with reminders of England's early history. Its rivers offer an ideal introduction to the landscape and its past, and a fine way to appreciate the untamed quality of the region. The next band includes the great industrial rivers of the north-east, the Tyne, the Wear and the Tees. These rivers may lack obvious appeal but they are well worth exploring, linking as they do the scenery of the Pennines with the traditional industries upon which England's Victorian wealth and power was based, coal, iron and steel, shipbuilding and international trade. A third, rather broader band comprises the beautiful wilderness of the Yorkshire Dales, and Moors, great tracts of upland divided by the wide valleys of the Derwent, the Ure, the Swale, the Wharfe and the other North Yorkshire rivers. These rivers not only flow through spectacular scenery but they also link together great churches, abbeys, castles and country houses, spanning several centuries of English history. Much of Yorkshire can be explored by water, either by following the river courses or by boat along the rivers that are still navigable. It is still possible to arrive in York by boat several weeks after leaving London.

The valley of the river Coquet in Northumberland, one of the hidden pleasures of England's lesser known rivers.

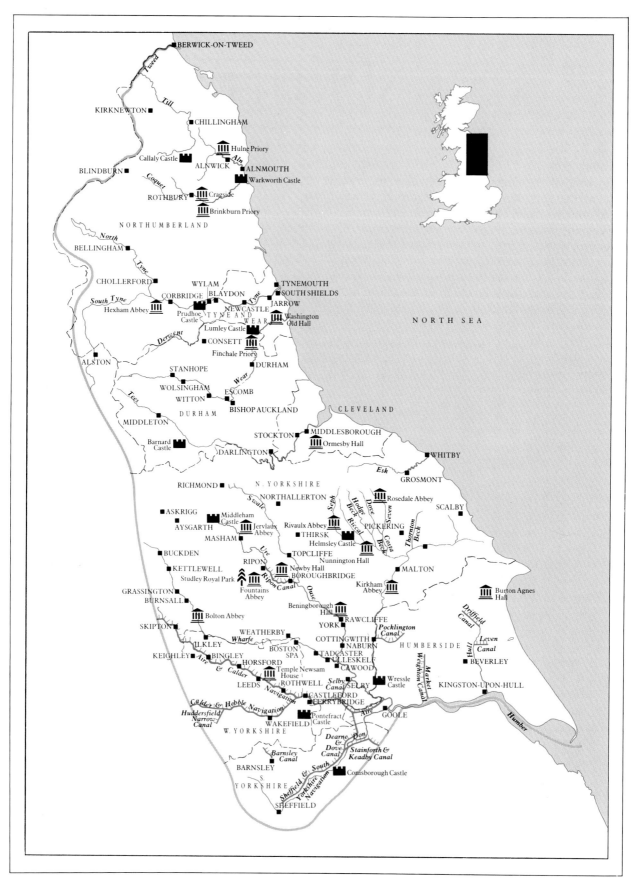

BERWICK-ON-TWEED

Tweed

Till

KIRKNEWTON

CHILLINGHAM

Hulne Priory

Callaly Castle

ALNWICK   *Aln*

BLINDBURN   ALNMOUTH

Warkworth Castle

Coquet

ROTHBURY   Cragside

Brinkburn Priory

NORTHUMBERLAND

North

BELLINGHAM

Tyne

CHOLLERFORD

WYLAM   TYNEMOUTH

South Tyne   CORBRIDGE   BLAYDON   SOUTH SHIELDS

Hexham Abbey   *Tyne*   JARROW

Prudhoe   NEWCASTLE

Castle   TYNE AND   Washington

Lumley Castle   WEAR   Old Hall

CONSETT

Derwent   Finchale Priory

ALSTON

STANHOPE   DURHAM

WOLSINGHAM   *Wear*

WITTON   ESCOMB

Tees   DURHAM   BISHOP AUCKLAND

MIDDLETON   CLEVELAND

Barnard   STOCKTON   MIDDLESBOROUGH

Castle   DARLINGTON   Ormesby Hall

WHITBY

Esk

GROSMONT

N. YORKSHIRE

RICHMOND

NORTHALLERTON   Rosedale Abbey   SCALBY

Swale   *Seph*

ASKRIGG   Middleham   *Hodge Beck*   *Dove*

AYSGARTH   Castle   Rivaulx Abbey   PICKERING

Jervlaux   *Riccal*   *Costa Beck*   *Thornton Beck*

MASHAM   Abbey   Helmsley Castle

BUCKDEN   *Ure*   THIRSK

TOPCLIFFE   Nunnington Hall

KETTLEWELL   RIPON   *Ripon Canal*   MALTON

Studley Royal Park   Newby Hall

GRASSINGTON   BOROUGHBRIDGE   Kirkham

Fountains   *Ouse*   Abbey   Burton Agnes

BURNSALL   Abbey   Beningborough   Hall

Hall   *Driffield Canal*

SKIPTON   Bolton Abbey   YORK   RAWCLIFFE

WEATHERBY   *Pocklington Canal*   *Leven Canal*

ILKLEY   *Wharfe*   COTTINGWITH   *Hull*

KEIGHLEY   BINGLEY   BOSTON   NABURN   HUMBERSIDE

Aire & Calder   SPA   TADCASTER   BEVERLEY

HORSFORD   ULLESKELF   *Market Weighton Canal*

Temple Newsam   CAWOOD

House   *Selby Canal*   Wressle Castle   KINGSTON-UPON-HULL

LEEDS   ROTHWELL   SELBY

Navigation   CASTLEFORD   *Humber*

Calder & Hebble Navigation   FERRYBRIDGE   GOOLE

Huddersfield Narrow Canal   Pontefract   *Aire*

WAKEFIELD   Castle

W. YORKSHIRE   *Dearne & Dove Canal*   *Don*

Barnsley Canal   *Stainforth & Keadby Canal*

BARNSLEY   *S.*   Comsborough Castle

Yorkshire   *Sheffield & South Yorkshire Navigation*

S. YORKSHIRE

SHEFFIELD

NORTH SEA

410

The final band is formed from two quite separate and distinctive regions. The first, Humberside, is a low-lying and little known area of small towns and villages. It is predominantly agricultural, a hidden corner of England overshadowed by the Humber estuary, a great seaway that gives waterway access to the second region, which comprises the industrial towns and cities of Yorkshire. The Humber leads directly to the heart of Yorkshire, an area rich in memorials to nineteenth-century ambition and technical skill. The industrial landscape is impressive and full of interest. Coal and iron are still the dominant forces, their traditional importance underlined by a large network of active commercial waterways. Here, on the Aire and Calder Navigation, on the Sheffield and South Yorkshire canals, at Goole and at Selby, it is possible to relive the atmosphere of the canal age at its height, an experience now unique to the north-east. The canals of Victorian England however, are part of a system of new waterways and docks that are being steadily expanded and improved to enable Continental barges to navigate directly to Sheffield, Doncaster and other centres of industrial activity. This blend of old and new is typical of the northeast and gives it its characteristic flavour.

The rivers of the Border and the Cheviots

The least developed, and correspondingly, the least known part of England is Northumberland. The north of the county is wild, remote and virtually unaffected by the activities of man. The scenery is spectacular and largely undomesticated; great bare hills, tracts of woodland and a mass of small, quick-

Thomas Bewick's eighteenth-century engraving of the bull of Chillingham, where the herd of wild white cattle have roamed for over 700 years.

The temple of Mithras at Carrawburgh, one of the best preserved Roman buildings associated with Hadrian's Wall.

flowing streams, most of which drain the Cheviot hills. One has to be hardy to survive here and so it is no surprise that the region has produced a number of distinctive, and highly self-sufficient animal species: Cheviot sheep, wild goats, and the Chillingham herd of wild cattle. Among the streams are a number of larger rivers, the most important of which is the **Tweed**. Much of this river is in Scotland, while a long stretch between Coldstream and the estuary actually marks the border. However, Berwick-on-Tweed and the last few miles of the river are in England and a number of interesting tributaries flow southwards into Northumberland. Berwick still has the feeling of a frontier town, underlined by the ruined twelfth-century castle, the town walls and the barracks, which were designed by Vanbrugh in 1717 and are apparently the oldest barracks in Britain still in active use. The **Till** is an attractive tributary of the Tweed, meandering through a valley at the foot of the Cheviots. It is a river surrounded by history. Near its source is Chillingham, which has a fine twelfth-century church and is the home of the white wild cattle, a herd that has lived enclosed in Chillingham Park for over 700 years. The Till passes near Kirknewton with its medieval sculpture, Heatherslaw Mill, and the site of the Battle of Flodden Field, while near its junction with the Tweed is the fifteenth-century Twizel Bridge, the widest medieval single span bridge in Britain. To the south is the river **Aln**, which flows past Callaly Castle, Hulne Priory, and Alnwick with its abbey and Norman fortress on the way to its sandy estuary at Alnmouth.

Perhaps the most dramatic of the Cheviot rivers is the **Coquet**. It rises high above Blindburn, its course through the hills followed closely by a remote road that eventually deteriorates into a track leading to the Scottish border. It is a fast-flowing trout river, like most of those in the region, and makes its way down from the hills into Coquet Dale past isolated little villages. The first town of any size is Rothbury, where the river is dominated by the tall towers of Cragside, a late Victorian mansion designed by Richard Norman Shaw, and the first house in the world to be lit by electricity generated by water power. Nearby, and deep in the wooded river valley, is Brinkburn Priory, which was founded in 1135, ruined in the sixteenth century, restored in the nineteenth century and is still richly endowed with medieval romance. Near the sea the Coquet opens out into a wide estuary, overlooked by the twelfth-century Warkworth Castle which appears to grow out from the precipitous hill. Nearby, cut out of solid rock and standing high above the river is its fourteenth-century hermitage.

The Tyne and its tributaries

One of the major rivers of England, the **Tyne** has been at the centre of English history for the last 200 years. The river witnessed the growth of the Industrial Revolution, the development of railways and the frenetic industrial development of the nineteenth century, when the ironworks, mines and shipyards totally dominated the river banks from Hexham to the sea. More recently the Tyne has watched the decline of these traditional industries as the north-east goes through a period of economic change in every way as far-reaching as the revolution that created the wealth of the region in the eighteenth century. The industrial rivers of the north-east, the Tyne, the Wear and the Tees, are losing their industrial importance but, once they overcome the inevitable tide of decay and dereliction, they may begin to return towards their pre-industrial state. Certainly all three are already rivers

Canoeing on the river Wear. The violent and dramatic courses of many northern rivers makes them particularly challenging for canoists.

of extraordinary contrast, flowing from their sources high in the Pennines through dramatic scenery and wild beauty, with no hint of the total dedication to industry that determines their nature a few miles further towards the east coast.

The Tyne enjoys two sources, which come together to form one large river near Hexham. The **North Tyne** rises in Kielder Forest, flowing from the huge Kielder Water reservoir, which is used extensively for water sports, leisure activities and fishing. It is a fairly remote river, passing through Bellingham and a number of smaller villages where it meets tributaries that drain the Wark Forest to the west. At Chollerford it is crossed by Hadrian's Wall, which is in a particularly impressive state in this area. Nearby are forts, notably Brunton Turret, a bath house at Chesters and a temple at Carrawburgh, sturdy reminders of the level of civilisation attained by the Romans in such primitive and inhospitable regions. The **South Tyne** follows a very different course, rising in the Pennines far to the south, by Alston Moor. Despite the remoteness of the region, exploration is not difficult. The river is accompanied by two little roads and by the Pennine Way and until fairly recently there was also a railway to Alston. Alston is an attractive hill village and market town, which is frequently cut off during the winter. There are a number of smaller villages beside the river on the way to Haltwhistle, where it becomes more accessible. There are plenty of castles, Blenkinsop, Bellister and Langley, reflecting the turbulent history of the region and just west of Hexham the South Tyne joins its northern

The transporter bridge across the Tees at Middlesborough is a unique survival of a once common example of Victorian engineering.

branch to become the Tyne. At Hexham the industry begins, but there are still a number of reminders of the pre-industrial Tyne, Hexham Abbey, the Saxon church at Corbridge and the fourteenth-century Prudhoe Castle. Industrial history is also well represented, there is the National Tractor Museum at Hunday and Wylam is the birthplace of George Stephenson. This mixture of medieval and industrial history continues along the banks of the Tyne as it widens into a tidal estuary, passing Newcastle, Jarrow and South Shields before meeting the sea at Tynemouth. A similar type of river is the **Derwent**, the major tributary of the Tyne. This rises in the wooded Derwent Reservoir and enjoys a short scenic route before meeting industry at Consett. Beyond Consett the Derwent takes an attractive, wooded course through Rowland's Gill, passing the ruined Gibside Estate, with its Elizabethan Hall, orangery, gardens and its eighteenth-century chapel with its fine three-decker pulpit. The Derwent joins the Tyne near Blaydon, at one time the home of the famous races.

The Wear

The **Wear** is in many ways a similar river to the Tyne. It also rises in the Pennines, to the south-east of Alston, in an area that was formerly the scene of extensive mining. Only old shafts and quarries remain, now looking a natural part of the landscape. Between St John's Chapel, Stanhope and Wolsingham the river passes through the scenic Weardale, where the fast-flowing waters are popular with canoeists. Beyond Wolsingham the Wear starts a huge loop that takes it southwards through Witton

The upper reaches of the Tees are characterised by waterfalls. The most spectacular of these is High Force, near Middleton-in-Teesdale.

Whitby harbour is attractively old-fashioned, its quays and fishing boats reflect the traditional flavour of the English seaside.

with its castle, Bishop Auckland and Escomb Saxon church before turning north towards Durham. The view of the Wear curving round Durham, with the cathedral raised high above on a steeply wooded hill is justly famous. It is relatively unchanged since the eighteenth century and provides an exciting introduction to a fine city. Despite the industrial nature of the region as a whole, the Wear manages to retain its historical associations and it has a predominantly rural nature. North of Durham much of its course is wooded and there are the remains of Finchale Priory and Lumley Castle, the latter, like so many of the country houses in this area, provides the setting for Elizabethan banquets and similar entertainments. Washington Old Hall, a Jacobean mansion that has earlier connections with the Washington family, links the Wear to the United States, and nearby is a wildfowl reserve, marking the start of the Wear's estuary. From here to the sea, industry and particularly ship-building have determined the nature of the Wear, although many other industries used to be associated with Sunderland, including the making of pottery and glass.

The Tees

The third of the great rivers of the north-east is the **Tees**. Rising in the Pennines, in the remote wilderness of Moor House Bird Reserve, the Tees flows into Cow Green Reservoir, which it leaves via the dramatic Caldron Snout waterfall and cataract. At the base of the waterfall its course is joined by the Pennine Way, which accompanies it for several miles through Teesdale to Middleton. There are several waterfalls of which the most spectacular is the High Force, the highest in England, and they can all be seen from the Alston-Middleton road, which follows the route of the Tees. After Middleton, the river becomes less dramatic, its wooded course leading to Barnard Castle. A fine town built high on a hill overlooking the river, Barnard Castle has a number of attractions, including the castle itself, Egglestone Abbey and the Bowes Museum, a rich and varid collection of works of art housed in a huge Victorian version of a French château. Between Barnard Castle and Darlington the Tees follows a rural course, forming the border between Durham and Yorkshire. East of Darlington the river becomes navigable, starting a 24 mile tidal estuary through Stockton and Middlesborough to the sea in Hartlepool Bay. This section is busy with shipping, and the banks are heavily developed, with steel, chemicals, ship-building and other industries. Despite these rather daunting surroundings, there is still plenty of interest, notably eighteenth-century Ormesby Hall, the Captain Cook Museum, and the Middlesborough transporter bridge, a unique example of Victorian engineering.

The Esk

One of the lesser known rivers of the north-east is the Esk, a salmon river that rises in the Cleveland Hills and flows eastwards in a steep valley through the North Yorkshire Moors. It can be explored by road but the best way to enjoy it is by rail. The branch line from Middlesborough to Whitby shares its valley and is a particularly scenic journey, while at Grosmont, one of a number of small riverside villages, there is a junction with the North Yorkshire Moors Steam Railway. The Esk meets the sea at Whitby, an attractive town with an abbey, a museum, a beach and a good old-fashioned atmosphere, particularly around the harbour.

The rivers and canals of Yorkshire

The river Humber, a great tidal waterway that carves its way deep into the north-east of England, is not only one of the great shipping rivers of England but it is also the backbone of a great network of rivers and canals that radiate throughout Yorkshire. Wherever they rise, most Yorkshire rivers make their way down to the Humber estuary by one means or another. The Derwent, the Ouse, the Ure, the Wharfe, the Swale, the Hull, the Aire and the Calder all mingle their waters in the Humber. For many centuries the very size of the Humber made it a natural barrier, dividing Yorkshire from Lincolnshire and the north Midlands and marking the distinctive change in the landscape. It is a huge river, wide and fast flowing, its banks isolated and relatively undeveloped. Until the opening of the Humber suspension bridge which incorporates the world's largest span (4626 feet between piers) it could only be crossed by ferry. Even today, wildfowl and bird reserves are as much a part of the Humber as oil terminals, container ports and shipyards. The importance of the Humber as a shipping river is also reflected by the many canals and waterways that connect with it. A great number of Yorkshire's rivers were turned into navigations and many are still open and active today, while the remains of others long closed or abandoned reveal how extensive the network was in its heyday. From the Humber boats can travel northwards to York

The Humber suspension bridge. It is the most recent and the most dramatic of the many exciting river crossings to be found in England.

and beyond, westwards to Leeds and thence across the Pennines to the narrow canals of Manchester and the west of England, and southwards along the Trent to the Midlands and ultimately to London.

Because they are so numerous and so varied, the rivers and canals of Yorkshire cannot be described as one great network, but must for convenience be separated into smaller groups or units.

The Derwent and its tributaries

The **Derwent** rises in the high moors west of Scalby and flows towards the sea before turning inland along the wide glacial valley that leads to Malton. North of Malton the Derwent is joined by a network of tributaries, all flowing south from the North Yorkshire Moors. This collection of fast-flowing rivers and streams leads not only to spectacular countryside and quiet, hidden valleys, but also to some remarkable buildings. The **Thornton Beck** leads to Stain Dale and Dalby Forest; the **Costa Beck** to Pickering and its castle; the **Seven** to Rosedale Abbey; the **Dove** to Farndale, the Dale of the Daffodils; the **Hodge Beck** to Bransdale, a land-locked valley; the **Riccal** to Helmsley Castle and seventeenth-century Nunnington Hall; and the **Seph** to Rievaulx Abbey, one of the most beautiful ruins in England. Exploration of these moorland rivers reveals many other delights, which are accessible by minor roads along the river valleys. Malton, a town with Roman associations, marks the former head of navigation of the river Derwent.

Opened in 1701, and briefly extended for a further 11 miles to Yedingham, the navigation ran for 38 miles to the junction with the Ouse at Barmby-on-the-Marsh. There are five locks, but the upper section from Stamford Bridge to Malton was closed in 1935. The Derwent is a particularly attractive waterway and so it is likely that the navigation will be restored through to Malton. It is a quiet river, flanked by small villages but there are plenty of historical associations, for example the ruins of Kirkham Abbey and Wressle Castle, and the site of the Battle of Stamford Bridge, won by King Harold before he marched southwards to meet his doom at the Battle of Hastings.

The Pocklington Canal

The **Pocklington Canal**, a pleasantly obscure waterway with nine locks, leaves the river Derwent at Cottingwith to wander gently towards Pocklington. Opened in 1818 it continued in use until the 1930s and then fell into decay. Although its route is through a remote landscape of marshland and fens,

The dramatic ruins of Rievaulx Abbey by the river Seph. The chief glory of the abbey now is the thirteenth-century choir, a splendid example of northern English architecture.

A pretty bridge over the remote Pocklington Canal in Yorkshire, a nine-mile waterway gradually being restored by volunteers.

it is an attractive canal, with well-built bridges and locks, its surroundings rich in bird life. The route of the canal is easy to follow and restoration plans make it likely that boats will one day be able to reach Pocklington again.

The Ouse and its connections

The **Ouse** is the major waterway of Yorkshire. A river of great contrasts, its waters flow from Wensleydale through constantly changing scenery to its junction with the Humber and the Trent at Trent Falls. The Ouse is actually two rivers for, from Ouse Gill Beck, a few miles north of York, it changes its name to the **Ure**, although the two are effectively the same river. The Ure rises near Askrigg in Wensleydale and takes a dramatic course through the Dales, tumbling over waterfalls, notably at Aysgarth, and passing the ruins of Middleham Castle and Jervaulx Abbey before reaching Masham. From here the river pursues a more sedate and rural route to Ripon, a fine and little known cathedral town, with Fountains Abbey and the Studley Royal landscape park and gardens nearby.

Ripon is linked to the Ure by the **Ripon Canal**, opened in 1773 to bypass a shallow and rocky stretch of the river. There are three locks, the upper two of which were abandoned in 1955, leaving the present terminus near Ripon race course. However, the canal can easily be followed to its original basin near the cathedral. Ripon is the most northerly point on the English inland waterway network; a boat setting off from Godalming on the river Wey, south of London, could moor at Ripon several weeks later. South of Ripon the Ure continues through beautiful country, passing Newby Hall and flowing through Boroughbridge, which once boasted 22 coaching inns, to its junction with the Ouse at Swale Nab. The Ouse winds its way through fields and woodlands, passing the early eighteenth-century Beningbrough Hall on its way to York. York is still an active inland port and its traditional waterfront is particularly attractive, with a variety of early warehouses and mills, and an interesting selection of commercial and pleasure boats. South of York the Ouse continues through rural surroundings to Naburn, where its character begins to change. From Naburn

*The river Ouse at York. The city built its prosperity on the river trade and its waterfront is
a rich and varied architectural delight.*

southwards the river is tidal and it becomes increasingly wild and unfriendly as it approaches the Humber. The muddy banks give way to bleak marshland that the river flows through at an alarming speed, apparently reaching nine knots in places. The river demands great care in navigation but there is plenty to be seen from the land. Cawood is a pretty riverside town, while Selby and Goole are busy inland ports, which retain the atmosphere of the Victorian period when their importance was first established. Selby, with its fine market place and twelfth-century abbey, is still predominantly a waterway town. The Selby Canal links the Ouse to the **Aire and Calder Navigation**, one of the busiest commercial waterways of the north-east. Goole also has a connection with the Aire and Calder, and indeed Goole was established by the Aire and Calder Company as a major canal port in the nineteenth century. South of Goole the Ouse becomes more like the sea than a river, with sandbanks, lighthouses and a wild tidal flow, rushing through a dramatic wilderness surrounded by marshland.

A number of other rivers of interest connect with the Ouse, notably the **Swale** and the **Wharfe**. The Swale rises, like the Ure, in the Dales and its upper reaches as far as Richmond are similar in character. Richmond is one of the most delightful small towns in England and it makes the most of its river, but south of Richmond the Swale becomes a curiously remote rural river, its banks unapproached by villages or roads. Despite its isolation, there were plans in the middle of the eighteenth century to turn the Swale and some of its tributaries into navigations, and thus link Northallerton and Thirsk to the Ouse. Some work was carried out during the 1760s, making the Swale navigable to Topcliffe and constructing a basin and wharf at Thirsk, but it is not likely that these proposed navigations were ever completed. The **Wharfe** is altogether a more attractive river, rising in Langstrothdale high in the Dales. It follows an exciting course through Wharfedale and offers many features attractive to canoeists. Its route through Wharfedale is followed by a road and the Dales Way footpath, making exploration easy and enjoyable. There are many pretty riverside villages, notably Buckden, Kettlewell, Grassington and Burnsall, there are the ruins of Bolton Abbey and, as the Dales descend to the moors, there is Ilkley. East of Ilkley, the river enters a more cultivated landscape as it skirts to the north of Leeds, passing through Weatherby and Boston

Spa on its way to Tadcaster. From Tadcaster to its junction with the Ouse at Cawood the Wharfe has periodically been navigable, although no formal navigation works have ever been carried out. Certainly trading barges regularly reached Tadcaster during the eighteenth century, and as late as the 1890s some Tadcaster brewers formed a company to improve the navigation. Today the river is often shallow and impassable above Ulleskelf, the tidal limit.

The canals and rivers of Humberside

A number of waterways flow into the north bank of the Humber, including some early navigations that are now mostly disused. One of the more remote of these is the **Market Weighton Canal** which was opened in the 1780s, partly to link Market Weighton to the Humber, and partly to drain the flat farmlands below the Yorkshire Wolds. Despite its undramatic quality this canal remained in commercial use until early this century, when the top three miles were closed, although the lower section was still in use as late as the 1950s. Since then, the canal has had a somewhat chequered history. In 1971 the sea lock

into the Humber was closed, thus closing the canal, but in 1978 the lock was restored and back in use, thus reopening the lower six miles of the canal. The route of the upper section to Market Weighton can still be traced, and a number of original canal buildings survive.

A more significant waterway is the river **Hull** which rises in the Wolds near Burton Agnes Hall and then flows south through Beverley to join the Humber at Kingston upon Hull. Twenty miles of this river, effectively the tidal section, are still navigable, and so the pleasant town of Beverley can be visited by boat. The landscape is not very exciting but the river has a number of connections with Hull docks and so there is plenty of activity. Two small canals link with the river Hull, the **Driffield Canal** and the **Leven Canal**. Of these, the former is the more interesting. Opened in 1770 and active until the 1940s, the canal has a number of attractive locks, some swing bridges and, at Driffield itself, a very attractive basin surrounded by fine early warehouses. Easy to explore, and extensively used by small boats, the Driffield Canal is well worth a visit.

An aerial view of Goole, showing the complex network of rivers, canals and docks that underline the town's importance in the Victorian era.

The commercial waterways of Yorkshire

Yorkshire still boasts a network of busy, commercial waterways making it, in effect, the only place in England where a great variety of trading vessels can still be seen. Here is the only English parallel with the commercial waterways of Europe, for it is only in this area that the waterways are sufficiently large and well-maintained to attract commercial traffic both from the Continent and from other parts of England. This network links Leeds, Wakefield, Castleford, Doncaster, Sheffield and other industrial centres with Goole, and thus with the Humber and the North Sea. The basis of the network is three rivers which have been navigable in part for several centuries: the **Aire**, the **Calder** and the **Hebble**. During the nineteenth century these navigations were greatly improved and expanded and the waterways of Yorkshire were among the few in England able to overcome the threat posed by the railways. Through the nineteenth century and into this century commerical traffic continued to increase, and some of these waterways still hold their own against competition from road transport.

The Aire is the largest of the three rivers, and also the most attractive. Rising in the Dales north of Skipton, it is for the first few miles a typical uplands river, fast flowing and scenic. It follows closely the course of the Leeds and Liverpool Canal, through Airedale to Keighley and then to Bingley, Horsford and Leeds itself where it becomes a navigation in its own right. From Leeds the Aire continues through Rothwell, Castleford, Ferrybridge and Rawcliffe to its junction with the Ouse north of Goole. Although still navigable, the winding course of the Aire between Ferrybridge and the Ouse has been bypassed by an artificial canal which takes a direct route to Goole. A branch canal leads to Selby and another, following the course of the river Calder to Wakefield, connects with the Calder and Hebble Navigation and continues to Sowerby Bridge, where it ends. Originally two trans-Pennine canals, the Rochdale and the Huddersfield Narrow, connected with the Calder and Hebble, thus linking Manchester with Leeds and the north-east, but these have been closed for many years (for further details see *The North-West*).

A view of the river Swale near Keld, showing North Yorkshire Swaledale scenery at its best.
The Swale is an attractively remote rural river.

A train of 'Ton Pudding' compartment boats. They have been used for transporting coal on the Aire and Calder Navigation since the Victorian period.

Although these waterways are predominantly industrial, there is plenty to see. The landscape itself is often quite dramatic, blending well with the powerful relics of Victorian development. There are also many echoes of an earlier period of civilisation, for example Wakefield Cathedral, Pontefract Castle and eighteenth-century Temple Newsam House. However, for many people the greatest interest is the commercial traffic that is still using these waterways. Barges loaded with chemicals, oil and petrol, industrial products, gravel and stone and above all coal can still be seen in plenty, particularly on the Aire and Calder Navigation. Coal was always the major traffic and even today a number of power stations are still supplied by water. The best place to watch this traffic from is Ferrybridge in West Yorkshire. Here the Tom Puddings can be seen, trains of compartment boats full of coal, each of which is physically lifted out of the water to be emptied at the power station by a huge mechanical hoist providing another example of Victorian ingenuity that is still in action.

The other great commercial waterway of Yorkshire is the river **Don**. The Don Navigation was opened from 1751 to 1819 to link Sheffield and Rotherham with Goole and the Humber estuary. Like the Aire and Calder, this navigation was continuously expanded and improved and so was able to remain successful throughout the nineteenth century and well into the twentieth century. In 1895 it was amalgamated to form the **Sheffield and South Yorkshire Navigation**, with branches connecting with the Aire and Calder, with the river Trent via the Stainforth and Keadby Canal and with Barnsley and Wakefield via the Deane and Dove and Barnsley Canals. The **Dean and Dove** and **Barnsley Canals** were closed during the 1950s and 1960s, and although parts of their route have been obliterated, they can still be traced. However, the other parts of the network continue to thrive, and the section between Doncaster and Rotherham has recently been entirely rebuilt and enlarged to take continental-sized barges and to enable commercial traffic to sail directly between the Continent, the Humber ports and the industrial centres of Yorkshire. This rebuilding programme, completed in 1982, represents the first major investment in commercial waterways in England since the 1930s. The Sheffield and South Yorkshire is above all a commercial network carrying heavy traffic through a predominantly industrial environment but it is not without interest. It has plenty of historical associations and a number of surprises. Among these are Conisborough Castle, a splendid twelfth century castle whose massive keep still looks nearly new, and the trolleybus museum at Sandtoft.

Liverpool's waterfront with the Liver Building, topped by its famous birds, the most traditional and familiar view of the Mersey.

THE NORTH-WEST

The north of England is divided into two by the Pennines, a great chain of hills which forms the geographical and physical backbone of the country. The Pennines are also a major watershed, separating the rivers that flow eastwards to the North Sea from those that fall westwards to the Atlantic. The north-west of England is a distinctive and highly varied region, its nature determined to a considerable extent by the waterways that run through it. The greatest of these waterways are the Eden, the Lune and the Ribble. These rivers are little known but their long courses warrant exploration for they reflect the changing character of the north-west itself, a landscape that ranges from the dramatic and isolated scenery of the north, full of echoes of Roman and medieval England, to the industrial heartlands of the south.

In the far north, the Scottish borderlands that surround Carlisle are not well known, yet they contain a number of pleasant rivers that follow quiet routes to the Solway Firth. Far better known are the waterways of the Lake District and the Cumbrian mountains, which have been attracting visitors since the eighteenth century. The pleasures of the Cumbrian coast should not be overlooked and they are easily explored via its rivers. To the south lies more splendid scenery, notably the Yorkshire Dales and the Forest of Bowland, and the contrasting coastline around Morecambe Bay, associated for centuries with fishing and shipbuilding. The waterways of south Lancashire reflect the impact of the Industrial Revolution. This area was radically changed by the growth of the textile industry, which was dependent upon rivers and canals for power and transport. Centres of industrial activity grew up along these waterways, creating a pattern still apparent today despite the changed nature of the industry and its environment. The Lancashire towns on the foothills of the Pennines are full of echoes from the eighteenth and nineteenth centuries, and the best way of

Cows grazing at Camboglanna Roman fort at Birdoswald, one of the best preserved Roman buildings associated with Hadrian's Wall.

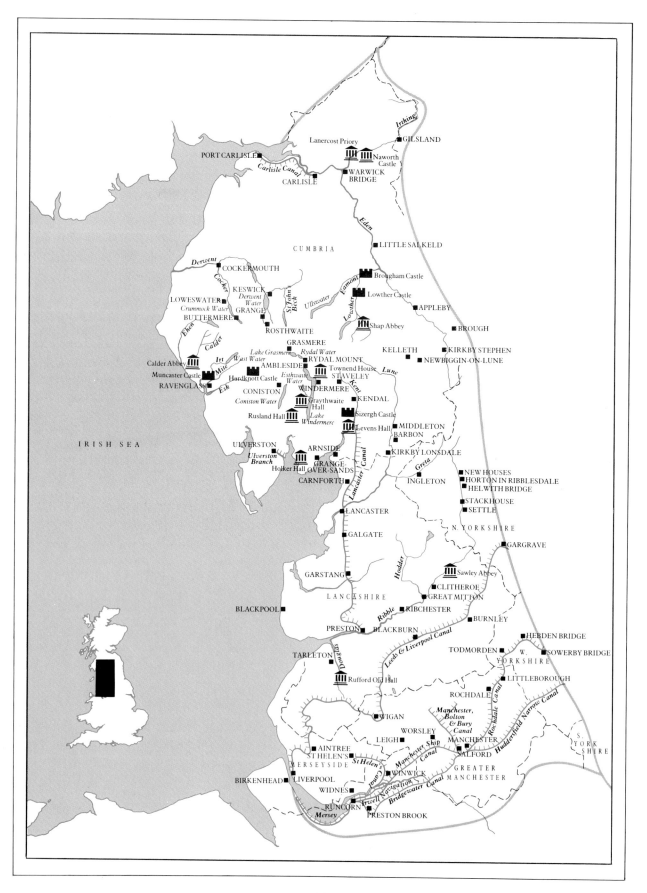

appreciating this is to travel along the waterways, especially the great trans-Pennine canals.

The wide estuary of the Mersey forms a sheltered seaway that enabled Liverpool to develop from the seventeenth century as a centre for international trade, particularly with America and the colonies, and ships are still a vital part of Liverpool's economy. Liverpool's neighbour, Manchester, is a great Victorian metropolis whose wealth was drawn from the corners of the British Empire. This corner of England is currently experiencing a painful period of change as the traditional pattern of industry is slowly dismantled, and now is the time to explore it, before centuries of history disappear. The waterways of the region are a direct historical link. The Duke of Bridgewater's canal was the first modern canal to be built in England and it inspired a network of canals that are now largely forgotten. There is still much to be discovered in the network of narrow canals that linked Manchester to the rest of England, in the docks, the Mersey, and along the Manchester Ship Canal, which connected British industry to the rest of the world.

The Eden and its tributaries

Rising high in the Pennines east of Brough, the **Eden** is for many miles a wild and remote river. For much of its course it drains the Pennines, flowing quickly through a dramatic landscape of hills, moorland and woods. Despite its relative isolation, the Eden is not a difficult river to explore. Minor roads frequently run close to it, but the best way to see it is from the Settle to Carlisle railway line. This is one of the most exciting railway journeys in Britain but the line is now threatened with closure. The wildness of the river is matched not only by its landscape, but also by the towns and villages that flank it. There are castles at Brough, Appleby and Corby, all built originally as medieval fortresses, while a stone circle near Little Salkeld is a reminder of a far earlier period of civilisation. Although there are a few old mills along its course, the Eden is a very undeveloped river and salmon and trout can still be seen among its rapids. The only town of any significance is Carlisle, traditionally a fortified town and still a famous garrison. Although rather gaunt, Carlisle wears its past well. There is a cathedral, a castle, a museum and plenty of strong stone buildings. West of Carlisle the Eden follows a more rural course, undulating gently to its tidal estuary on the Solway Firth.

One of the best known known features of northern England and the Borders are the Roman remains, and in particular Hadrian's Wall. A good way to explore the Wall and its associated musuems is to follow the river **Irthing**, for it is never far from the Wall on its way to join the Eden near Warwick Bridge, east of Carlisle. The Irthing rises in the

Lanercost Priory, one of the many historical landmarks along the course of the river Irthing. The Priory was founded in 1169.

inaccessible Wark Forest and then joins the Wall near Gilsland, passing two forts, the most famous of which is Birdoswald. However, not everything is Roman, for nearby is Naworth Castle and the romantic ruins of the twelfth-century Lanercost Priory, set in woods on the north bank of the river. Another interesting tributary is the river **Eamont** which connects Ullswater to the river Eden. It also has historical associations, notably the prehistoric earthwork known as King Arthur's Round Table, near Eamont Bridge, and nearby the ruins of Brougham Castle. Eamont Bridge marks the junction of the Eamont and the **Lowther**, the latter leading to the huge Haweswater reservoir, the isolated ruins of Shap Abbey and Lowther Castle with its wildlife park.

The Carlisle Canal

One of the most forgotten features of Carlisle is the **Carlisle Canal**, which once linked the town of Port Carlisle on the Solway Firth. This ambitious attempt to develop Carlisle into a seaport dates from the early 1820s. A wide canal with 8 locks, it enjoyed a modest success in transporting coal and building materials for 30 years. There was also a passenger service along the canal and travellers bound for Liverpool could spend the night in a specially built hotel in Port Carlisle. In 1853 the canal was closed and replaced by a railway, which in turn has disappeared. Traces of the canal can still be found, including warehouses and a fine customs house in Carlisle, and a lock, basins and wharves in Port Carlisle, as well as the hotel building formerly used by Liverpool-bound passengers.

The Derwent and the Northern Lakes

The Lake District is one of the most familiar leisure areas in England, its many lakes, rivers and streams have been enjoyed by generations of visitors. It is a region of mountains and high hills, with many large expanses of enclosed water, linked and drained by innumerable rivers and streams. The rivers tumble rapidly through steep, rocky valleys and there are plenty of dramatic waterfalls, or forces. Much of it is inaccessible except to the most dedicated and well-equipped of explorers, but there is still plenty to see and enjoy along the main rivers which connect the lakes together.

The major river of the region is the **Derwent**, which rises high in the mountains above Borrowdale. Tiny wooded villages, notably Rosthwaite and Grange, mark its course to Derwent Water, after which it flows on through remote woodlands to the long Bassenthwaite Lake. To the west is Cockermouth, a little town famous for its church and the house where Wordsworth was born in 1770. West of Cockermouth the Derwent becomes a placid river, wandering through farmland to its mouth near Workington, a traditional mining town with a

Autumn colours near Keswick, one of the most popular Lake District resorts.

strong Victorian flavour. The other northern lakes are connected to the Derwent by its tributaries. **St John's Beck** and the river **Greta** lead to the thickly wooded Thirlmere, a long narrow lake at the foot of Helvellyn mountain. The Greta also passes through Keswick, a popular Lake District resort whose local museum has a collection of Wordsworth mementos. Cockermouth marks the junction between the Derwent and the **Cocker**, the latter flowing through Lorton Vale to link Loweswater, Crummock Water and Buttermere. West of Buttermere village is the dramatic Scale Force, a waterfall that plunges over 120 feet through the rocks. To the south-east lies Seathwaite, reputedly the wettest place in England, with an average rainfall of over 160 inches.

The rivers of the Cumbrian coast

The cliffs and sand dunes of the Cumbrian coast between Whitehaven and Barrow-in-Furness are intersected by a number of small rivers which flow busily down to the sea from the mountains and fells.

A typical Lakeland scene, the valley of St John's Beck between Keswick and Thirlmere. This area abounds in superb walks.

Hire boats are available on the larger lakes and provide a good way to enjoy the scenery.

The **Ehen** links Ennerdale Water with Cleator Moor and Egremont, while the **Calder**, which shares its estuary with the Ehen, passes the ruins of Calder Abbey. The **Irt** flows west from Wast Water, the deepest lake in England, overlooked by Sca Fell. Between the rivers **Mite** and **Esk**, which flow into the sea either side of Ravenglass, is the track of the narrow gauge Ravenglass and Eskdale steam railway, its climbing route built originally in 1875 to transport iron ore to the coast. The Esk also flows past Muncaster Castle, a fortified house dating back to the thirteenth century, famed for its furnishings, ornamental gardens and tropical birds. Nearer its source, and 800 feet above the Esk is a much older structure, the Roman Hardknott Castle, built to defend England against the Picts and the Scots prior to the construction of Hadrian's Wall.

The southern Lakes

Flowing into Morecambe Bay from the north are the rivers that lead directly to the best known group of lakes in England: Coniston Water, Windermere, Esthwaite Water, Rydal Water and Grasmere. Apart from the natural pleasures of the landscape, this region offers a wide variety of other interests. The pretty lakeside towns and villages of Coniston, Windermere, Ambleside and Grasmere have managed to preserve their identity despite the thousands of visitors. There are fine houses and gardens, notably Townend House, Graythwaite Hall, Brockhole, Court House and Rusland Hall, and interesting literary associations, such as the Wordsworth Museum at Grasmere and his house at Rydal Mount, and John Ruskin's house at Brantwood, overlooking Coniston Water. For those attracted by the history of transport there is a steam railway, the Lakeside and Haverthwaite, at the southern end of Windermere, and Windermere also has a Steam Boat Museum. In this region of lakes there are unusually few rivers of significance, but the lakes themselves are easy to explore and enjoy. The best way to see them is by boat. On some, such as

Arnside on the estuary of the river Kent in Cumbria. The Kent estuary is flanked by wide sandy beaches, and Arnside is a popular holiday resort.

Originally built to carry iron ore, the miniature Ravenglass and Eskdale steam railway is now a major tourist attraction on the Cumbrian coast.

Windermere and Ullswater, there are scheduled passenger services, and on many others small boats, dinghies, canoes and sailing craft, can be hired.

To the south of the Lake District lie Cartmel Sands, which are overlooked to the east by Holker Hall with its gardens, motor museum and adventure park, and to the west by the town of Ulverston. For many years Ulverston was linked to Morecambe Bay by a short ship canal. Opened in 1796, this gave the town a new life as an inland port and it remained active until early this century. The **Ulverston Canal** was finally closed in 1945, but still survives virtually intact, and so can easily be explored.

The Kent

Although lacking the obvious drama of many of the Lake District rivers, the **Kent** should not be overlooked. It is relatively accessible throughout its course and passes a number of features of interest. Rising above the Kentmere Reservoir high in the mountains, the Kent is for its first few miles a typical uplands stream, wild and fast flowing. It passes

through Staveley, where traditional country furniture is made and then flows through a more open, agricultural landscape to Kendal. This town is the gateway to the Lake District and its many attractions include a castle, the eighteenth-century Abbot Hall Art Gallery and Museum, with its collections of furniture and paintings, the Lakeland Life and Industry Museum, and the local museum of natural history and archaeology. The Kent flows through the town, adding to its appeal. South of Kendal the river passes along a wide valley on its way to its estuary into Morcambe Bay, flanked at its mouth by Arnside and Grange-over-Sands. Although busy main roads run close to the river in this area it is still worth exploring. Two major country houses dominate the valley: Sizergh Castle, an Elizabethan mansion with a fourteenth-century tower and a seventeenth-century garden, which has been the home of the Strickland family for over 700 years; and Levens Hall, famed for its topiary garden, its furniture and, more unexpectedly, its collection of steam traction engines.

Bridge House, Ambleside, one of the most distinctive architectural features in this attractive village that has remained largely unspoiled despite its many visitors.

The Lune

The river **Lune** rises high in the Fells west of Kirkby Stephen and effectively marks the transition between the dramatic landscape of the Lake District and the more domestic countryside of north Lancashire. At first wild and remote, the Lune soon enters the wide valley which it shares with the M6 motorway and the main west coast railway to Scotland. This valley leads ultimately to the long curving finger of the river's tidal estuary west of Lancaster. Apart from Lancaster, which the Lune impressively divides into two, the only town of any size on its route is Kirkby Lonsdale. However, there are many attractive small villages to be discovered, for example Newbiggin on Lune, Kelleth, Middleton, Rigmaden Park and Barbon, the last named famous among car enthusiasts for its hill climbs. The Lune has a number of tributaries, most of which flow directly down from the hills to the east but one, the **Greta**, is particularly memorable. This river rises in Whernside and then flows westward through Ingleton to the Lune, its course dramatically marked by waterfalls, gorges and caves, into which it sometimes vanishes completely.

The Lancaster Canal

The **Lancaster Canal** was first planned in 1771 and it is one of the few major man-made waterways in the north-west of England. It was not finally completed until early in the nineteenth century when the main line between Preston and Kendal was opened. Isolated from the main canal network, the Lancaster has always had a character of its own, with distinctive bridges, elegant aqueducts, and a predominantly rural 57 mile route through pleasant countryside. When it was first built, there was a tramway link between Preston Basin and the Leeds and Liverpool Canal, five miles to the south, but this did not last long. Commercial traffic on the Lancaster Canal continued until the 1940s and then it quietly declined. In 1955 the upper section between Tewitfield and Kendal was abandoned, but the lower section of over 42 miles is still open to pleasure boats. Despite its rural nature, the Lancaster Canal has many features of interest. Preston itself is not too exciting, but within a few miles the canal becomes entirely rural, passing old stables, mills and lift bridges. At Garstang there is an attractive basin, while at Galgate there is a short branch canal leading to Glasson with its old-fashioned docks and the sealock into the Lune estuary. North of Lancaster is a most impressive stone aqueduct, which is 640 feet long, over the river Lune, after which the canal passes Hest Bank, coming within a quarer of a mile of the sea.

After Carnforth, the home of Steamtown, one of the largest steam railway centres in England, the canal comes to its present rather abrupt terminus, at the foot of the M6 motorway. Ironically, the most attractive part of the canal is the closed section to Kendal, where there are locks, a large number of fine bridges and aqueducts, and a short tunnel at Hindcaster, as well as a more interesting landscape. Although parts of this section still hold water, the best way to explore the canal is on foot, for the towpath is a right of way throughout its length.

The Ribble and its tributaries

The **Ribble**, Lancashire's largest river, actually rises in North Yorkshire, high in the Pennines. Its course through the Yorkshire Dales is marked by tiny villages, notably New Houses, Horton in Ribblesdale, Helwith Bridge and Stackhouse until it reaches Settle. The landscape is dramatic through Ribblesdale but gradually the character of the river changes as it approaches the fertile valley that carries it towards Preston and its estuary. The ruins of Sawley Abbey are followed by Clitheroe, with its Norman castle and museum, and the Roman fort at Ribchester, which serves as a reminder of a far earlier period of civilisation when Lancashire was a wild and undeveloped region. Just outside Preston the river passes Samlesbury Hall, a fourteenth-century manor house, and then industry takes over as the Ribble skirts the southern border of Preston. Still a port of some significance, Preston has exploited the tidal estuary of the Ribble since Roman times. This long natural expanse of water connects the town with the sea, several miles to the west. The Ribble has a number of tributaries, the most attractive of which flow down from the fells west of Ribblesdale. These include the **Hodder**, which rises above Stocks Reservoir and then passes remote villages hidden high in the Forest of Bowland on its way to join the Ribble near Great Mitton. There are waterfalls and a packhorse bridge. Nearby, but flowing from the south is the **Calder**. This rises in the moors south of Burnley, near Claviger Gorge, passes through Burnley itself, and thence to Cawthorpe Hall and Great Harwood Abbey and Gardens. Not strictly a tributary, but sharing the same estuary as the Ribble is the river **Douglas**. Not much to look at today, this was an important waterway in the eighteenth century when it was made navigable from its estuary to Wigan. The navigation fell into disuse after the building of the Leeds and Liverpool Canal, which duplicated much of its route, from Wigan to Burscough Bridge, and from Burscough to Tarleton via the Rufford branch. Today only the last few miles are still navigable, linking Tarleton with the estuary, and connecting the Leeds and Liverpool Canal with the sea.

This elegant eighteenth-century bridge over the Lancaster Canal near Galgate, is one of several fine bridges that cross the canal.

The marina at Galgate on the Lancaster Canal, which is linked to Glasson and the Lune estuary by an eight-mile branch canal.

The Trans-Pennine Canals

One of the greatest challenges facing the canal builders of the eighteenth century was the need to link the industrial towns of South Yorkshire with Manchester and Liverpool. Colossal feats of engineering were required, for the Pennines stood in the way, and the builders themselves faced extraordinary hardships and yet, by the early years of the nineteenth century, no less than three trans-Pennine canals were in operation. The first of these was the **Rochdale Canal**, opened in 1804 to link the Bridgewater Canal in Manchester with the Calder and Hebble Navigation at Sowerby Bridge. The second was the **Huddersfield Narrow Canal**, opened in 1811 to join the Ashton Canal in Manchester with Huddersfield. The third was the **Leeds and Liverpool Canal**, built between 1770 and 1816. Today only one of these canals, the Leeds and Liverpool, is open to traffic but the routes of the Rochdale and Huddersfield Narrow can still be traced and many of their most important and impressive features are still intact. Anyone wishing to understand the importance of canals in the eighteenth and early nineteenth centuries should explore these trans-Pennine routes.

The Rochdale Canal, with 92 locks in 33 miles, is a dramatic piece of engineering. It starts from the heart of Manchester, passing beneath Piccadilly and other familiar landmarks. The first nine locks are still in use, as this part of the Rochdale operates as a vital link between the Ashton and Peak Forest Canals, but the remainder is impassable. Between Manchester and Rochdale the surroundings are gloomy and industrial but full of history. After Rochdale the scenery improves, as the canal passes through Littleborough and Todmorden, climbing all the time. After reaching its summit, the canal descends the dramatic Calder valley, through Hebden Bridge to its terminus basin in Sowerby Bridge. Traffic continued to use the Rochdale Canal until it was finally closed in 1952.

The Huddersfield Narrow Canal is equally dramatic, with 74 locks in under 20 miles, and at Standedge is the longest canal tunnel ever built in England. This astonishing structure, over 5600 yards long, was cut through solid rock and must have been a nightmare for the early Victorian boatmen, for its passage took over 3 hours. The route of the Huddersfield Narrow is partly industrial and partly through impressive Pennine scenery and, although parts have been filled in, it can easily be followed. Despite the ambitions of its builders, the Huddersfield Narrow Canal was never really successful, and regular through traffic had largely ceased by about 1904, although it was not

finally closed until 1944. There are plans to restore and reopen both these canals and work has begun, but it will be many years before boats can once again pass through Standedge tunnel. In the meantime, both can be explored on foot and the towpath is readily accessible by road in many places. To explore these canals is to understand the impact of the Industrial Revolution on the predominantly agricultural economy of England in the late eighteenth century.

The third route, the Leeds and Liverpool, is not only still open but also enjoys the most dramatic Pennine scenery. The canal is 127 miles long with 91 locks, and commercial traffic was active until the 1960s. The architecture of the canal itself and its surrounding buildings is impressive, with locks, bridges and mills all built from the local sandstone, hard, dark and impenetrable. There is a tunnel at Foulridge and many of the locks are grouped into

A fisherman on the Leeds and Liverpool Canal near West Marton. Canal fishing is very popular and many stretches are leased to fishing clubs.

The dramatic staircase of five locks at Bingley, one of the most exciting features of the Leeds and Liverpool Canal.

flights, with 23 close together at Wigan, and at Bingley the famous 5 locks staircase, one of the wonders of the waterways. The route of the canal is from the river Mersey by Liverpool docks, through Liverpool and Aintree to Wigan, then through Blackburn, Burnley, Gargrave, Skipton, Keighley, Saltaire to Leeds and the junction with the Aire and Calder Navigation. Branches also connect the Leeds and Liverpool to the Bridgewater Canal at Leigh, and to the sea via the Ribble estuary at Rufford. The scenery is wild and remote, a mixture of spectacular Pennine beauty. Victorian industry mingles with urban development and there are plenty of features of interest that have little to do with the canal itself, for example Kirkstall Abbey and Rufford Old Hall, besides all the surrounding towns and villages of the Yorkshire Dales.

The canals and rivers of Manchester

Although rarely recognised as such today, Manchester was once the centre of a great network of waterways that linked the city with many other parts of England. Some of these waterways date back to the Middle Ages, and the growth of Liverpool as a major trading port. Heavily industrialised since the eighteenth century, Manchester and its surrounding towns have inevitably swallowed up the wild and undeveloped countryside still so abundant further north. As part of the same process, the rivers and streams have been turned into commercial waterways, sources of power or basic drains. Clearly this is not an area of unspoilt countryside and gently flowing streams, yet there is plenty to see, for in many ways the Manchester region is a mirror of English history over the last two centuries.

At the heart of the region and the original cause of its prosperity, are two great rivers, the **Mersey** and the **Irwell**. Since the Middle Ages the Mersey has carried boats as far south as Warrington, and long before then Liverpool had begun to develop as a seaport. The long curving estuary of the Mersey provides a natural deep water and relatively sheltered harbour, and Liverpool and Birkenhead have been associated with ships and the sea for centuries. The growth of Manchester in the early eighteenth century created the need for adequate transport links with the port of Liverpool and this led to the development of the waterways. Manchester expanded around the river Irwell, a tributary of the Mersey and so the first step was to turn this into a navigation. The **Mersey and Irwell Navigation** was duly opened in 1736, and throughout the eighteenth century, as trade increased and the rival waterways came into being, it was steadily improved. It remained Manchester's main trade link with Liverpool and the sea until 1894 when the Manchester Ship Canal was opened. The first major rival to the Irwell Navigation was the **Bridgewater Canal**, part of which was opened in 1761. This canal, built to link Manchester with the Mersey at Runcorn, was the first major artificial waterway in the modern sense to be built in Britain and it effectively launched the canal age. The canal's instigator, the third Duke of Bridgewater, originally planned the canal, which was designed by the engineer James Brindley, to transport coal from his mines at Worsley Delph. As a commercial venture it

A view of the Leeds and Liverpool Canal passing through Saltaire, Sir Titus Salt's splendid Victorian industrial estate.

The Barton Aqueduct. This remarkable bridge swings on its central pivot, still full of water, to allow the passage of larger vessels on the Manchester Ship Canal.

was immediately successful and it was steadily expanded to connect with other canals, the Trent and Mersey at Preston Brook, the Leeds and Liverpool at Leigh and the Manchester Ship Canal. It continued to carry commercial traffic into the 1970s. Today the canal is largely used by pleasure boats but it is an interesting canal to explore, partly because of its associations with the start of the Industrial Revolution, and partly because the Bridgewater and its connections offer an unusual way to see the Manchester region. It also has two features of remarkable interest. The first of these is the Barton Aqueduct. When the canal was built, a brick aqueduct carried it over the river Irwell. This was demolished in the 1890s during the construction of the Manchester Ship Canal and replaced by the Barton Aqueduct. This unique and extraordinary device is a huge steel aqueduct that swings on a central pivot to allow ships to pass. To see this great machine in operation is to understand the ingenuity of the Victorian mind. The second remarkable feature is the original basin at Worsley where the Duke of Bridgewater shipped his coal to Manchester and elsewhere. Here, from a basin dramatically cut out of solid rock, are the entrances to a series of tunnels that linked the coal mines with the canal. This was a complete underground network, with locks, inclined planes and over 40 miles of waterway connecting the various coal mines and seams. Special narrow boats were built for this network and some can still be seen in the basin.

There are a number of other canals in the Manchester region that are now derelict but the enthusiast will find plenty to see. One of the earliest canals of the eighteenth century was built to connect St Helen's with the Mersey. The **St Helen's Canal** was not finally closed until the 1940s and much remains, including locks at Widnes and St Helen's and workshops and warehouses at Winwick. However, the canal is rapidly disappearing under various development schemes. More substantial but less easy to explore, requiring foot work rather than a car, is the **Manchester, Bolton and Bury Canal**. Opened in 1797, this canal was built to serve the coal trade and continued to trade commercially until the 1930s. It also operated a successful passenger service during its early years. Today, its route can still be traced. There are locks to be seen near Salford and Prestolee, aqueducts over the river Irwell (the best of these is also at Prestolee) and the towpath provides an interesting walk into Bury.

The final waterway, and obviously the most important, is the **Manchester Ship Canal** itself. Opened in 1894, this major undertaking turned Manchester from a canal city into an international port. Ships up to 600 feet long, 65 feet wide and drawing 28 feet of water can still sail into the heart of the city, 36 miles from the sea. Although part of its route followed the river Mersey and Irwell, much of the Ship Canal was dug from scratch. There are five

The Manchester Ship Canal under construction. The largest man-made waterway in England, it is also the first to have been built with mechanical equipment.

The unexpected sight of a coaster sailing through the fields miles from the sea, one of the more dramatic pleasures of the Manchester Ship Canal.

huge locks and a number of bridges, which either swing to allow the passage of ships or, like the M6 motorway bridge, cross the canal at high level. In some ways the canal itself is a linear dock, lined with quays, jetties and terminals from its connection with the Mersey at Eastham to Manchester docks. The Manchester Ship Canal is the only waterway in England to have been built on this scale and, although traffic today is gradually diminishing, it is still worth a visit, for its engineering, and for the spectacle of huge ships sailing through the country-side west of Manchester.

ACKNOWLEDGMENTS

Photographs were supplied and are reproduced by kind permission of the following institutions, museums and photographers:

ENGLISH CASTLES

Aerofilms Ltd: 12 left and right, 15, 20, 34, 38, 54, 56, 57, 79, 80, 121 top, 127, 147 bottom
James Austin: 88 left and right
John Bethell: 17, 24, 46 left and right, 47, 49, 51, 59 top, 60, 61 top, 64, 65, 66 left, 67, 82, 84, 87, 96, 98 top and bottom, 99 top and bottom, 105, 109 top and bottom, 114-5, 126, 134 bottom, 135 bottom, 142-3
Bodleian Library: 121 bottom
Jane and Colin Bord: 110 right, 112 left, 113 top and bottom
British Tourist Authority: 107
Cambridge University Aerial Survey: 27, 144
Peter Chèze-Brown: endpapers, opp. title page, 13, 14 left, 22, 23, 25, 32, 33 bottom, 37, 41 bottom, 70, 71 bottom, 73, 74 left, 75 top and bottom, 76 left and right, 78 top and bottom, 92, 93 bottom, 100 left, 101, 122, 131, 134 top, 135 top, 139 top, 141, 145 bottom, 148, 149
Fotobank/ETB: 62, 89 bottom, 123, 129, 133, 137, 138, 139 bottom.
Michael Holford: 9 (Ianthe Ruthven), 16, 33 top, 36, 63, 69 (Ethel Hurwicz), 90-1, 93 top
Angelo Hornak: 28
Jarrolds, Norwich: 68 top, 108
A. F. Kersting: 35 left, 41 top, 61 bottom, 68 bottom, 72, 77, 83, 97, 104, 106, 116, 118, 125 left, 132, 136, 145 top, 146, 147 top
Lithograve (Birmingham) Ltd: 102
S. & O. Mathews: 19, 45 top
National Trust: 14 right, 42 left and right
Walter Scott, Bradford: 128 right
Kenneth Scowen: 30 top, 35 right, 39, 40 right, 39 top, 40 left, 44 right, 58 left, 81
Edwin Smith: 43 bottom, 55 top and bottom, 95, 103 left and right, 110 left
Tate Gallery: 86
Derek Widdicombe: copyright page, 21, 59 bottom, 119, 120, 124, 130 left and right, 140
Andy Williams: 52-3
Trevor Wood: 85, 88 left, 94 left and right, 111
Woodmansterne Ltd: 45 bottom (Clive Friend FIIP), 50 (Nicholas Servian FIIP)
Weidenfeld and Nicolson Archives: 29, 30 bottom, 31

Castle plans by Line and Line

GREAT ENGLISH HOUSES

The author and publishers would like to thank the owners or tenants of these houses for permission to include them in this book.

Aerofilms 262-3, 285; John Bethell Endpapers (Blenheim Palace), 162 above, 163, 164-5, 211, 239 below, 274 below, 216, 282 below, 283 above, 291; Janet and Colin Bord 212 below left, 213; Neil Burton 204; Country Life 192 above; Christopher Dalton 172 left, 224, 269 below, 273; English Life Publications Ltd 167, 174, 175, 207, 277, 278 left; Fotobank/English Tourist Board 161, 176 (Trevor Wood), 198, (Jon Wyand); Hever Castle 214, 215 below; Michael Holford 208; Angelo Hornak (Sarah, Duchess of Marlborough), 218-9, 255 left (by kind permission of the Marchioness of Cholmondeley); Jarrolds 160, 168, 169, 225, 244, 245, 250; A. F. Kersting Frontispiece (Stone Hall, Houghton Hall), 170 left, 171, 176 below, 179 below, 185, 186, 193, 199, 202, 203, 215 above, 222, 223, 227, 231 above, 234, 240, 241, 243, 246, 249, 252 left, 253, 254, 255 right, 268, 272 above and left, 278 right, 284, 286; Loseley House 206; Sally and Oliver Mathews 271, 289 above right, 290; National Motor Museum, Beaulieu 177, 178, 179; National Portrait Gallery 236 right; National Trust 180 (John Bethell), 184 above right, 184 below (Olive Kitson), 212 above left, 217 below, 230 (Jeremy Whitaker), 232-3 (Jeremy Whitaker), 238 (Horst Kolo), 239 above (John Bethell), 269 above (Jeremy Whitaker), 274 above, 275 (Angelo Hornak), 282 above (John Bethell), 283 below (John Bethell), 288, 289 left, 292 (Peter Mansfield), 293; Photo Precision Ltd 210 right; Edwin Smith 156, 187, 205, 210 above left, 216, 229 below, 236 above left, 247, 248, 289 below; Transglobe 200; Trustees of the Chatsworth Estate 242; Weidenfeld and Nicolson Archives 158 (Jeremy Whitaker), 170 right, 172 right (Cressida Pemberton Pigott), 173 (Cressida Pemberton Pigott), 176 above, 182, 183 (Kerry Dundas), 184 above left (Kerry Dundas), 188-9, (Cressida Pemberton Pigott), 192 left (Cressida Pemberton Pigott), 194 (Cressida Pemberton Pigott), 195 (Susan Lund), 196, 197 right, 209 (Kerry Dundas), 210 below left (Derrick Whitty), 220-1 (Cressida Pemberton Pigott), 228 (Derrick Whitty), 229 above (Derrick Whitty), 231 below, 236 below left, 237, 251, 252 right (Kerry Dundas), 256-9 (Cressida Pemberton Pigott), 260, 261, 264-5 (John Bethell), 266-7 (Cressida Pemberton Pigott), 270, 272 below right, 279 (Cressida Pemberton Pigott), 280 (Jeremy Whitaker) 281, (Cressida Pemberton Pigott), 287 (Cressida Pemberton Pigott); Jeremy Whitaker 197 left; Whitbread Collection 154 (Bridgeman Art Library); Andy Williams 181, 201, 217 above, 226; David Worth Regional Map 152; Woodmansterne Publications Ltd 162, 212 right

ENGLISH RIVERS & CANALS

Aerofilms: 317, 333, 335, 339
John Bethell: 301, 303, 348-9, 351, 352, 374, 376, 390, 393, 394 397, 405, 416
Janet and Colin Bord: 298, 304, 312, 323, 325, 326-7, 329 bottom, 350, 352, 356, 362, 365 right, 385, 391, 411 right, 414, 423, 427 top
British Museum: 396
British Waterways Board: 368 bottom left, 378, 379, 382, 387, 388, 431, 435
Fotobank: endpapers, 426-7
Gainsborough Library, Lincolnshire: 302 bottom
Angelo Hornak: 321
Lady Lever Art Gallery: 338
Manchester Ship Canal Company: 437
Mansell Collection: 302 top, 411 left
Sheila and Oliver Mathews: copyright page, 320, 327 right, 332 bottom, 418
National Trust: 311, 360
Derek Pratt: 308, 310, 316 top, 319 top, 324 top, 334, 342, 344, 345 left, 346 top, 347, 361, 363, 366, 367, 368 top left, 369, 371, 373 380-1, 383, 384, 386, 401, 407, 412, 417, 421, 433, 434, 436, 438
Arthur Oglesby: 328
Royal Academy: 395
Brian and Sally Shuel: 309 bottom, 316 bottom, 346 bottom, 403, 413 right, 415, 419, 430
Edwin Smith: 364
Swanston Graphics: 306-7, 322-3, 336-7, 354, 368 top right, 372, 392, 410, 424
Patrick Thurston: frontispiece, 314, 340 bottom, 377, 400, 409, 428, 429
Michael Turner/The Sunday Times Magazine: 299
Roy Westlake: 300, 309 top, 313, 318, 345 right, 358, 365 left, 389, 399
Derke Widdicombe: 330, 398, 402, 420, 422
Trevor Wood: 315, 340 top, 375, 404
Wookey Hole: 319 bottom
Weidenfeld and Nicolson Archives: 357, 359